Photographs by

J. Allan Cash

T. H. Everett

Andreas Feininger

Gottlieb Hampfler

Emil Javorsky

Josef Muench

Ivan Polunin

Winston Pote

Darwin Van Campen

and others

Line drawings by

Charles Fracé

A CHANTICLEER PRESS EDITION

LIVING TREES OF THE WORLD

Thomas H. Everett

DOUBLEDAY & COMPANY, INC. · NEW YORK

Planned and produced by Chanticleer Press, New York

Printed by Amilcare Pizzi S. p. A., Milano, Italy

Library of Congress Catalog Card Number 68-25989

Contents

Introduction

Trees are perennial plants that have one, or rarely few, persistent, self-supporting main stems or trunks, usually of considerable height. The group does not stand apart but merges imperceptibly into the class of plants we call shrubs. The latter are lower than most trees and ordinarily have several or many branches arising directly from the ground or from close to the ground. Trees are an extremely important element in the flora of the world. Where they occur in great numbers over large areas they profoundly modify environmental conditions and, in turn, their ability to survive, endure and perpetuate themselves is dependent upon favorable environments. An especially important factor is availability of sufficient moisture, and thus annual precipitation is usually of outstanding importance to them. Other crucial factors include mean annual temperature, length of the growing season, character of the soil and exposure to wind. Where conditions are optimal for tree growth, as in tropical rain-forest regions and over great areas of the Temperate Zone, they dominate the flora, and vast, dense forests result. In other places, where the environment favors the growth of grasses and other herbs, as for instance in savanna regions, it often does not do

so to the complete exclusion of trees, and trees often occur there as solitary specimens or in groups with open areas between. Even in certain deserts, a few trees prosper. These kinds are distinctly xerophytic, that is, drought resistant, and are often confined to locations where underground supplies of water are available. In polar regions and above certain heights in many mountain areas there are no trees, even though a wide assortment of other plants may prosper.

It seems certain that during some earlier geological periods trees dominated the flora of the world to a much greater extent than they do now, and most surely they once flourished in regions where they are presently of lesser importance or where they do not grow at all.

Like all plants, trees are classified and named in accordance with orderly systems. The most natural systems attempt to reflect the true relationship of plants to one another and probable lines of descent and evolution. In such systems trees form no special group, often occurring in genera, families and orders that include herbaceous species as well as shrubs and vines. Whether a plant is a tree or not is of no significance in classifying it. Systems of classification that reflect evolutionary processes are called phylogenetic. At best they are imperfect because we are not yet able to work out in incontestable detail the long history of plants on earth. That, however, does not excuse us from attempting to trace the "family trees" of trees.

Of one thing we can be certain, no straight-line development continued over vast geologic ages. The phylogenetic "tree" has so many branches that the points of origin of many groups of plants are unknown or vague, and often the lines separating related groups are indistinct. So plant classification must be to some extent pragmatic. In this book the classification closely follows that of *Taxonomy of Vascular Plants* by George H. M. Lawrence (1951), which in turn is based on *Syllabus der Pflanzenfamilien* by Engler and Diels (1936).

Under this system, the higher or vascular plants (which does not include such kinds as bacteria, algae, liverworts and fungi) are broken down into divisions, classes, orders, families, genera and species. Each Division contains several Classes and these are divided into Orders. Each Order consists of one or more Families and each Family of one or more genera.

The name of the genus forms the first part of the name of the plant, whereas the second part of the name of the plant is called the specific epithet or trivial name. Thus, the cedar of Lebanon is *Cedrus libanii.* In this case *Cedrus* is a generic name that is applied to all true cedars including the Atlantic cedar and the deodar cedar as well as the cedar of Lebanon. When the specific epithet *libanii* is added to the generic name *Cedrus,* the combination *Cedrus libanii* identifies the cedar of Lebanon specifically and is applied to no other plant.

A height of about twenty feet has been established as the minimum for plants to be included as trees in this book. Heights and trunk diameters given are the maximums or near maximums for the species; ordinarily most members of a species will be smaller. Very often tree species occur in stunted or dwarfed form toward the highest altitude at which they grow, toward their northern limits in the Northern Hemisphere, and toward their southern limits in the Southern Hemisphere. Regions of inadequate rainfall may also prevent specimens from attaining average size for the species.

Filicanae (Ferns)

This division of the plant kingdom contains a vast number of genera and species that bear no flowers or seeds. Each plant develops a non-sexual spore that grows into a plant called a prothallium, which looks completely unlike the plant that produces the spores. The prothallia of ferns are tiny, flat organisms which develop female gametes or egg cells and male gametes or sperms. The latter are motile; by swimming through films of water they reach the female gametes and fertilize them. As a result, a new generation of spore-bearing plants begins.

Ferns and their allies exhibit, then, a distinct alternation of generations. For example, the Boston fern produces on the underside of its mature leaves a pattern of scalelike bodies, easily visible, which, when ripe, release many dustlike spores. Under suitable conditions each spore grows into a green liverwort-like or scablike body, a fraction of an inch in diameter, lying flat on the soil or other medium and not at all like a fern in appearance. Each of these produces both eggs and sperms which unite to form a new individual fern of the familiar sporophyte type.

Of the Pteridophyta only the order Eufilicales of the class Filicanae include tree ferns and not all of these are tall enough to warrant inclusion in this book. All taller tree ferns belong in the families Cyatheaceae and Dicksoniaceae.

CHAPTER 1

The Eufilicales

If you know ferns only as delicate-foliaged denizens of North Temperate Region woodlands and perhaps in a few tropical forms favored as indoor pot plants, it may come as some surprise to learn of others that grow as tall as six-story buildings and form quite sizable forests. Yet there are such tree ferns.

More than three hundred species of tree ferns inhabit the tropics and subtropics of most parts of the world as well as certain mild Temperate Regions of the Southern Hemisphere. They grow

Tree ferns. Cyathea arborea (Emil Javorsky)

Tree ferns. Cyathea arborea (U. S. Forest Service)

species that flourished in great numbers and over vast areas of the world when coal beds were being laid down more than 200 million years ago. Arboreal representatives of their close relatives, the seed ferns, now long extinct, were even more abundant. Some grew to a height of 100 feet. It was these early tree ferns that formed, many eons ago, the first forests of our evolving world.

The chief use of tree ferns is as cultivated ornamentals in gardens and conservatories, but they have, and have had, other uses. Sections of their trunks are frequently employed as supports on which to grow epiphytic orchids. Their trunks, very termite resistant, are employed as posts to support huts and other buildings. The abundant silky hairs called pulu that clothe the leaf buds of the Hawaiian *Cibotium chamissoi*, the Hapu'u, were once used as dressings for wounds, for embalming the dead and as stuffing for mattresses and pillows, and a considerable amount of pulu was shipped to the Mainland United States. The Hawaiians fed the stems of the young fronds and the nearly pure starch of the trunks to hogs and even ate the starch themselves in time of famine. For a brief period a laundry starch industry was based on the use of Hawaiian tree ferns. As tinder for transporting fire from place to place, the Carib Indians used dried tree fern trunks. The Maoris ate the baked mucilaginous pith of the ferns.

CYATHEACEAE—CYATHEA FAMILY

This family, containing the greatest numbers of tree ferns, has its natural distribution mostly in mountain forests from New Zealand and Australasia to Malaysia, from Chile to Mexico and the West Indies, and in Africa. The family is considered to have originated in the Antarctic when milder climates prevailed there and to have spread northward. The most important genera are *Alsophila* and *Cyathea*.

Numerous species of *Alsophila* occur in both the Old World and New World tropics. Their trunks are often covered with a mat of roots or have hairs or scales at their tops. *A. excelsa*, native of Australia and Norfolk Island, is reported to attain a height of 80 feet. From Australia and Tasmania comes *A. australis*, which reaches 20 feet in height, and from tropical Asia the tall-growing and prickly *A. glauca*. An attractive South American species is *A. oligocarpa* from Colombia.

in cool, humid localities usually at fairly high elevations, in some places ascending to ten thousand feet, and in New Zealand some kinds grow at sea level. They prosper wherever they are bathed by mists, fogs and rains.

The trunks of tree ferns are very different from those of our more familiar trees. They lack a central core of wood and have no cambium layer to add annual rings of tissue to the outside of the trunk; growth takes place only at the apex of the stem. The material of which the trunk is formed is fibrous and tough. Often, the outside of the trunk is concealed beneath a layer of interlacing aerial roots that provide numerous niches from which sprout mosses, small ferns and other epiphytes.

The leaves or fronds of tree ferns form lacy patterns and are easily recognized, even by one who has never seen them before, as belonging to ferns. When young, they are coiled tightly in fiddlehead fashion. The foliage forms a many-leaved crown that spreads parasol-like from the top of the stem. Many tree ferns are much too small to be included in this book, some being less than ten feet in height and others less than three feet. But there are a goodly number of truly tall kinds.

The tree ferns of today are descendants of

10

Tree ferns. Dicksonia antarctica (Robin Smith)

The genus *Cyathea* consists of many species in the tropics and warm temperate regions of both hemispheres. Some are under 20 feet high but most species are 20 to 30 feet high and a few grow to 50 feet or higher. All are handsome. Among the best known are *C. dealbata* from New Zealand and Lord Howe's Island, called the silver tree fern, because of the milky whiteness of the undersides of its fronds, *C. smithii* of the West Indies, Mexico and Venezuela, and *C. medullaris*, from New Zealand, Australia, Tasmania and islands of the Pacific, which grows to 50 feet or more and in New Zealand withstands more cold than most tree ferns, surviving even a few degrees of frost.

DICKSONIACEAE—DICKSONIA FAMILY

Most members of this family are tree ferns with fronds generally very large and often hard and somewhat leathery. The trunks are furnished with hairs but do not have scales. The family has a somewhat spotty natural distribution; it is represented in New Zealand, Australia, Malaysia, Hawaii, Juan Fernandez and Central America.

Cibotium is a small genus from Mexico, Central America and Polynesia that includes several stout tree ferns, most of which have three-part fronds. Commonly cultivated in greenhouses in North America are young specimens of *C. schiedei*, which in its native Mexico grows to 15 feet high or sometimes higher. Another Mexican, *C. regale*, attains twice this height and has fronds 12 feet long. Until recently about 400,000 acres of the island of Hawaii were forested with tree ferns. The Hapu'u, one of the commonest tree ferns of Hawaii, is *C. spendens*, which attains a height of 16 feet. From Hawaii, too, comes *C. chamissoni*, an even taller tree with a thick growth of near-black hairs on the stems of its fronds.

Dicksonias are mostly natives of the Southern Hemisphere and generally withstand cooler temperatures than the majority of tree ferns. In New Zealand, some grow within sight of glaciers, and snow occasionally falls on *D. antarctica*. Dicksonias have firmer and harder foliage than most other tree ferns. Of the eight or nine New Zealand species the slender tree fern, *D. squarrosa*, is most common. Growing to 20 feet high, it has a slender, blackish trunk that is sometimes branched.

11

Gymnosperms

The Spermatophytes or seed plants differ from Pteridophytes in that they exhibit no easily observed alternation of generations. More obviously, Spermatophytes produce flowers and seeds. True, in some the flowers are not showy developments but much reduced, as, for instance, in pines⁻ and pandanuses. Nevertheless, they are technically flowers and their female elements or ovules after fertilization develop into seeds which give rise to new plants essentially like the one that bore the seeds. The Spermatophyta consists of two subdivisions, the Gymnospermae and the Angiospermae.

The Gymnosperms differ from Angiosperms in that their ovules are not enclosed in an ovary but are borne naked on the scale of a cone or carpel. Their flowers are extremely simple, consisting of just ovules and pollen sacs—no sepals, petals, stamens or stigmas, the organs which give character to flowers as the term is commonly used. In addition, resin canals are evident in the stems and there are no vessels in the secondary wood. Certain exceptions or partial exceptions can be found to each of these criteria.

Gymnosperms are but the remains of a highly varied group that dominated world flora in Mesozoic times. They nevertheless are an extremely important element in our flora, being especially abundant in forests in temperate regions both north and south of the equator. They include many well-known trees, among them some of the most important economically. The living Gymnosperms, numbering about 675 species, are divided into four orders. One of these, the Cycadales, consists of only one family, the cycads.

CHAPTER 2

The Cycadales

CYCADACEAE—CYCAD FAMILY

Living cycads are curious remnants of an ancient flora once plentiful in the vegetation of the world. Well-defined fossils from the Triassic period, 175 to 200 million years ago, testify to the antiquity of the group, their wide distribution and common occurrence during the Jurassic, 125 to 150 million years ago. Today nine genera and less than ninety species survive, all in the tropics and subtropics; of these, only three species exceed 20 feet; others have distinct trunks of lesser heights but many have only very low or subterranean stems. To the non-botanist, cycads may resemble palms, and in America they are often called sago-palms, but the two groups are not even remotely related. Those who see them as similar to ferns are much closer to the truth. The cycads are the most primitive family of the Spermatophyta or seed-producing plants extant; they represent a connecting link with the Pteridophyta, the ferns and fern allies. As in the ferns, sexual reproduction is accomplished by means of ovules and motile male sperms, but, unlike the ferns, cycads produce seeds.

Every cycad plant is strictly male or female, the sexual manifestations being conspicuous cones. Reports that individual plants sometimes change their sex do not seem to be substantiated. Cycads are classified as an "irregular" family of the Gymnospermae or cone-bearing plants.

Those which develop obvious trunks—the only ones with which we are concerned—do superficially resemble certain palms. They have stout columnar stems, usually unbranched, to which the stubs of old leaf stalks remain attached. The large pinnate or feather-like leaves form, like tree ferns, a beautiful spreading crown at the top of the trunk. The leaves, dark green, tough and leathery, remain on the plant for one to three years or sometimes longer, depending upon the species and the conditions. Flushes of new leaf growth, each consisting of a circle of leaves, occur every year or two, occasionally at longer but rarely at shorter intervals. The foliage of some kinds, and perhaps of all, is poisonous to certain animals; in Australia *Macrozamia* causes a paralysis known as the "wobbles" that affects the hind legs of cattle.

The cones of cycads are large; in fact, certain cycads produce the largest cones of any plant. *Macrozamia peroffskyana* is reported to have developed a female cone 2 feet long and weighing 84 pounds and one cone of *Encephalartos caffer* weighed 92 pounds. The seeds, orange, scarlet, or white, resemble small plums; inside a fleshy coat each has a large stone in which is stored a starchy material. Starch from the seeds and also from the stems of some kinds is used locally for food. The starch contains a poison but this can be eliminated by roasting. In Australia

Cycads (South African Railways)

Macrozamia has been used as a source of laundry starch.

Cycad roots are of peculiar interest. In addition to a vertical tap root and rather weak branch roots, they develop masses of upward-growing-roots near and at the ground surface. This is the result of profuse branching stimulated by bacterial infection and very often by a blue-green alga. It is not known whether the relationship between the cycad and the invaders is symbiotic, that is, of mutual benefit, or whether it represents parasitism; but cycads show no ill effects from the relationship.

The tallest cycad, *Macrozamia hopei*, is one of several handsome macrozamias, all natives of Australia. Western Cuba, the mountains of Pinar del Rio, is the native home of *Microcycas calocoma*, called colloquially "Corcho." Sometimes 30 feet tall and with the greatest trunk diameter of any cycad, it has a dense crown of glossy dark green leaves up to 3 feet in length and cones up to 2 feet long. A Mexican rain-forest species, *Dion spinulosum*, grows to a height of 50 feet. It occurs in limestone soils, shaded by other tall-growing trees. This cycad has female cones more than 20 inches long and weighing more than 30 pounds; its seeds are processed into meal for tortillas.

13

Cycad. Dion spinulosum (T. H. Everett)

A few other cycads reach a height of 20 feet or even slightly more. Here belong two Australian species, *Cycas media,* the Australian nut-palm, and *C. rumphii.* Cycases are remarkable in that the female cones are extremely primitive and scarcely recognizable as cones; they consist of a large number of leaves of reduced size arranged loosely and, like the seed ferns of Paleozoic times, bearing seeds on their edges. Thus cycases are the most primitive seed-bearing plants extant.

Much shorter, ordinarily not exceeding 10 feet, but among the best-known cycads, are *Cycas revoluta* and *C. circinalis,* the former Japanese, the latter of the Old World Tropics. These are fairly commonly cultivated in conservatories and out in the open in warm climates; their leaves are often cut and used in florists' decorations.

CHAPTER 3

The Ginkgoales

GINKGOACEAE—GINKGO FAMILY

The order Ginkgoales consists of only one family, the Ginkgoaceae. The *Ginkgo biloba,* or maiden-hair tree, the sole survivor of a large family and genus, is the oldest species of tree extant. Paleobotanists trace it back in its present form to the Triassic era, 175 to 200 million years ago, when great dinosaurs roamed the earth.

In those days many kinds of ginkgo abounded, as sedimentary rocks in America, Europe, Asia and Australia provide much fossil evidence. Yet today no wild specimens of this noble tree exist—unless we accept the report of a reliable investigator that genuine spontaneous stands grow in northern China. In the last great ice age, the advancing ice cap destroyed the ginkgoes of North America and Europe; but it did not glaciate China, Korea or Japan, and there a solitary species, *Ginkgo biloba,* survived. Just what caused its later possible disappearance from the wild is not known, but fortunately it was preserved by the Chinese chiefly as a tree to plant near temples, tombs and similar sites. From these the present world population of ginkgoes is derived. The earliest mention of the ginkgo in Chinese literature was in the eighth century A. D. About 1730 the tree was introduced to Europe, the first specimen being planted in the Botanic Garden at Utrecht in Holland. The first tree brought to America was reportedly set in the garden of William Hamilton near Philadelphia in 1784.

Under favorable conditions the ginkgo attains a height of 120 feet and a girth of 30 feet or more. Its rather sparse and erratic branching produces a loose, spirelike effect in young specimens, but as it matures it develops a heavier crown supported by several massive ascending or spreading branches. Especially characteristic are the leaves which have unique parallel veins. They are fan- or wedge-shaped, which accounts for an early Chinese description of it as the tree "with leaves like a duck's foot" and for the English name, maidenhair tree, which refers to the similarity of the leaf to a leaflet of the maidenhair fern. In fall, the foliage turns bright yellow before it drops off. The leaves, like those of larches and the true cedars, grow on two kinds of branches or shoots, one elongating several inches each year and having rather scattered leaves, the other being spurlike laterals that lengthen infinitesimally each season and have leaves clustered at the tips.

Ginkgo trees are male or female but cannot be differentiated visually until they bloom. The flowers are inconspicuous, the females in pairs on slender stalks, the males in catkins. The male cells propel themselves through films of moisture

to the egg cells and effect fertilization. Seeds then develop, each an oval nut about three-quarters of an inch long surrounded by a thin fleshy layer which becomes bright orange and of evil odor, caused by the presence of butyric acid. Cleansed of the enveloping pulp, washed and roasted, the thin-shelled pure white nuts are a favorite food in China, where they are called *pai-kuo,* or *yin-kuo* (whence the name ginkgo), that is, white nuts, or *yin hsing,* silver apricot.

The ginkgo thrives in many temperate parts of the world, withstands city conditions extremely well and is often planted in parks and along boulevards. It is remarkably free from all pests and diseases and quickly reestablishes itself after transplanting.

CHAPTER 4

The Coniferales

Plants of the important order Coniferales differ from cycads and ginkgoes in that their sperm cells are not motile. Their leaves are typically needle-like, linear or scalelike, rarely oblong to elliptic, and are never divided into separate leaflets. They are always parallel-veined. Their fruiting organs are usually woody cones but in a few kinds are fleshy and berry-like. Nearly all conifers are evergreen; the exceptions are *Larix* (Larch), *Pseudolarix* (Golden-Larch), *Taxodium* (Swamp-Cypress), *Metasequoia* (Dawn-Redwood) and *Glyptostrobus*.

TAXACEAE—YEW FAMILY

This family is sometimes split into three families, the Taxaceae, Cephalotaxaceae and Podocarpaceae, based on technical differences in the anthers, ovules and seeds. The family consists of about a dozen genera and a hundred species, but many are shrubs rather than trees. The taxads are resinous evergreens with leaves usually alternate and usually two-ranked or apparently so.

Above: Ginkgo fruits (John H. Gerard: National Audubon) Left: Ginkgo tree (W. Strojny)

The flowers are ordinarily unisexual, the males conelike. The ovules, usually solitary, are borne on rudimentary carpels and develop into seeds either partly or completely surrounded by fleshy coverings.

Athrotaxus—Tasmanian-Cedar

These three very similar species endemic to the mountains of Tasmania are related to *Cryptomeria*, a genus of evergreen trees of the pine family, and, like it have ultimate branchlets that are deciduous. The tallest, the King William-pine (*A. selaginoides*), grows to a height of 100 feet with a trunk diameter of about 3 feet. Its leaves, up to one-half inch long, are much larger and more loosely arranged than those of *A. laxifolia* and *A. cupressoides;* and the latter grow only to a height of about 45 feet.

Tasmanian-cedars are densely branched, bisexual trees with short, stem-hugging or somewhat spreading scalelike leaves and small woody cones. The trees have slightly furrowed bark which peels in shreds; they are pyramidal and shapely when young but eventually become irregular and unkempt. The wood is light in weight, straight-grained and easy to work and is valued for cabinet work and interior finish.

Cephalotaxus—Plum-Yew

These are small Asiatic trees that closely resemble yews but are more graceful. They have opposite branches, leaves marked on their undersides with two broad white stripes, and seeds completely surrounded by pulp. Their common name refers to the plumlike appearance of their fruits. Although in their native habitats they become trees 30 feet or more in height, in cultivation they are usually shrubby. Of the five or six recognized species the most noteworthy are the Japanese plum-yew, *C. drupacea*, its variety *C. d. pedunculata (syn. C. harringtonia)*, and the Chinese species *C. fortunei*.

Dacrydium

The largest number of species of this evergreen genus is found in New Zealand but it is also found in Australia, Tasmania, New Caledonia, Borneo, Malaya and Chile. Young specimens and the lower branches of older trees have needlelike leaves, whereas the leaves on adult trees are scalelike and closely overlap. Male and female flowers occur on separate trees. The only New World representative of the genus is *D. forkii*, a native of Chile, and since it grows less than a

foot high, it is probably the smallest of all conifers. *D. laxifolium* of New Zealand, sometimes bears seeds when only 3 inches tall!

Known as rimu and as red-pine, *D. cupressinium* is pyramidal when young, attains 100 feet in height and almost 5 feet in trunk diameter in its native New Zealand, where it is an important timber tree. Its leaves are little more than small prickles pointing along the slender drooping stems. The fruit consists of a blue-black seed set in a red cup, after the manner of an acorn. Its straight-grained wood serves many building purposes both indoors and outdoors, and its bark is used in tanning.

The huon-pine, *D. franklinii*, is a pyramidal tree of Tasmania that grows up to 100 feet tall. It has been called the teak of Tasmania and is greatly valued for its fine, fragrant, canary-colored wood, light in weight, durable, tough, and easy to work. Tasmania's most distinctive and valuable tree, it is unfortunately becoming scarce.

Phyllocladus

These curious trees and shrubs of the Southern Hemisphere have their true leaves represented by scales; the organs that look like and function as leaves are cladodes or flattened branchlets. Along the margins of the latter, the female flowers and seeds appear, with the seeds in cuplike sheaths like tiny acorns. Male and female flowers appear sometimes on the same and sometimes on different trees.

The celery-top-pine of Tasmania, *P. rhomboidalis*, grows to 100 feet high with a trunk diameter up to 3 feet. It produces the hardest and heaviest wood of the island's native conifers. Available only in small quantities, it is valued for flooring, doors, boat construction and similar uses. It grows from sea level to 2500 feet in an equable, cool climate; it tolerates snowfall and wet, acid soils better than any other Tasmanian tree. At higher elevations it is much stunted.

The tanekaha (*P. trichomanoides*), which has a limited distribution in lowland forests in New Zealand, grows to 70 feet tall and in many instances develops a trunk 3 feet in diameter. Its wood is used for such purposes as flooring, doors and boat construction. Its bark is used for tan-

Tree fern. *Cyathea arborea (Emil Javorsky)*
Overleaf left: Norway spruce. Picea abies (Gerhard Klammet) Right: Red fir. Abies magnifica (Tom Myers)

ning. Another New Zealand species, the taotoa (*P. glaucus*), grows up to 40 feet high and has a maximum trunk diameter of about 2 feet. It has a limited distribution, chiefly in the Auckland district, and the male and female flowers are usually found on separate trees.

Podocarpus

This genus and its near relatives, both living and fossil, are predominantly of the Southern Hemisphere although species occur north of the equator. Podocarps, but not necessarily *Podocarpus*, were abundant in Jurassic times, 130 to 175 million years ago, and then competed with araucaria as the dominant tree in the Southern Hemisphere.

Podocarpuses are evergreen, resinous, mostly tall, dense-foliaged trees with narrow leaves. Their berry-like fruits grow on stalks that are usually purple or red and much swollen; those of some species are edible.

In South Africa *Podocarpus* is the only common representative of the conifers, the one other indigenous genus of that group being *Widdringtonia*. Several species occur and a South African has said that they are "the most magnificent of all our forest trees. Standing sometimes 150 feet high, with trunk diameters up to 11 feet, these giants tower above the surrounding forest." In South Africa they are called yellow-woods, are widely distributed, and extend even as far north as Ethiopia. The commonest are upright yellow-wood (*P. latifolia*) and Outeniqua yellow-wood (*P. falcata*). Others of interest are *P. henkelii* and *P. elongata*, a more bushy kind prized for use in ornamental plantings.

The upright yellow-wood is said to have yielded more lumber than any other South African tree; so plentiful was it that it was used in early days for railroad ties as well as for flooring, construction and furniture. Similar to it and with similar uses for boat building is the Outeniqua yellow-wood. It is a quick-growing tree and an excellent decoration for large gardens and for planting along avenues. *P. henkelii* is like the others and is valued as a garden tree.

In Australia, *P. alata*, known as brown-pine, and *P. amara*, called black-pine, are rain forest species that produce finely textured, golden brown wood adaptable for turnery and carving.

A number of podocarpuses are native to New

Yellow pine. Pinus ponderosa (Lola B. Graham: National Audubon)

Tasmanian-cedar. Athrotaxis cupressoides (Michael Sharland)

Zealand. Dominant in low wetland is the kahikatea or white-pine (*P. dacrydioides*). Specimens more than 200 feet tall have been recorded but more often they attain a maximum of 80 to 120 feet. They have straight trunks sometimes unbranched for 70 feet or more and up to 4 feet or more in diameter, well buttressed at their bases, and tiny, scalelike leaves. The seeds are carried on conspicuous, bright red, succulent peduncles, or stems, which are eaten by the Maoris. The tree called black-pine or matai in New Zealand is *P. spicata*, which grows up to 80 feet tall, has a bluish-black glossy bark, but no great trunk diameter. This is a lowland species that produces very good lumber. The miro (*P. ferruginea*), another inhabitant of lowland forests, is a somewhat smaller tree which has falcate or sickle-shaped leaves, one-half inch or more in length, and red, plumlike fruits that have a turpentine odor and are much liked by native pigeons. The totara (*P. totara*) is a massive tree that occasionally reaches a height of 100 feet. Its nuts are seated on large succulent peduncles. It occurs in lowland and montane forests and is a very valuable timber tree. The Maoris hollowed out war canoes,

sometimes seventy feet long, from whole trunks. The wood is durable in water and highly resistant to the teredo worm, a marine mollusk; for this reason it is preferred for wharf piles.

About a quarter of all *Podocarpus* species are natives of the New World. They occur mostly in mountain regions from the West Indies and Mexico to southern Chile and Argentina, and are sources of good lumber. The more northern kinds include *P. coriacea*, which grows in the West Indies and Central America, and *P. montana* and *P. oleifolia*, which range from Bolivia to Costa Rica. In Chile several species are logged, one of the most valuable being *P. nubigens* or manihu, trees which grow to a height of 80 feet and up to 3 feet in trunk diameter. Smaller trees of some local importance as sources of lumber are *P. andina* and *P. saligna*.

Of the Oriental species, one of the best known is *P. macrophylla* from Japan. This attains a height of 60 feet and has handsome glossy leaves. A more shrubby variety of it, *P. m. maki*, is much favored for growing in containers. *P. nagi*, also Japanese, grows up to 90 feet high and has comparatively broad leaves.

Saxegothaea—Prince Albert-Yew

This southern Chilean tree, *S. conspicua*, is the only one of its genus. It resembles a small-leaved yew, grows to a height of 60 feet and has spreading or pendulous branches. Its seeds occur in cone-like heads. Prince Albert-yew inhabits swampy rain forests. Although its wood is of high quality, the usable trees per acre are too few to warrant extensive exploitation.

Taxus—Yew

These attractive evergreens comprise ten Northern Hemisphere species so closely related that perhaps they should be regarded as variants of a single species. Some are trees but a few are shrubs. Of the trees, by far the most important are the English yew (*T. baccata*) and the Japanese yew (*T. cuspidata*), the former most commonly planted in gardens in Europe, the latter in America, each in numerous horticultural varieties.

The English yew, a native of Europe, North Africa and western Asia, grows up to 60 feet high and has a short, very thick trunk and a spreading or rounded head of branches with

Kahika-tea. Podocarpus dacrydiodes (J. H. Johns: New Zealand Forest Service)

leaves arranged spirally but on twisted stalks in approximately two ranks. The unisexual flowers are nearly always borne on separate trees. The decorative fruit consists of a seed set in a juicy, fleshy red cup. The flesh is sweet and edible but the seed itself contains a poisonous alkaloid.

Until the invention of firearms, the wood of this yew was valued above all others for the manufacture of bows, and many laws regarding their planting and preservation were enacted in England, Italy, Normandy and other parts of Europe. And in early times it was held sacred by many peoples including the ancient Britons. Its evergreen nature symbolized eternal life; its poisonous qualities and the usefulness of its wood lent it added mystery and interest. At one time yews were very commonly planted in English churchyards, and they have long been valued in England for hedges and topiary. It is a curious fact that under some conditions the foliage of the English yew is poisonous to livestock, yet many instances are recorded where animals have eaten the leaves without harm. Apparently wilted foliage from cut branches is the most deadly and it may be that virulence is increased if the poison is taken into an empty stomach. The English yew lives to a great old age, surely more than a thousand years. There are many noble specimens in Great Britain, including the Ankerwyke Yew, near which the Magna Charta was signed.

The Western yew, *T. brevifolia*, ranges from Montana to British Columbia and California where, at its best, it reaches 50 feet in height with a girth of 15 feet; it has wide-spreading branches. On the western slopes of the Sierra Nevada it occurs at elevations up to eight thousand feet. Asiatic species include *T. chinensis*, the Chinese yew, which is known from central and western China and Taipan, and the Himalayan yew, *T. wallichiana* which occurs in the mountains at elevations of six to eleven thousand feet and also in Burma, Malaya, Sumatra and the Philippines. This species is reported to reach a maximum height of 100 feet.

Under favorable conditions the Japanese yew grows as big as the English yew and can withstand colder winters. "Chinese" Wilson, the great

Above: Australian kauri-pine. Agathis australis (K. and J. Bigwood) Right: Australian hoop pine (Australian News and Information Bureau)

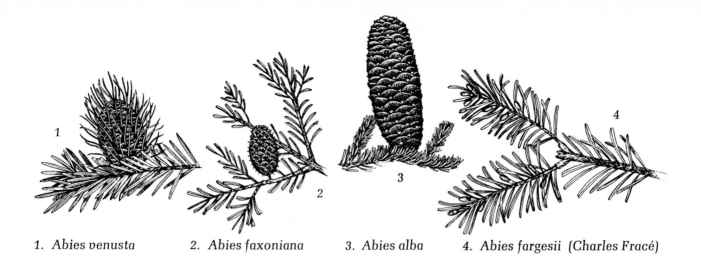

1. *Abies venusta*   2. *Abies faxoniana*   3. *Abies alba*   4. *Abies fargesii* (Charles Fracé)

plant explorer, reported seeing the finest specimens, 40 to 60 feet tall and from 6 to 10 feet in girth, in the Diamond Mountains in central Korea. Both there and in Japan this species is thinly scattered in woods among other kinds of trees. The Ainus of northern Japan and other peoples of regions where *T. cuspidata* grows made bow staves of its wood. Japanese yew was introduced to America in 1862, and is the only yew commonly grown in eastern North America.

Torreya

This genus has an interesting natural distribution, with two species in the United States, two in China, one in Japan. The stinking-cedar (*T. taxifolia*) of Florida and Georgia rarely attains 40 feet in height, but its American West Coast relative, the California-nutmeg (*T. californica*) may grow to twice this height or more; the Japanese *T. nucifera* and the Chinese *T. grandis* are also tall. Torreyas are handsome trees. They have opposite branches and stiff, sharp-pointed leaves in opposite spreading ranks. The foliage has a pungent, disagreeable odor. The egg-shaped fruit is a large bony seed covered with a tough fleshy layer.

ARAUCARIACEAE—ARAUCARIA FAMILY

Few trees look as "prehistoric" as these, and some botanists believe they are the most ancient and primitive of the conifers. Be that as it may, the family today consists of two genera, *Araucaria*, confined in the wild to the Southern Hemisphere, and *Agathis*, mostly from south of the equator but with some representation to the north. Usually trees of this family are unisexual, rarely bisexual. Their branches are characteristically in tiers. The family differs from *Pinaceae*

in that the cone scales are without distinct bracts and each bears only one ovule.

Araucaria

Most curious of this genus is the Chilean-pine or monkey puzzle (*Araucaria araucana*). Native both east and west of the Andean divide between latitudes 37° and 40° south, its name refers to the southern Chilean province of Arauco. It attains a height of 150 feet, or sometimes more, and a trunk diameter at breast height of up to 5 feet. In forests the trees lose their lower branches and present tall straight trunks with rounded or flattened candelabra-like crowns that occupy less than a third of the height of the tree. In the open, specimens develop much larger crowns and pendulous branches that come well down the trunk and even to the ground. This species is highly popular as an ornamental in parks and gardens, and good specimens may be seen in California and the Pacific Northwest, Great Britain, southern Europe and in other mild temperate areas.

The dark green leaves of the monkey puzzle are broad, stiff, leathery and sharp-pointed. They overlap each other and clothe the curious, rather brittle snakelike branches closely, forming a protection discouraging to boys and other ambitious climbers; hence the name monkey puzzle. The thick bark, broken into various-sized polygons, contains a resin used medicinally by the local Indians. The male catkins are 3 to 5 inches long, the female cones almost as big as a man's head. The latter contain up to 180 large edible seeds, called piñones, which are delicious when roasted. The pale yellowish lumber is of fine texture and good quality.

The most important timber of Brazil is *A. angustifolia*, the parana-pine. This species covers

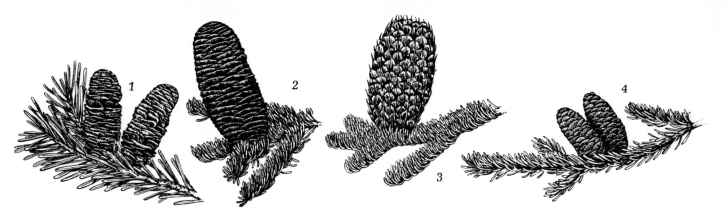

1. *Abies grandis*   2. *Abies magnifica*   3. *Abies nobilis*   4. *Abies balsamea* *(Charles Fracé)*

great areas in the southern part of the country and extends into Argentina, Paraguay and Uruguay. The tree grows to a height of 120 feet and has clear trunks and candelabra-like heads of upturned branches that form flattened crowns. Its leaves are attenuated and sharp-pointed; its seeds are edible.

From Queensland, Australia, comes the bunya-bunya (*A. bidwillii*), valued both for ornamental gardening in subtropical climates and for cultivation indoors as a pot plant. Its sharp-pointed leaves grow in two rows and are smaller than those of the monkey puzzle. The bunya-bunya may grow to a height of 140 feet and is a valuable forest tree. Its female cones grow up to a foot long and may weigh as much as ten pounds. The seeds are edible. This tree is planted in Hawaii, on the Riviera and in other warm temperate regions. Another Australian species is the Richmond-river-pine or hoop-pine (*A. cunninghamii*), the latter name deriving from its bark, which has horizontal cracks in encircling bands. A producer of resin and valuable lumber similar to that of the bunya-bunya, this tree attains a maximum height of 200 feet and diameter of 5 to 6 feet.

The Norfolk Island-pine (*A. excelsa*) is one of the best known and most handsome conifers. It grows natively only on the Pacific island from which it takes its name and there may exceed 200 feet in height. Of exceptionally symmetrical growth and with light green foliage, it is popular as an indoor pot plant and for outdoor planting in such mild climates as those of southern California and Hawaii.

Confined to New Caledonia and the nearby Isle of Pines, another species, *A. cookii*, was named after Captain Cook. Of somewhat similar habit to *A. excelsa* but more columnar, it grows to a height of 200 feet and has a perfectly straight trunk.

Agathis—Dammer-Pine and Kauri-Pine

Of about twenty species of this genus, the kauri-pine of New Zealand, the Queensland kauri-pine of Australia, and *A. orientalis*, a native of the East Indies, are best known. The kauri-pine (*A. australis*) has been called the monarch of the New Zealand forests. Its lumber is of great economic importance and the source of kauri gum, which is not obtained from living trees but is dug up in fossilized form from regions once covered with forests of the tree. Fresh resin taken from the trees is used in manufacturing varnish, paint and linoleum. Kauri-pines ordinarily reach a height of 120 to 150 feet, with trunk diameters up to 12 feet; exceptional specimens with trunks 24 feet in diameter and estimated to be four thousand years old have been reported. This species has comparatively small and narrow leaves.

The Queensland kauri-pine (*A. robusta*) of Australia may attain a height of 150 feet and a diameter of 7 to 9 feet. It has a straight, smooth, slightly tapering trunk ordinarily free of branches for up to two-thirds of its height and the crown is spreading and heavily branched. Essentially an inhabitant of rain-forest regions, the lumber produced by this species is of good quality although rather soft. It also produces gum resin, both fresh and fossil. Related species, *A. palmerstonii* and *A. microstachya*, known as North Queensland kauri, attain slightly larger dimensions.

PINACEAE—PINE FAMILY

This important family consists chiefly of trees; only a few members are shrubs. By some authorities it is divided into three families, the Pinaceae, Taxodiaceae, and Cupressaceae. It consists of about 32 genera and 376 species, chiefly of temperate and subtropical regions, nearly all evergreens and usually bisexual (*Juniperus* is unisexual). The leaves are needle-like, lanceolate or scalelike. The fruits are cones or, rarely, berry-like as a result of the union of fleshy cone scales. This family differs from Taxaceae and Ginkgoaceae in having pistillate cones.

Abies—Firs

Firs and spruces are much confused in the popular mind yet are easy to distinguish. Firs—*Abies*—have upright axillary cones that disintegrate as soon as ripe, and their leaves pull or fall away from the twigs leaving smooth, circular, dislike scars but without taking any of the bark of the twig with them and without leaving tiny projections, whereas spruces—*Picea*—have pendulous cones, usually at the ends of their branches, which remain intact at maturity, and twigs roughened by the presence of retained leaf bases. If a live leaf of a spruce is pulled off a small piece of the bark of the twig comes with it.

Firs are among the most useful timber trees although less important in this respect than spruces. They are natives of the Northern Hemisphere, the southern limit of the genus being just within the Tropic of Cancer in Guatemala. They are trees of pure atmosphere, responding badly to the polluted air of cities and industrial regions. As a group they need ample moisture and humid conditions and are intolerant of aridity either of soil or atmosphere.

Firs are among the most handsome of conifers and where they thrive they rank with the finest evergreens for creating landscape effects. They are beautifully symmetrical, of stately appearance and, in many cases, attain great heights. Their trunks are strictly erect, furnished with branches that are more or less tiered and form flat sprays. In open situations the lower limbs are retained and the trees are foliaged to the ground but under forest conditions the tapering trunks are without branches for a considerable height. When bruised, the leaves are aromatic. They are always arranged spirally on the twigs but because of twisting at their bases they often appear to form opposite rows.

The firs number about fifty species. Commercially, they are sources of lumber, pulp and resins; some are used as Christmas trees. Because their wood is not odorous it is favored for use in packing boxes for foods such as butter and lard. About forty species of *Abies* are recognized.

American Firs

Of the dozen or so species native to North America, those from the Northwest include the tallest, *A. grandis*, which may approximate 300 feet, with a trunk diameter of 4 feet, *A. concolor*, up to 250 feet, with a trunk up to 6 feet through, and *A. nobilis*, up to 250 feet, with a trunk up to 8 feet in diameter. The giant fir (*A. grandis*) ranges from Vancouver to central California, Montana and Idaho, the finest specimens occurring near the coast. Its trunk tapers slightly, its branches are downswept, its flexible leaves are green on their upper surfaces, silvery white beneath, notched at their tips and spreading in a single plane in two ranks at nearly right angles to the twigs. The cones, from 2 to 4 inches long, are green. The wood is coarse-grained, white and weak.

The white fir or Colorado fir (*A. concolor*) ranges from Colorado to Mexico and is the most adaptable *Abies* for comparatively dry conditions. Of the western American species it is best suited for the eastern states, with the Rocky Mountain type better for this purpose than the westernmost form.

Abies concolor reaches its greatest dimensions in the California Sierras. It forms a stiffish narrow spire of short branches bearing ample foliage, the leaves longer than those of other kinds—a pale blue-green when young, and dull green as they age. Its cones, up to 5 inches long, are gray-green, yellow or purple. The lumber has properties similar to those of the giant fir. It is one of the most satisfactory for landscape planting in the northeastern United States.

The noble fir (*A. nobilis*) has a reddish trunk and short, stiff branches the lower of which are somewhat pendulous. In old age it usually develops a broad, rounded head. The upper surfaces of its leaves are deeply grooved; the leaves are crowded in several rows. The wood of this species (together with that of *A. magnifica*, it is called red fir and is sometimes known as larch) is of superior quality, being light, strong and rather close-grained. It is valued for interior finishing and for packing cases.

The red fir (*Abies magnifica*) is found in Oregon and California, and sometimes grows up to 200 feet with a trunk diameter up to 10 feet. Its branches are horizontal, slender and short so that the tree is narrowly pyramidal. The leaves, quite blue during their first season, and blue-green later, are decidedly four-angled. The cones, up to 9 inches long, are purplish brown. A variety, *A. m. shastensis,* has somewhat smaller cones. The wood of the red fir, which is soft and light, but weak, is used for packing cases and some construction purposes.

The western American *Abies* natively distributed most widely is the alpine fir, *A. lasiocarpa.* It occupies high mountain regions from the Yukon to New Mexico and Arizona at elevations up to ten thousand feet. Variety *A. l. arizonica,* the corkbark fir, which is the southern form of this species, is distinguished by its thick, creamy white, soft, corky bark and its smaller cones. *Abies lasiocarpa* sometimes grows to 175 feet high and has a trunk diameter of 5 feet. It is dense and spirelike and has silver-gray bark and crowded short branches, the lower usually slightly drooping. The bluish-green leaves are crowded and nearly erect. The cones are dark purple and up to 4 inches long and the wood is similar to that of the red fir.

The cascade fir *(Abies amabilis)* reaches a maximum height of 250 feet with a trunk diameter of 6 feet. When grown under open conditions it is clothed to the ground with short, somewhat pendulous well-foliaged branches, but in forests often has a clear trunk to a height of 150 feet. The rough bark is silvery white until middle age but darker on old specimens. The cones are up to 6 inches long and purple. This fir grows from Alaska to Oregon at sea level in the northernmost part of its region and at high elevations farther south. Its wood is light, hard and close-grained but lacks strength. Lumbermen often call it larch. The Santa Lucia fir *(Abies venusta)* is in its wild state confined to the Santa Lucia Mountains of California where it becomes 150 feet high with a trunk sometimes 3 feet in diameter. Its branches, usually pendulous, often sweep to the ground. This pyramidal tree tapers abruptly into a slender spire. The long lateral branches are distantly spaced, sinuous and sparse of foliage. The leaves are sharp-pointed. Altogether, it is a tree of very distinct and ornamental appearance. Its coarse-grained wood is heavy and also fairly soft.

Sometimes called sacred fir, *Abies religiosa* is a Mexican species which locally provides rosin and lumber for construction not requiring great strength. Specimens grow to 150 feet tall and have a trunk diameter of 5 feet. The name "religiosa" refers to the use of branches in decorating places of worship for religious festivals. Closely

White fir. Abies concolor (U. S. Forest Service)

similar species are *A. hickelii* of Mexico and *A. guatemalensis* from Guatemala, the latter representing the most southerly natural range of the genus *Abies.*

The principal fir of eastern North America and the species of widest natural distribution of all American firs is the balsam fir *(A. balsamea).* This often grows in swampy land in nearly pure stands; its wood, mixed with spruce, is used for pulp. It is a favorite Christmas tree and its abundant resin is the Canada balsam of commerce. Occasionally this kind reaches a height of 75 feet and a trunk diameter of 2 feet or more. Its branches spread to form an attractive pyramidal tree but the lower ones soon die under forest conditions. The fragrant leaves are dark green on their upper surfaces, silvery white beneath, and the cones are a rich purple. Unfortunately, the balsam fir is not amenable to cultivation except possibly in localities where it grows naturally, that is, in certain areas from Labrador to West Virginia and to Minnesota and Iowa. Of more local distribution, being confined to the Allegheny Mountains, is the closely related southern balsam fir *(A. fraseri).* A difference between the two species is that the young shoots of *A. fraseri* are covered with short, reddish hair whereas those of *A. balsamea* are gray; the leaves of the southern balsam fir are shorter and are whiter beneath.

European Firs

The mountains of central Europe and the Pyrenees and Corsica are the chief homes of the silver fir (*A. alba*), a quite magnificent tree that towers to 150 feet or more and may have a trunk nearly 7 feet in diameter. Its leaves are ranged in two comblike rows. In many parts of Europe it is an important forest tree, a source of light, soft, rather weak lumber well suited for interior trim but not durable enough for outdoor use. It serves many other purposes, including carving and, because of its resonant qualities, as sounding boards for musical instruments. It is also the source of Strasbourg turpentine, used in varnishes and artists' paints. Splendid cultivated specimens are to be seen in Scotland but this species does not prosper in most parts of Great Britain and North America.

Abies nordmanniana is not unlike the silver fir but its leaves spread in many directions instead of remaining in one plane; they are a rich glossy green above and marked with conspicuous white bands underneath. It is a very handsome tree and one of the most satisfactory for planting in the central United States. A native of the southern and southeastern shores of the Black Sea and the western Caucasus Mountains, it sometimes grows to 225 feet high and has a trunk diameter of 5 feet. It closely resembles *A. cilicica* but has more crowded foliage and its cone bracts extend beyond the scales of the cone. Its lumber has the same uses as that of *A. alba*.

The Greek fir (*A. cephalonica*) inhabits the higher mountains of Greece, attaining 100 feet and a trunk diameter of almost 5 feet. The sharp-pointed leaves stand out at right angles all around the stems and are glossy green above, marked with two conspicuous white lines below. The Cilician fir (*A. cilicica*) is a native of Asia Minor and northern Syria. Together with the cedar of Lebanon, it is found in Lebanon and in the Antitaurus Mountains. It grows up to a height of 100 feet, has a trunk diameter of about 2 feet and foliage arranged like that of *A. nordmanniana* but less crowded on the twigs; the bracts of the cones are completely hidden by the cone scales.

Indigenous only to the mountains of Granada and always on limestone soils, the Spanish fir (*A. pinsapo*) is an excellent tree for landscape use wherever it thrives. Given ample room and

Noble fir and male flowers. Abies nobilis (U. S. Forest Service)

light it retains its lower branches well. It grows to a height of 100 feet and has a trunk diameter of 4 to 5 feet. The short, stiff, blunt leaves at right angles to the twigs spread in all directions and distinguish it from all other firs except perhaps *A. cephalonica,* but the leaves of the latter are longer and sharp-pointed. Across the Mediterranean in North Africa is the home of the Algerian fir *(A. numidica),* a 70-foot-tall densely branched tree with a trunk diameter of 2½ feet. It has short, thick leaves which are usually arranged more or less vertically on the twigs. This species is known only from the Babor and Tababor mountains.

Asiatic Firs

The great majority of firs are natives of Asia, many originating in the mountains of western China and unlikely ever to be seen growing naturally by many Westerners. A goodly number have, however, been cultivated and are grown in America and Europe.

Among the Asiatic firs are five Japanese species. The Nikko fir *(Abies homolepis),* reaching a height of 100 feet and a trunk diameter of 6 feet, is common in the mountains of central Japan. Stiff, pyramidal and with horizontal branches and crowded foliage, it is a splendid landscape subject. Its pointed leaves, glossy green above and silvery white beneath, stand at right angles to the twigs and have a wide V-shaped opening between the two upper rows. The cylindrical cones are purple. An important diagnostic characteristic is deep grooves in its branchlets. Another Japanese species, *A. veitchii,* is stiffly pyramidal, branches horizontally, and grows to 100 feet high with a trunk diameter of 4 feet. It generally forms a narrow specimen with short branches. With chalk-white undersides to its dark green leaves, this is a good landscape tree. The cylindrical cones are a bluish purple ripening to brown.

Inhabiting high elevations in the mountains of Japan is the 80-foot-high *A. mariesii* with a trunk diameter of 2 feet. The tree forms a dense pyramid with branches stout, stiff and spreading and bark a light gray almost to white. The moni fir *(Abies firma),* plentiful in southern Japan, supplies wood for pulp and for carpentry where high quality is not required. It is the largest and one of the most beautiful of Japanese firs, forming broad pyramidal specimens up to 150 feet high with trunks 5 feet in diameter. It has massive horizontal branches and slightly grooved

branchlets. Its leaves, which are glossy green above and have two grayish bands on their undersides, are arranged in two rows pointing upward. In young trees the leaves end in two sharp points. The cone bracts extend well beyond the scales of the cone.

The Sakhalin fir, *A. sachalinensis,* which inhabits northern Japan and nearby islands, growing to 130 feet high with a trunk diameter of 3 feet, has slender needles and closely resembles *A. sibirica* but has slightly grooved branchlets and dark green foliage. Its wood is used for pulp.

The Korean fir *(A. koreana),* discovered in 1907 at alpine elevations on the volcanic island of Quelparet and thought to be endemic there, was later found growing on the Korean mainland. It attains 50 feet and up to 2 feet in trunk diameter. In old trees the bark is rough. The leaves, glossy green above and intensely white beneath, spread radially from the twigs. The tree is of stiff, formal, pyramidal habit and is a good landscape subject.

From Korea and Manchuria comes the needle

Atlantic cedar. Cedrus atlantica (Othmar Stemmler)

fir (A. holophylla), an attractive species that grows up to 150 feet and has a trunk 4 feet in diameter. It is closely related to A. firma but the leaves on young trees have one rather than two points and the bracts of the cones are completely enclosed by the scales.

Tremendous areas in Russia and Siberia are naturally forested with the Siberian fir (A. sibirica); indeed this is the most widespread of any Abies. It grows to 100 feet tall and has slender leaves; it may be distinguished from its near relative A. sachalinensis by the lack of grooves in its branchlets and its light green foliage. Its wood serves the same purposes as that of A. alba and is used in making pulp.

Two closely allied Himalayan Abies are important, A. pindrow and A. sepctabilis, the latter most commonly called Himalayan fir, the other sometimes known as West Himalayan fir. Both attain imposing proportions, up to a height of 200 feet and trunk diameters of 8 to 9 feet, and both produce purple cones. They form great forests in their native mountains, A. pindrow up to elevations of 12,000 feet, the other to 13,000 feet. At the highest altitudes these form pure one-species forests but lower they are mixed with spruces and other trees. Both have straight-grained wood much used locally in general carpentry and for box making, matchwood and similar purposes. A. spectabilis has deeply grooved branchlets whereas those of A. pindrow are smooth.

In the first few years of the present century a number of firs from the mountains of western China were introduced in America and Europe and are seen occasionally in botanic gardens and similar collections. Among these trees are A. chensiensis, 120 feet; A. ernestii, 180 feet; A. fabri, 120 feet; A. fargesii, 120 feet (which has proved one of the most satisfactory for growing in eastern North America); A. faxoniana, 120 feet; A. forrestii, 60 feet; A. recurvata, 180 feet; and A. squamata, 120 feet, which is remarkable in having bark that flakes off to display the red underbark.

Callitris—Cypress-Pine

The native flora of Australia is poor in conifers; not more than a dozen species have been of commercial importance. Among these are certain

Above: Cryptomeria japonica (T. H. Everett)
Left: Cypress. Cupressus arizonica (Janet Finch)

Callitris or cypress-pines. The genus is confined to Australia and Tasmania but botanists once included it in certain African species now named *Widdringtonia. Callitris* differs from *Widdringtonia* in having scalelike leaves in threes and cones usually with six scales. Several callitrises are valued for their lumber and as sources of resin, aromatic oil and tanning materials. Most widely distributed is the white cypress-pine (*C. glauca*), which ranges from the western slopes of the coastal mountains and in scattered areas far to the west, north and south. Its green or silvery-greenish blue foliage distinguish this 100-foot tree with a trunk diameter up to 3 feet from other species. Its wood is popular for interior trim and other decorative purposes; it is durable, very resistant to termites, and can withstand hot, dry conditions.

The mountain-pine or black-pine (*Callitris calcarata*), which occurs in eastern Australia, is pyramidal and attains a height of 80 feet and a trunk diameter of 1½ feet. Its wood is prized because it is not affected by borers or aquatic insects and is durable in the ground. It is a source of tanbark. The northern cypress-pine (*C. intratropica*) occupies a belt almost completely across northern Australia and grows up to 80 feet high and a trunk diameter up to 2½ feet. Its leaves range from gray-green to bright green. This is the most valued tree of its territory; its lumber is highly resistant to termites.

In Tasmania the Oyster Bay-pine (*C. tasmanica*) is a large tree but on the mainland is less impressive. A handsome, somewhat spreading form, it thrives near the sea and produces wood similar to that of the white cypress-pine.

The coastal cypress-pine or stringybark (*C. macleayana*) has a very characteristic fibrous or stringy bark. Native to the coastal areas of New South Wales to Queensland, it is narrowly pyramidal and can reach a height of 150 feet. Its foliage gives the effect of great tufts and its wood is handsome and durable.

Cedrus—The True Cedars

Cedar is applied as a common name to several very different kinds of trees and shrubs as well as to some other plants. Thus, we have red-cedar (*Juniperus virginiana*), stinking-cedar (*Torreya taxifolia*), West Indian-cedar (*Cedrella odorata*)

Above: Deodar cedar. Cedrus deodara (Janet Finch)
Right: Norway spruce. Picea abies (Gerd Däumel)

Cedar of Lebanon. Cedrus libani (Anna Riwkin: Full Hand)

and ground-cedar *(Lycopodium complanatum)*. Most specifically and most properly, cedar designates any one of the four species of the genus *Cedrus:* the Atlas cedar *(Cedrus atlantica),* the Deodar cedar *(C. deodara),* the cedar of Lebanon *(C. libani)* and the Cyprian cedar *(C. brevifolia).* These species differ only in minor details and undoubtedly represent survivors of a common ancestral type that once formed more or less continuous forest throughout the mountains from the western Mediterranean as far as the western Himalayas.

The surviving species occur in isolated groups. The Atlas cedar, confined to the northwestern corner of Africa, is abundant in the mountains of Morocco and Algeria. About 1500 miles to the east, on the island of Cyprus, occurs the Cyprian cedar, the entire population limited to a few hundred acres. On the nearby mainland, both in the mountains of Lebanon and in the Taurus Mountains of Asia Minor is the cedar of Lebanon. Approximately another 1500 miles eastward great forests of Deodar cedar extend from the easternmost Himalayas almost to Nepal.

Most famous of the cedars is that of Lebanon to which so frequent reference is made in Holy Writ. It was of the fragrant, durable wood of this species that King Solomon built his Temple, his adjoining palace, the house of the Forest of Lebanon, as well as a house for his wife who was a Pharaoh's daughter, and the massive Porch of Judgment. King Hiram of Tyre and rulers of other neighboring countries also drew upon the cedar forests to provide embellishment for their palaces. Extensive though the original forests were, they could not survive such exploitation. To reinforce a slave army of King Hiram of Tyre, Solomon conscripted as many as 30,000 Israelites and 150,000 slaves together with 3300 supervisors, all of whom were set to cutting lumber in Lebanon. The effect of such massive assaults could not be less than disastrous. So only tiny remnants of the ancient glory of Lebanon's cedar forests remain. The best-known groves occupy a tiny part of the Kedisha Valley at an elevation of over six thousand feet. The species is more plentiful in the Taurus Mountains.

The Cedar of Lebanon, the tallest, most majestic and most massive tree known to the Israelites, can attain a height of about 125 feet and a maximum girth of almost 50 feet. Its great horizontal branches spread majestically and are clothed in dark green needle leaves which, like those of the larch, radiate from the tips of short, spurlike lateral branches that lengthen only a fraction of an inch each year. Unlike larch, cedars are evergreen.

The other species of *Cedrus* are only slightly different from *C. libani.* Together they form a natural group not closely related to any other existing genus. Their closest affinity is, perhaps, with the larches. As cultivated trees, cedars are most common in England. There, the cedar of Lebanon as well as the deodar and Atlantic cedars grow into magnificent specimens. In America, except in California, true cedars are less common, partly because they are not adaptable to the climate over great areas. The hardiest kind is the bluish-leaved variety of the Atlantic cedar, *Cedrus atlantica glauca.*

Chamaecyparis—False Cypress

These large pyramidal trees of North America, Japan and Taiwan are closely related to *Cupressus* except that their cones ripen the first season and each cone scale has two or rarely up to five seeds. As a group these trees withstand cold better than *Cupressus.* Except for some horticultural varieties that retain juvenile foliage perma-

32

nently, seedling specimens have needle-like leaves quite different from the flat scalelike leaves arranged in fronds that develop with maturity.

Of the seven known species of *Chamaecyparis*, three are American. The white-cedar (*C. thyoides*) has leaves without white or glaucous markings on their undersides and slender, compressed, irregularly arranged but not pendulous branchlets. A native of swamplands throughout eastern North America, this tree attains a height of 80 feet and a trunk diameter of about 3 feet. Its wood is utilized for many purposes, including boat and building construction, shingles and poles. In New Jersey, logs buried for centuries are common in peat bogs and provide excellent, durable, straight-grained lumber.

The Nootka false-cypress (*C. nootkatensis*) has quadrangular, drooping branchlets and leaves without white markings on their undersides. A native from Oregon to Alaska, this slender tree is often 120 feet tall with a trunk up to 6 feet in diameter. It is one of the most ornamental of its genus. Its wood is used locally for a variety of purposes and is preferred by Alaska Indians for canoe paddles. Because much Nootka false-cypress forest is inaccessible, the lumber is not exploited to any great extent.

An area of about forty miles wide from Eureka, California, to Coos Bay, Oregon, is the native home of Lawson's false-cypress (*C. lawsoniana*), an important timber tree that provides wood used in building and boat construction, flooring, Venetian blinds, matchsticks, railroad ties, millwork and posts and poles. A narrow pyramidal, it reaches an imposing height up to 200 feet and a trunk diameter of 12 feet and, where it has room, branches and foliage down to the ground. The flattened, frondlike branchlets grow in horizontal planes. The bright green to glaucous leaves are marked, often indistinctly, on their undersides with white lines. Regarded as one of the most beautiful conifers, this tree has given rise to about one hundred horticultural varieties, many of them prized in landscape planting. Unfortunately, they thrive only in humid climates.

Most important of the Japanese native kinds is the Hinoki false-cypress (*C. obtusa*), which is greatly appreciated in its home country for the superior lumber it produces. Like some of its

Incense-cedar. Libocedrus decurrens (American Forest Products)

American relatives, it has given rise to numerous horticultural forms valued by gardeners and landscapers. Its typical form is a broad pyramidal that may attain a height of 150 feet, with horizontal branches and flattened, pendulous, frondlike branchlets. The blunt-tipped, stem-hugging leaves are bright glossy green above and have white lines forming a Y shape underneath. One of the most important lumber-producing trees of Japan, it sometimes has a trunk 6 feet in diameter. It does not prosper in alkaline soil.

The Sawara false-cypress (*C. pisifera*) may be distinguished from the Hinoki false-cypress by its sharply pointed, stem-hugging leaves of nearly equal size and marked on their undersides with an X in white lines. Both as a garden tree and as lumber it is decidedly inferior to *C. obtusa* and is valued much less in Japan. At maturity it may be 150 feet tall and have a trunk diameter of 5 feet. It is of narrow pyramidal outline. The Sawara false-cypress grows faster than the Hinoki false-cypress and will adapt to alkaline soil. This species, too, is represented in cultivation by many horticultural forms.

Cryptomeria

This occurs as one species, *C. japonica*, in Japan and southern China, the mainland form being distinguished as variety *C. j. sinensis* and differing in being of looser growth and having spiny cones. The most important conifer of Japan, it is valued for its high quality and durability as lumber and for its beauty. It has been extensively used for planting on avenues, notably in Japan, but it does not do as well in America and Europe.

C. japonica grows up to a height of 150 feet, with a trunk diameter up to 15 feet, is narrowly pyramidal in form and has whorled branches and spirally arranged leaves. Its cones are ¾ to 1 inch long. In Japan the leaves of *Cryptomeria* are used for making incense sticks.

Cunninghamia—China-Fir

This group comprises two handsome broad pyramidal eastern Asiatic evergreen trees allied to cryptomeria. *C. kronishii* is endemic in the mountains of Taipan at altitudes of 4,500 to 6,000 feet. At its best it exceeds 150 feet in height and has a trunk up to 8 feet in diameter. *C. lanceolata*, the better-known kind, found from

Lawson's cypress. *Chamaecyparis lawsoniana* (John Markham)

34

southern and western China, grows to a height of 80 feet and has larger leaves and larger cones. The leaves of cunninghamias, flattened, stiff and sharp-pointed, are spirally arranged; their undersides are marked by two broad white bands.

Cupressus—Cypress

Although frequently applied to other genera, the name cypress most properly belongs to *Cupressus,* a genus of splendid evergreen conifers represented naturally in the floras of North America, Europe and Asia. Essentially, they are inhabitants of mild climates. With the possible exception of *C. macnabiana,* they will not, unlike many conifers, survive harsh winters. Most cypresses are known for their graceful appearance and beautiful, more or less feathery, aromatic foliage, but some varieties are as strict and formal in outline as an exclamation point. Characteristically the genus has almost quadrangular branchlets furnished with small, opposite pairs of scalelike leaves set close against the twigs, but in young seedlings the leaves are needle-like and spreading. The almost spherical cones have three to seven pairs of scales; except for the sterile lower ones each scale bears many seeds, which differentiates it from the nearly related *Chamaecyparis,* each cone scale in the latter having two or, more rarely, from three to five seeds. The cones of *Cupressus* usually exceed half an inch in diameter and ripen in their second year, while those of *Chamaecyparis* are less than half an inch across and mature in their first year.

One of the most familiar species is the Mediterranean cypress (*C. sempervirens*), which is native through southern Europe and western Asia. It is up to 80 feet tall and quite variable in habit. One of its best-known variants is *C. s. stricta,* the Italian cypress, which has erect branches, forms a very narrow column of greenery and is frequently planted in formal gardens. But the Italian cypress is really a horticultural form of venerable ancestry, its exact origin unknown. It can be increased only by vegetative propagation and by carefully selecting appropriate seedlings from the very variable progeny that results if its seeds are sown. When raised from seeds most of the plants revert to the types of the wild population which characteristically are not columnar but have more or less horizontal branches and become massive trees of great spread. They occur intermingled with cedars of Lebanon but have a much wider range than that conifer. At maturity they may become 100 feet or more high.

Monterey cypress. Cupressus macrocarpa (Josef Muench)

The wood of the Mediterranean cypress is fragrant, fine-textured and lasting. From it were constructed the gates of Constantinople and the massive doors of St. Peter's church in Rome.

Not unlike *C. sempervirens* is the Monterey cypress (*C. macrocarpa*), restricted to a very small area on the coast of central California. This picturesque tree sometimes is as much as 90 feet tall; it has horizontal branches that support a broad, spreading crown. When old, it looks very much like aged cedars of Lebanon. Furnished with juvenile needle foliage, young specimens are quite different in appearance from older ones that have developed mature scale-leaf foliage; when these plants are repeatedly sheared to form hedges, they tend to produce juvenile foliage permanently.

Were one to rely on names, the Portuguese cypress (*C. lusitanica*) would be indeed misleading. Its natural range includes parts of Mexico, Guatemala and Honduras but botanists first learned about it from a cultivated specimen found in a monastery garden in Portugal in the seventeenth century; presumably this had been brought home by an early voyager to the New World. It is somewhat scarce and its fragrant and durable wood is valued highly through its native range. The Portuguese cypress grows to a maximum height of 100 feet and is a wide-spreading tree with graceful, pendulous branchlets and cones that

Left: Italian cypress. Cupressus sempervirens stricta (W. Rauh) Above: Mediterranean cypress. C. sempervirens (Wilhelm Schacht)

are very glaucous, especially during their first year. The branchlets of *C. lusitanica* are arranged in irregular spiral fashion; *C. benthamii*, which is regarded by most authorities as a variety of *C. lusitanica*, has flattened branchlets in two rows in the same plane.

Nearly related to these is *C. torulosa*, the Himalayan cypress, a native of Nepal, 150 feet high and narrowly pyramidal in outline. Its deep green scalelike leaves are on more or less drooping branchlets. The cones, when young, are purplish. One of the most beautiful of all conifers is *C. cashmeriana*; despite its name, there is doubt about its native habitat or that it is found in Kashmir; the best evidence suggests that it hails from Tibet. Nonetheless, it is remarkably graceful, with ascending branches and long, completely pendulous sub-branches and branchlets, the latter flattened and having leaves of a lovely bluish-green hue. There are no true scalelike leaves. A very fine specimen of *C. cashmeriana* grows on Isola Madre, Lago Maggiore, in Italy. Another handsome, but smaller, example is cultivated in the Temperate House in Kew Gardens, England.

Occurring in Arizona, New Mexico and Mexico and ranging further east than any other American species is *C. arizonica*, a tree much valued for landscape planting in the Southwest. It sometimes becomes 70 feet tall and develops a heavy bole. Other New World cypresses are *C. forbesii*, a slender thirty-footer; *C. goveniana*, which rarely reaches 75 feet; and *C. macnabiana*, rarely exceeding 30 feet, with a dense, pyramidal head. All are natives of California.

Several outstanding cypresses are natives of Asia. Here belongs the mourning cypress (*C. funebris*) of central China which has widespreading branches from which hang in vertical planes long, slender lateral branches and flattened branchlets. This elegant tree, much planted in China, grows to a height of 70 feet and has uniformly gray-green leaves arranged on its twigs in four rows; its juvenile foliage is very distinct, consisting of pale green needle-shaped leaves grouped in threes or fours. In the small size of its cones, one-third to one-half inch across, and the comparatively few seeds, from three to five, in each cone scale, this species closely resembles a *Chamaecyparis*. The wood of the mourning cypress is valued for building and boat construction. *C. duxlouxiana* is a Himalayan native that is reported to grow up to 150 feet tall. It, too, has drooping branchlets and bright green or bluish foliage.

Fitzroya

The single species of this genus, *F. cupressoides*, a native, often of swampy lands, in southern Chile, is remarkable because it is the only Chilean conifer that forms dense, almost pure stands over thousands of acres. It is exploited for its lumber, which is the best produced in Chile and is used in carpentry and for other purposes such as making lead pencils, cigar boxes, and musical instruments. The logs are formed into rough planks in the forest by being split with wedges of the hard wood of *Mytus luma*, and natives then carry them on their backs through swamps and over poor roads, often for long distances. In Chile, the tree and wood are called "Alerce," the Spanish name for larch, but *Fitzroya* is quite different from *Larix*, the true larch of the Northern Hemisphere. The inner bark is used in caulking boats.

Fitzroya cupressoides has a maximum height of 240 feet and a maximum trunk diameter of 15 feet. It grows rather slowly and attains an age of at least one thousand years. When young the trees are broad, pyramidal and very dense, but with age they develop tall trunks topped by small heads of foliage; so many of the branches are dry that from a distance a forest of these trees appears to lack life. The tiny leaves occur in

alternating whorls of three; on their undersides they have two white bands. The cones, each of nine scales, ripen the first season.

Glyptostrobus

One small tree of southern China, *G. pensilis*—closely related to the swamp-cypress and the dawn-redwood, and like these, the larches and the golden-larch—remarkable among conifers for being deciduous. On non-fruiting branches the leaves occur in three rows, while on the cone-bearing branches they are scalelike and overlapping. In fall, before leaf drop, they become yellow and brown. The cones, pear-shaped and on stalks one-half inch or more long, are different from the very short-stalked round or ovoid cones of nearly related *Taxodium*. In its native Canton this species grows at stream sides and in moist soil.

Juniperus—Juniper

Junipers are chiefly Northern Hemisphere evergreens and cross the equator only in the mountains of East Africa. Their fruits are cones, but because each consists of several succulent, united scales and looks like a berry, they are commonly known as berries. Each fruit contains one to six seeds, rarely more. In most kinds the fruits are bluish-black, often glaucous. According to species, the fruits ripen in their first, second or third year. Botanically, *Juniperus* is closely related to *Cupressus* and it is not always easy to distinguish one from the other without seeing the fruits. Both produce two distinct types of leaves, needle-like and scalelike. On young specimens, the former only are borne, hence this type of foliage is referred to as juvenile. However, some junipers retain the juvenile foliage throughout their lives. Mature plants, according to kind, may have all opposite scale leaves, all needle leaves (arranged in threes) or some branches with one and some with the other. Juvenile foliage is of help in distinguishing *Juniperus* from *Cupressus*; the needle leaves of the former have whitish lines or markings on their upper sides, those of *Cupressus* on their lower surfaces.

Junipers have a pungent aroma. Because of this, fruits of *J. communis* are used to flavor gin, and the wood of many types is valued as a moth repellent in lining clothes closets and chests. The wood of several, notably *J. lucayana, J. macropoda, J. procera* and *J. virginiana*, is preferred above all others for making lead pencils.

Outstanding American junipers are the red-cedar of the eastern states and southern Canada (*J. virginiana*), which sometimes reaches a height of 100 feet and a trunk diameter of 4 feet. Often the lower trunk is buttressed. This tree is characteristically narrowly pyramidal or columnar, but becomes irregular in old age. The southern red-cedar (*J. silicicola*), from the southeastern United States and the West Indies is very similar. More massive in the trunk, although not reported as growing more than 80 feet high is *J. occidentalis* of the West Coast. Diameter at breast height has been measured at 14 feet and at ground level at 21½ feet. The specimen so measured was estimated to be at least three thousand years old. This kind has spreading branches. Another Westerner, closely related, is *J. monosperma*, the berries of which usually contain only one seed. Also in western North America is western red-cedar (*J. scopulorum*), which forms an irregular-topped tree, usually with a short trunk that divides into several ascending branches. Perhaps the handsomest of American junipers, *J. pachyphlaea*, called alligator juniper because of its checkered bark, is a native of Arizona, Texas and New Mexico. The foliage of young specimens is almost silvery white and very beautiful, and the fruits are a reddish brown.

In the West Indies grows *J. barbadensis*, once the dominant tree in Bermuda but now very seriously reduced through infestations of scale insects. The Bermuda-cedar is a xerophyte, well adapted to dry, windy locations and limestone soils. It is short-boled and differs from *J. virginiana* specifically in its branching habit, in longer leaves and in fruits containing more than one seed. Of other kinds in the West Indies and in Mexico, the best known of the latter, *J. mexicana*, provides wood for local building, railroad ties and telegraph poles.

Of the European and western Asiatic natives, the Syrian juniper (*J. drupacea*) is of interest because it thrives in limestone soil and produces edible fruits. *J. thurifera* and *J. oxycedrus* are indigenous to lands bordering the Mediterranean, and so also is the Phoenician juniper (*J. phoenicia*), which has yellow or reddish brown fruits. The common juniper (*J. communis*) in its tree form is most abundant in Europe; in North America it usually occurs as a shrub. Notable varieties of it are the Swedish juniper (*J. c. suecica*), with light bluish green leaves and the Irish juniper (*J. c. hibernica*), which is dark green and columnar. *J. excelsa*, with upright or spreading branches and up to 70 feet tall, ranges through southwest Europe, Asia Minor and the Caucasus. The closely related *J. procera*, mightiest of the clan, reaches its maximum height of 150 feet in the mountains of East Africa.

Eastern Asia, including Japan, is the home of several fine species. One of the best, *J. chinensis*, has brownish-violet fruits and attains a height of 70 feet or more, but in some of its forms it is shrubby or even prostrate. Lower-growing, up to about 30 feet tall, is *J. recurva* which inhabits the Himalayas and southwestern China.

Keteleeria

These are Asiatic evergreens with spreading tiered branches and stiff linear leaves that are usually sharp-pointed on young specimens and blunt on older trees. They resemble and are closely related to firs but differ in that their leaves are not grooved on their upper sides and are pale green underneath, and their male catkins are borne in flower clusters known as umbels. In youth they are pyramidal but in old age they become flat-topped. Their upright cones mature the first year and fall when ripe. They prefer mild climates but can withstand dry conditions better than firs. Keteleerias grow to a height of 100 feet or more and up to 7½ feet in trunk diameter, and have furrowed or corky bark. They are apparently scarce even in their native lands. The known kinds are *K. fortunei* and *K. davidiana* from China, and *K. davidiana formosana* from Taiwan.

Libocedrus

The dozen or so species of Libocedrus have by some authors been split into five genera, but the group is considered here as one genus. The incense-cedar (*L. decurrens*), the only North American representative of the genus and the best known, occurs in mountain regions from Oregon to Baja California. Attaining a maximum height of more than 180 feet and a trunk diameter of 8 feet, its trunk tapers sharply. In youth and middle age specimens tend to be broad-columnar but in age they become less regular. The foliage is dark green; the leaves are scalelike, of even size and arranged in flat sprays like those of arborvitae. The cones, slender and up to an inch long, consist of two small and two larger scales. The wood is pleasantly aromatic and is valued for making lead pencils and in building. Unfortunately, large trees are usually infected with a fungus dry rot which reduces their value as lumber sources.

Two other species occur in South America. *L. uvifera* grows slowly to a maximum height of 90 feet and is greatly prized in southern Chile for its excellent lumber. On dry, rocky remote mountain sides in southern Chile and Patagonia where, it is said, no other trees can thrive, is found *L. chilensis*. Pyramidal in youth, flat-crowned and up to 60 feet high at maturity, its lumber is of good quality but, because of the inaccessibility of the trees, not of commercial importance.

In southwest China and Taiwan the 100-foot *L. macrolepis* is indigenous. Notable in New Zealand are *L. bidwillii*, the kaikawaka or mountain-cedar, and *L. plumosa*, the kawaka. The latter is taller, sometimes attaining 100 feet and has broader, feathery, juvenile shoots and compressed but not quadrangular adult shoots. The lumber of both species is useful and durable, with that of *L. plumosa* deep red and beautifully grained.

Larix—Larch

This is one of five genera of conifers all or most of which are deciduous; the others are *Pseudolarix*, *Metasequoia*, *Taxodium*, and *Glyptostrobus*. In fall all larches lose their leaves and in spring present delightful fresh green foliage well before most other trees leaf out. At this time, too, they are spangled with bright red or purple-red pistillate flowers; the staminate flowers are silvery and less conspicuous. The cones are erect and ripen the first year but after they have spent their seeds they remain attached to the branches indefinitely. Before leaf drop in the fall the foliage assumes an attractive yellow hue, that of *L. leptopus* being especially brilliant. The species number about ten and inhabit the cooler regions of the Northern Hemisphere; they are found chiefly in the mountains and as far north as trees grow. In Siberia they reach 72° north, in North America 67° north.

Larches are handsome trees with tapering trunks, regular pyramidal crowns and an almost delicate appearance. Only in old age do some assume irregular outlines. Their branches occur generally in tiers and are horizontal or somewhat pendulous. The needle leaves, except on

Above: Aged juniper (Josef Muench) Right: Redcedar. Juniperus virginiana (T. H. Everett)

Dawn-redwood. Metasequoia (T. H. Everett)   *European larch. Larix decidua (Wilhelm Schacht)*

the leading shoots of the branches, where they are scattered and spirally arranged, sprout in crowded clusters from short spurs spaced along the branches. These spurs, like those of *Cedrus* and *Ginkgo,* elongate only a fraction of an inch each year.

Most important of the American species and most magnificent of all larches is the western larch *(L. occidentalis),* native of the Northwest, where, at its best, it attains a maximum height of 200 feet and a trunk diameter of 8 feet. Its bark, normally dark colored, becomes bright cinnamon red on old trunks. The tree is of slender, pyramidal outline. The bracts of its cones are markedly longer than its cone scales. This species favors moist, well-drained soils. Its wood is suitable for a great variety of construction work.

The American larch *(L. laricina),* known also as tamarack and hackmatack, is widely distributed from Alaska to Labrador and southward to Minnesota, Illinois and Pennsylvania and is most abundant in swampy areas. A height of 75 feet and a trunk diameter of 2 feet approximate its

maximum dimensions. The bracts of the female inflorescence are completely enclosed by the cone scales. The principal uses of its wood are for poles, fence posts, and railroad ties.

The only other American species, *L. lyallii,* is found near timberline elevations and has approximately the same distribution as *L. occidentalis.* It is distinguished by its four-angled, bluish-green leaves. It grows to a height of 50 feet with a maximum trunk diameter of 4 feet.

As an ornamental for landscape uses the Japanese larch *(L. leptolepis)* probably ranks first among larches. It may grow to 100 feet tall with a trunk diameter up to 4 feet and, where allowed ample room, develops a fairly broad pyramidal head. Its needles have two white bands on their undersides, more distinct than those of the European larch, and the cone scales reflect outward at their tips. The older branches are orange-colored. The high slopes of Mt. Fuji in Japan are clothed with dwarf examples of this larch which, at the highest elevations at which they grow simply hug the cindery ground with their gnarled branches. It was thought that these dwarf trees represented a genetically distinct race, but it is now known that their form is caused by environmental conditions, and that seedlings raised from them under more normal conditions develop to normal size.

The European larch *(L. decidua)* is greatly valued in Europe for its durable lumber, extensively used in construction and for posts and poles. The tree is also exploited as a source of turpentine. This species, native of the European Alps and western Carpathian Mountains, grows to 140 feet tall and has a pyramidal or, when aged, an irregular outline; its trunk may measure 5 feet in diameter. Its yellowish-gray branches and branchlets are somewhat pendulous, which gives the tree a quite distinctive appearance. The cone scales, unlike those of the Japanese larch, do not flare outward at their tips.

Other larches, of considerable value in their home territories as sources of lumber, occur in Asia. The Chinese larch *(L. potaninii)*, like the American *L. lyallii*, which has its leaves ridged on their upper as well as their lower surfaces, has much the aspect of the European larch and is the most important timber tree of western China. The Siberian larch *(L. sibirica)*, a close relative of the European larch, grows to 120 feet tall and inhabits northeastern Russia and Siberia. In Sakhalin, Manchuria and Siberia the Dahurian larch *(L. gmelini)* grows to 70 feet high, becoming irregular and developing wide-spreading branches. It is grown for lumber in northern Europe.

The Himalayan larch *(L. griffithii)* ranges through Nepal, Sikkim and Bhutan and has distinctly pendulous branches and its cones, 2½ to 3 inches long, are much larger than those of other species.

Metasequoia—Dawn-Redwood

Numerous kinds of trees living today have persisted with little or no change since remote geologic times and are well represented by ancient fossils. But the term "living fossil" seems to be applied chiefly to *Metasequoia* because it was described and named from fossil records before it was known to exist in present world flora. The first living specimens—three of them—were discovered by a Chinese forester in 1941 not far from Chungking, but it was not until

Western larch. Larix occidentalis (U. S. Forest Service)

Norway spruce. Picea abies (Wilhelm Schacht)

Norway spruce (J. Allan Cash)

1946 that the tree was identified as of a genus previously unknown in a living state. Then a Chinese botanist, Dr. H. H. Hu, determined that it was identical with *Metasequoia*, which had been described just a few years earlier by a Japanese botanist from Pliocene fossils found near Tokyo; the new find was named *M. glyptostroboides* and given the popular name of dawn-redwood. It is now known that the dawn-redwood grows natively over an area of about 250 square miles, centering in western Hupeh, and that in one valley alone there are more than one thousand specimens. Within a very few years, through the combined efforts of the Arnold Arboretum of Harvard University and Chinese scientists, seeds were distributed to botanical gardens and other growers of trees, and from these were raised specimens in most temperate regions of the world. *Metasequoia* has proved most amenable in cultivation, with trees in America and Europe already 40 feet or so high and producing cones. As a young specimen, at least, this species grows very fast and appears to be free of pests and diseases. It is very easy to

propagate by cuttings. In its native home there are specimens over 100 feet tall and 3 feet in trunk diameter at a height of four or five feet from the ground; at their buttressed bases the diameter is, of course, greater. In the part of China where it grows naturally the foliage of *Metasequoia* is used for feeding cattle and many of the trees are repeatedly pruned to supply this fodder. The natives of the locality in which it grows call it the *shui-sa,* which means water-fir.

Metasequoia is a deciduous conifer very similar in appearance to *Taxodium* and has the same habit, in fall, of shedding the short shoots which produce most of its leaves. The short shoots of *Metasequoia* are opposite each other on the branches, whereas those of *Taxodium* are alternate. In fall, before leaf drop, the leaves turn a warm yellowish brown. The cones are small.

Picea—Spruce

To the non-botanical eye the spruces are sometimes difficult to distinguish from their near relatives the firs, but the points of difference are definite. The leaves of spruces have peglike bases attached to the twigs from which they fall so that the bare parts of the young branches are rough; the leaves of firs drop cleanly, leaving nothing but level, circular scars on smooth twigs. Furthermore, the cones of spruces are pendulous and usually at the tips of branches; those of firs are erect and lateral on the branches.

Spruces number about fifty species, widely distributed through the Northern Hemisphere in temperate and subarctic regions and most abundant in Asia. They are among the most useful of evergreen trees but because they do not age gracefully, old specimens often becoming unkempt, they are less valuable for ornamental than for commercial purposes. Many grow to heights of 200 feet with strictly vertical trunks and branches arranged in distinct tiers.

American Spruces

Seven species of *Picea* are native to North America, four in the West and three in the East. All of the eastern and two of the western have distinctly four-angled leaves but those of *P. breweriana* and *P. sitchensis* are flat. The wood of the eastern American kinds is of great importance as a source of pulp and is used for construction, packing boxes and sounding boards for pianos and other musical instruments. The sitka spruce *(P. sitchensis)* is also important for building purposes, packing boxes and crates. The lumber of the other American species, *P. pungens* and *P. breweriana,* is not much exploited.

Under favorable conditions the sitka spruce— up to 180 feet high, with a trunk diameter up to 10 feet—forms imposing specimens with buttressed bases and gradually tapering trunks. Under forest conditions the latter are bare of branches for much of their length but when grown in the open, the lower branches are retained and the tree is broadly pyramidal in outline. The stiff, blue-green, sharp-pointed leaves have two white bands on their upper surfaces; they are strongly keeled on their lower sides. They project in all directions from the twigs, distinguishing this tree from all other flat-leaved spruces. Native from Alaska to California, the sitka spruce is rarely found more than fifty miles from the coast.

The Brewer spruce *(P. breweriana),* is remarkable for its whiplike branchlets, often 6 to 8 feet long, which depend gracefully from spreading branches. Confined naturally to a few isolated localities of southern Oregon and northern California, this is a comparatively rare species. It is

Norway spruce flowers (Ingmar Holmåsen)

distinguished from other flat-leaved spruces by its weeping branchlets and hairy shoots. Specimens form slender pyramids up to 120 feet high with a trunk diameter of 3 feet. The dark green leaves spread in all directions from the branchlets.

The Colorado spruce *(P. pungens)* is also called blue spruce because of the color often exhibited by its foliage. As a matter of fact the color ranges from dull green to almost silvery light blue. Horticultural varieties, selected for their coloring, are propagated by grafting and are often considered superior for landscape planting.

The Colorado spruce forms a stiff, very symmetrical and dense pyramid, its tiers of branches rather distantly spaced on the trunk. Its rigid, very prickly leaves are slightly incurved. The Colorado spruce inhabits elevations of from six to ten thousand feet in Colorado, New Mexico, Utah and Wyoming and was first found on Pikes Peak in 1862. Of spruces, this is one of the best adapted for dryish climates.

The other Western American species, the Engelmann spruce *(P. engelmannii),* resembles the

Colorado spruce but its branchlets are covered with fine hair and its four-angled, bluish-green leaves are less rigid. Its foliage, when bruised, emits a disagreeable odor. *P. engelmannii* grows to 150 feet with a trunk diameter of 3 feet. It ranges in high mountains from British Columbia and Alberta to New Mexico.

Two spruces of eastern North America have a much wider natural distribution than the designation Eastern spruces suggests, yet their lumber is usually marketed as "Eastern spruce." The ranges of the white spruce (*P. glauca*) and the black spruce (*P. mariana*) almost coincide, but the latter extends into the southern Appalachians. These two kinds occur plentifully from Labrador to Alaska southward to New York, Minnesota and Montana. The only species confined to the eastern part of the continent, the red spruce (*P. rubens*), occurs from Nova Scotia to the high mountains of North Carolina and Tennessee. The black spruce, of slender outline and up to 90 feet high with a trunk diameter of almost 3 feet, often has an irregular, open head and pendulous branchlets bearing crowded blue-green leaves on densely haired shoots. The red spruce attains 100 feet and a trunk diameter of nearly 3 feet. It has a narrow pyramidal outline and is readily recognized by its lustrous bright green, nearly straight leaves carried on hairy twigs. It has smaller cones, 2 inches or less in length, than the Oriental spruce (*P. orientalis*), with which it is sometimes confused.

Favoring the banks of streams and lakes is the white spruce, up to 100 feet tall and up to 3½ feet in trunk diameter. It is extremely hardy and it grows in stunted form even where permafrost grips the ground to depths of three or four feet. This species can be easily recognized by its bluish foliage which has a malodorous mousey scent. Its leaves are tetragonal and unlike *P. mariana* and *P. rubens*, its twigs are not hairy. A variety, *P. g. densata*, the Black Hills spruce, is noteworthy for its dense, compact habit and slow growth and, in some individuals, for distinctly blue foliage; ordinarily it does not exceed 40 feet in height.

European Spruces

Probably the best-known European species is the Norway spruce (*P. abies*). A native of mountain regions of central and northern Europe, but not

Sitka spruce. Picea sitchensis (Kenneth S. Brown)

of Great Britain, and extending eastward to the Volga River, it is the most northern tree of Lapland and eastern Russia. It is widely planted for lumber and in eastern North America is quite commonly used in landscaping. It has been employed far too frequently for the latter purpose since it becomes thin and is likely to lose its top as it ages. Sometimes becoming 200 feet tall, of pyramidal form, and with a trunk diameter of up to 7 feet, this tree is densely branched and foliaged; its leaves are dark green. The twigs are either smooth or covered with very minute hairs. The Norway spruce is one of the most important timber trees of Europe. Vast amounts of its light, soft, straight-grained lumber are employed for a great variety of purposes, including carpentry, pulping and the sounding boards of violins. This species is also the source of Burgundy pitch and of spruce beer.

The Serbian spruce (*P. omorika*) is sometimes 100 feet high, with a trunk diameter of 1½ feet, a very slender trunk and spirelike outline. The lowest of its short branches are often drooping. A native only of limestone soils in a very limited area of Yugoslavia, this is one of the most graceful of spruces. Its shining green leaves have whitish undersides and as a landscape tree it ranks high. It prospers in northeastern America.

The Oriental spruce (*P. orientalis*) occurs naturally in the mountains of Asia Minor and the Caucasus, where it attains heights up to 180 feet and a trunk diameter up to 7 feet. It is a compact, graceful tree of dense pyramidal outline and has dark green glossy foliage; its leaves are shorter than those of all other spruces except certain dwarf horticultural forms. Its branches are pendulous, its branchlets densely hairy.

Asiatic Spruces

The native spruces of Asia number many more than those of America and Europe together. In Japan, Sakhalin, Taiwan, and the vast continental reaches that extend westward from the coasts of China, Korea and the Pacific U.S.S.R. they are found almost everywhere in the colder, moist, northern and mountainous areas. Some are of comparatively local distribution; others grow over vast regions and in the west overlap the territories of European kinds. Of the two score

Above: Brewer spruce. Picea breweriana (P. H. Brydon) Right: Serbian spruce. Picea omorika (Gerd Däumel)

Yellow pine. Pinus ponderosa (Darwin Van Campen)

or so species of *Picea,* just about half are wildlings confined to the mountains of central and western China. It is unlikely that many Westerners will see them growing there, but through the efforts of the great plant hunters of this and the previous century, a goodly number are cultivated in America, Europe and other temperate lands.

Japan is the homeland of several fine spruces. Outstanding is the tigertail spruce *(P. polita),* which grows to 130 feet high, may have a trunk diameter of 3 feet and forms a dense, stiff pyramid. Its stout sickle-shaped leaves, which spread from all sides of the twigs and end in hard points, are distinct from those of any other spruce. A comparatively rare species, it is not exploited for lumber but is much planted in Japan for decorative purposes. The only flat-leaved spruce of eastern Asia (all others of the region have distinctly four-angled leaves) is the Yeddo spruce *(P. jezoensis),* which attains its largest dimensions on the northern island of Japan and has a very wide distribution on the mainland. It is distinct from other flat-leaved species in having pale twigs and dark green leaves with bluish or silvery white undersurfaces. The leaves are crowded on the upper

sides of the shoots. Of spirelike or pyramidal outline, it is the tallest Japanese spruce, sometimes attaining 150 feet with a trunk diameter of 7 feet.

Four Japanese kinds of lesser importance are the Alcock spruce *(P. bicolor),* the Sakhalin spruce *(P. glehnii),* the Japanese bush spruce *(P. maximowiczii)* and *P. koyamai.* The Sakhalin spruce is found in northern Japan and Sakhalin Island where it forms pure forest stands. Growing to 120 feet high with a trunk diameter of 4½ feet, it is a handsome, narrowly pyramidal tree. Related to it, but having smooth, rather hairy shoots is the only spruce that is a native of Taiwan, *P. morrisonicola.* The Japanese bush spruce, although usually seen in cultivation as a small bushy tree, sometimes attains 120 feet or more and a trunk diameter of 4½ feet in its native Japan. It was originally discovered on Mt. Fuji and is known to occur elsewhere but is extremely local. *P. koyamai,* which rarely exceeds 50 feet and a trunk diameter of 1½ feet occurs in Japan and Korea. It has a narrowly pyramidal outline.

The Himalayan spruce, *P. smithiana,* from Nepal to Afghanistan, is a broadly pyramidal tree of noble and somber aspect that grows up to a height of 200 feet or more and a trunk diameter up to 7 feet. It has spreading branches and conspicuously pendulous branchlets furnished with long, dark green, sharply pointed incurved leaves which radiate from all around the twigs. Its cones are 4 to 7 inches long. The wood, similar to that of the Norway spruce, is exploited for pulp wood, match wood and other purposes.

Central Asia, especially Turkestan and adjacent regions, is the home of *P. schrenkiana,* a narrowly pyramidal or columnar tree that sometimes exceeds 100 feet in height. Its leaves radiate from all sides of the twigs and the tree closely resembles the Himalayan spruce except that it is much narrower in outline and its cones, 3 to 4 inches long, are smaller.

The Sikkim spruce *(P. spinulosa),* another handsome kind that sometimes exceeds 200 feet in height, is the only spruce native to the western Himalayas, where it ascends to over ten thousand feet. Its branchlets are decidedly pendulous and the tree is of rather open, broadly pyramidal habit. Its flat leaves have a central ridge on both sides and are pointed.

The Siberian spruce *(P. obovata),* might just as well be included with the European as with the Asiatic kinds, for it is native from Scandinavia

Italian stone pine. Pinus pinea (Gerhard Klammet)

to Kamchatka and Manchuria. In habit, appearance and size it resembles the Norway spruce and is sometimes treated as a subspecies of it, but it is distinguished by having shorter leaves and hairy shoots. Intermediates between the two species occur. An inhabitant of very severe climates, this is the most widely spread of all spruces in their native state. Its wood is used for the same purposes as the Norway spruce.

Of the western Chinese species, the dragon spruce *(P. asperata)* is valued for landscaping because it withstands seaside conditions better than most spruces, an unexpected attribute of a tree that grows naturally so far from the ocean! It is pyramidal, up to 100 feet tall and resembles the Norway spruce in habit; it is dense-foliaged and has hairy twigs. It was introduced to cultivation as recently as 1910. Western Chinese species closely allied to this are *P. aurantiaca, P. meyeri* and *P. retroflexa,* all brought into cultivation at about the same time as *P. asperata.*

Picea likiangensis is a 100-foot western Chinese tree with somewhat compressed, overlapping leaves and more or less hairy shoots. Very closely similar are *P. purpurea* and *P. montigera.* All of these were first brought to Western gardens from 1908 to 1910. *P. wilsonii,* named after that superb collector of Asiatic plants, "Chinese" Wilson, onetime keeper of the Arnold Arboretum, differs from all other cultivated Chinese spruces in its slender branchlets and slender, dark glossy green leaves. It is of good appearance and may grow up to 75 feet.

Pinus—Pine

Pine trees are of ancient lineage. Species distinct from those extant, but still clearly recognizable as belonging to the genus *Pinus,* occur as fossils in cretaceous rocks over 100 million years old. They were widely distributed in the Tertiary Era.

Today, pines are predominantly natives of the Northern Hemisphere. Only one, *Pinus merkusii,*

47

extends natively south of the equator, into Sumatra. Many kinds, however, have been transplanted by man to parts of the Southern Hemisphere and are important there in forestry plantings. Pines form natural stands from the equator to the Arctic Circle and from sea level to as high in mountain regions as trees survive. They tend to be gregarious and in many places cover vast areas as single-species forests; elsewhere they intersperse with other trees to form mixed forests. In some ways pines in temperate regions are of as much economic importance as are palms in the tropics, for among them are many of our finest lumber producers as well as sources of pulpwood, turpentine, rosin, pitch, tar and essential oils. The seeds of some are valued as food for humans. More than eighty well-defined species are recognized and it is probable that others have not yet been described.

As a group, the pines favor open, windswept, sunny locations and well-drained soils. They have no need of rich earth; in fact they prosper on lands too lean in nutrients and too stony and steep for most agriculture. For this reason as well as for their valuable products and speed of growth, they are much used for reforestation.

Among coniferous trees, pines are by far the most important group. They are evergreen and resinous. As young specimens they are conical, at maturity they often become irregular in outline and extremely picturesque; between-times they are likely to have less character. Their branches occur in tiers. The leaves or needles are usually in bundles of from two to five according to species, their bases enclosed in a sheath; in *Pinus cembroides monophylla* they are usually solitary. They are always solitary, too, on very young pines, the leaves being scattered singly along the shoots; the adult arrangement appears only with the development of second or third year shoots. shoots.

The flowers of pines are unisexual and borne in conical clusters. The female clusters, which, after fertilization, develop in their second or third year into the well-known cones, are borne near the apices of the year's growth; the male catkin-like clusters develop from the bases of the year's shoots. At maturity the male flowers release great clouds of wind-borne pollen, easy to see if a branch is shaken vigorously.

Above: Torrey pine. Pinus torreyana (Bill Stackhouse) Left: Southern pine (Emil Javorsky)

Almost half the known species of pines are natives of North America and these include some of the very best.

American Pines

Especially noteworthy among American species is the white pine (*Pinus strobus*), a beautiful tree, which originally covered vast areas of the Northeast and is highly valued for its lumber. Although now scarce in truly large sizes, it is still a conspicuous feature in northeastern American landscapes and is much planted for forestry and decoration. Its foliage is a lovely gray-green, its needles are slender and soft and grow in bundles of five. Taken to England in 1705, it was freely planted by Lord Weymouth for forestry and became known as the Weymouth pine; in France the name became Pin du Lord. The white pine occasionally attains a height of more than 200 feet, with a trunk diameter of 6 feet. It is planted for lumber in central Europe.

The mountain white pine (*P. monticola*) of the Western mountains resembles the Eastern white pine and has the same uses; it is a somewhat smaller tree and it has stiffer leaves and is of heavier appearance. The limber pine (*P. flexilis*) is another Westerner belonging to the five-needled group of pines. Its common name derives from its tough and pliant branches which, when clothed with foliage, are distinctively plumelike.

The whitebark pine (*P. albicaulis*) rarely exceeds 60 feet in height and has wide-spreading branches and tough, very flexible branchlets. Its leaves are short and stiff. In parts of the Rocky Mountains and other mountain ranges of the American Northwest it grows abundantly and often forms the timberline. Its seeds are large and edible.

Another splendid member of this genus in the Northwest, the sugar pine (*Pinus lambertiana*) grows to almost 250 feet and has a trunk up to 12 feet in diameter in its native country. It is one of the most valued timber trees of the region. Its wood may be had in large, defect-free sizes and has a sweet resinous odor. When it is fresh, it often yields sugary exudations. Its leaves occur in fives and its cones are long, measuring up to 20 inches. Closely related to the sugar pine is the Mexican pine (*P. ayacahuite*), which provides the best timber of any Mexican conifer. Although nowhere abundant, it is widely distributed from Guatemala to the United States. It has cones up to 15 inches long. Other five-leaved American pines are the torrey pine (*P. torreyana*) of south-

White pine. Pinus strobus (Gottscho-Schleisner)

ern California, which has needles up to 13 inches long, and the bristle cone or hickory pine (*P. aristata*), a short-needled small tree of the Southwest.

Several American pines have their needles always or nearly always in clusters of three. Among these is one of the most important and one of the tallest pines of the West, the yellow pine or bull pine (*P. ponderosa*). Occasionally reaching 230 feet in height, it has long, dark green foliage and is an important source of excellent lumber. Although its needles are usually in threes, they range from two to five in a bundle. Closely related to it is Jeffrey's pine (*P. jeffreyi*), which grows to a height of 180 feet, is native from California to Oregon, and has considerable ornamental value because of its long pale bluish-green leaves, which occur in clusters of three.

A native of southern California and a handsome tree of up to 100 feet or more in height is the Monterey pine (*P. radiata*), which grows rapidly and has bright green foliage. At maturity it has a round-topped, irregular open head of wide-spreading branches. Its leaves are arranged

in bundles of three or in pairs. This species has been successfully introduced as a forest tree into Australia and New Zealand. It is of particular value for planting at seasides.

The piñon or Mexican stone pine (*P. cembroides*) is small and spreading and, like its variety *P. c. edulis*, the nut pine, produces delicious edible seeds or "nuts." Both are natives of the southwestern United States and Mexico, the nut pine extending north to Wyoming; both have their leaves in bundles of three or, more rarely, in pairs.

Other western American pines with their leaves in threes are the digger pine (*P. sabiniana*), a very distinct round-headed California species, loose of habit and sparse of foliage, with foot-long light bluish-green leaves and 10-inch-long cones, and *P. coulteri*, also loose-growing and sparse-foliaged and with dark bluish-green leaves 12 inches long and cones up to 14 inches long. From the West, too, comes the knob-cone pine (*P. attenuata*) which usually has three but sometimes only two leaves in each bundle; indigenous from Oregon to California, it sometimes grows 100 feet tall.

Noteworthy among Eastern American pines which have leaves in threes are longleaf pine (*P. palustris*), loblolly pine (*P. taeda*), and pitch pine (*P. rigida*). The first two are important sources of lumber which together with that of *P. echinata*, is known collectively as Southern pine. The wood of pitch pine is inferior for carpentry but is an excellent fuel. The longleaf pine, an open-headed kind that reaches 120 feet in height and has a natural range from Virginia to Florida and Mississippi is the most important timber tree of the southeastern United States and is also a useful source of turpentine and rosin. Another, the loblolly pine, indigenous from New Jersey to Florida and Texas, sometimes exceeds 150 feet in height and forms a compact, round-topped crown of branches and foliage. Pitch pine, rarely more than 75 feet high, has an open irregular head and often becomes very picturesque with age. It thrives on dry, stony soils. The trees are frequently furnished with whisker-like tufts of green leaves that sprout on very short shoots directly from adventitious buds that lie under the bark of trunks and branches.

The slash pine (*P. caribaea*), the principal pine of Central America, occurs also in the West

Red-cedar. Thuja plicata (U. S. Forest Service)

Indies and the southeastern United States. Under good conditions it attains 100 feet or more in height with a trunk diameter sometimes exceeding 3 feet. Its leaves occur in clusters of three or sometimes two. Its lumber is of considerable value and it is a source of turpentine and rosin.

American pines with leaves in pairs are not numerous. The shore pine (P. contorta), a round-headed tree that ranges from Alaska to California merges eastward into its variety, the lodge pole pine (P. c. latifolia), which is common throughout the Rocky Mountains. The latter forms a narrowly pyramidal head, has longer leaves and is much hardier than the shore pine. Also, it sometimes reaches 150 feet, whereas the shore pine rarely exceeds 30 feet in height. The shore pine is one of the few pines that grows in wet soil. It has been introduced to Great Britain and is there used in forestry plantings. The bishop pine (P. muricata) of California is handsome, growing to a 90-foot-height, pyramidal when young, densely round-topped when aged. The cones usually remain unopened on the trees for several years before spilling their seeds.

Eastern American species with paired leaves include the red pine or Norway pine (P. resinosa). It may at first seem to be misnamed, but its popular designation refers to the Maine village of Norway and not to the land of the Vikings. It is handsome, has reddish bark and sometimes becomes 120 feet tall with a trunk 3 feet in diameter. It is popular for forestry planting. Its natural range is from Newfoundland to Pennsylvania, westward to Manitoba and Minnesota. Another handsome kind is the shortleaf pine (P. echinata), which is found from New York to Florida and Texas and has dark bluish-green foliage. Occasionally its leaves occur in threes. It forms a broad oval head and may reach a height of 120 feet. The range of the jack pine (P. banksiana), the most northern of eastern American pines, extends south from near the Arctic Circle to New York and Minnesota and reaches a maximum height of 70 feet. Its wood is used for pulp. The scrub pine (P. virginiana), cedar pine (P. glabra) and sand pine (P. clausa) are other eastern American two-leaved pines but they have no great merit either as ornamentals or as producers of lumber; their chief use is as fuel.

Above: Pinus cembroides monophylla (U. S. Department of Agriculture) Right: Foxtail pine. Pinus balfouriana (Bill Stackhouse)

European Pines

The native pines of Europe include many notable kinds, several of which are popular for planting in temperate regions. One of the best known and most valuable for its lumber as well as for turpentine and other "naval stores" is the Scotch pine (P. sylvestris). A two-needled kind, this species occurs throughout the length and breadth of Europe and across Siberia; no other pine is naturally so widely distributed. Among its varied habitats are swampy lands in Scandinavia, dry infertile soils in central Europe, and the mountains of the Mediterranean region. Rarely does it much exceed 100 feet in height or 5 feet in trunk diameter. The foliage is dark bluish-green and the bark over large areas is a warm reddish orange color; older specimens are very picturesque.

The Austrian pine (P. nigra) is a two-needled tree that occurs sporadically in southeast Europe and Asia Minor. Occasionally it becomes 150 feet tall with a trunk diameter of 6 feet. Typically, it is very symmetrical and pyramidal but in age it sometimes becomes broad-headed and flat-topped. It is very well adapted for planting close to the sea and it is much used for landscaping in northeastern America, as for example in the extremely poor soil at Kennedy Airport in New York. The Austrian pine has longer and darker green needles than the Scotch pine and its bark is dark gray. Several geographical forms of this species are recognized, notably the Crimean pine (P. n. caramanica) and the Corsican pine (P. n. poiretiana). These, like the typical kind, are used extensively in forestry.

The Swiss mountain pine (P. mugo) is best known to many Americans in its dwarf variety, the mugho pine (P. m. mughus). The typical kind may attain a height of 45 feet and, like P. m. mughus, inhabits the mountains of central Europe. In its bushy form this pine occurs in its native mountains at above 10,000 feet—higher elevations than any other tree or shrub. Its paired leaves are markedly twisted, dark green, stiff and pointed; its cones are glossy.

An extremely picturesque tree is the Italian stone pine (P. pinea), a native throughout southern Europe. It grows up to 100 feet tall and has

Above: Longleaf pine. Pinus palustris (Andreas Feininger) Right: Canary Island pine. Pinus canariensis (Wilhelm Schacht) Far right: Chir pine. pinus roxburghii (Janet Finch)

52

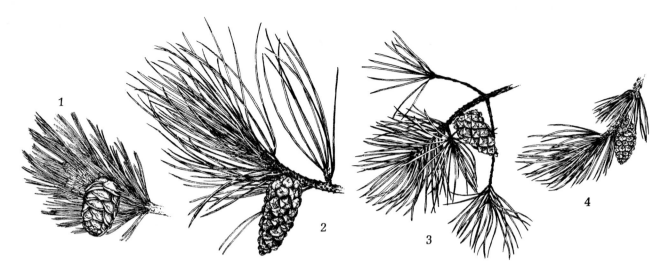

1. *Pinus cembra* 2. *Pinus nigra* 3. *Pinus sylvestris* 4. *Pinus mugo (Charles Fracé)*

long horizontal branches which form broad flat heads on old specimens. This species is a characteristic and conspicuous element of the landscape in many parts of Italy, and it forms fairly extensive forests in some places. *Pinus pinea* usually has two but sometimes three leaves in each bundle. It bears big edible seeds in large glossy cones which do not mature until their third year. Husks found in refuse heaps of ancient Roman camps in Britain are evidence of how long these seeds have been valued as food.

Of all two-needled pines, the species with the longest leaves, reaching up to 8 inches, is the cluster pine or maritime pine (*P. pinaster*), a southern European tree that thrives in coastal areas. At its tallest it may be 120 feet high and is highly decorative when old and rugged. Its cones, which remain on the tree for many years, come in clusters. It is a source of rosin but its lumber is of inferior grade. It is planted to bind sandy soil.

With its leaves usually in pairs, the Aleppo pine, or the Jerusalem pine as it is sometimes called (*P. halapensis*), is a very handsome species. A native of southern Europe, North Africa and Asia Minor, it commonly occupies coastal areas where it forms round-topped heads with great plumose masses of gray-green foliage. The Aleppo pine, which rarely exceeds 80 feet in height, is one of the most important producers of turpentine and since earliest time has been exploited for this as well as for rosin and tar; its wood is of inferior quality.

Endemic to dry, exposed slopes in the Canary Islands is the attractive Canary Island pine (*P. canariensis*), with glossy, more or less drooping, grass-green leaves up to a foot long and in clus-

ters of three. It is valued for landscape planting in mild climates. Under favorable conditions it attains a height of 100 feet and a trunk diameter of 3 feet; it has a broad round-topped head with spreading branches and somewhat pendulous branchlets. It is distinguished from all other three-leaved pines by its yellow shoots, long leaves and large cones, the latter up to 9 inches long.

Sometimes 120 feet high, the Swiss stone pine (*P. cembra*) is pyramidal when young but ages into a broad, open-topped specimen of great picturesqueness. This five-needled species inhabits the Alps of central Europe and frequently forms the dominant woody species at timberline altitudes. Its numbers are being seriously reduced by fires and by grazing but, fortunately, its range extends far beyond the European Alps, well into Russia and Siberia. The excellent wood of this tree, known as Arolla, is much used for wood carving, construction and the manufacture of furniture. Its seeds are edible.

Sometimes called the Balkan pine, *P. peuce* of southeastern Europe is a densely branched ornamental tree that forms a slender pyramid and attains an eventual height of perhaps 80 feet. Its needles, which come in bundles of five, stand erect.

Asiatic Pines

The pines of Asia are valued in their native lands as sources of lumber and other forest products and some for their ornamental qualities. Several are cultivated in America and Europe in gardens and others in forestry. Outstanding among Asiatic five-needled pines are *P. parviflora, P. nepalensis, P. armandii,* and *P. koraiensis.* The first

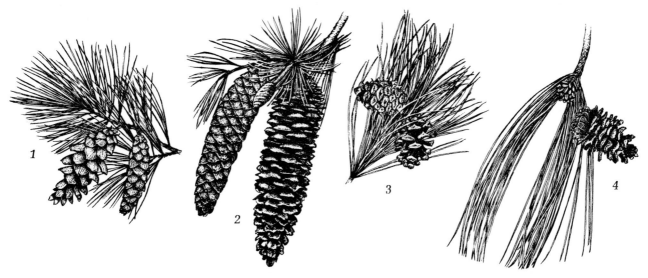

1. *Pinus strobus* 2. *Pinus lambertiana* 3. *Pinus ponderosa* 4. *Pinus palustris (Charles Fracé)*

named is the Japanese white pine, a highly ornamental tree that may grow to 80 feet tall and that forms a broad spreading head of horizontal branches with brushlike tufts of foliage at the ends of its twigs. Under cultivation it develops quite rapidly; when planted for ornament it requires ample room. Its gray-green leaves are quite short, soft and twisted. Its cones grow in clusters and remain on the branches for several years. The Himalayan white pine *(P. nepalensis;* also called *P. excelsa)* is surely one of the loveliest of pines. In a wild state it may exceed 150 feet in height and it forms a broad, loose pyramid of branches handsomely furnished with long, drooping grayish or bluish green leaves. It grows rapidly as a young specimen and begins to bear cones, slender and sometimes up to 10 inches long, at an early age. The Himalayan chir pine *(P. roxburghii),* which grows up to 180 feet tall, differs only in a few minor details from the species *P. canariensis.*

The Chinese white pine *(P. armandii),* a 60-foot native of China, Korea and Taiwan, has wide-spreading horizontal branches and bright green leaves. The Korean pine *(P. koraiensis)* occurs both in Korea and Japan, and under favorable circumstances it may grow to 150 feet high. Its leaves are straight and dark green. It is pyramidal in outline and densely branched and foliaged. Because of its handsome appearance and slow growth it is excellent for planting in small gardens. It is related to *P. cembra* but its 5-inch cones are twice as big as those of its European relative. It produces the best lumber of any oriental pine, quite as good as that of the eastern American white pine.

Completely distinctive is the lacebark pine

(P. bungeana) of northwest China, which often develops more than one trunk from its base. Of particular interest is bark that peels or flakes off in large irregular patches, exposing the pale cream-colored underbark, much in the manner of plane trees. Growing to about 100 feet tall and with a trunk diameter up to 12 feet, this species has a rounded to pyramidal head and short, rigid, light green leaves in bundles of three. It grows slowly and is much planted by the Chinese in burial grounds and near temples. Another Chinese species, *P. tabulaeformis,* has stiff leaves in pairs, or occasionally in threes, and may grow 70 feet high; a variety *P. t. densata* has two leaves in each cluster.

Outstanding two-needled Japanese pines are the Japanese black pine *(P. thunbergii)* and the Japanese red pine *(P. densiflora).* The former may exceed 100 feet in height and 5 feet in trunk diameter. Its dark gray or nearly black bark is deeply fissured; its straight, stiff leaves are paired and dark green. The stiff, crooked branches spread horizontally and usually are of varying lengths and irregularly disposed. This develops into an extremely picturesque tree, which accounts for its appearance in numerous Japanese prints and other works of art. It is excellent for planting in seaside locations and is one of the chief lumber-producing trees of Japan. The other Japanese species, the red pine, reaches 120 feet in height, develops an irregular, broad head, has reddish, scaling bark and a trunk up to 4 feet in diameter. It is an important source of lumber in its native country and is favored by Japanese experts for training as bonsai, the dwarfed trees grown in containers. A dwarf variety, the Japanese umbrella pine *(P. d.*

Swiss stone pine. Pinus cembra (W. Rauh)

Pinus coulteri (Gerd Däumel)

umbraculifera) forms a low, rounded head and is planted in gardens.

Two pines closely related to the preceding are natives of Burma, the Indo-Chinese peninsula and the Philippines, *P. insularis* and *P. merkusii*; the latter also extends into Borneo and Sumatra and is the only species native to the Southern Hemisphere. The most obvious difference between them is in the leaves: those of *P. insularis* occur in pairs, those of *P. merkusii* in threes. *Pinus insularis* attains 80 feet in height in the dry, exposed mountain ridges it inhabits in northern Luzon. In Sumatra *P. merkusii* grows up to 100 feet tall and forms flat, umbrella-like heads after the fashion of *P. pinea*.

Pseudolarix—Golden-Larch

The only species, *P. amabilis* of China, is closely related to the larches and like them is deciduous. It differs in that its male catkins are clustered rather than solitary and its woody cone scales, which are much larger than those of *Larix*, separate and the cone disintegrates at maturity. The cones of *Larix* remain intact, their scales persisting. In addition, the leaves of *Pseudolarix* are larger and stouter than those of any larch

and the cones face more or less downward and are not erect. The golden-larch is indigenous only to a very limited area in the coastal mountains of eastern China. A handsome, ornamental tree of pyramidal outline, which grows to 130 feet high and has a maximum trunk diameter of 3 feet, it has wide-spreading branches that tend to be pendulous toward their ends. As with larches, the leaves on terminal shoots are scattered in spiral fashion, but most of the foliage grows in radiating clusters at the ends of very short and very slow-growing, spurlike laterals. The foliage in spring is yellowish green. As summer advances, it becomes more distinctly green and in fall, before leaf drop, it changes to a rich golden yellow. The cones are composed of thick, triangular scales and are almost as broad as high. As the cones approach maturity the scales spread outward and the cones then bear a gross resemblance to plants of *Sempervivum*.

Pseudotsuga

The best known of this genus is the Douglas-fir (*P. taxifolia*). Another North American is the bigcone-spruce (*P. macrocarpa*). Four other species are natives of eastern Asia. In western

56

North America there are good examples of fossilized specimens from the Miocene. In Ginkgo Petrified Forest near Vantage Bridge, Washington, silicified logs of *Pseudotsuga* occur along with those of *Ginkgo* and other trees.

Pseudotsuga consists of tall pyramidal trees with branches in irregular whorls, two-ranked linear leaves with a white band paralleling each side of the prominent midrib on their undersides. The pendant cones, which mature in one season, have conspicuously protruding bracts; these, together with the pointed winter buds, are positive identifications of the genus and distinguish it from the nearly related *Abies*; it can be readily told from *Tsuga* by its smooth branches and because it is not roughened by attached and persistent leaf bases.

Douglas-fir (*P. taxifolia*), named after the early nineteenth century British plant collector David Douglas, is surely one of North America's most magnificent and useful trees. Its natural range extends from British Columbia to New Mexico, eastward to Colorado. The Rocky Mountain form, often distinguished as variety *P. t. glauca*, is quite distinct from the coastal species; it has shorter needles that are bluish rather than green, it is more compact and slower-growing, has cones with spreading or reflexed scales, and, most important to landscape planters in cold regions, withstands much lower temperatures than the coastal type. For this reason it is highly favored in northeastern America; in Great Britain the coastal form does better. Whereas the more western form sometimes grows to over 300 feet and has trunks up to 15 feet in diameter, the other rarely attains a height of 100 feet and a trunk diameter of 3 feet. Specimens 200 feet or more high with 6-foot trunks are common; they occur sometimes in pure stands, more often admixed with other conifers, their huge trunks close together and rising perpendicularly and without branches to great heights. The finest stands occur between the coast and foothills of the Cascade Mountains and not much above sea level on Vancouver Island and the nearby mainland. Douglas-fir is greatly valued as a source of lumber and is used for a wide variety of purposes. It is a favored species for forestry planting in Europe. Because it holds its needles well when cut, young specimens make very satisfactory Christmas trees. As a garden tree it withstands city conditions better than most conifers. It has given rise to numerous horticultural varieties.

Pitch pine bark. Pinus rigida (Rutherford Platt)

The bigcone-spruce (*P. macrocarpa*) inhabits mountain slopes in southern California and Baja California. Its popular name refers to its cones, which are larger than those of any other *Pseudotsuga*, measuring up to 7 inches long. The tree has more or less downswept branches and bluish green foliage. It attains a maximum height of perhaps 80 feet and a trunk diameter of about 3 feet. The chief use of its wood is as fuel.

The Japanese *Pseudotsuga japonica* reaches a maximum height of about 100 feet and is different from the American species in that the tips of its leaves are slightly notched. Two closely related kinds come from western China, *P. sinensis* and *P. wilsoniana*, and a variety of the latter, *P. j. formosana*, is endemic to Taiwan.

Sciadopitys—Umbrella-Pine

One of the most distinctive evergreen trees is the Japanese *Sciadopitys verticillata*, the only representative of its genus. It is a handsome, slow-growing kind with whorled branches, a dense, narrow, conical form and, in its native land, reaches a height of up to 110 feet and a trunk diameter of up to 4 feet. It bears leaves of two kinds, one being triangular brown scales

scarcely a quarter of an inch long, disposed along the lower parts of the shoots and in two or more rings near their tips, and the other being a long, narrow, flattened, glossy green kind grouped in twentys to thirtys at the ends of the shoots and spreading like the ribs of an umbrella. Actually each green leaf consists of a joined pair; the line of fusion is visible in grooves in the upper and lower sides of the compound. The cones mature in their second season and are from 3 to 4 inches long. The umbrella-pine is valued chiefly as a garden tree. Its lumber is of good quality but little of it is available. It is very resistant to decay; timbers used in the Sensu Bridge in Tokyo lasted without painting for three hundred years. Several fossil species of *Sciadopitys* have been described from as far back as the Jurassic and Cretaceous. Once the genus was widely distributed in the Northern Hemisphere.

Sequoia—Redwood

The groves of one of America's most noble native trees, the redwood, occupy a narrow coastal belt almost five hundred miles long and never more than thirty-five miles wide from southern Oregon to California; it occurs only in areas influenced by sea fogs. This magnificent evergreen was named for Sequoyah, a halfbreed Indian who devised the Cherokee alphabet. Although the statement has been challenged, there seems little doubt that the tallest of all trees is a redwood; the champion, discovered in 1966 in Redwood Creek Valley, California, measures 385 feet; it is a double tree with a trunk diameter of 16.8 feet. Specimens less tall but with considerably thicker trunks are known. The maximum age of redwoods has been reliably estimated as about two thousand years. The geologic records of *Sequoia* are beclouded because it is often impossible to distinguish their fossilized remains from those of *Sequoiadendron, Taxodium, Taxus* and some other genera, but there is no doubt that in the Tertiary a species not materially different from *S. sempervirens* was widely distributed. The redwood at maturity has a slender head and horizontal or down-sweeping branches. The linear leaves of lateral shoots have two white lines on their undersides and are arranged in flat sprays. The scalelike leaves of

Above: Douglas-fir. Pseudotsuga taxifolia (U.S. Forest Service) Left: Big-trees and sugar pines (Bill Stackhouse)

terminal shoots are arranged spirally and either lie close to the stems or spread slightly. The pendulous cones are up to 1 inch long and mature the first year. The bark is very thick, furrowed, fibrous and reddish. Redwoods possess remarkable powers of reproduction both from seed and from sprouts that spring very freely from stumps of felled trees. One factor that has helped preserve this species in its tiny remaining domain through untold millennia is its remarkable resistance, largely due to the insulating effect of its thick bark, to damage from fire.

Redwood lumber is highly valued for a wide variety of construction purposes, especially where resistance to humid or wet conditions is important. Dense, mature groves of redwood contain more cubic feet of lumber to each acre than any other known forest.

Sequoiadendron—The Big-Tree or Giant Sequoia

Formerly included in the genus *Sequoia*, this species is now given a genus of its own, *Sequoiadendron giganteum*. The distinction is based on the fact that the leaves are of only one kind and are spirally arranged on the twigs, the winter buds are naked, the cones have twenty-five or more scales, and other details. In addition, the cones of the big-tree are from 2 to 3 ½ inches long (at least twice as big as those of *Sequoia sempervirens*) and mature in their second rather than in their first season. This species (*Sequoiadendron giganteum*) does not have sprouts springing from its bases.

The big-tree attains a greater total bulk than any other tree, although it is neither the tallest (its relative, the redwood, exceeds it) nor of the greatest girth (the baobab and Mexican swamp-cypress exceed it). Specimens 325 feet high are known, and trunk diameter, measured a few feet from the ground, above the flaring base, may approximate 25 feet.

Sequoiadendron is one of the rarest and at the same time one of the best known of trees. It is confined in the wild to an area about 280 miles long and less than twenty miles wide on the western slopes of the Sierra Nevada in California at elevations of five thousand to 8400 feet. There this majestic species persists in a few dozen groves, some of which, fortunately,

Redwood. Sequoia sempervirens (Darwin Van Campen)

are preserved in national parks. Like the redwood, it is well represented by close relatives in fossil records of trees that flourished in ancient geologic times. A petrified wood sample from Cretaceous deposits in the Isle of Wight off the southern shore of England closely resembles *S. giganteum,* and similar vestiges have been found from Greenland and elsewhere. In times past both *Sequoia* and *Sequoiadendron* where much more widely distributed on the earth.

Many statements have been made about the age attained by big-trees, some of them unquestionably extravagant. The soundest estimates indicate that specimens may live to 2500 or possibly 3000 years.

Sequoiadendron giganteum is uniformly pyramidal in youth and well furnished with branches and foliage to the ground. In age it develops an irregular, rounded crown, and very old specimens may have trunks without branches to a height of 150 feet. The branches are comparatively short and horizontal or drooping. The trunk is covered with deeply furrowed, spongy bark, 1 to 2 feet thick on old specimens. When the species was discovered in 1841, it created extraordinary interest among botanists and horticulturists. In 1853 seeds were sent to England; it proved a great success and plantings more than 150 years old on avenues and elsewhere can be found there. In 1853 the British botanist Lindley named the genus *Wellingtonia,* where upon the American botanist Winslow renamed it *Washingtonia;* alas for national pride, an earlier name, *Sequoia,* rightfully took precedence. Then, in 1939, the big-tree was segregated from *Sequoia* and placed in a new genus, *Sequoiadendron.*

The wood of the big-tree is light, brittle and very durable. At one time it was commercially exploited, and much destructive lumbering took place. Today it is of slight commercial importance because so little of it is left; many of the remaining trees are in protected groves.

Taiwania

Best known of two species that comprise this genus is *T. cryptomerioides,* an endemic of the mountains of Taiwan at elevations of six thousand to eight thousand feet. When young, it is pyramidal and has pendulous branches, whereas in age it exhibits a bare trunk and small dome-

Bald-cypress. Taxodium distichum (V. R. Johnston: National Audubon)

shaped crown. It may exceed 180 feet in height and have a trunk diameter of 9 feet or more. In southwestern and central China there is a closely related species, *T. floussiana.*

Taxodium—Bald-Cypress or Swamp-Cypress

Taxodium, abundant in Tertiary times in Europe, Asia and North America, as fossil records so clearly prove, is now a native only of the southeastern United States and Mexico. But there it is widespread and relatively abundant. It is the only genus of the Coniferales that includes both deciduous and evergreen kinds. It consists of three closely related species, all handsome. Like the *Metasequoia,* these trees have two kinds of young shoots: persistent terminal or leading ones with axillary buds and leaves arranged spirally, and deciduous slender lateral shoots with leaves in two ranks. The latter drop off at the end of their first or in their second year, according to species. These deciduous shoots of *Taxodium* are alternate on the branches, whereas those of *Metasequoia* are opposite.

Bald-cypresses are also remarkable because in swamps or areas regularly inundated their roots at various distances from the trunk develop astonishing conical protuberances, called "knees," which rise to a height of 3 or 4 feet or even 10 feet. They consist of spongy, light wood covered with spongy bark and often become hollow when old. The purpose served by these "knees" has been much debated. The most popular theory is that they supply air to the submerged roots. The root system is of interest because it consists of stout horizontal roots that radiate from the buttresses (often hollow in old age) of the trunk and send large anchor roots downward to very considerable depths. The "knees" most often rise directly above these anchor roots. This rooting system goes far to assure the survival of trees in soft, swampy earth.

In early years and middle age bald-cypresses are rather narrowly pyramidal in outline but in advanced age they often develop broad, round heads, sometimes with a spread of 100 feet or even more. Their foliage is light and feathery, and that of the deciduous kinds becomes a warm, rich brown before it is shed in fall. The nearly globular cones ripen in their first year.

Above: Arbor-vitae. Thuja occidentalis (T. H. Everett) Right: Chinese coffin tree. Taiwania cryptomerioides (Paul Popper Ltd.)

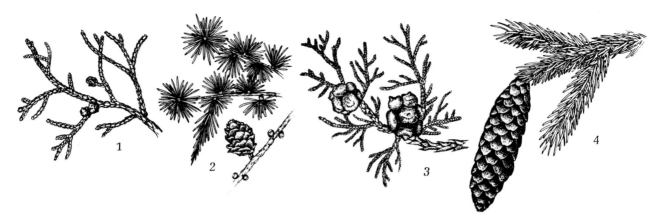

1. *Juniperus chinensis* 2. *Larix decidua* 3. *Cupressus duxlouxiana* 4. *Picea abies* (Charles Fracé)

The most important bald-cypress is *T. distichum,* which occurs from Delaware to Florida westward to Illinois, Missouri, Arkansas and Louisiana. Although primarily a tree of wetlands and swamps, it thrives when cultivated under drier conditions. Its tapering trunk, usually prominently buttressed at its base, grows up to 150 feet high and has a diameter, above the broadened basal portion, of up to 12 feet.

The wood of *T. distichum,* known simply as cypress (not to be confused with that of the true cypress or *Cupressus),* is of very considerable commercial importance. It is known for its ability to resist decay and is used for parts of structures exposed to weather or likely to remain moist; it is a preferred wood for greenhouse construction. Because of the highly attractive grain of much of the wood, it is greatly valued for use as panels, interior trim and similar purposes. The wood of older trees is often invaded by a fungus which forms narrow channels through it. Lumber from such trees exhibits decorative patterns by this and is known as pecky cypress; although not as strong as uninfected wood, it is as durable because the growth of the fungus ceases with the felling of the tree. In southern Europe *T. distichum* is planted for lumber.

Altogether a smaller and more slender tree is *T. ascendens,* sometimes called pond-cypress, which occurs from Virginia to Florida and Alabama. Unlike *T. distichum,* this species has branches that are erect rather than upright and leaves appressed to the twigs.

The Mexican bald-cypress (*T. mucronatum*) is usually evergreen, shedding its branchlets and leaves in their second season. It is found in wet soils on the high tableland of Mexico and into Guatemala and under favorable circumstances attains great size. Its lumber is lighter, softer, and inferior to that of its northern relatives and is of only local importance. Several really huge specimens of this species are known, one of which, the famous "El Gigante," which grows in the churchyard of the village of Tule, Oaxaca, has been described by a botanist as "one of the largest living things on earth." It is only about 140 feet tall but it has a huge, approximately spherical head and an enormous trunk. Because of the buttresses the trunk does not make an even circle but its average diameter is 25 feet. One diameter exceeds 50 feet, and following the ins and outs between the buttresses, it measures 150 feet in circumference at the base. An outstanding Mexican botanist, Dr. Cassiano Conzatti, sets the age of this giant at between 1500 and 2000 years. It is noteworthy that this tree grows in a dry location, but there is evidence that the course of a nearby river has changed since the tree was young; furthermore, there is ample water about 5 feet below the ground.

Thuja—Arbor-Vitae

This genus includes five species of symmetrical columnar and narrow, pyramidal evergreen trees of North America and eastern Asia that have rather short branchlets on which the adult scale-like leaves are arranged in opposite pairs to form four longitudinal rows; each pair of lateral leaves almost covers the facial pair. The cones are not more than 1 inch long, each with eight to ten scales. All parts of these trees are resinous and give off a strong aroma if rubbed or bruised.

Young specimens of arbor-vitae have spreading needle-shaped leaves, quite distinct from the scalelike adult foliage. Some of the horticultural varieties of *T. occidentalis* and *T. orientalis* always retain their juvenile foliage.

1. Larix laricina 2. Tsuga mertensiana 3. Picea breweriana 4. Sequoia sempervirens (Charles Fracé)

Giant arbor-vitae or western red-cedar *(Thuja plicata)* is native along the Pacific Coast of North America from Alaska to northern California and eastward to western Montana. Specimens are sometimes 200 feet tall with trunks up to 12 feet in diameter at their buttressed bases. They attain a maximum age of about one thousand years. The scalelike leaves of this species are without conspicuous glands and usually have whitish markings on their undersides. Because the light, soft wood splits easily it is especially valued for making shingles, lining closets and other carpentry and for greenhouse benches and other purposes where resistance to moisture and decay is more important than strength. Slender trunks are much used as fence posts and poles. The Indians carved the trunks of this arbor-vitae into totem poles and used rough planks, split from the trunks without sawing, in constructing their huts. There are many horticultural varieties of *T. occidentalis.*

American arbor-vitae or northern white-cedar, *T. occidentalis,* is much hardier than any other species. It inhabits swampy land from Nova Scotia and New Brunswick to New Jersey and, in the mountains, to North Carolina and Tennessee. It grows to a maximum height of about 60 feet and develops a stout, buttressed trunk which may become 6 feet in diameter. Its scalelike leaves on the main axes have conspicuous glands but have no white markings beneath. In winter its foliage assumes a rather unpleasant yellowish brown color which reduces its appeal as a garden planting; nevertheless, in harsh climates it is valued for landscaping because of its great resistance to cold. It is especially useful as a windbreak or hedge. The chief uses for the lumber are as poles and fence posts.

A handsome species is Japanese arbor-vitae *(T. standishii),* a native of central Japan that generally resembles *T. plicata.* It is rather broadly pyramidal and looser branching than other species, and up to 50 feet tall. Its scale leaves have whitish triangular marks on their undersides and are without glands; when crushed they emit a eucalyptus-like odor.

Considerably smaller, usually not more than 50 feet tall, is the oriental arbor-vitae, *T. orientalis,* from China and Korea. This species is represented in cultivation by many horticultural varieties. The typical plant has more or less upcurved branches and has its foliage sprays in vertical planes; the leaves are of the same color on both surfaces. *T. orientalis* and its varieties are sometimes referred to by the name *Biota.*

Only rarely does the Korean arbor-vitae *(T. koraiensis)* assume tree form; more usually it is shrubby. As a tree its maximum height is about 25 feet. It is slender and has glandular leaves that are bright green above and glaucous on their undersides. It is, as its name implies, a native of Korea.

Thujopsis—Hiba Arbor-Vitae

The only species of this Japanese genus, *T. dolobrata,* is segregated from *Thuja* because each of its cone scales has three to five instead of two seeds. It is also very distinctive in having much broader branchlets and rounded cones with thick, woody scales. The frondlike branchlets are arranged in horizontal planes and bear opposite scale leaves in four rows; the leaves are shining dark green on their upper surfaces and have conspicuous patches of white beneath.

The Hiba arbor-vitae and its varieties are best adapted to cool, humid climates. In cultivation it is sometimes shrubby but at its best in its native country it becomes a splendid ornamental tree of

Mexican bald-cypress. Taxodium mucronatum (Lorus and Margery Milne)

formal, pyramidal habit up to 50 feet tall, while its variety, *T. d. hondai,* of more northern distribution in Japan, attains twice this height. Its lumber is straight-grained and durable and is valued in Japan for bridge and boat building.

Tsuga—Hemlock

This genus comprises a dozen or more graceful North American and Asiatic evergreen trees with horizontal or pendulous branches and elegant foliage. The flattened, narrow, linear leaves are predominately two-ranked or approximately so, and have a pair of whitish bands on their undersides. In most kinds the cones are 1 inch or less long. Each cone scale enwraps two seeds. Hemlocks are splendid decorative trees for planting in areas not subject to sweeping winds; unlike many conifers, they can stand part shade. They do not thrive in dry soils.

The name hemlock is a variation of hemlock-spruce, the colloquial name in Great Britain for *Tsuga canadensis.* The trees have no relationship to the hemlock used by the ancient Greeks as a poison and famous for causing the death of Socrates. That hemlock is *Conium maculatum,* a weedy relative of the carrot and parsnip, a member of the family Umbelliferae.

The eastern North American *T. canadensis* reaches a maximum height of 100 feet and diameter of 4 feet and is widely distributed from southern Canada to Alabama. It is a source of tanbark and of a rather poor splintery lumber used for rough carpentry and paper pulp. The more compact Carolina hemlock (*T. caroliniana*) of more southern range in the Appalachian Mountains has similar uses. From Alaska to California, in humid coastal regions, occurs the Western hemlock (*T. heterophylla*), a fast-growing kind that may exceed 250 feet in height and 8 feet in trunk diameter; it is narrowly pyramidal and is one of the principal trees of the region. Its wood is distinctly superior to that of *T. canadensis.* Another western American, the usually bluish-leaved mountain hemlock (*T. mertensiana*) occurs at high altitudes from Alaska to California; its wood is of medium quality, its bark rich in tannin, its maximum height 150 feet. The mountain hemlock differs from all others in having lines of stomata on the upper as well as the lower leaf surfaces. Two graceful Japanese hemlocks are *T. sieboldii,* which grows up to 100 feet high, with very dark green glossy foliage, and *T. diversifolia,* usually shorter. The former is easily distinguished from other hemlocks by its completely glabrous shoots. *T. chinensis*, which reaches a maximum height of 150 feet, is from western China, and a variety, *T. c. formosana*, is endemic to Taiwan. Its cones are erect and have a varnished appearance. A similar species from the same region, *T. yunnanensis*, has dull cones and is whiter on the leaf undersurfaces. The Himalayan hemlock *(T. dumosa)* grows to a height of 120 feet in its native mountains and individual trees have been measured with a trunk diameter of nearly 8 feet.

Widdringtonia

Although in South Africa these are called cedars and they have also been named cypress-pines, they are neither cedars, cypresses nor pines but are closely related to *Callitris*, from which they differ in having smaller leaves in pairs and cones, usually of four scales. All are natives of Africa or Madasgascar; all are evergreens with small, scalelike leaves, male flowers in catkins and cones that produce seeds, and all are very resinous.

The Clanwilliam-cedar is found in a limited region of wild mountains called the Cedarberg, about 150 miles north of Cape Town. It grows up to 70 feet high and has a trunk up to 5 feet in diameter. In youth it is pyramidal but it becomes ragged and irregular with age. Much damage has been done to the Cedarberg by fire and by overexploitation but it is now a government conservation agency. The sweetly scented wood is of high quality, very insect-resistant and withstands decay under moist conditions.

From East Africa comes the magnificent *W. whytei*, called the Milanji-cedar, up to 140 feet tall and almost 5 feet in trunk diameter. Symmetrical when young, it becomes irregular and wide spreading as it ages. This species has suffered much from forest fires. It wood makes excellent lumber.

One other kind of *Widdringtonia* must be mentioned: the Willowmore-cedar *(W. schwarzii)*, which grows in spectacular and almost inaccessible mountain terrain 350 miles east of the Cedarberg and attains heights up to 100 feet and a trunk diameter of over 4 feet. It closely resembles the Clanwilliam-cedar but has smaller cones and thicker, blunter leaves.

Mountain hemlock. Tsuga mertensiana (Sumner: Monkmeyer)

Angiosperms: The Monocotyledons

In this category belong all plants commonly thought of by laymen as flowering plants and some that may not seem to belong in it. The Angiospermae together with the Gymnospermae include all seed-producing plants. Unlike the gymnosperms, their ovules are enclosed in an ovary that becomes the seed container and they have vessels in the stem tissues. Exceptions to either of these characterizations occur.

The angiosperms are the most prominent forms in the world's flora. They include 200,000 or more species in orders variously estimated to number from fifty-five to over one hundred.

One of the great mysteries of botany is the comparatively sudden appearance of the angiosperms. Botanically, they are a recent development. Not until the Lower Cretaceous Era, 120 to 135 million years ago, did plants resembling modern angiosperms appear but they then began a rapid distribution so that by the end of the Cretaceous, seventy million years ago, they were well represented all over the world. Neither their ancestral lines, geographic origin nor patterns of migration are well understood. The Angiospermae is divided into two classes, the Monocotyledonae and the Dicotyledoneae.

The Monocotyledonae contains the plants called monocotyledons, or sometimes just monocots, names derived from the fact that the seeds have but one cotyledon. When the seed germinates it produces a solitary seed leaf. Other distinguishing features are the vascular bundles throughout the stems, the parallel veining in almost all leaves, and flower parts in threes or multiples of three. None of these features is definitive, since there are occasional exceptions to all of them. The vast majority of monocots are herbaceous; woody kinds are uncommon and few of these attain tree size.

CHAPTER 5

The Pandanales

PANDANACEAE—SCREW-PINE FAMILY

Of the three families in the order Pandanales only the Pandanaceae includes woody plants. The Pandanaceae in turn is an Old World family

Above: Fruits of screw-pine (Paul Popper Ltd.)
Right: Screw-pine stilt roots (Robin Smith)

that contains three genera, only one of which, the *Pandanus*, contains trees. Morphological evidence suggests that these plants are more primitive than palms, but there is no fossil record to support this conclusion.

Pandanus—Screw-Pine

The name screw-pine derives from the fact that the leaves are arranged in spirals and the fruits and foliage resemble those of pineapples. The leaves are long and narrow, like those of dracaenas or gigantic sedges, and are often spiny along their margins; they grow in dense clusters at the ends of the branches. Many kinds of *Pandanus* are low and bushy but some are tall trees with many-branched trunks; they usually have stilt-roots originating well up on the trunk or on the branches and extending down into the ground.

Screw-pines are natives of tropical Asia, Indian Ocean islands and Polynesia, with a few kinds in Africa. They are the only monocotyledons that offer palms serious competition in

Screw-pine (Paul Popper Ltd.)

CHAPTER 6

The Principes

The Order Principes consists of only one family, the Palmaceae or palms. Palms are among the most ancient of flowering plants; fossils date back to the early Triassic. Today, the family flourishes in most tropical and subtropical regions.

PALMACEAE—PALM FAMILY

Although the many kinds of palms vary in form and size, they have a characteristic appearance that enables even laymen to recognize most of them without difficulty.

We are not concerned here with those palms that have no systems or trunks of appreciable height or those that are slender climbers. Our interest is in the kinds that attain heights of at least 20 feet. These have woody columnar trunks usually without branches but topped by a crown of large, persistent stiff leaves. The leaves are either feather-like (pinnate) or hand-like (palmate); a few palmate kinds are nearly or quite undivided and unlobed. In bud, palm leaves are folded in longitudinal pleats which "shake out" as the leaf unfolds and splits into lobes or leaflets.

The flowers of palms are small or even minute, individually inconspicuous, greenish, yellowish or reddish, mostly arranged in large clusters, either simple or branched according to species, and usually enclosed during early development by an obvious spathe. The flowers may be unisexual or bisexual. Palm fruits are technically berries, drupes or nuts; they vary tremendously in size and other details.

Palms are of immense economic importance as producers of foods, wax, oils, sugar, wine, fibers and material for building construction, as well as for the fabrication of furniture and other articles. They are highly prized, too, for their

the struggle for growing space. In many places in tropical Asia and in islands of the Indian Ocean *Pandanus* predominates, sometimes even completely excluding palms. *Pandanus* trees are male or female. Their fruits are large, more or less globose and somewhat woody, with the whole somewhat resembling a large cone.

The tough, pliable leaves of screw-pines are plaited into mats, baskets, screens, fans, sandals, hats and other articles. From the fragrant flowers perfumes and native medicines are prepared. The fruits of some kinds are edible.

Among the common species are *P. odoratissimus*, which is known as hala in its native Hawaii and also occurs on other Pacific islands, Australia and southern Asia. This is a spreading tree, up to 20 feet tall. *P. utilis,* from Madagascar, one of the tallest kinds, attains a height of 60 feet. Its leaf spines are red. *P. leram,* the Nicobar Islands breadfruit, has especially large fruits which are said to be edible. From India comes *P. furcatus,* which grows to a height of 40 feet and is said to have leaves up to 20 feet long.

Right: Sugar pine. Pinus lambertiana. (Ralph Cornell)
Overleaf left: Coconut palms. Cocos nucifera (Marvin W. Schwartz) Right: Colorful sheaths of sealing wax palm. Crytostachys lakko (W. H. Hodge)

ornamental qualities as shade trees and landscape features and are often cultivated as decorative plants in containers. Some, such as the sealing-wax palm (*Crytostachys lakko*), which forms clumps of tall, thin stems, have brilliantly colored sheaths. Because of the extraordinary variety of ways in which they are used, palms in some areas influence the whole way of life of a people.

Areca

The best known of these slender, feather-leaved palms of tropical Asia, the Pacific islands and Australia is the betel palm (*A. cathecu*). Its seeds, cut into pieces and wrapped in a leaf of betel pepper (*Piper betle*) with a little lime and a little cutch, are chewed as a stimulant and a narcotic uses resulting in a flow of red saliva. The betel palm, growing up to 100 feet high but with a trunk diameter of only 6 inches, has a comparatively small crown of leaves and fragrant flowers. It may live up to one hundred years. This species is widely planted in India and Malaya, but no clearly wild specimens have been discovered. Its native habitat is presumed to be Malaya.

Arenga

The most important of this tropical Asiatic group of bisexual feather-leaved palms is *A. pinnata*, the sugar palm of Malaya, which grows to a height of 40 feet. Like other species, it has a crown of very large, erect and spreading leaves and a short trunk usually clothed with old, hairy leaf bases. The leaves of the sugar palm may be 30 feet long. This is not a long-lived tree and after flowering once it dies. Its flower clusters open in succession from the top of the tree downward. The young flower stems are tapped for their sugar-rich sap which is evaporated into jaggery or palm sugar and is also used to make palm wine. The trunk contains excellent palm starch or sago.

Attalea

This is a South American genus of feather-leaved palms very closely allied to *Orbigna, Scheelea, Maximiliana, Markleya* and *Parascheelea*. It includes both bisexual and unisexual species. Collectively, these form a major element in vast forest, savanna and plains regions and are extremely important to local peoples as sources of building material, thatch, fiber, wine, oil and

Bald-cypress. Taxodium. (Douglas Faulkner)

Palmyra palms. Borassus flabellifer (M. Krishnan)

edible young leaves. *A. funifera*, for example, is a source of a long flexible fiber called piassava used to make brushes, whisks and brooms; fibers called by the same name are obtained from certain other South American and African palms. Another species, the cohune nut palm, formerly named *A. cohune*, but now *Orbignya cohune*, is a handsome tree especially suited as an ornamental for avenue planting. Its crown of enormous leaves arches gracefully upward from the tops of trunks up to 50 feet tall. Its seeds, almost as big as hens' eggs, yield an oil that is similar to coconut oil and is used in cooking and in making margarine, soap and candles.

Borassus

Of these large fan-leaved palms of Asia and Africa, the most important is the palmyra palm (*B. flabellifer*). It attains 100 feet in height and a trunk diameter of 3 feet or more. Its huge rounded leaves divide about halfway along their length into many slender strips which are forked at the tips. Each tree is completely male or female. Native to India and Malaya, it is widely

used. A Tamil poem recites 801 such uses or products, including the production of a drink called toddy (from the sap, fermented or unfermented), edible seeds, construction timber, leaves for thatch, matting and baskets, and fibers for cords and ropes.

Caryota—Fishtail Palms

The common name of this group refers to their leaflets, which are triangular with squared and eroded ends resembling the tails of fishes. The leaves are feather-shaped and, unusual in palms, twice pinnate. These trees are native from Asia and Malaya to Australia. They bloom but once. Flowering begins near the top of the trunk and continues downward until the foodstuffs stored in the trunk are exhausted; then the tree dies. Another species, *C. urens*, the wine palm or toddy palm of India and Malaya, grows up to 60 feet high and has broad leaves 20 feet long. Its great hanging flower clusters are tapped to produce a sugar sap called toddy, yielding up to twenty-four pints in twenty-four hours. The tree is also a source of sugar, wood, fiber and of edible starch, which is obtained from the pith. Still another, *C. rumphiana*, of Malaya, grows to 100 feet high, while the more common *C. mitis* of Burma, which renews itself by suckers from its base, rarely exceeds 40 feet in height.

Ceroxylon

This Andean genus contains the tallest species of palm, *C. andicola*, with a trunk that may exceed 200 feet in height. It grows west of Bogota at an elevation of ten thousand feet. Another species, *C. utile,* grows at the highest Colombian-Equadorian border. At night the temperature there drops below freezing and occasionally snow falls.

Ceroxylons are wax palms; their trunks are covered with a film of this material and their huge feather-like leaves are coated on their undersides, giving them a silvery appearance. The wax is employed locally for making candles. The fruits, bright orange-red, grow in large clusters.

Chamaerops—European Fan Palm

Rarely as much as 20 feet tall, the European fan palm (*C. humilis*) is of interest because it represents the most northerly extension of the

Palm groves, Australia (Robin Smith)

palm family. It is the only palm native to Europe, occurring north as well as south of the Mediterranean Sea. Its trunk is ragged with persistent leaf bases and coarse hairlike fibers, which are harvested commercially. The segments of its deeply cut, semiorbicular leaves stand out stiffly and do not droop.

Cocos—Coconut

Only one species, the coconut palm (*C. nucifera*), is now included in this genus. It occurs throughout the tropics, chiefly along seashores and mostly for limited distances inland. There is doubt as to its original habitat, the most generally accepted conclusion being that it is of Indo-Pacific origin, but another theory has it a prime native of the Pacific coast of South America. In any event, it is now ubiquitous in cultivation, and in many areas to which it was undoubtedly introduced by man or ocean currents.

The coconut palm frequently has a leaning trunk, thickened at its base and curving upward, sometimes to a height of 100 feet. Its crown consists of up to thirty-six gracefully disposed, dark green pinnate leaves, each of which may be 20 feet long. Each flower cluster consists of numerous minute males that open for about two hours in the very early morning, and then fall, and much fewer and larger females, the ovaries of which become, five to six months after fertilization, the familiar fruits. The fruits, which ripen in ten to twelve months, are green, orange-yellow or reddish but finally turn brown. The large seed or "nut" is surrounded by a thick, fibrous husk. The entire fruit floats and can remain unharmed in sea water for about four months, which makes its distribution by ocean currents possible and probable.

The coconut has countless uses and is the most valuable of all palms. Its trunks are used locally in construction and cabinetwork, its leaves for thatch, baskets and matting; the fiber of the husk of the fruit, coir, is made into mats, ropes and other articles; the shells of the nuts are fashioned into bowls and other utensils and are burned to give the best medicinal charcoal. Palm wine or toddy, from which comes the alcoholic beverage arrack, and palm sugar are obtained by tapping the flower clusters; the liquid in unripened fruits is a refreshing drink; the

European fan palm. Chamaerops humilis (W. Schacht)

"meat" of ripe nuts is edible and nutritious, and when dried it becomes the coconut used in confectionery and baking. But by far the most important commercial product of the coconut palm is copra, the dried "meat" or endosperm of the seeds, which yields a harvest of three million metric tons annually. From it is expressed coconut oil, which is basic to the preparation of margarines, cooking oils, soaps and candles.

Copernicia

The most important of this genus of fan-leaved wax palms is the carnauba palm (*C. cerifera*) of Brazil, which occurs in vast numbers in the tropical lowlands of the dry northeasters portion of the country. Even more abundant is the caranda palm (*C. alba*) of southwest Brazil. Described as forming "solid stands hundreds of square miles in extent," this species inhabits low ground that is subject to periodic flooding and where high temperatures prevail. Twenty-one other species of *Copernicia* occur in the West Indies and South America, most of very local distribution.

The carnauba palm may reach a height of 40 feet and has a trunk somewhat thickened above its base and a spherical crown. The undersides of the leaves are coated with a wax which is an important article of commerce. It is used for shoe polish, furniture and floor polishes, fine candles and other purposes.

Corypha

Of about eight species of these large fan-leaved palms, the best known is the talipot palm (*C. umbraculifera*), which is thought by some to be native to Ceylon and the Malabar coast. A massive tree, it grows up to a height of 80 feet and has a trunk diameter of 3 to 4 feet. Its huge leaves, much divided to their centers, may measure 16 feet across and have stalks 10 feet long or more. The panicle of creamy white flowers, developed when the tree is from thirty to seventy-five years old, is gigantic, measuring from 30 to 40 feet across and up to 20 feet high; when it first emerges from among the foliage it looks like a pole. The tree dies after flowering and fruiting once. The hard, marble-like seeds are used in making buttons.

Above: Germinating coconut (Lorus and Margery Milne) Left: Doum palm. Hyphaene theobaica (Emil Schulthess)

Elaeis

An inhabitant of lowlands and swamps throughout the humid tropics of Africa and Madagascar, *E. guineensis*, the African oil palm is, next to the coconut palm, the most important source of palm oil; and it is extensively cultivated for this oil. The African oil palm attains 100 feet in height and has feather leaves of very many leaflets. Its trunk is roughened by the persisting stubs of fallen leaves. Male and female flowers occur in separate inflorescences, with as many as 140,000 male flowers and 3500 female flowers in each cluster. The fruit, which takes four to six months to ripen, consists of a stone surrounded by a pulpy covering. Palm oils of different types are obtained from both pulp and stones and are used for the same purposes as the oil of the coconut palm. Except for *Raphia*, this is the only genus of palms native to both the Old and New Worlds. One other species of *Elaeis* occurs in tropical America.

Erythea—Hesper Palms

About ten species of this bisexual fern-leaved palm are native to northwestern Mexico. With the exception of *E. edulis*, which has green leaves, the leaves of most of these palms are conspicuously glaucous blue on their undersides. Among those that exceed 20 feet in height are the big blue hesper palm (*E. armata*), which has a thick trunk; the short-arm blue hesper palm (*E. brandigeei*), a slender-trunked tree; and the Guadalupe palm (*E. edulis*).

Howea

Howeas are perhaps best known as pot and tub plants cultivated by florists. (Often they are called kentias, although this name rightfully belongs to another kind of palm.) There are two species, both endemic to Lord Howe's Island in the Pacific. They are medium-sized, feather-leaved, graceful trees of value as ornamentals. *H. belmoreana* can be distinguished from *H. forsteriana* by the leaflets which arch upward from the midrib instead of diverging horizontally and by the fact that the leaves themselves are more distinctly arched. Because the trees on Lord Howe's Island are the only reliable sources of seeds for florists the trees are well protected and the seeds carefully harvested and marketed.

Above: Coconut palm. Cocos nucifera (Emil Javorsky) Right: Coconut fruits (Paul Popper Ltd.)

Hyphaene

The doum palm (*H. theobaica*) of Upper Egypt and the Sudan has been cultivated since earliest historic times, and probably before then, for its nourishing and diuretic edible fruits. Its seeds provide a vegetable ivory that is made into needles and buttons and is used in carving. A tree that was sacred to the ancient Egyptians, it is frequently depicted in their arts and it is easily recognized in such representations by its freely branched trunk, a characteristic extremely rare in palms.

The doum palm can get along under the hottest sun and under desert conditions, but does best only where fair supplies of ground water are available. It grows to a height of about 30 feet. Other species of *Hyphaene* occur in the open, drier areas of Africa, Madagascar and India.

Livistona

Included here are about thirty species of tropical and subtropical fan-leaved palms of Asia, Indonesia, the Philippines and Australia. Some are lofty but others are of more moderate height. Their deeply lobed leaves are approximately spherical. For some distance beneath the foliage the trunks are clothed with persisting fibrous leaf sheaths. The orange, red, blue, purple or black fruits, borne in loose bunches, are quite attractive.

Among the best-known species is *L. australis*, a tall Australian tree called cabbage palm in its native country, where it grows up to 80 feet or more. The aborigines used its wood for spearheads and ate the young leaves. The leaves are made into hats and baskets and the wood serves for building and other purposes. The Chinese fan palm (*L. chinensis*) from central China is a popular ornamental often misnamed *Latania borbonica*. It rarely exceeds 30 feet in height and has a dense, globular crown of leaves. Its leaves, wider than long, may measure 5 feet across and are divided to the middle into many segments. The Malayan biroo palm (*L. rotundifolia*) has a slender trunk that may exceed 100 feet in height; its leaf blades are divided from the point of their stalk attachment to within a third of the distance from their margins.

Above: Talipot palm. Corypha umbraculifera (Max Hemple) Left: Chinese fan palm. Livistonia chinensis (T. H. Everett)

African oil palm. Elaeis guineensis (Lorus and Margery Milne)

Lodoicea—Double Coconut

One of the most remarkable trees in the world grows on two tiny islands of the more than thirty islands of the Seychelles group in the Indian Ocean. The seeds of *L. maldivica*, the double coconut or coco-de-mer, are the largest of any plant and were known long before the plant that bore them was discovered. The enormous fruits, weighing up to fifty pounds, dropped from the trees for untold ages, rolled off the islands into the ocean and were washed up in the Maldive Islands. There they were found by Indians and Europeans who conjectured fancifully about their origin and ascribed to them enchanting magical properties. Inside the husk, which is scarcely an inch thick, is a huge, heart-shaped seed resembling two coconuts joined like Siamese twins. The fruits are said to take up to ten years to ripen. *L. maldivica*, the only species, is fan-leaved and reaches heights up to 100 feet, has a trunk diameter of 1 foot, and is believed to live for one hundred years or more. Its huge leaves have stalks up to 30 feet long and blades up to 16 feet long and 8 feet wide. Male and female flowers are borne on separate trees.

Metroxylon—Sago Palms

These, the true sago palms (various species of cycads are often called by this name in America), are indigenous to Malaya and Polynesia and form vast forests there. Each tree flowers once and then dies; the flower clusters are terminal and very large, towering high above the foliage. Sago is the starch stored in the trunk before the flowering, which usually occurs when the tree is about fifteen years old. The sago, used in making puddings, is harvested two or three years before the flower cluster forms because flower production reduces the amount of available starch. Despite the huge reserves of sago palms in areas where these plants grow naturally, most of the sago used in America and Europe comes from a different plant named manihot.

Best known of the sago palms is *M. sagus*, a 4-foot-tall, pinnate-leaved tree that favors

swampy ground. It increases chiefly by suckers, rarely producing seed. Another species, *M. rumphii*, which has spiny rather than smooth leaf bases, is one of several other kinds that are exploited for their starch.

A somewhat different palm, one that does not die after its first blooming and does not sucker, and which is valued not for sago but for its hard, horny seeds, which are used as vegetable ivory, is *M. amicorum*, a native of the Caroline Islands. The chief source of vegetable ivory, used for making buttons, ornaments and similar articles, however, is the trunkless ivory-nut palm (*Phytelephas macrocarpa*) of South America.

Phoenix

This genus of about seventeen species of fan-leaved palms is endemic to Africa and Asia. The trees are unisexual and vary greatly in size according to species. One, *P. roebelinii*, attains a height of only 9 feet; others rarely achieve 20 feet. Phoenixes are easily recognized because they are the only feather-leaved palms with leaflets pointed at the tips and folded downward along the centers. Identifying the various species is sometimes difficult, for some exhibit considerable variation and hybrids are common.

The date palm (*P. dactylifera*) is by far the most useful kind and, second only to the coconut, is the most important of all palms commercially. To the peoples of North Africa, India and areas in between it has been a valuable resource since prehistory. A special virtue is its ability to thrive in arid climates with minimal soil water. It is the palm of desert oases.

The date palm has a stout trunk that reaches up to 100 feet in height and is covered with persisting leaf bases. Sucker shoots develop from the bottom of the trunk. The crown is a heavy canopy of stiffish, pinnate, gray-green leaves, each being up to 20 feet long. The trees live and yield for two hundred years or more. To ensure fruit, growers hang branches of male flowers in blooming female trees or collect and dust pollen on the female flowers. A flower cluster may contain ten thousand flowers. Date fruits are highly nutritious and in parts of Africa are the prime food of man and beast. Numerous varieties are cultivated. Dates are also grown commercially in the American Southwest.

Above: Date palm. Phoenix dactylifera Left: Date fruits. (Both, W. Rauh)

1. *Phoenix dactylifera* 2. *Caryota urens* 3. *Cocos nucifera* 4. *Sabal causiarum* 5. *Washingtonia filifera* 6. *Roystonea borinquena* 7. *Chamaerops humilis* (Charles Fracé)

In addition to supplying food, the date palm has, according to one tabulation, more than eight hundred other uses. In some areas the fruits even serve as money. Sugar and wine are prepared from the sap and the leaves are used for matting and baskets.

The wild date palm (*P. sylvestris*), a native of India, does not have edible fruits but is a quite important source of toddy, sugar, wine and arrack. It also supplies fiber and tannin. It grows to 40 feet tall and has a trunk surrounded by a huge head of gray-green leaves. Other noteworthy species of *Phoenix* include *P. canariensis*, endemic to the Canary Islands but widely cultivated in warm countries as an ornamental. Its non-suckering trunk supports a huge head of up to one hundred or more handsome leaves, towering to a height of 50 or 60 feet. An attractive African species, *P. reclinata*, normally does not exceed 20 feet in height but grows twice as tall if the suckers at the base of its trunk are removed. The Indian *P. rupicola*, which does not have suckers, is a decorative tree that grows to a height of 20 feet.

Pritchardia

This is the only genus of palms native to Hawaii, where it is represented by more than thirty closely related species or geographical variants. In addition, two species inhabit Fiji and two the Tuamotu Islands near Tahiti. They are decorative bisexual trees, 30 feet or less tall, with a fairly heavy trunk topped by a round head of stiff, unusually broad, wedge-shaped, fan-type leaves that are shallowly indented at the margins. In Hawaii the unripe seeds, called hawane or wahane, are eaten and the leaves are used to make fans and hats.

Among taller growing species are *P. affinis*, *P. hillebrandii* and *P. insignis*, all from the Hawaiian Islands, and *P. pacifica* from Fiji. The genus is sometimes named *Eupritchardia*.

Raphia—Raffia Palms

Members of this African or Madagascan genus have the largest leaves of any known plant—sometimes as much as 70 feet long! There are supposed to be about twenty species but their botany is not well understood and there is much yet to learn about them. Most have stout trunks up to 40 feet tall but some have no trunks. They produce huge flower clusters and apparently at least a few die after flowering once. One scholarly study says that "the inflorescences emerge from among the leaves as enormous worms covered with spathes, and they branch into enormous centipedes with the bracts set regularly in two rows as if they were trousers to the legs; the whole construction may be twelve feet long and hang menacingly overhead." The leaves are the source of raffia fiber. Wine is derived from *R. vinifera* and *R. taedigera*. The seeds of some species are employed as fish poison but those of certain other kinds are edible when young.

Roystonea

This group consists of about seventeen species in the Caribbean region and Central America; they were formerly called *Oreodoxa*. All are lofty,

feather-leaved and bisexual. They have majestic light-colored columnar trunks, usually with swollen and constricted outlines. Their flowers and fruits are borne in huge clusters that spring from the trunk just below the foliage. The young leaves are edible. Because of their straight trunks and noble appearance, roystoneas are greatly prized for planting on ornamental avenues. Notable examples of such avenues are in the botanic gardens at Rio de Janeiro and in Ceylon.

The cabbage palm or palmiste (*R. oleracea*) of Trinidad and other West Indian islands may grow to a height of 120 feet and is different from all other kinds in having its leaflets arranged in two rather than four rows. Its trunk is swollen only at its base. Its leaves spread in all directions except downward. The Cuban royal palm (*R. regia*) has its trunk thickened at its base and at or above its middle. It grows up to a height of 70 feet and has a crown of 10-foot-long leaves which arch in all directions. In its native Cuba its fruits are used as food for hogs. The Florida royal palm (*R. elata*) grows somewhat taller than *R. regia*. It is now restricted in the wild to wet places in and near the Everglades, but is commonly planted elsewhere for ornament. Its trunk is thickened at the base and usually narrows and thickens again to a broad shoulder at the top.

The Puerto Rican royal palm (*R. borinquena*) attains a height of about 50 feet. Its trunk expands at about three-quarters of its height from the ground and tapers below and above that point. It has leaves about 10 feet in length and ovoid, yellowish brown fruits. It is a native of Puerto Rico and St. Croix.

Sabal—Palmetto Palms

Found primarily in Central America, the West Indies and Mexico, this genus extends northward into the southern United States. Its twenty-five species include tall trees as well as scrub palms usually without appreciable trunks, all fan-leaved and bisexual. The leaf stalks of the tree types continue well into the blade portion of the leaf. In those leaves that are held more or less horizontal the midrib curves downward. Slender threads or filaments hang from the leaf margins. Several species are endemic to particular islands or to limited mainland areas and

Above: Phoenix palm. Phoenix sylvestris (M. Krishnan) Left: Raffia palm. Raphia ruffia (W. Rauh)

Washingtonia palms (Union Pacific Railroad)

perhaps should be considered geographical variants of other species. Arboreal species of *Sabal* have trunks clothed with leaf bases in their upper parts and sometimes to the ground; the crevices between these often harbor ferns, bromeliads, orchids and other epiphytes, and the trunks frequently support vines.

The cabbage palm or palmetto of the southeastern United States (*S. palmetto*) is a familiar native of Florida and occurs along the coast to North Carolina, often in poor, sandy soils. Sometimes becoming 90 feet tall, it has a smallish globular crown of leaves segmented halfway to their midribs, the divisions drooping or curving downward. The flowers and the small, round, shiny black fruits occur in many branched clusters. Besides being ornamental, this palm produces useful wood, edible hearts of young leaves, material for hat-making and thatch, and its roots contain tannin. Another species, the Texas palmetto (*S. texana*) attains

a height of 50 feet, has a bright reddish brown trunk and makes its home in the lower Rio Grande Valley and Mexico. Its fruits are bigger than those of *S. palmetto*, which are about a third of an inch in diameter. Perhaps the most stately kind is *S. umbraculifera*, an endemic of Hispaniola with a massive trunk, leaves and fruits conspicuously larger than those of *S. palmetto*, and usually a heavy shag of old leaf beneath the crown. It grows to a height of 60 feet or more. The Puerto Rican hat palm (*S. causiarum*) is a stout tree up to 50 feet tall, its trunk often free of old leaf bases. Endemic to Bermuda, the Bermuda palmetto (*S. bermudiana*) reaches a height of 40 feet and often has a leaning or crooked trunk which usually is soon bare of old leaf bases.

Trachycarpus—Windmill Palm

This eastern Asiatic palm is one of the hardiest; it can be grown outdoors in South Carolina and

in Great Britain. It has a slender trunk, up to 30 feet tall, covered with black, hairlike fibers. Its nearly round leaves are about three feet in diameter and have drooping segments, in which respect it differs from the lower-growing *T. wagnerianus,* of unknown origin. An allied kind, *T. caespitosus,* also of unknown habitat, has multiple trunks.

Washingtonia

Two species that grow naturally only in isolated patches in canyons in Arizona, California and Mexico, and probably represent relics of vast forests of Cretaceous times, are *W. filifera* and *W. robusta.* The former has gray-green, the latter shining green, foliage. Except in young specimens, the mature leaves of *W. robusta* do not have the many hanging threadlike filaments that characterize *W. filifera.* Both are massive, the trunk of *W. filifera* the thicker of the two but the latter the taller. *W. filifera,* the more northern species, may be 80 feet or more tall.

A characteristic feature of *Washingtonia* is the dead, drooping leaves which clothe the entire trunk of younger trees, and much of the upper part of the trunk of older trees, in a cylinder of dried brown foliage. This skirt or mane adds greatly to their ornamental qualities. The Indians used the seeds, the pulp of the fruits and the leaf buds for food and utilized the fibers and leaves for cordage thatchery and other purposes. *W. robusta* is confined to Mexico; *W. filifera* occurs in both Mexico and the United States.

CHAPTER 7

The Liliales

LILIACEAE—LILY FAMILY

The Liliales is an order that includes very few trees, and the Liliaceae or lily family is pre-

Above: Cabbage tree. Cordyline australis (Robin Smith) Left: Dragon tree. Dracena draco (Alfred Ehrhardt)

dominately herbaceous, but some of its members have woody stems and a few of these are trees.

Aloe

This large group of succulent-leaved plants includes a few of tree size. The largest and tallest is *A. bainesii* of South Africa, which attains a height of 60 feet with a trunk up to 5 feet in diameter. When about 6 feet high its trunk forks into two branches, each of which divides into two and so on as the tree grows. The fleshy, sword-shaped leaves are clustered toward the ends of the branches. The flowers, salmon pink fading to cream and with green tips, occur in dense, many-flowered racemes.

The kokerboom (*A. dichotoma*) of South Africa was named in 1776 by Francis Masson, the first professional plant collector to visit South Africa. A flat-topped tree of curiously rigid aspect, it is slow-growing and rarely exceeds 25 feet in height or a trunk diameter of from 2 to 3 feet. Its whitish gray bark peels in large patches. The leaves, short, flat, lanceolate and glaucous gray-green, are carried in rosette-like bunches at the ends of the branches. The kokerboom's bright yellow flowers are so well supplied with nectar that they are a great attraction to bees, birds and baboons. Other tree aloes include *A. africana, A. candelabrum* and *A. pillansii*, all of South Africa.

Beaucarnea

These trees of the warm, dry parts of North America and Central America have dracaena-like foliage and panicles of small whitish flowers. Their trunks are erect, tapering and conspicuously swollen at and just above ground level. The best-known species is *B. recurvata* from southeast Mexico, which grows to a height of 30 feet, branches near its top and has thin recurved leaves up to 6 feet long. *B. stricta*, also from southern Mexico, is similar but has straight leaves. *B. gracilis*, a native of the same region, differs chiefly in having a very much swollen trunk base and very glaucous leaves.

Cordyline

Cordylines are different from dracaenas only in technical details. Somewhat palmlike in appearance, they have long, narrow leathery leaves

Above: Dragon tree (E. Aubert de la Rue) Right: Joshua trees. Yucca brevifolia (Josef Muench)

which form bushy crowns at the ends of branches and panicles of small greenish or yellowish flowers followed by berry-like fruits. In New Zealand the native *C. australis* is called cabbage tree because early settlers used the young leaves as a vegetable. It grows to a height of 40 feet and is one of the largest plants of the lily family. Its cream-colored, fragrant flowers are succeeded by milky white berries which are a favorite food of pigeons. At night decaying leaves of the cabbage tree are phosphorescent. A botanist tells of a living specimen which had a hollow trunk so large that a Maori had fitted a door to it and used it for tool storage. The leaves are suited for paper-making; they also have a very strong fiber that is used as rope.

Dracaena

The dragon tree of the Canary Islands (*D. draco*) grows to a height of 60 feet or more and is very distinctive. It attains a great age, one specimen, on Teneriffe, which was blown down in 1868, was famous for centuries and was long believed to be the oldest tree in the world. When blown down it was 70 feet high and had a trunk girth of almost 45 feet. This species has sword-shaped

Joshua tree blossoms (Hubert A. Lowman)

glaucous green leaves, about 2 feet long and 1³/₄ inches wide, all crowded near the ends of the branches. Its tiny greenish flowers are succeeded by orange berries. The dried sap, called dragon's blood, is used for coloring varnishes and at one time was employed medicinally.

Nolina

These natives of the southwestern United States and Mexico are desert and dry country plants, mostly of less than tree dimensions. Closely related to and resembling *Beaucarnea* is *N. beldingii* of Baja California, which reaches heights up to 25 feet and branches near the top.

Yucca

Yuccas are North American and West Indian plants, predominantly of desert and semidesert regions; a few, with rigid stems, grow to tree size. They have stiff, sword-shaped leaves and large, usually erect panicles of nodding, waxy, creamy-white flowers which open at night and are sweetly fragrant. The developing seeds provide food for the larvae of a small white moth which is found wherever yuccas grow natively; this moth reciprocates by gathering the pollen of the plant and depositing it in the stigmatic chamber of the flower. Yuccas are sources of a coarse fiber used to make mats, cordage and other wares. In Mexico the flowers are eaten raw or cooked, and a saponaceous material in the roots is used for washing and, in extract form, as a foaming agent in beverages.

The Spanish bayonet (*Y. aloifolia*), a native of the southern United States, Mexico and the West Indies, grows up to a height of 25 feet, has a single or branched trunk and leaves that are up to 2¹/₂ feet long. Its flowers are often tinged with purple.

The Joshua tree (*Y. brewifolia*), which may attain 30 feet in height and when old is of grotesque shape, is localized in areas bordering the Mojave and nearby deserts, where it adds greatly to the picturesqueness of the landscape.

A native Mexican yucca is *Y. australis*, which becomes quite a large tree and, unusual among its kind, has drooping flower clusters. Another tall kind, *Y. elephantipes*, has a trunk swollen at the base like that of *Beaucarnea*. *Y. elata*, of the southwestern United States and Mexico, sometimes becomes 20 feet tall. Its narrow gray-green leaves are narrowly margined with white. In southern Texas and Mexico occurs *Y. treculeana* which grows to a height of 25 feet.

CHAPTER 8

The Scitaminae

This order of four tropical and subtropical families includes such familiar plants as bananas, gingers and cannas. Only one of its genera, *Ravenala*, contains species that can be regarded as trees. The order is considered to be highly developed and possibly to represent the ancestral stock of the orchids.

MUSACEAE—BANANA FAMILY

Contrary to popular belief, bananas do not grow on trees. The plant that produces this tropical fruit is herbaceous and has a trunk that is a cylinder of encircling leaf stalks pressed close together. But some plants belonging to the same botanical family as the banana, the *Musaceae*, have woody trunks; among these is *Ravenala*.

Ravenala

This genus has a somewhat unusual natural distribution, with one species in Madagascar and one in South America. The Old World *R. madagascarensis*, the traveler's tree, is the better known. Its common name derives from its having hollow bases to its leaf stalks from which it is said that travelers obtained drinking water. The travelers' tree has a palmlike trunk up to 30 feet in height and immense long-stemmed, paddle-shaped leaves arranged in two ranks spread in one plane like a gigantic fan. Although the leaves do not naturally divide, they are usually more or

Traveler's tree. *Revenala madagascariensis* (T. H. Everett)

less shredded by wind action. The white flowers, contained in boat-shaped bracts, and succeeded by blue seeds, are borne in racemes that arise from the leaf axils. In Madagascar the seeds are used as food, the sap for sugar production, the leaves for thatching and the wood of the trunk for construction purposes.

Angiosperms: The Dicotyledons

Angiosperms that typically have seeds containing two cotyledons and produce two seed leaves upon germination constitute the class Dicotyledoneae. Members of this group are called dicotyledons or simply dicots. In addition, such plants have vascular bundles arranged as cylinders, net-veined leaves and flower parts in fours, fives or multiples thereof or in large numbers. In woody dicots a layer of cambium tissue just beneath the bark produces secondary layers of new tissue each year so that trunks and branches increase in thickness by the addition of wood that forms annual rings.

CHAPTER 9

The Verticillatae

The order Verticillatae consists of only one family, the Casuarinaceae, which is not closely related to any other family of living plants and contains only one genus. Its tiny flowers have neither sepals nor petals.

CASUARINACEAE—CASUARINA FAMILY

Casuarina—She-Oak, Beefwood, Ironwood, Australian-Pine

This curious genus consists of about forty-five species, most of them Australian, but a few Polynesian, Malayan or African. The trees appear to be leafless, the leaves being reduced to small scales that form toothed collars around the nodes or joints of slender branchlets. These branchlets contain chlorophyll and function as leaves for the purpose of photosynthesis and other normal leaf processes. Actually the branchlets look like leaves; they are needle-like and grooved and give to casuarinas the gross aspect of pine trees. For this reason they are often called Australian-pines. The branchlets are deciduous and when shed form a mulch beneath the trees like the leaves of pines. The flowers are unisexual; both sexes are usually on the same tree. Male flowers appear in spikes at the branchlet tips, females in round heads at the bases of the branchlets. The fruits are cones. Casuarinas are valued for planting in warm regions as landscape features. They are useful as windbreaks, on avenues and for planting ner the sea.

Perhaps the best known is *C. equisetifolia*, the swamp she-oak. It is sometimes called horsetail

Above: Drooping she-oak. Casuarina stricta (T. H. Everett) Right: Horsetail tree. Casuarina equisetifolia (B. J. H. Moon)

tree because its branchlets resemble the stems of the common *Equisetum* or horsetail. Of rather somber appearance because of its long, drooping gray-green stems, bunched in great plumes, this species is pyramidal and has duller and darker she-oak in Australia. It grows very rapidly (one specimen is recorded as having reached a height of 80 feet in ten years) and may eventually be 150 feet high. There is no accurate data on the life span of these trees but it is surely some hundreds of years. They have hard red wood (the name beefwood refers to this), which is used for furniture and a variety of other purposes. It was favored by the Australian aborigines as a material for war clubs and by Fijians for making tapa-cloth beaters. Its bark has properties that make it useful for tanning and dyeing and as an astringent. *C. equisetifolia* inhabits saline swamps and tidal estuaries; it is well adapted for planting in seashore locations and is much used for this purpose in warm regions.

One of the largest of the casuarinas is *C. cunninghamiana* of New South Wales and Queensland. It occurs on banks of freshwater streams and rivers and is known as river she-oak and fire she-oak. Its wood is hard, close-textured and durable and is used for making shingles,

paneling, furniture, poles and similar articles. Young seedlings are eaten by livestock but they are too woody and astringent to provide good fodder. Another casuarina, *C. glauca* (also called swamp she-oak), grows in saline swamps to a height of 50 feet or more. It is an erect tree of sparse appearance with handsomely figured, strong and durable wood which has similar uses to that of *C. cunninghamiana*. The drooping she-oak *(C. stricta)* grows up to 30 feet high and has long, pendulous, prominently grooved branchlets and deep red, handsomely grained soils, its slightly acid young growths form useful stock feed. Its hard, tough, reddish wood lacks durability but is good for turnery and furniture.

Other casuarinas include *C. torulosa*, or forest she-oak, of fairly erect growth and with slender branchlets and deep red, handsomely grained wood that is prized for furniture manufacture; the belah *(C. lepidophloia)*, a fairly quick-growing tree that has considerable ornamental value, is of use for fencing and fuel but is not durable in moist ground, and has branchlets usable for stock feed; and the black she-oak *(C. suberosa)* which thrives in poor soils and has dark brown wood that is of use for shingles, staves, handles and similar purposes.

CHAPTER 10

The Salicales

The very distinct order of Salicales has the characteristics of its only family, the Salicaceae. It appears to have developed from advanced ancestral stocks comparatively late in geological time.

SALICACEAE—WILLOW FAMILY

Willows and poplars are the only representatives of the family Salicaceae. Botanical differences which caused some authorities to transfer *Salix eucalyptoides* to a separate genus, *Chosenia*, are not accepted by others as being sufficiently important to warrant that treatment. All of the family have simple deciduous leaves and unisexual flowers—without calyxes or corollas—in dense catkins. Except in rare instances, male

Cottonwood seeds (Henry Mayer: National Audubon)

and female flowers are found on separate trees. The fruits are capsules containing many hairy seeds. The bark is bitter.

Populus—Aspen, Cottonwood and Poplar

These are quick-growing, soft-wooded trees of considerable commercial and some ornamental importance. There are thirty to forty species widely distributed through the Northern Hemisphere where, especially in northerly parts of their ranges, they often form sizable forests. Their wood is valued for such purposes as making paper pulp, excelsior, containers for food, matchsticks, crates and boxes. Hybrid kinds are numerous and some have been bred to develop desirable commercial qualities to the fullest. Because of the prevalence of hybrids, because male and female flowers are on separate trees (the flowers are wind-pollinated), and because flowers and foliage are usually not present at the same time, the identification of poplars is frequently difficult. It is correct to refer to all members of the genus *Populus* as poplars, but in the United States and Canada *P. deltoides* and those of its close relatives which

Cottonwood in California (Josef Muench)

have deeply furrowed grayish bark are usually called cottonwoods, and the name aspen is applied most frequently to two species with smooth greenish or grayish bark.

As ornamentals, poplars have the disadvantages of being brittle, and thus being subject to storm damage, and of having wide-spreading, searching roots that may clog drains, lift street paving and damage foundations of buildings. In general they should be used for landscaping only in regions where better trees do not prosper. Among those suited for areas where hot, dry summers and cold winters prevail are *P. alba, P. berolinensis, P. deltoides* and *P. fremontii.*

Poplars fall readily into six quite distinct groups. White poplars have leaves white-woolly or gray-hairy on their undersurfaces and leaf margins coarsely toothed or lobed, especially on young vigorous shoots and on young trees. Their leaf stalks are usually round. The bark at first is smooth and pale-colored. White poplars are all natives of Europe. The black poplar and cottonwood group have unlobed leaves, green on both sides and leaf margins thickened and cartilaginous. Their leaf stalks are flattened, at least near the blade, or cylindrical. The bark is deeply fissured like that of oaks. These are the latest to leaf out in spring. The large-leaved poplars and cottonwoods are distinguished by exceptionally big leaves which lack cartilaginous margins and have cylindrical or channeled but not flattened stalks. Their bark is rough. Balsam poplars have their winter leaf buds and young leaves coated with a sticky substance having the fragrance of

Black poplar. Populus nigra (Gerhard Klammet)

balsam. The undersides of the leaves, which are unlobed, are usually whitish but not woolly. The leaf stalks are either cylindrical or four-angled. The aspens are characterized by unlobed leaves, usually with long, flattened stalks, which are responsible for the restless fluttering of the foliage in response to even the slightest breeze. Variable-leaved poplars are distinguished by the great leaf variation that occurs on the same plant. The leaf stalks are not flattened.

Prominent among the black poplar group is the cottonwood *(P. deltoides)*, which ranges from Quebec to North Dakota, Florida and Texas. An open, broad-headed tree growing up to 90 feet high, it is valued for pulpwood and in some regions is much planted for windbreaks and shade. Its hairy-margined leaves have flattened stalks and coarse curved teeth. Varieties of this species go by the name of southern cottonwood. Quite similar but smaller is the Great Plains cottonwood *(P. sargentii),* which has lighter

yellow branches and yellow-green leaves. Closely related species are *P. wislizenii*, which grows as large as *P. deltoides* but is without the glands at the bases of its leaves characteristic of the latter, and, in the Southwest, *P. fremontii* of similar size. This and some other species from that region differ only in minor characteristics from *P. deltoides.*

The black poplar proper *(P. nigra)* is a tree of wide distribution through Europe and western and central Asia. It grows up to a height of 90 feet and has leaves resembling those of *P. deltoides* but usually smaller, less deeply toothed, without basal glands or hairy margins, and with very compressed stalks. Like aspens, the foliage dances in light breezes. Typically this species is pyradmidal and has duller and darker foliage than the cottonwood but, like so many poplars, it is variable and has given rise to several named varieties. The best known of these is the Lombardy poplar *(P. nigra italica)*, a very narrow, erect kind. It was introduced in America by 1784. Another variety, *P. n. thevestina*, which is exactly like the Lombardy poplar except for bark that is as white as that of a white birch, is much planted in Algeria and in Kashmir.

A hybrid complex between the American *P. deltoides* and the European *P. nigra* has been given the name *P. canadensis*. The cross that resulted in the original hybrid is presumed to have been made in France about 1750 but some of the many forms of *P. canadensis,* such as *P. c. serotina, P. c. regenerata, P. c. eugenei, P. c. marilandica* and several others, probably had independent origins. The Carolina poplar *(P. c. eugenii)*, a male form that has coarse, glossy leaves and is much narrower in outline than typical *P. canadensis*, has often been planted as a street tree but is not well suited for that purpose; it is thought by some to be a hybrid between a form of *P. canadensis* and the Lombardy poplar *(P. nigra italica)*. It grows to a height of 150 feet.

In its typical form *P. canadensis* becomes 100 feet high and has spreading or somewhat ascending branches. Its coarse, glossy leaves, toothed and somewhat hairy at the margins, may or may not have the glands typical of its cottonwood parent.

The white poplar or abele *(P. alba)* is a rapid-growing, many-branched tree up to 100 feet tall, with the bark of its young branches whitish and the undersides of its variably toothed leaves woolly white. The leaves on its vigorous shoots are distinctly lobed. In variety *P. a. nivea* the lower leaf surfaces are covered with a felt of snow-white hairs. A variety that is used for landscape planting and thrives near the sea is *P. a. bolleana*, which is tall and narrow in outline. It originated in Turkestan.

The gray poplar *(P. canescens)* is generally similar to the white poplar but its leaves are not lobed; they are gray-hairy beneath. It has the same geographical range as the white poplar and is considered by some to be a hybrid between it and the European aspen.

The Chinese white poplar *(P. tomentosa)* is similar to *P. alba*, may become 90 feet tall and has leaves that are gray tomentose beneath. Its leaves are not lobed but those on long shoots are doubly toothed.

The American aspen *(P. tremuloides)* and the European aspen *(P. tremula)* are very similar. Both attain maximum heights of about 90 feet and both have such flattened leaf stalks that their nearly circular leaf blades quiver with the slightest movement of air. Both are widely distributed geographically, the American from Labrador and Alaska to Pennsylvania, Missouri and, in the mountains, into Mexico; the European through Europe, North Africa, western Asia, Siberia, northeastern Asia and China. The Chinese manifestation, variety *P. t. davidiana*, has smaller leaves that have shallower teeth and are reddish when they unfold.

The American aspen, which is believed to have the widest natural distribution of any North American tree, has conspicuously whitish-gray bark when young. It is most abundant in the northern part of its range, where it tends to take over clearings. Its lumber is valued only where other wood is scarce. The European aspen differs from the American kind in having more circular, less abruptly pointed leaves, which, when young, are whitish rather than green beneath and have deeper marginal teeth. This species blooms earlier in spring than any American poplar; its profusion of long catkins makes an extremely attractive display. It produces suckers freely.

The American large-toothed aspen *(P. grandidentata)* ranges from Nova Scotia and Minnesota to North Carolina, Tennessee and Iowa. Reaching up to 75 feet in height, it is straight-trunked and has a rather narrow, rounded head. Its leaves resemble those of the European aspen but are larger, thicker, more coarsely toothed and have stouter leaf stalks; it differs from the Euro-pean aspen also in having downy rather than smooth young shoots.

Two Asiatic aspens, the Japanese *P. sieboldii* and, from China, *P. adenpoda*, attain heights of about 70 feet. They closely resemble the European aspen but usually have conspicuous glands at the bases of their leaves. The ends of the leaves of the Chinese kind have longer points than those of other aspens.

The balsam group of poplars is most numerous. The balsam poplar or tacamahac *(P. tacamahaca)* is a narrow, upright-branched tree that grows up to 90 feet high and ranges across North America from Labrador to Alaska and southward to New York, Michigan, Nevada and Oregon. Its firm leaves are dull whitish on their undersides and finely toothed. Like all of its group, its large, very resinous buds exude a balsamic fragrance in spring. The Western balsam poplar *(P. trichocarpa)*, also called black cottonwood, is the largest deciduous tree of Pacific North America. Native from Alaska to southern California, it sometimes attains a height of 225 feet. It differs from *P. tacamahaca* in having slightly angled branchlets that are sometimes pubescent and in having three-valved rather than two-valved seed capsules. Other American poplars of this group include the narrow-leaved cottonwood *(P. angustifolia)*, which may reach a height of about 60 feet, is slender-branched and has orange-colored twigs. This kind is native from Saskatchewan to Arizona. Somewhat smaller and round-headed is *P. acuminata*, which ranges from Saskatchwan to Arizona; it attains 45 feet in height.

Several balsam poplars are indigenous to eastern Asia. Notable among them are *P. simonii* of northern China, a rather narrow, handsome tree that grows to a height of 50 feet and has small bright green leaves; *P. yunnanensis*, of southwestern China, with angled branchlets and red midveins to its leaves; *P. szechuanica*, of western China, growing up to 125 feet high, with angled young branchlets and large handsome leaves; *P. cathayana* of northwestern China, Manchuria and Korea, which attains a height of 120 feet and has upright branches and large leaves; and *P. maximowiczii*, a handsome kind that grows up to 120 feet tall and has branches that spread widely. *P. maximowiczii* is also native in Japan where it is much planted to form windbreaks and as a roadside tree.

From central Asia comes the small-growing *P. tristis*, and from Siberia *P. laurifolia*, a 45-

American aspen. Populus tremuloides (Union Pacific Railroad)

foot tree with strongly angled branchlets which are pubescent toward their tips.

Prominent among hybrid and supposed hybrid kinds in the balsam poplar group is *P. candicans,* the balm of Gilead or Ontario poplar. This probably originated in Europe before 1755, but its parentage, if indeed it be of hybrid derivation, is not known. It grows to a height of 90 feet and has stout wide-spreading branches. Another hybrid balsam poplar is *P. berolinensis,* the Berlin poplar, a tree of columnar growth and bright green foliage believed to have the Lombardy poplar and *P. laurifolia* as its parents.

Three large-leaved poplars must be noticed: *P. heterophylla,* the swamp cottonwood, is a 96-foot tree native from Connecticut to Illinois, Georgia and Louisiana. The Chinese *P. lasiocarpa* is one of the most decorative of poplars; it grows to a height of 70 feet, is round-headed and has bright green leaves decorated with red petioles and midribs. *P. wilsonii* is similar to *P. lasiocarpa* but has smaller, duller leaves.

A poplar with interesting Biblical associations is the variable-leaved *P. euphratica.* This is the "willow" of the Old Testament. It is remarkable for the great diversity of leaf shapes that occur on the same plant. Reaching up to 50 feet high, with spreading branches and a trunk diameter of 2 feet or more, it grows natively from Egypt and Syria to central Asia and China.

Salix—Willow

Willows are trees and shrubs—some hugging the ground and only an inch or two high—mostly of the Northern Hemisphere. They are natives of all continents except Australia. Most species grow in moist or wet soils, but a few favor drier places. Their minute, insect-pollinated flowers are borne in catkins. Many kinds bloom in late winter or spring before the leaves appear, others after the plants are foliaged. Although immense numbers of seeds are produced, comparatively few are fertile and they soon lose their ability to germinate. Propagation is often effected by twigs that are transported by wind or water and take root in moist or wet soil. The species number between four hundred and five hundred; there are also numerous hybrids. Identifying willows is often as difficult as distinguishing poplars, and for the same reasons.

The pliable young stems of willows, called withes or osiers, are used for making baskets and wickerwork; their wood is made into boxes, excelsior and a fine grade of charcoal as well as Dutch clogs and English cricket bats. The frames of Eskimo kayaks are of willow and English bee skeps (hives) are framed of the same material. Willow bark contains a high percentage of tannin and, like all other parts of the plant, is bitter.

In many parts of Europe willows, cultivated for the production of osiers, are planted in marshy areas little adapted to other kinds of agriculture. When grown for this purpose they are pruned to the ground every year or two. Planted along river, pond and canal banks, each has a stout trunk several feet high with shoots growing only from its top. The shoots, periodically cut off close to the trunks, are used for stakes and other purposes. Such pollarded willows give character to some European countrysides; they become quite old and then are decidedly picturesque.

References to willows in the English translations of the Bible have led to a popular misconception. It seems certain that Israelite captives in Babylon did not hang "their harps upon the willows" (Psalms 137:2) when they wept about

Pollarded willows (Paul Popper Ltd.)

Permanent wave tree. Salix matsudana tortuosa (P. H. Brydon)

their sufferings but on the branches of the poplar tree *(Populus euphratica)*. The legend that the tree involved was the weeping willow *(Salix babylonica)* and that its branches, previously erect, were thereby weighed down and have since been pendulous has no basis in fact. The weeping willow is of Chinese origin and could scarcely have been brought to the Holy Land as early as 500 B.C. However, the great Swedish botanist Carl Linnaeus, under the impression that the weeping willow was the tree referred to in the Psalms, named it *Salix babylonica*, the Babylonian willow, and so it remains.

Country people in Great Britain have long called the stems of willows carrying plump male catkins "palms" and have used them with religious significance on the Sunday before Easter to substitute for true palms. In Russia, too, and probably elsewhere in Europe, willows have been used in Palm Sunday observances.

In the first century A.D. the Greek physician Dioscorides wrote that a decoction of leaves of the white willow was an excellent treatment for gout. For centuries afterward, Europeans used infusions of willows to treat gout, neuralgia, toothache and other pains but because of its bitterness did not take the medicine internally. In

1827 a French chemist, attempting to isolate the pain reliever believed present in willows and some other plants, discovered in *Spiraea* a glucoside he called salacin, a name derived from *Salix*, the name of the willows. About a decade later a refined product, salicylic acid, was prepared from salicin. This acid, still employed in the treatment of athlete's foot and dandruff, cannot be taken internally. In 1899 a German chemist isolated from the bark of willows acetylsalicylic acid, which has proved to be an almost universal pain reliever and one that is safe to take internally. He named this asperin, deriving the word from *spirsaure*, the German name for salicyclic acid. So the name aspirin commemorates the fact that its precursor, salicin, was first obtained not from a willow but from a *Spiraea*.

Since the dawn of history willows have served man for many other purposes. The frames of Roman coracles and battle shields, as well as their paddles and oars, were fashioned of willow. Wherever willows grew they were used to make hunting and fishing equipment. Dyes and tanning materials derived from willows have been used since earliest times. The foliage and young stems of willows provide much forage for antelope, caribou, deer, moose, reindeer and other cud-chewers. Lastly, willows are of immense importance for stabilizing riverbanks and wetlands and preventing erosion by water and wind, as their roots spread widely and hold the soil, thus preventing it from washing away.

American Willows

The black willow (S. nigra) has a wide range through much of North America. Its wood is exploited for making boxes, crates, charcoal and excelsior. It grows to a height of 40 feet and usually develops several trunks and a broad open crown. It blooms after its leaves appear. A variety, S. n. altissima, of Arkansas, Louisiana and Texas, is reported to be sometimes 120 feet high and is the tallest of American willows.

Other tall-growing American kinds are the peach-leaved willow (S. amygdaloides) and S. lasiandra. Both reach maximum heights of 60 feet. The former, with a single trunk up to 2 feet in diameter, is widely distributed across northern North America, whereas the latter grows naturally from British Columbia to New Mexico. It has ascending branches and a trunk diameter up to 3 feet. The peach-leaved willow differs from the black willow in that its leaves are glaucous on their undersides and from the European almond-leaved willow in having glandless leaf stalks. S. lasiandra, a very handsome kind, is closely related to the European bay or laurel willow and, like it, has shining dark green leaves with wavy-toothed margins; the midribs of the leaves are yellow.

Among lower-growing American willows the following are of tree size: the red or polished willow (S. laevigata), the arroyo willow (S. lasiolepis), and S. scouleriana. All grow to a height of 30 feet or occasionally more. The first two are confined to the West Coast from Washington southward, with the arroyo willow extending into Mexico. S. scouleriana ranges from Alaska to California and New Mexico; in the north it withstands temperatures of about 75° F. below zero; in the southern part of its range temperatures may exceed 120° F. above zero—quite a variation for any plant species to be able to endure!

One of the best-known American willows is the pussy willow (S. discolor), native of the northeastern and north-central states and adjacent Canada. It differs from the European goat willow in having smaller, less ovoid and more cylindrical male catkins, and female flowers with short but distinct styles, leaves that are smooth rather than roughened on their upper surfaces and branchlets that do not retain their downy coating until fall. The pussy willow grows to a height of about 20 feet and thrives better in dryish ground than most willows.

European Willows

The white willow (S. alba) of Europe, Asia and North Africa has a thick trunk and spreading yellowish brown branches that form an open head up to a height of 80 feet. It blooms before it leafs out in spring. Its light grayish green foliage produces a whitish effect which accounts for the common name of the tree. The leaves have silky hair, especially on their undersides. This is one of the handsomest willows and one of the most important as a source of lumber. The wood of one variety, S. a. calva, which has more upright branches than the type, is prized above all others for making cricket bats. Variety S. a. vitellina, with yellow branchlets and leaves glaucous on their undersides, provides osiers of good quality. Of the several other varieties of this species the most important is S. a. tristis, an extremely hardy, yellow-twigged weeping willow.

The crack willow (S. fragilis), native to Europe and Asia, has escaped from cultivation in eastern North America and reproduces itself there spontaneously. It grows rapidly to a maximum height of 90 feet. This species acquired its colloquial name from the readiness with which its branchlets break off at their junctions with the branches. A distinguishing characteristic is the wide angle (60° to 90°) at which the branchlets spread from the branches; in the nearly allied white willow the angle of divergence is 30° to 40°.

One of the handsomest willows, S. pentandra of Europe and northern Asia, is called the bay willow because its comparatively large, broad, brilliant green leaves resemble those of the sweet bay (Laurus nobilis). This species has escaped from cultivation and reproduces itself spontaneously in eastern North America. It sometimes attains a height of 60 feet, and bears its catkins after its leaves unfold.

The almond-leaved willow (Salix amygdalina) is a native of Europe and Asia that sometimes is 30 feet tall. Of erect growth, it is commonly cultivated in Europe for osiers. Another European willow much used for basketmaking is the common osier (S. viminalis), which sometimes attains 30 feet but is usually shorter. Its natural range, too, extends into Asia. The leaves of the common osier are covered with silky hairs on their undersides and their margins are without teeth. Those of the almond-leaved willow are hairless beneath and finely toothed at their margins.

Yet another Eurasian is the violet willow (*S. daphnoides*). This is sometimes 40 feet tall and is of erect, vigorous growth. It is distinguished by the beautiful violet or purple waxy coating that covers its young shoots. Its finely toothed leaves are glaucous beneath. Its male catkins are almost as handsome as those of the goat willow. The osiers of this willow are called "violets" by basket makers.

Quite distinctive is the 45-foot tall *S. elaeagnos* of the mountains of southern Europe and Asia Minor. The very narrow leaves of this species produce an elegant feathery effect; they are white-hairy beneath and their upper surfaces are gray-hairy at first but later become green and hairless. Because of the size and handsome appearance of its silky male catkins, which are bright yellow at maturity, the goat willow (*S. caprea*) of Europe and northern Asia is the most decorative of the pussy willows; it is the willow commonly called "palm" in Great Britain. It attains a height of about 25 feet.

Asiatic Willows

The best known of this group is the Babylonian weeping willow (*S. babylonica*), a native of China. Its long, pendulous branches and fine-textured foliage gives it a special grace that makes it the most ornamental of all weeping willows. Unfortunately, it is less cold-hardy than the weeping variety of the white willow (*S. alba tristis*), and so is not suitable for planting as far north. A hybrid of *S. babylonica* and *S. fragilis* is the Wisconsin or Niobe weeping willow (*S. blanda*), which is also much hardier than the Babylonian weeping willow. Its lustrous leaves are conspicuously broader than those of *S. babylonica*. Probably of the same parentage is the Thurlow weeping willow (*S. elegantissima*), which is as hardy as the Wisconsin weeping willow and has much longer pendulous branches. Despite the fact that its leaves are duller than those of the Wisconsin weeping willow, the Thurlow weeping willow is the best substitute for *S. babylonica* wherever it is too cold to grow the latter.

Salix matsudana of northeastern Asia grows to a height of 40 feet. It is best known perhaps in its variety *S. m. tortuosa*, which is sometimes called the permanent-wave tree and is planted as an ornamental by lovers of the unusual and grotesque. Its branches and twigs are conspicuously twisted spirally and contorted.

Two large willows of Asia are *S. jessoensis*, growing up to 90 feet tall, and *S. cardiophylla*, attaining to 75 feet in height. The former is a native of Japan. The latter grows in Korea. The leaves of *S. jessoensis* are hairy on their lower surfaces, those of *S. cardiophylla* are quite smooth.

CHAPTER 11

The Myricales

One family comprises the order Myricales: The tiny flowers have neither calyxes nor corollas. The members of this family, which includes a few small trees as well as shrubs, have aromatic foliage, yellowish resinous dots on their leaves, and one-seeded berry-like fruits which are often coated with wax. Individual plants may be completely male, completely female or bisexual; whole plants and sometimes individual branches may change sex from year to year.

MYRICACEAE—SWEET GALE FAMILY

Myrica

This genus, numbering thirty-five species, occurs in many temperate and tropical regions. Its members have tiny unisexual or bisexual flowers in short spikes and undivided leaves. *Comptonia*, the other genus of the family, has divided fernlike leaves.

Among the more important species are California bayberry (*M. californica*), wax-myrtle (*M. cerifera*) and the nearly related *M. mexicana*. All are low trees, or sometimes shrubs, usually less than 35 feet tall and evergreen or partially evergreen. The wax from the fruits of *M. cerifera* and *M. mexicana* is used for candle-making, as is that of *M. arguta*. As its name implies, *M. californica* is a native of western North America. *M. cerifera* occurs naturally from New

97

Jersey to Florida, Texas, the West Indies and Central America, while *M. mexicana* has its home in Mexico, often in high mountains. *M. arguta*, of Venezuela and Colombia, is called laurel and *olivo* locally. The tree, which has slender stems and open crowns, is the commercial source of a wax marketed as cera de laurel. *M. faya*, the fire tree of the Canary Islands, Madeira and the Azores has edible red fruits. Introduced into Hawaii for reforestation, this species has there become something of a pest. Another species, *M. rubra*, of China and Japan, is sometimes cultivated for its edible fruits.

CHAPTER 12

The Juglandales

Only one family, the walnuts, comprises the order Juglandales. The tiny flowers have neither petals nor sepals. These are deciduous trees or occasionally shrubs, usually with alternate, pinnate leaves that are aromatic. The unisexual flowers are in catkins or spikes.

JUGLANDACEAE—WALNUT FAMILY

Carya—Hickory

All members of this genus of twenty-five species are deciduous and except for one in southern China all are American. They are easily distinguished from *Juglans* and *Pterocarya* because the pith of their branchlets is solid, not divided into thin transverse plates. Their male catkins are three-branched whereas those of *Carya* are unbranched.

Hickories grow rather slowly. Their wood has great strength and elasticity and is used for the handles of tools subject to impact shock such as axes and hammers, and also for wheels, implements, machinery and baseball bats. It is excellent fuel and is much used for smoking meats, giving them a flavor that is highly prized.

The largest species is the pecan (*C. pecan*) which sometimes attains a height of 180 feet and may have a trunk diameter of 6 to 7 feet a few feet above the ground. Growing in the open, it develops a broad, rounded crown. It has thin-shelled edible nuts and many selected varieties are cultivated for commercial use. The pecan grows naturally in low fertile ground from Iowa and Indiana to Alabama, Texas and Mexico.

The shagbark or shellbark hickory (*C. ovata*) and the big shellbark hickory (*C. laciniosa*) attain maximum heights of 120 feet and have thick-shelled nuts. The former develops an irregular, narrow crown, a trunk 3 to 4 feet in diameter, and bark which flakes in large, loose plates. Its edible nuts are highly regarded, several selected varieties being cultivated. The big shellbark hickory, native from New York to Iowa, Tennessee and Oklahoma, chiefly inhabits rich, deep, fairly moist soils. It has a straight trunk rarely 3 feet in diameter, shaggy bark that flakes off in plates, and a narrow, oblong crown. Its large nuts are usually not separated for commercial purposes from those of the shagbark hickory. The leaves of *C. laciniosa* have seven or nine leaflets; those of *C. ovata* usually have five.

The bitternut (*C. cordiformis*) and the water hickory (*C. aquatica*) have thin-shelled, bitter nuts. Both sometimes attain 100 feet in height. A handsome tree with a rather broad crown, the bitternut grows from Quebec to Minnesota to Florida and Texas. It is slender-trunked and narrow-headed.

The mockernut (*C. tomentosa*) forms a handsome specimen that grows up to 90 feet high with a trunk up to 3 feet in diameter. Its head may be narrow or broad. Its nuts have thick, hard shells that contain a very small amount of sweet meat. It is native from New England and Ontario to Nebraska and Florida and Texas.

The pignut (*C. glabra*), which occurs as a native in dryish soils from New York to Missouri and Florida, grows up to 100 feet high with a trunk up to $2\frac{1}{2}$ feet in diameter and, typically, a narrow head. Its nuts have thick, hard shells that contain small sweet meats. The closely related sweet pignut (*C. ovalis*) differs in that its leaves have seven leaflets rather than the usual five of *C. glabra*. It grows to a height of 100 feet and is narrow in outline. The Chinese species, *C. cathayana*, was first brought into cultivation in Western gardens in 1917. It grows to a height of 60 or 70 feet.

Juglans—Walnut

These are deciduous nut-bearing trees of the Old and New Worlds. As ornamentals they are generally less attractive than hickories but they are sources of excellent cabinet woods and all have edible nuts. The pith cavities of the young shoots are divided into chambers by transverse walls or plates of pith, so that the pith does not form continuous, solid cylinders. The name *Juglans* is derived from *Jovis glans* (Jupiter's acorn), the ancient Latin name for *J. regia*, the Persian walnut. There are fifteen species.

The nuts of the Persian walnut are commonly known as English walnuts in the United States. The valuable lumber of the tree is called by names that indicate its geographical origin, such as Circassian walnut, Italian walnut and French walnut. It is considered the best wood for the making of gunstocks. The Persian walnut is native from southeastern Europe to China. A variable species, it typically forms a spreading round-headed, densely foliaged specimen up to 100 feet high.

The black walnut of eastern North America is *J. nigra*, a native from Massachusetts to Florida and Texas. Growing up to 150 feet high with a trunk diameter up to 6 feet and developing a wide-spreading head, this species is more ornamental than *J. regia* and is one of the most valuable of lumber trees. From its burls and stumps an especially fine-figured wood is obtained. This tree differs from the Persian walnut in that its leaves are toothed and are pubescent beneath and its nuts, which are edible, do not split naturally. Several varieties have been selected and propagated to provide commercial supplies of nuts. Hind's black walnut, native to the central part of California, is commonly planted as a street tree on the West Coast and is also used as an understock upon which to graft the Persian walnut. Occasionally growing up to 75 feet high, it forms a round-headed specimen. Its leaves are toothed and at maturity are essentially smooth on their under surfaces.

The butternut *(J. cinerea)* is less handsome and not as valuable as the black walnut; nevertheless it is the source of excellent lumber for general carpentry, interior trim, and furniture. The tree grows up to 100 feet tall with a trunk diameter of 2 to 3 feet; in open locations it develops a wide-spreading head. Its nuts are clothed with sticky hairs and the scars that mark the places

Above: Shagbark hickory. Carya ovata (T. H. Everett) Right: Shagbark hickory. (Michigan Department of Conservation)

Pecan. *Carya pecan* (United States Department of Agriculture)

on the branches from which leaves have dropped have conspicuous bands of hairs on their upper edges. The butternut is native from New Brunswick to Georgia to the Dakotas and Arkansas.

Other New World *Juglans* include a few smaller trees of the western United States such as *J. rupestris*, *J. major* and *J. californica*, as well as *J. jamaicensis* of Puerto Rico and other West Indian islands and *J. insularis* of Cuba. A few species occur in Mexico. In South America walnuts are native in the Andes and are prized there locally for their lumber. The important species of Peru is *J. neotropica*, which grows up to a height of 50 feet or more and has trunks 3 feet in diameter. The Argentine walnut is *J. australis*, a kind that rarely is as much as 60 feet high and has trunks 3 feet wide.

The most important walnuts of Asia include the Japanese *J. sieboldiana* and its variety *J. s. cordiformis*, the latter called heartnut because of its smooth, flattened, sharply edged, thin-shelled heart-shaped nuts; those of typical *J. sieboldiana* are sticky pubescent, thick-shelled and more globose than those of the heartnut. *J. sieboldiana* and its variety attain heights of about 60 feet, and have massive branches and rounded heads. Selected varieties of the heartnut have been propagated and planted for nut production. Closely related to *J. sieboldiana* is the Chi-

nese *J. cathayensis* and *J. mandshurica* from northern China. They grow 60 to 70 feet high, are round headed and have sticky pubescent fruits.

Pterocarya—Wingnut

Here belong about eight Asiatic deciduous trees that differ from walnuts and hickories in that their fruits are small, winged nutlets borne in long, drooping racemes. The pith of the young stems is laminated like that of walnuts. The best-known species is the Caucasian wingnut, *P. fraxinifolia*, which is native from the Caucasus to Iran. It reaches an ultimate height of 100 feet with a trunk diameter of 4 feet, and develops a spreading head, often wider than high. This tree favors moist soils.

The Japanese wingnut, *P. rhoifolia*, is one of the largest deciduous trees growing in the vicinity of Mt. Hakkoda, in Japan, where it is abundant in moist soils between altitudes of 2500 and 4000 feet. It grows to a height of 90 feet. Chinese species of *Pterocarya* include *P. hupehensis* of the western mountains, which differs from the Caucasian wingnut chiefly in that its leaves have five to nine rather than eleven to fifteen leaflets. It attains a height of 70 feet or more.

CHAPTER 13

The Fagales

All members of this order, the Fagales, which consists of two families only, are trees or shrubs.

BETULACEAE—BIRCH FAMILY

The Betulaceae consist of bisexual, alternate-leaved trees and shrubs with simple leaves and tiny flowers, the latter lacking petals and sepals. The male flowers grow in catkins, the females in conelike clusters or spikes. The family is confined chiefly to the temperate and cold regions of the Northern Hemisphere and consists of six genera and about one hundred species.

Alnus—Alder

Thirty-five deciduous trees and shrubs, chiefly in the Northern Hemisphere but also represented in the Andes, constitute the genus *Alnus*. Most bloom in late winter or early spring. The male flowers come in long pendulous catkins, the females in short conelike catkins. They differ from the birches in that the female catkins are woody and persistent and do not disintegrate when the seeds are ripe but fall to the ground whole, and also in that each tiny male flower has four rather than two stamens. They are primarily trees of moist soils and cool climates. Alders do not rank high as ornamentals for landscape planting but some kinds are exploited commercially for their forest products.

The most imposing North American species are the white alder *(A. rhombifolia)* and the red alder *(A. rubra)*. The former, which is sometimes more than 100 feet tall with a trunk diameter of 2 to 3 feet, is indigenous from Washington to California; the latter, usually not more than 70 feet tall, ranges from Alaska to Idaho and California, reaching its greatest size in the vicinity of Puget Sound. The wood of the red alder is of considerable local importance in furniture manufacture. The speckled alder *(A. incana)*, native to Europe and Asia as well as to North America, forms a round-headed tree that sometimes attains a height of 65 feet and a trunk diameter of 2 feet. It is extremely hardy to cold.

There are a few smaller North American species. *A. sinuata*, which grows to a height of 40 feet or sometimes more and a trunk diameter up to 8 inches, is plentiful from the Arctic Circle to northern California and Montana. The smooth alder *(A. rugosa)*, rarely exceeding 25 feet in height, is native from Maine to Florida and Texas. The seaside alder *(A. maritima)*, about as tall as the smooth alder, inhabits moist soils in Delaware and Maryland and in Oklahoma and differs from most kinds in that it blooms in fall. In the mountains from British Columbia to New Mexico and Baja California occurs the mountain alder *(A. tenuifolia)*, growing to a maximum of about 30 feet in height.

From Mexico several species of *Alnus* have been described and one, *A. glabrata*, is reported to attain considerable size. The barks of the Mexican kinds are used locally for tanning and dyeing and in medicines. In Central America *A. acuminata* is plentiful in the mountains, in some places forming forests of one species; it grows up to 35 feet high and its wood is used locally for building. The South American alders all seem to be variants of *A. jorullensis*, which itself may merge imperceptibly into *A. acumi-nata*. In the Andes it is greatly valued as a source of fuel and for lumber, which is used in carpentry, cabinetmaking, boxes and packing cases. The bark serves in tanning and dyeing and the leaves medicinally. In Ecuador, *A. jorullensis* becomes 60 feet or more high and has a maximum trunk diameter of more than 2 feet.

European Alders

The most important native European alder is the black alder *(A. glutinosa)*, which in central Europe forms extensive forests from valley bottoms to above four thousand feet. Its range extends across most of the continent and into Siberia in the north and North Africa to the south. It occasionally occurs spontaneously in an escape from cultivation in northeastern America. The black alder forms a rather narrow specimen up to 90 feet tall, with a trunk diameter up to 4 feet. Its bark is black and fissured. Its dark green leaves retain their color without much change until they drop late in the fall. When young, its shoots and leaves are decidedly sticky, which accounts for the name *glutinosa*. This quite important timber tree produces lumber in soils too wet for most trees. From it are made boxes, engineers' models and wooden clogs. The ancient Romans employed it for piling and boat making. *Alnus incana*, discussed above with the native American trees, is the second commonest species in Europe and is there called the gray alder. It is readily distinguished from the black alder by leaves that are typically gray-downy beneath. The Italian alder *(A. cordata)*, confined naturally to Italy and Corsica, is a round-headed tree up to 75 feet tall. Pyramidal in outline and with attractive glossy leaves, it is one of the handsomest alders and thrives in drier soil than most. Its mature female catkins, from 1 to 1 1/4 inches long, are larger than those of other alders.

Asiatic Alders

Asia is the home of several tree-sized species, such as *A. pendula* and *A. firma hirtella*, which are Japanese endemics. Typically, the former does not exceed 10 feet in height but the variety *A. f. hirtella* may be three times that height. The latter is graceful and has long, slender branches. Its leaves characteristically have from twelve to eighteen pairs of veins which, together with its grayish or yellowish brown twigs, distinguish it from *A. pendula*; the leaves of *A. pendula* have from eighteen to twenty-six pairs of veins and the twigs are dark reddish brown. *A. pendula*

grows up to a height of 25 feet. The Japanese alder (*A. japonica*) is a native of northern Japan and the Asiatic mainland. Reaching a height of 80 feet and forming a pyramid with dark green foliage, it is one of the largest and most handsome members of the genus. Another species that occurs both in Japan and on the mainland is *A. hirsuta*, which is a broad, pyramidal tree that grows up to 60 feet high. In the western Himalayas is the remarkable *A. nitida*, the Himalayan alder, which is reported to attain a height of 100 feet and a trunk diameter of 5 feet. It has blackish bark and leaves that are glossy green above and paler on their undersides. This species shares with the American *A. maritima* the distinction of blooming in the fall.

Betula—Birch

Birches are comparatively short-lived deciduous trees and shrubs of light, elegant appearance; many kinds are remarkable for the beauty of their bark. Their leaves are typically oval or rhomboidal, have longish stalks and usually toothed margins. In the far north and at high altitudes birches form extensive forests. Their wood is valued for flooring, interior trim, doors, plywood and furniture; it is also an excellent fuel. When exposed to moisture it rots quickly unless treated with preservatives, but after treatment it is sufficiently resistant to be used for railroad ties. The bark is impervious to water and for this reason the wood is used locally in northern Europe and Asia for roofing shingles. North American Indians wrote on it and used it to make wigwams and canoes. Some species of birch contain an aromatic oil which is extracted by distillation. Species of *Betula* number about sixty.

American Birches

About nine native species of *Betula* in North America attain tree size. Most important as a source of lumber is *B. lutea*, the yellow birch, which is round-headed at maturity, but is pyramidal when young. It grows up to 100 feet high and attains a trunk diameter of 3 to 4 feet and is spontaneous from Newfoundland to Manitoba to the high mountains of the southern Appalachians, usually in moist or wet soils. Its bark, silver-gray on young branches, becomes yellowish or reddish brown with age and peels in thin

Silver birch. Betula pendula (Ingmar Holmåsen)

Above: Flowers of the European silver birch
Right: European birch. Betula pubescens (Both
Ingmar Holmåsen)

flakes; that of the young shoots is aromatic and
has a bitter taste.

The cherry birch or sweet birch (*B. lenta*) ranks
second only to the yellow birch as a producer of
lumber. From its wood and bark is distilled
sweet birch oil, used medicinally and as a substitute for oil of wintergreen in flavoring, and
birch beer is made from its sap. It attains a maximum height of about 80 feet with a trunk diameter up to 5 feet and ranges from Maine to
Alabama and westward to Ohio. It is less tolerant of heat than the yellow birch and will not
ordinarily succeed where hot summers occur
regularly. The cherry birch is distinguished from
the yellow birch by its darker brown bark,
remindful of that of a cherry tree, by the sweeter
taste of the bark of its young shoots, and by the
lack of hair on the scales of its catkins. In fall
its foliage becomes brilliant yellow.

The river birch (*B. nigra*) is a pyramidal tree
of rugged appearance that attains a height of
about 90 feet. Its trunk often divides low down
into two or three erect trunklike branches, and
quite often the lower trunk, which may be 5 feet
in diameter, is crooked. The bark is reddish

Gray birch. Betula populifolia (T. H. Everett)

brown to orange-brown and peels in papery flakes. The leaves, which are whitish beneath, turn yellow in fall. The river birch grows in lowlands from Massachusetts to Florida and west to Minnesota and Kansas and favors moist soils; it prospers even where the land is inundated for a part of each year.

One of the best and handsomest American species is the canoe or paper birch (*B. papyrifera*), which reaches an extreme height of 125 feet and has a trunk diameter of 2 to 3 feet. Its head is typically rather narrow and open. This birch is remarkable for the almost pure whiteness of its flaking bark, a feature which is displayed to best advantage against a background of evergreens such as pines or hemlocks. The paper birch occurs spontaneously from Labrador to British Columbia and Washington and into Montana, Nebraska and Pennsylvania. Some of its varieties extend beyond this range, one, *B. p. neo-alaskana,* occuring from Saskatchewan to the valley of the Yukon.

Quite different is the gray birch (*B. populifolia*). Rarely as high as 40 feet or with trunks more than 1½ feet in diameter, this native of dry, barren soils as well as of pond and swamp margins is one of the first invaders of abandoned farms and of timberlands devastated by fire. Typically, it forms a clump of several crooked trunks, the crookedness resulting from

winter burdens of snow and ice. Under such conditions the trunks bend until their tops touch the ground but, although their recuperative powers are great, they often fail to regain completely their former positions. The bark of this birch is white with conspicuous black triangular markings; it does not peel as freely as that of the paper birch. The chief use of its wood is as fuel.

European Birches

Only two species of birch are indigenous to Europe and these are so similar that some authorities consider them one. They are distinguished by the fact that the twigs of the silver birch (*B. pendula*) are warty and hairless whereas those of the common European birch (*B. pubescens*) are covered with fine down but lack the rough protuberances. These grow farther north than any other trees and are the only trees native to Iceland. Even at latitude 70° north they become forest trees and they extend south to mountainous areas bordering the Mediterranean and eastward well into Siberia. Of pyramidal growth, under favorable conditions they reach a height of 75 feet or occasionally more, but in the far north they are much less impressive. Their bark, which peels in papery layers, is white, that of the silver birch more intensely so than that of the common European birch. In old specimens the bark on the lower part of the trunk often becomes ragged and dark. These are graceful, pyramidal trees, with the branches of older specimens, especially those of *B. pendula*, drooping at their ends. The European birches provide lumber for the making of fine furniture and barrels and for turnery. Beer is prepared from their sap.

Asiatic Birches

The greatest number of birches are Asiatic but many occupy territories unlikely to be visited by many Westerners. Some are cultivated in Europe and America.

Outstanding among endemic Japanese kinds is the monarch birch (*B. maximowicziana*), described by one authority as "probably the most beautiful of all birches." It has larger leaves than any other species—heart-shaped and up to

Right: A typical feather palm (Walter Dawn) Overleaf left: Spanish bayonet. Yucca aloifolia (Emil Javorsky) Right: Cottonwood. Populus deltoides (Bill Stackhouse)

7 inches long and 5 inches wide. The tree grows to a maximum height of 100 feet and has orange-gray peeling bark.

The Japanese cherry birch (*B. grossa*) is similar to the American cherry birch (*B. lenta*) but has more coarsely toothed leaves. It grows to a height of about 100 feet. On old specimens the bark becomes deeply fissured and changes from brown to near black. An interesting native of central Japan is *B. globispica*, a 60- to 70-foot species that has nearly white, peeling bark and broad oval leaves.

A few birches occur both in Japan and on the Asiatic mainland. Of these, *B. davurica* grows to a height of 70 feet, has wide-spreading branches, and purplish brown bark which peels in thin strips and clothes the trunk with curling flakes so that the trunks generally resemble those of the American river birch (*B. nigra*). Of about the same height but with grayish or creamy white, flaking bark is *B. ermanii*. It forms a handsome, round-headed tree.

Another attractive species is *B. schmidtii*, which attains 100 feet in height and has dark gray to nearly black bark divided into small plates. One of the finest of the birches native to both mainland Asia and Japan is *B. mandshurica*, which occurs in several varieties. The island form, the Japanese white birch, has larger leaves —not wedge-shaped at their bases—and is distinguished as *B. m. japonica*. Perhaps the finest of the *B. mandshurica* varieties is *B. m. szechuanica* from the high mountains of western China. A tree with wide-spreading branches and up to 60 feet tall, its white bark has the appearance of American canoe birch and also peels.

The Chinese paper birch (*B. albo-sinensis*) is an open-headed tree up to 100 feet high. Its bright orange to orange-red peeling bark is seen to excellent advantage in winter. It is a native of western China. From the same region comes *B. luminifera*, which grows up to 60 or 70 feet in height, is handsome and has comparatively large leaves. Its brown bark does not peel.

Sometimes called the Himalayan birch, *B. utilis*, is not so hardy as most birches. It has a brown bark which peels in papery flakes, and its young shoots are orange-brown and densely covered with gray down. This kind, in its native Himalayas, grows up to 60 feet tall. Another

Quaking aspen. Populus tremuloides (James R. Simon)

Paper birch bark. Betula papyrifera (Andreas Feininger)

Himalayan kind that associates with *B. utilis* is *B. jacquemontiana*. It has white, peeling bark and warty twigs. Still another, *B. medwediewii*, has its home in the region south of the Caucasus. A tall, handsome tree, one of its distinctive features is the large size of its leaves, which are 4 to 5 inches long and up to 3 inches wide.

Carpinus—Hornbeam

Hornbeams are slow-growing, characteristically round-headed, deciduous trees of the Northern Hemisphere, chiefly of Asia but with representatives in North America and in Europe. There are about thirty-five species. They have zigzag twigs and broad, conspicuously parallel-veined, double-toothed leaves. Their flowers, which are insignificant, appear with the foliage and occur in catkins. The catkins of male flowers arise from shoots of the previous year and generally resemble the male catkins of birches. The female catkins are terminal on the shoots of the current year, erect at first but becoming pendent as they approach the fruiting stage, and with small leafy bracts which, attached to the small fruits, enlarge and serve as wings in seed dispersal.

The only New World hornbeam, *C. caroliniana*, also called the blue-beech, has a wide distribution from the east coast of North America

Gray birch bark. Betula populifolia (Andreas Feininger)

Yellow birch bark. Betula lutea (Andreas Feininger)

to Minnesota, Texas, Mexico and Central America. Often developing several trunks, which are fluted and covered with thin gray bark, it rarely grows as high as 40 feet. Its foliage turns splendid shades of orange and red in fall. Its wood is very hard but of little commercial importance.

The European hornbeam (*C. betulus*) is much more imposing than its American counterpart. Pyramidal when young, at maturity it becomes a round-headed specimen up to 80 feet high and is ranked among the most handsome of European trees, more elegant in appearance than the beech with which it is sometimes confused. It is conveniently distinguished from the beech by the muscle-like flutings of its trunk and by more coarsely saw-toothed and less shiny leaves, which in fall turn an agreeable yellow. This hornbeam occurs through all of western, central and southeastern Europe and in Asia Minor but its range does not extend as far north as that of the beech (*Fagus sylvatica*). Its extremely hard, almost bony wood is not easily worked. It has been used for making small objects which must have great strength, such as axles, spokes, yokes, cogs and parts of the striking mechanisms of pianos; it is also excellent fuel. In landscape plantings this species is of especial value for creating tall hedges. When sheared regularly such hedges retain their dead leaves until spring, a feature which increases their effectiveness as

windbreaks. The European hornbeam does not adapt well to coastal regions.

The Japanese hornbeam (*C. japonica*) differs from the American, European and some other Asiatic kinds in having leaves with fifteen to twenty-four instead of seven to fifteen pairs of veins. Its young shoots are hairy, its foliage handsome. It becomes about 50 feet tall. Another native of Japan, and also of continental Asia, is *C. tschonoskii*, a graceful tree that grows to about the same height as the Japanese hornbeam. Yet a third, of similar origin and dimensions, is *C. laxifolia*. The last two species have leaves with seven to fifteen pairs of veins each, which separates them from *C. cordata*, also of mainland Asia and Japan, the leaves of which have fifteen to twenty pairs of veins. The densely hairy young shoots of *C. tschonoskii* distinguishes it from the American and the European hornbeams. From the latter *C. laxifolia* can be told by its sharp-pointed leaves.

Corylus—Hazel

The hazels consist of fifteen species of wind-pollinated deciduous woody plants, mostly shrubs but including a few trees, all of the Northern Hemisphere. The male flowers, which grow in pendulous catkins, mature in spring; the females are enclosed in small scaly buds from which, in spring, red styles protrude. From hornbeams (*Carpinus*) and hop-hornbeam (*Ostrya*) hazels differ in that their fruits grow in clusters rather than pendent spikes and their leaves usually have not more than nine pairs of veins. The fruits (nuts) are enclosed or partly enclosed in a husk of leafy bracts.

The Turkish hazel (C. colurna) is the best-known Corylus of tree size. When fully grown it may be 80 feet high and have a trunk exceeding 2 feet in diameter. It is pyramidal and usually its trunk is very short and divides so low down that the branches rest or almost rest on the ground; the bark is gray and corklike. This native of southern Europe and Asia Minor has nearly circular leaves and is the source of edible nuts as well as of excellent lumber that has a great variety of uses. As an ornamental the Turkish hazel has much to recommend it. It is of fine appearance, it is attractive in bloom, and it stands dry soil conditions well.

The Chinese hazel (C. chinensis) is very similar to the Turkish hazel and is regarded by some botanists as a variety of that species. It has darker young shoots and its leaf margins are evenly and less coarsely toothed. The great plant explorer Ernest H. Wilson told of seeing specimens 120 feet high in western China.

Ostrya—Hop-Hornbeam

Here belong ten species of deciduous trees primarily of the Northern Hemisphere but extending into Central America. The common name refers to the fruits, which are born in hoplike clusters, each nut inside a bladder-like container formed of light green bracts. Except for their fruits, these trees closely resemble hornbeams. The differences are these: the lateral buds of hornbeams lie flat against the twigs whereas those of hop-hornbeams are erect, the male catkins of hop-hornbeams develop in fall while those of hornbeams are not evident until spring, and the leaf veins of hop-hornbeams are sometimes branched toward their ends.

The American hop-hornbeam (O. virginiana) is sometimes called ironwood because of the hardness of its wood. It is a slow-growing, pyramidal or round-headed tree that reaches an ultimate height of about 60 feet and a trunk diameter of 2 feet. Its durable lumber has no substantial commercial importance but is used locally for a variety of purposes such as fence posts, tool handles and mallets.

The European hop-hornbeam (O. carpinifolia) closely resembles the American species but has broader nutlets. Also, its leaves are commonly rounded at their bases; those of O. virginiana are usually somewhat heart-shaped.

Somewhat taller, and attaining a maximum height of 80 feet, is the Japanese hop-hornbeam (O. japonica), a native of China and other parts of northeast Asia including Japan. It differs only slightly from the American and European kinds, the most notable distinction being that the undersides of its leaves are conspicuously pubescent instead of being, like the other tow, without or almost without hairs.

FAGACEAE—BEECH FAMILY

This important family contains between eight hundred and nine hundred deciduous and evergreen trees and shrubs that have unisexual flowers, usually with both sexes on the same plant. The fruits (nuts) are partially or completely surrounded by a husk called a cupule. The Fagaceae is closely related to the Betulaceae and is one of the oldest families of the dicotyledonous trees. Fossil specimens from the Cretaceous Period are known.

Castanea—Chestnut

The twelve trees, or rarely shrubs, of this genus have handsome, furrowed bark and coarsely toothed, parallel-veined, undivided leaves unlike those of any other trees of North Temperate regions except for a few oaks. The leaves grow in two ranks. The edible seeds (nuts), usually found in clusters of one to three but sometimes

Chinese chestnut. Castanea mollissima (T. H. Everett)

up to seven, are contained in a prickly, burrlike envelope (cupule) which at maturity splits and releases them. The flowers grow in long, slender catkins and are so abundant in early summer that, although of an undistinguished yellowish hue, they make quite an attractive display. They have a decided odor that some people consider unpleasant. Those of the lowest catkins on the shoots are all males; the uppermost catkins consist mostly of male flowers but close to their bases each bears from one to three female flowers.

Two tree-sized species of *Castanea* are native to North America, the American chestnut (*C. dentata*) and the chinquapin (*C. pumila*). The natural range of the former is from Maine to Michigan to Alabama and Missouri, and that of the latter from Pennsylvania to Florida and to Texas. The American chestnut occasionally attains 100 feet in height and has a trunk 4 feet or more in diameter. It is straight-trunked and broad-headed, its crown rounded in outline. Unfortunately this species has almost been eradicated by a parasitic fungus that has proved uncontrollable. Called the chestnut bark disease fungus, this organism also attacks the Spanish chestnut and some other kinds; it was discovered in 1904 after it was introduced to the United States from Asia. Infected trees frequently develop sprouts from their bases and these may grow for the first few years, seem healthy and even bear fruit, but within a very few years of their first cropping they inevitably succumb to the disease. Although the chinquapin (*C. pumila*) sometimes grows to a height of 50 feet and may have a trunk diameter of 3 feet, it is often no more than a tall shrub. Its nuts, borne singly, or rarely in pairs, are small but sweet. Its lumber is used locally for a variety of purposes.

The Spanish chestnut (*C. sativa*) does not differ markedly from the American chestnut. The most obvious variations are in leaves that are, at least when young, pubescent on their undersides, and winter buds that are hairless or nearly so. This tree may exceed 100 feet in height and have a trunk 10 feet or more in diameter. A native of southern Europe, North Africa and Asia Minor, it has long been valued as a source of food and lumber. It is believed to have been brought to Great Britain by the Romans as food for their troops and horses and has since made itself so much at home there that it reproduces spontaneously. In southern Europe, selected named varieties are cultivated for their nuts.

European hornbeam. Carpinus betulus (Wlodzimierz Puchalski)

There are several Asiatic chestnuts and some are resistant to the chestnut bark disease. The Chinese chestnut (*C. mollissima*), indigenous to the mountains of western China, is outstanding in this respect because it also produces nuts of a commercially valuable size and quality. It is widely cultivated in China for its nuts. It becomes a dense, round-headed tree up to 60 feet high with a trunk about 2 feet in diameter. Like the chinquapin, its leaves are finely hairy beneath but, unlike that species, each burr usually contains two or three nuts. The young, vigorous shoots are also furnished with long, spreading hairs. This native of China and Korea is about as hardy as the American chestnut. Two other Chinese species are worthy of mention: *C. henryi*, which grows to a height of 90 feet, with a trunk diameter up to 3 feet, hairless shoots, leaves without hairs on their undersides, and burrs that contain only one nut; and *C. seguinii*, a 30-foot tree that has pubescent shoots, leaves with hairs on their undersides on the veins only and usually three nuts in each burr.

The Japanese chestnut (*C. crenata*) is often shrubby but may grow to a height of 30 feet or more. Botanically, it is closely related to the American and Spanish chestnuts. At one time all three were considered mere geographical variants of one species. It differs from the American kind in that its leaves are hairy beneath, at least when young, and from the European species in that its leaves are less coarsely toothed and its fruits are often borne laterally rather than terminally on the branches. This species is the source of the biggest pieces of commercial lumber of any Chinese chestnut.

Castanopsis

This important group of trees, which inhabits tropical and subtropical Asia, except for one species which is a native of western America, links the chestnuts (Castanea) with the oaks (Quercus). The relationship is so close that no characteristic absolutely distinguishes the two genera, and some species have been variously assigned to Castanopsis, Castanea and Quercus by different authorities. Indeed, the Chinese C. cuspidata has been considered by various botanists to be a Quercus, a Lithocarpus, and a Castanopsis, while C. fissa of China has been described as a Quercus and as a Castanea. As now interpreted, species of Castanea are all deciduous while Castanopsis are all evergreen. The distinction between Castanopsis and Quercus is less clear. Castanopsis have their male and female flowers usually in separate catkins and, unlike Castanea, their fruits do not ripen until their second year. The nuts of some species are edible, those of others poisonous. In some species they are completely enclosed by the burr, in others only partly so, in which cases they form a transition to acorns. There are about 120 species of Castanopsis.

The giant chinquapin (C. chrysophylla) of the northwestern United States grows to a maximum height of 100 feet with a trunk diameter of 6 feet, but at high elevations it is often shrublike. Pyramidal or rounded in outline and with attractive dark green lustrous foliage, it thrives on dry, poor soils. In summer it bears catkins of cream-colored flowers and later fruits that consist of a spiny burr that nearly encloses the usually solitary nut. The young shoots and leaves are covered with golden yellow scurfy scales. The lumber of this species is of some local importance; it is soft, close-grained and not strong.

Of thirty or more species that occur in China, C. hystrix serves much the same purposes in sub-

Hop-hornbeam. *Ostrya carpinifolia* (Andreas Feininger)

tropical areas as do oaks in temperate climates. It attains a height of about 50 feet and a trunk diameter of 2 feet. It is indigenous from China and Taiwan to the Himalayas. C. fargesii grows up to 100 feet high; its trunk may measure 4 feet through. With wide-spreading branches and attractive flowers, this handsome tree is common in western China.

The 60-foot-high C. sclerophylla of eastern and central China has solitary nuts only partially enclosed by the non-spiny cupule, which is much like an acorn. Its somewhat bitter nuts are made into an edible paste called tou-fu. Probably the largest of the Chinese species is C. diversifolia, which reportedly attains a height of 150 feet at altitudes of five thousand feet in its native Yunnan. Eight species of Castanopsis are indigenous to Taiwan; some are endemics. Of the species known only from that island, C. kamakamii is described as a large tree of the central mountains and C. carlesii as a straight-trunked tree abundant in all forests.

The Castanopsis of Malaya are locally called Malayan-chestnuts, and the nuts of C. wallichii are quite as good to eat as those of the Spanish

chestnut; each is enclosed in a burr covered with unbranched spines. Another edible nut-bearing kind of Malaya and also of Sumatra is C. *inermis,* which has curious wart-covered burrs and flowers and an odor of rancid fat that is attractive to pollenizing insects. The greater Malayan-chestnut (C. *megacarpa)* has solitary nuts, reputed to be poisonous, completely enclosed in a burr covered with branched spines.

Fagus—Beech

Here belong some of the most magnificent and useful trees of the North Temperate zone. About ten species are recognized, most of them Asiatic and all of them having a strong family resemblance. In parts of America, Europe and Asia they form extensive forests. *Fagus* differs from its near relation *Nothofagus* in having its male flowers in many-flowered heads and its female flowers usually in pairs and enclosed by bracts from which protrude the red stigmas of the flowers. The flowers appear with the leaves. The fruits are small, triangular, edible nuts enclosed or partially enclosed in woody husks by twos. Beeches are deciduous and have thin, smooth, gray bark and simple flat, parallel-veined leaves. Beeches produce dense shade and many surface roots; few plants will grow beneath them.

Two beeches are natives of North America. The American beech (F. *grandifolia)* occurs throughout the eastern half of Canada and the United States; the Mexican beech (F. *mexicana)* is confined to Mexico. The American beech, densely oblong-pyramidal in outline, sometimes grows to a height of 120 feet with a trunk diameter up to 4 feet. Attractive at all seasons, it is a splendid landscape tree where space for its adequate growth is assured. It is hardier than the European beech but is more difficult to transplant successfully. It often produces colonies of new trees from suckers which spring from the roots of old specimens.

The wood of the American beech is used principally for flooring, interior trim, furniture, crates and boxes, and brushes. The Mexican beech attains a height of 120 feet and may have a trunk over 3 feet in diameter. Its wood is of high quality, durable and very hard. The tree differs from the American beech in having longer fruits and leaves that are wedge-shaped at their bases.

Silver-beech. Nothofagus menziesii (New Zealand Forest Service: J. H. Johns)

The European beech (*F. sylvatica*) grows to a height of more than 100 feet and may have a trunk up to 8 feet in diameter. It differs from the American beech in having leaves with coarser teeth and with only five to nine veins and in not producing suckers from its roots. The European beech is a native from Great Britain and Norway to the Mediterranean and Iran. Its wood is greatly valued for a variety of purposes, particularly for furniture, butchers' blocks, carpenters' planes, and carved bowls; it is also excellent fuel, giving little smoke and much heat. The printing blocks used by Johann Gutenberg, the first inventor of movable type, may have been carved out of beech wood, a fact commemorated in the German word for letters, *Buchstaben*, which is derived from the German name of the beech, *Buche*. There are several very distinct horticultural varieties of this tree, one of the most handsome being the copper beech (*F. s. atropunicea*), all specimens of which are descendants of a few trees that were found growing naturally in Switzerland and date back at least to 1660. In Asia Minor, the Caucasus and Iran is found the oriental beech (*F. orientalis*), which grows to a height of 120 feet and differs from the European beech in having leafy, bractlike instead of awl-shaped appendages beneath the female flowers.

Two Japanese beeches are important, *F. japonica*, which is called Japanese beech, and *F. sieboldii*. The trunk of the former is typically divided near its base into several trunklike branches and the tree forms a broad, rounded head. It grows to a height of 75 feet and has leaves that lack hairs on their undersides. *Fagus sieboldii* grows up to a height of 100 feet and more closely resembles the American and European beeches than does *F. japonica*. It has the leafy bracts surrounding the female flowers characteristic of *F. orientalis* but differs from that species in that its leaves are broadest below the midsection instead of above it. The Chinese *F. lucida* resembles *F. sieboldii* but the bracts around the female flowers are very short and triangular. This tree, a native of western China, does not exceed 35 feet in height; the undersides of its leaves have a slight waxy blue coating. From central China comes *F. engleriana*, which grows to a height of 70 feet and also has leaves that are slightly waxy blue beneath. This same characteristic is typical of *F. longipetiolata*, a 75-foot-tall beech that inhabits central and western China. In this kind the leaves are pubes-

cent beneath, whereas those of *F. engleriana* and *F. lucida* are hairless.

Lithocarpus

Of about 300 species of *Lithocarpus*, all except one, which is indigenous to Oregon and California, are natives of eastern and southeastern Asia. They are evergreen trees botanically intermediate between oaks (*Quercus*) and chestnuts (*Castanea*); their flower clusters generally resemble those of chestnuts, the male flowers being in erect or semi-erect catkins. The female flowers and fruits, which mature in their second year, come in stout, stiff spikes. The fruits, like those of oaks, are acorns. By some authorities the group is divided into three genera, *Cyclobalanus*, *Pasania* and *Lithocarpus*.

The American species, *L. densiflora*, sometimes becomes 150 feet tall, but at the higher altitudes at which it grows it is usually shrubby. It has several common names, including California chestnut-oak and tanbark-oak. The usefulness of its lumber is somewhat limited because it tends to split and warp badly during seasoning, but the tree is an important source of tanbark. In China and Taiwan *L. amygdalifolia* reaches a height of 150 feet and sometimes has a trunk 5 feet in diameter. Many smaller species occur in China, including *L. spicata*, a variable kind that ranges from western China to India and Java. Other *Lithocarpus* from the mountains of western China are *L. cleistocarpa*, a 50-foot tree the acorns of which have nuts almost completely enclosed by their cups, and the nearly related *L. henryi*, which grows slightly taller and in which about two-thirds of each nut of its acorns protrudes from its cup.

Nothofagus—Southern-Beech

This genus of thirty-five evergreen and deciduous trees is closely related to beech (*Fagus*) but differs botanically in that both its male and female flowers are solitary or in threes. The group occurs naturally only in temperate regions of the Southern Hemisphere and there has the distinction of being one of the two most important genera of native timber trees (the other is *Eucalyptus*). In general aspect *Nothofagus* differs more markedly from *Fagus* than mere technical differences suggest; usually its leaves are much smaller, have shorter stalks than those of true beeches and are set much more closely together on the twigs.

South American species of *Nothofagus* number about a dozen. In the more humid parts of the mountains of Chile and Patagonia they form extensive and dense forest and are of much importance locally as sources of lumber and as protection for watersheds.

The Antarctic-beech or nire (N. antarctica) is a deciduous tree that is native to a narrow strip along the Chile-Argentine boundary from about latitude 37° to 55° south. When young it grows rapidly and is of elegant appearance. At maturity it may exceed 100 feet in height. Its minutely toothed leaves are 1¼ inches or less in length and nearly as broad; its four-lobed fruits each contain three nuts. The lenga (N. pumilio) has about the same natural range and deciduous habit as the nire and often grows taller. Growing at lower elevations than the Antarctic-beech and extending from Tierra del Fuego to about latitude 38° south is the evergreen guindo (N. betuloides), which has sticky young shoots and toothed leaves up to 1 inch long. It may grow to 100 feet high. Beginning at the northern limit of the range of this species and extending northward along the coast and in valleys is the coihue (N. dombeyi), a massive tree that reaches a height of 130 feet or more and a trunk diameter of up to 8 feet. Its leaves are dark green above, paler and sprinkled with tiny black dots on their undersides. The guindo is extensively exploited as a source of good lumber; the wood of the coihue is less valued because it lacks durability and has a tendency to warp. The roble (N. obliqua), which is deciduous and may reach a height of 100 feet, is distinguished from the Antarctic beech by quite smooth instead of decidedly downy young shoots and by four-lobed fruits which contain two rather than three nuts. It occurs from Valdivia to Valparaiso, often in dense pure forest stands, and occasionally it attains a height of 160 feet and a trunk diameter of 5 feet or more. Its wood is used for heavy construction.

A deciduous species with a cherry-colored wood that is highly esteemed for cabinetwork, furniture, flooring, interior trim, cooperage, and many other purposes is the rauli (N. procera). This tree, which yields the most important hardwood in Chile, grows to a height of about 100 feet. Its leaves are up to 4 inches long and have fourteen to eighteen pairs of veins; those of the closely related roble, which are up to 3 inches long, have eight to twelve pairs of veins.

In New Zealand Nothofagus, unlike most indigenous trees of that country, forms extensive one-species forests of great beauty. The identification of species is sometimes difficult because natural hybrids occur. Many New Zealanders call these trees birches and designate them by such colloquial names as white-birch, silver-birch, black-birch and so on, without much regard to the actual species. They are also, more appropriately, known as beeches.

The commonest New Zealand Nothofagus is N. solandri, which reaches heights up to 100 feet, may have a trunk diameter of 5 feet and has leaves up to three-fourths inch long, with margins not toothed. The bark of young trees is white but on older specimens it becomes black, hence the name black-beech that is sometimes applied to it. Another species, N. menziesii, is sometimes 100 feet high and is called silver-beech because of its silvery bark. Its bluntly toothed leaves grow to a length of one-half inch and differ from those of N. cunninghamii in having double-toothed edges and one or two tiny pits of hairs near the leaf stalk on their undersides. The red-beech (N. fusca) may attain a height of 100 feet and a trunk diameter of 12 feet. It has coarsely toothed leaves up to 1½ inches long. A much smaller tree, usually not exceeding 50 feet in height, is the subalpine N. cliffortioides which has smooth-edged, toothless leaves no more than one-quarter inch long. The evergreen N. cunninghamii is a native of Tasmania, where it sometimes reaches 200 feet in height and may have a trunk diameter of 12 feet or more. Its leaves, which are about one-half inch long, have blunt teeth above their midsection. The Australian-beech (N. moorei) is an evergreen with pointed, sharply-toothed leaves up to 3 inches long. It may grow to a maximum height of 150 feet and is a native of New South Wales.

Quercus—Oak

The oaks form an immensely important genus of about 450 species in North America, South America, Europe, North Africa and subtropical Asia. They are closely related to Lithocarpus and Castanopsis. Those from warmer regions are usually evergreen; the leaves of colder-climate species die at the approach of winter, but, as if some lingering memory of the undoubted tropical origin of the group persists, they often remain brown and sere, clinging to the twigs well into the winter; this is especially true of young trees. The leaves are borne mostly in crowded clusters toward the tips of the branches, a feature helpful in recognizing oaks.

The flowers of oaks are unisexual, with both sexes on the same tree. The males form slender, drooping catkins in tassel-like clusters, the females are in short spikes. The most characteristic features are the fruits (acorns), each of which consists of a single large egg-shaped or rounded seed seated in a cuplike container. Another characteristic, shared with very few other trees, is that the twigs when cut cleanly across show a distinctly five-rayed pith.

Oak lumber is remarkable for its strength, beauty and durability. It has conspicuous medullary rays which are responsible for the fine figuring of the wood when it is cut on radial section, as is manifest in good oak paneling. Among the many uses of oak lumber are cabinetwork, furniture, interior trim, heavy construction, fence posts, railroad ties, cooperage and fuel. The bark of one species provides commercial cork and that of others the finest grade of tanbark. Dyes and inks are obtained from galls which develop on certain species, and the fruits (acorns) provide food for swine and for some peoples.

American Oaks

The oaks of the New World are numerous. About fifty species inhabit Canada and the United States. There are many kinds in Mexico and some are found in Central America, northern South America and Cuba. Both evergreen and deciduous kinds are represented. American oaks belong in two groups: the white oaks, nearly all of which have acorns that mature in their first year and leaves that in most kinds lack a bristle at the end of each lobe, and the black oaks, with acorns that do not ripen until their second year and leaves that invariably have bristle-tipped lobes. American oaks include some extremely important trees, especially for lumber.

White Oaks

One of the most massive American species is the white oak (Q. alba), which may reach 150 feet in height and has spreading, horizontal branches that form the framework of a huge, rounded head. The typical white oak has a trunk which may be 4 feet or more in diameter. Its leaves are lobed almost to their midribs and are whitish

Above: European beech. Fagus sylvatica (Andreas Feininger) Right: Roble. Nothofagus obliqua (T. H. Everett)

on their undersides. The natural range of this oak is the entire eastern United States. Its strong, hard, heavy, durable wood is used for shipbuilding, interior trim, cabinetmaking, construction and many other purposes as well as for fuel. The swamp white oak *(Q. bicolor)* has leaves much less deeply lobed than the white oak and forms a narrower head with less massive limbs, the lower branches usually pointing downward. It favors moist and wet soils and rarely attains a height of 100 feet but may have a trunk up to about 3 feet in diameter. Its wood is used for the same purpose as that of the white oak. This tree is native from Quebec to Georgia and Arkansas.

The burr oak or mossy cup oak *(Q. macrocarpa)* is sometimes 170 feet tall with a trunk up to 7 feet in diameter which may be bare of branches for 70 feet or more. Like the white oak, it has a broad, rounded head, spreading branches, and leaves with a terminal lobe much bigger than the lateral ones. It grows chiefly in fertile lowlands from Nova Scotia to Manitoba, Pennsylvania and Texas. Its wood has the same uses as that of the white oak.

Live oak. Quercus virginiana (Andreas Feininger)

The overcup oak *(Q. lyrata)* is so called because the cups of its acorns almost or quite enclose the nuts. This tree attains a height of 100 feet, with a trunk that may reach 3 feet in diameter and usually divides into pendulous branches that fork to form a round head. It ranges from New Jersey to Florida and Texas, and its wood has the same uses as that of the white oak.

A quite variable species is the post oak *(Q. stellata)*, which is widely distributed in dryish uplands from Massachusetts to Nebraska, Florida and Texas. It is sometimes nearly 100 feet high with a trunk up to 3 feet in diameter. Its branches are stout and spreading. Its leaves are characteristically deeply five-lobed. The wood of the post oak is hard, heavy and close-grained, and is used for construction, railroad ties, cooperage, fencing and fuel.

The chestnut oak *(Q. montana)* and the yellow chestnut oak *(Q. muhlenbergii)* are closely related kinds that owe their common names to the resemblance of their leaves to those of chestnuts *(Castanea)*, a similarity close enough to mislead the casual observer. Very much like them is the basket oak *(Q. prinus)*. All are handsome deciduous trees that may exceed 100 feet in height, and all have hard, strong, durable wood, useful for construction, cooperage, fences, railroad ties and fuel; that of the basket oak is also used for basketmaking. The yellow chestnut oak, which forms a rather narrow head, occurs from Vermont to Nebraska, Virginia, New Mexico and Texas; the chestnut oak, which develops a more iregular outline, is native from Maine and Ontario to South Carolina and Alabama; the dense, round-headed basket oak occurs from Delaware to Indiana. All three species have leaves with long, slender stalks and margins that are regularly and coarsely toothed. Those of the chestnut oak and the basket oak are broader above than below the middle, whereas those of the yellow chestnut oak are broader below the middle. The upper sides of the leaves of the basket oak are dark green; those of the chestnut oak are yellow-green.

Western North America is the home of several deciduous white oaks. One of the most important as a timber tree is the Oregon oak *(Q. garryana)* which ranges from British Columbia to California and becomes 100 feet high with a trunk up to 3 feet in diameter. It has upright or spreading branches which support a broad, round head. Its young twigs are orange-colored,

its leaves lobed almost halfway from their margins to their midribs. Its strong, hard lumber is valued for cabinetwork, shipbuilding, cooperage and fuel. The valley oak of California (*Q. lobata*) is impressive. It has stout, wide-spreading main branches and long, slender, pendulous smaller branches which sometimes reach to the ground. It may attain a height of 100 feet and a trunk diameter of 4 feet.

The Rocky Mountain white oak (*Q. utahensis*), which rarely exceeds 40 feet in height, has dark green foliage and branchlets densely covered with short yellow hairs. Its leaves are lobed halfway or more to their midribs. This oak has a narrow head of thick, erect branches. It is a native of dry soils in the mountains of Colorado, Utah, Arizona and New Mexico. Favoring dry slopes and valleys, the mountain white oak or blue oak (*Q. douglasii*), occasionally is 80 feet high and may have a trunk up to 3 feet in diameter. Its round head of stout, horizontal branches is densely furnished with blue-green, shallowly or deeply lobed leaves that are pubescent on their undersides. The chief use of its wood is as fuel.

Evergreen oaks are commonly called live oaks in America. The native kinds are included in the white oak group, although not all ripen their acorns in one year and some have bristle-tipped leaves. The live oak of the southern United States is *Q. virginiana*, a handsome, massive tree up to 75 feet in height with a trunk diameter up to 4 feet or more and a branch spread that may exceed 150 feet. It has glossy dark green leaves that are whitish on their undersides and scarcely toothed. The trunk usually divides a few feet from the ground and branches almost horizontally. This oak, with a natural range extending from Virginia to Florida and Mexico, is often planted as a shade and avenue tree. Its lumber is of high quality.

The California or coast live oak (*Q. agrifolia*) inhabits a coastal belt from northern California to Baja California. Up to 100 feet tall, it develops a broad dome-shaped crown that may be 150 feet through. It has a short trunk up to 4 or more feet in diameter and stout crooked branches, the lower ones frequently resting on the ground. Specimens crowded by other trees

Above: White oak. Quercus alba (Rutherford Platt). Right: European holm oak. Quercus ilex (T. H. Everett)

119

have more slender branches and less spreading crowns. The leaves resemble those of English and American hollies, which led early explorers to refer to this tree as the "holly-leaved oak." Usually the leaf margins are spiny; occasionally they are smooth. The upper leaf surface is glossy green, the lower side paler. The old leaves fall in spring about the time the new crop of leaves is developing, and individual leaves do not last more than one year. The heavy, hard, brittle wood of the California live oak is used chiefly as fuel. Its bark has been employed to adulterate the much superior tanbark of the California tan-bark-oak (*Lithocarpus densiflora*).

The canyon live oak or maul oak *(Q. chryso-lepis)* attains about 40 feet in height. It has massive, nearly horizontal branches and a crown up to 150 feet in diameter. Its trunk is short and may be 5 feet or more in diameter. The thick ovate to elliptic evergreen leaves, especially on young trees, are often spiny-toothed at their margins; their undersides are at first covered with yellowish hairs. Individual leaves live for three to four years. The acorns, usually solitary, mature at the end of their second year, which is unusual among American white oaks. The most handsome of Western oaks, this species has a natural range from Oregon to California. Its close-grained, hard, strong and tough wood is used by wheelwrights and for farm implements.

Black Oaks

The subgenus *Erythrobalanus*, the black oak group, is entirely American. Its acorns ripen at the end of their second season and the leaves and leaf lobes are tipped with distinct bristles. Black oaks, which include many kinds valued for street, avenue and other landscape purposes, are easier to transplant than white oaks. Typical is the common black oak *(Q. velutina)*, a native from Maine to Minnesota, Florida and Texas that grows up to a height of 150 feet with a maximum trunk diameter of about 4 feet. Its slender branches form an open, narrow crown. Its lustrous leaves, which are more variable than those of any other American black oak, are usually seven-lobed; in fall they become red or orange-brown. Because the inner bark of the twigs is orange, this species is sometimes called the yellow-bark oak. Its hard, heavy, coarse-grained wood is used as fuel.

Similar, but more handsome, is the California black oak *(Q. kelloggii)*, a native of Oregon and California that grows to a height of 100 feet and

may have a trunk 4 feet in diameter. Quite distinct in appearance from all other West Coast oaks, this species has leaves that show much variation in size and shape and are lustrous deep yellow-green above and paler below. The acorns are on thick, short stalks and are 1 to 1½ inches long, about twice as long as those of the black oak of eastern North America. The wood is porous, brittle and fairly heavy. It has no importance other than as fuel.

An outstanding oak for use as a street tree and shade tree, but one that will not thrive on alkaline soils, is the pin oak *(Q. palustris)*. This handsome kind, native from Massachusetts to Delaware and Arkansas, is pyramidal when young, irregular in outline at maturity. It attains a maximum height in excess of 100 feet and a trunk diameter of 5 feet. The leaves have from five to seven deep lobes and are conspicuously bristle-pointed. The lower limbs of the pin oak point downward, the middle limbs outward and the upper limbs skyward; the branches are not massive. One of the quickest growing oaks is the red oak *(Q. borealis)*. With its variety *maxima*, a taller tree with larger acorns, it ranges from Nova Scotia to Florida and Texas, the variety occupying the southern part of this territory. The red oak grows up to 70 feet in height and may have a trunk 3 feet in diameter. It has a rounded head of stout branches and dull green leaves with seven to eleven bristle-tipped lobes; in fall the leaves become orange or brown. The wood, hard, strong and heavy, is used for furniture, interior trim and construction.

Native to a wide area of the southeastern United States, as far north as Pennsylvania and New Jersey and west to Texas, the Spanish red oak *(Q. falcata)* becomes 80 feet tall and has an open, round-topped head of stout, spreading branches. The dark green, usually drooping leaves are deeply divided into five or seven untoothed lobes; they are paler beneath than on their upper sides. In autumn they turn dull orange or brown.

Differing from the red oak in that its leaves are lustrous above, and from the pin oak in having much larger acorns, ¾ to 1½ inches long, *Q. shumardii*, a native from North Carolina to Michigan, Florida and Kansas, grows up to 120 feet in height with a trunk up to 5 feet in diameter. It has an open crown and stout, wide-spreading branches. The scarlet oak *(Q. coccinea)* is so called because of the brilliant scarlet coloring of its glossy foliage in fall. The leaves have seven or rarely nine narrow bristle-tipped lobes. The acorns are solitary or in pairs. The scarlet oak, which is native from Maine to Florida and Missouri, grows up to 80 feet tall and may have a trunk 3 feet in diameter. Its branches, which are not massive, form an open, round-topped crown. The coarse-grained wood is hard and strong.

Several black oaks have unlobed leaves that to the casual observer may appear very unlike those of an oak. One of the most distinct of these is the willow oak *(Q. phellos)*, aptly named because its leaves, which turn yellow in fall, look something like those of a willow. When young they are pubescent but they become glabrous as they mature. This native of the Eastern seaboard and Gulf states is a splendid landscape tree. Pyramidal or round-topped and with slender branches, it becomes 90 feet high.

With semi-evergreen glossy leaves that are sometimes slightly lobed, quite hairless and dark green above and paler beneath, the laurel oak *(Q. laurifolia)* rarely attains 90 feet in height and forms a dense, round-topped tree. It is native from Virginia to Florida and Louisiana.

The leaves of the shingle oak *(Q. imbricaria)*, are glossy dark green above and are pubescent on their undersides even at maturity. They are of firm texture and are elliptic to oblong lanceolate, resembling in general appearance rather large leaves of mountain laurel. This tree attains a maximum height of 90 feet. It ranges throughout the eastern and central United States from New York to Missouri southward. The water oak *(Q. nigra)* forms a pyramidal round-topped crown of rather slender branches and has tardily deciduous small leaves that are often three-lobed at their ends. It grows to 80 feet in height and in the southern United States is freely planted as an avenue and street tree.

European Oaks

The oaks of Europe all belong to the white oak group. They include many noble species, several of classical significance. One of the best known in the English oak *(Q. robur)*, a species which despite its common name ranges through Europe, North Africa and western Asia. It was from the wood of this tree, before the days of steel ships, that the famous "wooden walls" of England were built. The English oak develops a spreading head of rugged branches up to 100 feet in height. The stalkless or nearly stalkless leaves have two earlike lobes at their bases. The durmast oak

Ancient English oaks. Quercus robur (National Audubon: V. R. Johnston)

(Q. petraea) of Europe and western Asia is very similar to the English oak, obvious differences being its longer leaf stalks and nearly stalkless acorns. Since ancient times the oaks of the Mediterranean region have been important. More than half a hundred references to them are made in the Bible. The valonia oak *(Q. aegilops)* was undoubtedly one of the best known to the ancients and was held sacred by them. Growing up to 80 feet tall, this tree has edible acorns which are ground into flour and made into bread; they are also used for tanning. Its leaves have bristle-tipped lobes.

The pubescent oak *(Q. pubescens)* has about the same geographical distribution as the English oak but is a smaller tree, rarely exceeding 50 feet in height and has leaves that are distinctly hairy on their undersurfaces. Very handsome is the round-topped and open-headed Hungarian oak *(Q. frainetto)*, which is endemic to a limited area in the Balkans and Hungary and is sometimes 120 feet tall. Its deeply lobed leaves are dark green above, grayish green and pubescent beneath, and have earlike lobes at their bases.

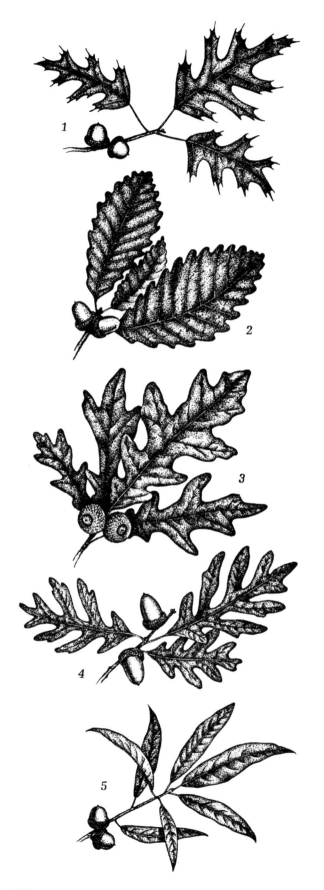

One of the latest deciduous trees to shed its leaves is the Turkey oak (*Q. cerris*) of southwest Europe and Asia Minor. It has handsome sharply cut leaves, and acorns covered with a mosslike growth of scales. The Turkey oak becomes 100 feet high, has rather slender branches and forms a broad, pyramidal crown. The cork oak (*Q. suber*), from which cork and corkbark are obtained, is unique. It is similar to the holm oak (*Q. ilex*) but has somewhat lobed leaves and a more open crown. A native of southern Europe and North Africa, this 60-foot evergreen has extraordinarily thick bark which has been used by man since ancient times and is still an important commercial product, especially in Spain, Portugal and Algeria. Cork is the outer bark and is stripped, without injury to the tree, every nine years. Cork oak trees may live for 500 years.

The most characteristic evergreen oak of Europe, and the hardiest, is the holm oak (*Q. ilex*). Confined naturally to lands bordering the Mediterranean, this species is commonly planted as far north as England and Ireland. It has a dense, rounded crown of dark green foliage. The young leaves are grayish yellow. A peculiarity is that on young specimens the leaves are toothed and holly-like but on mature specimens are smooth-edged; often both forms appear on trees of intermediate age. The leaves are pubescent on their undersurfaces. The holm oak attains a height of 60 feet and is closely related to the live oak of the southeastern United States. A variety, *Q. i. rotundifolia*, has sweet, edible acorns that in western Europe are a much appreciated article of diet.

Asiatic Oaks

The oaks in the subgenus *Cyclobalanopsis*, all Asiatic, are distinguished by the fact that the scales of their acorn cups are not separate but are joined in concentric rings. Here belongs *Q. myrsinaefolia* of Japan and China, which grows up to 60 feet in height and has evergreen lanceolate toothed leaves that are glossy green above and glabrous and glaucous beneath. The acorn cup has about six concentric rings, is hairless and is one-third as long as the nut. Another evergreen, widely distributed in eastern Asia including Japan and highly valued for its lumber

1. Quercus phellos 2. Quercus alba 3. Quercus lyrata 4. Quercus prinus 5. Quercus palustris (Charles Fracé)

is *Q. glauca.* This handsome, broad-crowned tree grows up to a height of 70 feet. Its elliptic to ovate oblong leaves, toothed above their middles, are shining green above and glaucous beneath; when young their undersides are silky hairy. The acorns, which mature in one year, are edible, their cups have four to eight concentric rings and are covered with silky hairs. The evergreen *Q. acuta* becomes 40 feet tall in its native Japan and has a rounded crown. It is a beautiful tree with pointed, ovate-oblong or lanceolate-oblong leaves that usually have wavy margins. They are glossy green above and yellowish green on their undersides. When they first expand they are covered with a brownish pubescence. The pubescent acorn cups, consisting of about six concentric rings, are about a quarter as long as the nut. Another member of the *Cyclobalanopsis* group is *Q. lamellosa* of northern India, a magnificent evergreen that grows up to 120 feet in height and may have a trunk 5 feet in diameter. It has pointed-ovate, sharply toothed leaves that are glossy green above and glaucous on their undersides and acorns with about ten concentric rings.

Prominent among Asiatic oaks that are allied to the white oaks of Europe and America is the Oriental white oak *(Q. aliena).* A native of Japan, Korea and China, this deciduous tree occasionally exceeds 60 feet in height and may have a trunk that measures 2 feet in diameter. It has blunt-toothed, dark yellowish green leaves covered with short hairs on their paler undersides. Several more or less distinct varieties of this variable species have been described and named by botanists. The Daimyo oak *(Q. dentata),* a native of Japan, Korea and China that is sometimes 80 feet high, is round-headed and has large, handsome leaves and very hairy twigs. The leaves are downy beneath and pubescent on their upper surfaces when they are young; in Japan, Korea and China, this deciduous tree are covered with conspicuous, spreading scales. The Daimyo oak is commonly planted near temples and burying grounds. Its bark is used for tanning and silkworms are fed on its foliage. A species, *Q. glandulifera,* from the same geographical region may reach 50 feet in height. It has lustrous bright green leaves that remain

1. *Quercus nigra* 2. *Quercus petraea* 3. *Quercus cerris* 4. *Quercus robur* 5. *Quercus falcata* (Charles Fracé)

123

English elm. Ulmus procera (John Markham)

until very late in fall; each leaf has seven to twelve pairs of gland-tipped teeth. The acorns mature in their second year. The Mongolian oak (*Q. mongolica*), which attains 90 feet in height and 3 feet in trunk diameter, is a common native of eastern Siberia, China, Korea and Japan and is distinguished by its extremely short leaf stalks and usually blunt-toothed, almost hairless leaves. The acorns mature in their first year. The lumber of this tree is of high quality. Dull green chestnut-like foliage characterizes *Q. variabilis*, an attractive native of China, Korea and Japan that is sometimes 80 feet in height with a trunk 3 feet through. Unlike most white oaks, its leaves have conspicuous bristle-like teeth; they are dark green above and densely white tomentose beneath. The acorns mature in their second year. This species has a fairly open crown and deeply furrowed corky bark that is used in China to make floats for fishnets and as a substitute for cork. In some parts of China an edible fungus is cultivated on felled saplings of this oak and its wood is employed for general construction. Easily distinguished from *Q. variabilis* by its leaves, which are hairless on their undersides except for axillary tufts, *Q. acutissima* has chestnut-like bristle-toothed leaves. Its acorns ripen in their second year. Silkworms are fed on

its foliage in China and its wood is used for general construction and shipbuilding. This oak ranges as a native from India to China and Japan.

Rarely exceeding 30 feet in height, the evergreen *Q. phillyraeoides* of Japan and China is closely related to the European holm oak (*Q. ilex*). Its broad-elliptic, shining green leaves are toothed except near their bases. Its acorns take two years to mature. In northern India the evergreen *Q. leucotricophora* is a native and becomes 80 feet tall. A very distinct species, it has narrowly oval or lanceolate leaves with toothed or wavy margins that are dark green above and have their undersides clothed with a felt of pure white hairs.

CHAPTER 14

The Urticales

The order Urticales represents the highest development of an evolutionary line from which the Fagales are also derived. It includes three families in which trees are represented.

ULMACEAE—ELM FAMILY

Here belong about two hundred species of trees and shrubs of tropical and temperate regions. Their typically unlobed leaves are arranged in two ranks.

Celtis

This is a genus of about eighty deciduous and evergreen trees and shrubs, mostly natives of the Northern Hemisphere. Their small, greenish flowers are unisexual, both sexes occurring on the same tree. Their leaves resemble those of elms (*Ulmus*). *Celtis* differs from elms in having three main veins rather than one arising from the base of each leaf and in having one-seeded fleshy

Right: Birch trees in New England (Gottlieb Hampfler) Overleaf left: Silver birch. Betula pendula (E. R. Degginger) Right: European birch. Betula pubescens (Gerhard Klammet)

fruits. Unless otherwise described, the species discussed are deciduous.

Native American *Celtis* includes the hackberry *(C. occidentalis)*, which ranges from Quebec to Manitoba, North Carolina, Alabama and Kansas and sometimes attains a height of 120 feet with a trunk diameter of 3 feet, and the closely related sugarberry *(C. laevigata)*, native from Indiana and Illinois southward, which has a maximum height of 90 feet and a trunk that may reach 3 feet in diameter. Both have dense round heads and produce lumber that is marketed as soft elm. The hackberry frequently has on its branches unsightly dense clusters of small twigs. These "witches brooms," the result of irritation by microscopic mites, by a fungus or by both, rarely occur on the sugarberry. Both hackberry and sugarberry are popular street trees in the southern United States. In the West Indies the slender-trunked *C. trinervia*, up to 50 feet tall, provides tough lumber for construction, tool handles and other purposes. The tala *(C. tala)*, of Argentina, is a comparable species with similar uses.

From southern Europe, western Asia and North Africa comes the nettle tree *(C. australis)*, a round-topped kind, sometimes 80 feet tall but often shrubby, with smooth gray bark like that of a beech. It is believed to live for as long as a thousand years. Several *Celtis* are natives of tropical Africa, among them the giant *C. adolphi-friderici*, which in Nigeria attains a height of 150 feet and a trunk almost 3 feet through. The trunk is widely buttressed at its base. The lumber of this tree, although not very durable, is in large demand locally for pestles and other purposes.

Best known of the South African species is the white stinkwood *(C. africana)*, which is widely distributed from the Cape of Good Hope to Ethiopia. In the forest it grows as tall as 80 feet and has a straight, clean trunk; in open areas it is shorter, its head more spreading. The name stinkwood refers to the unpleasant odor of its newly cut lumber which, after seasoning, is used for planks, furniture and other purposes. It is called white stinkwood because of the conspicuous grayish white color of its trunk and

Left: Beech forest (National Audubon: P. Berger) Right above: Scotch elm. Ulmus glabra (F. B. Grunzweig) Right: Scotch elm flower (Ingmar Holmåsen)

branches. This species is an excellent ornamental and is much used as a street tree. It has edible fruits and in India its foliage is used as fodder.

Among Asiatic *Celtis* worthy of note is *C. bungeana* of China and Korea, which has glossy dark green foliage and becomes 45 feet or more high. Apparently free of the "witches broom" condition that mars *C. occidentalis*, this species is perhaps the most satisfactory for planting in the northeastern United States. From Japan and Korea also comes the 70-foot *C. jessoensis*, which is less dense in habit than *C. bungeana*. It has been suggested as a possible good substitute for elms destroyed by the Dutch elm disease. Other Asiatic kinds are *C. julianae* of central China which is large-leaved, up to 80 feet high and is distinguished by yellowish green pubescence on the undersides of its leaves, and *C. koraiensis*, of Korea and northern China, remarkable for its nearly orbicular leaves and fruits more than one-third inch in diameter.

Several evergreen species occur in the warmer parts of Asia and the Pacific Islands. One such is *C. philippensis*, which ranges from Taiwan to Australia. Another is the stink celtis of Ceylon which becomes 100 feet tall and has foliage closely resembling that of the cinnamon tree; hence its name *C. cinnamomea*. Its common name derives from the unpleasant odor of its heartwood, which is used for construction.

Ulmus—Elm

Elms number about forty-five species, mostly deciduous trees of noble stature and appearance. None has showy flowers; their ornamental values rest in their growth habits and foliage characteristics, features that have caused several kinds to be highly regarded for landscape planting. This suitability is now seriously challenged by the prevalence of two death-dealing fungus diseases for which neither cures nor reliable, practical controls are known—Dutch elm disease and phloem necrosis disease. These have caused the deaths of vast numbers of majestic trees. Although not prevalent everywhere where elms are grown, these diseases occur over large areas and are constantly extending and increasing their ranges. As producers of lumber, elms rate highly; their wood is hard, tough, heavy and unusually resistant to splitting. It is used for cooperage, agricultural implements, crates and furniture.

Comprising the genus *Ulmus*, elms form a Northern Hemisphere group which reaches its southern limits in Mexico and the Himalayas.

In North America it does not occur natively west of the Rocky Mountains. Characteristically, the leaves of elms are asymmetrical, coarsely toothed and arranged alternately in two ranks. Most species bear small, brown or greenish brown, bisexual flowers, without petals, in early spring; a few kinds bloom in fall. Three of six species native to Canada and the United States are of commercial importance for lumber. They are the American or white elm (*U. americana*), the slippery or red elm (*U. fulva*), and the cork, rock or hickory elm (*U. thomasii*). The winged or wahoo elm (*U. alata*) has local importance as a lumber tree and is an interesting ornamental. European and Asiatic elms are greatly valued for their lumber.

The American elm is undoubtedly one of the most magnificent ornamental trees. No other elm of the temperate regions has such a majestic branching habit; none can completely replace it as a shade tree for planting in avenues and as specimens in parks and large estates. Early settlers and their descendants planted elms in front of homesteads and along roadsides, a pleasant custom responsible for the distinctive character of many New England towns and villages. The American elm, which reaches a height of 120 feet, is typically vase-shaped, with a few widely arching trunklike branches. But there are other forms; indeed, no other American tree is so variable in its appearance. Sometimes it has a round top of massive erect trunks each furnished with spreading branches and drooping branchlets; other specimens have many stout wide-spreading branches that branch and rebranch; and there also are many intermediate shapes. This species is a native of the eastern half of the United States and Canada. The slippery elm (*U. fulva*), so called because of its mucilaginous inner bark, produces lumber that is licorice-scented. It grows to a height of 60 feet and forms a broad, open head. Its flowers differ from those of the American elm in being upright rather than pendulous. This species is native from Quebec to the Dakotas, Florida and Texas. The wahoo elm (*U. alata*), which grows to a height of about 50 feet and ranges from Virginia to Illinois, Florida and Texas, is usually characterized by branchlets having two broad corky wings. This kind is sometimes planted as a street tree in the southern United States. The cork, rock or hickory elm (*U. thomasii*) also usually has winged branchlets but its leaves are not fringed with fine hairs (unlike those of the wahoo elm) and its buds are pubescent. This species ranges naturally from Quebec to the Dakotas, Florida and Texas.

The English elm (*U. procera*) is a noble tree that sometimes is 150 feet tall with a trunk 6 feet or more in diameter. It is peculiar in that it very rarely bears fertile seed and normally propagates by suckers from the roots. It forms an oval or oblong head and has rugged, deeply fissured bark. The base of the bole is often surrounded by a brushwood-like growth of twiggy branches. This tree, native to Great Britain and western Europe, has the unfortunate habit of shedding large branches unexpectedly and so is undesirable as a street tree. Growing up to 125 feet high and having a trunk sometimes 6 feet in diameter, the Scotch elm or wych elm (*U. glabra*) forms a rather open, broadheaded specimen. One of the noblest trees of northern Europe, it has rough, markedly asymmetric leaves that are often lobed toward their tips. Its branchlets are never corky and it does not produce sucker growths around its bole. Because of this, it is favored as an understock upon which to graft horticultural varieties of elms.

Among Asian elms the Japanese elm (*U. japonica*) ranks high. A broad-headed tree up to 110 feet tall, it resembles the Scotch elm, differing in that its leaves are larger and its twigs often possess corky wings. The Ainus, aborigines of northern Japan, regard this as the most important of trees and the first to be created. They cover their huts with its outer bark and use its mascerated inner bark for the manufacture of cloth and its dried roots as tinder. The Japanese elm is a native of continental Asia and Japan. Two small-leaved Asiatic elms are especially noteworthy, the Chinese elm (*U. parviflora*) and the Siberian elm (*U. pumila*). Both attain maximum heights of 80 feet and have leaves that are simply toothed, that is to say, the major marginal teeth are not again conspicuously toothed. The bases of the leaves of the Chinese elm are markedly asymmetrical but those of the Siberian elm are nearly equal-sided; the Chinese elm bears its flowers in fall, the Siberian kind in spring. The bark of old specimens of Chinese elm is rugged and handsome, that of the Siberian elm thin and scaling. Despite these differences, the two are often confused in gardens. The Chinese elm is the better ornamental and the more massive tree. At its best its trunk may calliper 3½ feet, whereas that of the Siberian elm rarely is 2 feet in diameter. In southern China and southern Japan the Chinese elm is evergreen and a variety called *U. p. sempervirens* with this characteristic is cultivated in southern California.

Closely resembling the American white elm (*U. americana*), but native from central Europe to central Asia, is the European white elm (*U. laevis*). It grows 100 feet or more high with wide-spreading branches that form an open head. Other European elms are the smooth-leaved elm (*U. carpinifolia*) and the Dutch elm (*U. hollandica*). The last-named, a hybrid between the Scotch elm and the smooth-leaved elm, was discovered in Belgium in 1694. It is commonly planted in Holland and Belgium and forms a handsome specimen. The smooth-leaved elm, a native of Europe and western Asia, attains a height of 100 feet, is quite variable in form but typically is pyramidal. Its branchlets are often distinctly corky. Its very asymmetrical leaves are glossy green and hairless above; their undersurfaces are pubescent along the midrib and in the vein axils.

Zelkova

Half a dozen deciduous trees of eastern Asia, the Caucasus, and the eastern Mediterranean region comprise this genus. They resemble small-leaved elms but have smooth, scaling bark and, unlike elms, their flowers are unisexual; both sexes are borne on the same twig, the males at the base and the females in the leaf axils above.

The keati (*Z. serrata*), native to Japan, Korea and Taiwan, produces high-quality, beautifully grained lumber that is greatly esteemed for furniture and, because of its durability, is much used for gateways, pillars and posts. It attains a height of 100 feet and characteristically branches low to form several arching limbs and a broad, round-topped head. Its leaves are sharply toothed; each has eight to fourteen pairs of veins. In China an edible mushroom grows on the wood of this tree. Attaining a maximum height of about 80 feet, the Caucasian *Z. carpinifolia* differs from the keati in having round-toothed leaves with six to eight pairs of veins. It forms an ovoid head that is narrower than that of the preceding species.

MORACEAE—MULBERRY FAMILY

Most of the fourteen hundred members of this family are trees and shrubs, all of which contain milky latex; the few without latex, such as the

131

Breadfruit. Artocarpus communis (Camera Hawaii: Werner Stoy)

Jakfruit. Artocarpus integra (M. Krishńan)

hop plant (Humulus), used in making beer, and the hemp (Cannabis), the source of marijuana, are herbaceous plants. Members of the family have simple leaves and unisexual flowers; some produce edible fruits and useful fibers.

Antiaris—Upas Tree

Of the four evergreen trees of tropical Asia, Africa and Madagascar that comprise the genus Antiaris, the upas tree (A. toxicaria) is most notable. In the eighteenth century extravagant stories of its deadly effects were published and are sometimes resurrected by writers of "plant wonder" stories for Sunday newspaper supplements. According to these legends, animals and men who approached an upas tree died of a noxious emanation from it, and no other plant life could exist for a considerable area around each tree. There is no truth in such stories, but the upas tree does contain a poisonous milky juice and this may have given rise to these travelers tales. The upas tree is a native of Malaya, Burma, India, Ceylon, Java and southern China, it becomes 150 feet or more high. For a long time, often until it reaches 100 feet in height, its branches are comparatively short and subsidiary to the central trunk; only when it has attained considerable height do a few of the larger limbs form a spreading head. Despite the fact that the juice is used in arrow poisons, the red-brown pear-shaped fruits, about three-quart-

ers of an inch in diameter, are said to be eaten by children. The female flowers of the upas tree are solitary, the males are in dense heads that resemble small green mushrooms. The fibrous inner bark, like that of its African counterpart, A. africana, is used to make bags, blankets and clothing; the wood of the African species is made into plywood, and decoctions of its bark are used medicinally.

Artocarpus—Breadfruit and Jakfruit

The breadfruit (A. communis) and the jakfruit (A. integra) are the best known and most important members of this group of forty-seven species of southeastern Asia and the Pacific Islands. It was in search of the breadfruit that Captain Bligh made his famous but disastrous voyage in the Bounty. Bligh was commissioned by the British Government to collect young breadfruit trees and introduce them to the West Indies as a possible source of food for slaves. On a later voyage Bligh succeeded, and breadfruit trees resulting from his efforts now flourish in the Americas. Like other members of the genus, both the breadfruit and jakfruit have tiny flowers crowded into heads that look like stalked burrs. Most kinds are evergreen but some, including the breadfruit, are deciduous in regions where dry seasons occur. The breadfruit is a handsome spreading tree about 60 feet tall. Its oval dark green, deeply lobed leaves are up to

2 feet long and are thick and leathery. The flower heads develop from leafy twigs, the females standing erectly, the males suspended on short stalks. The nearly globular fruits weigh up to four pounds and may be a foot in diameter. Covered with rough rind, they contain a stringy flesh rich in starch and sugar; some varieties contain seeds, others are seedless. The breadfruit, an important food in the tropics, is eaten raw, boiled, baked and roasted, and it is dried and made into flour.

The jakfruit tree, a native of India and Malaya which grows to a height of 70 feet, is at first pyramidal but with age becomes round-topped. Its elliptic or obovate unlobed leaves are up to 9 inches long. Unlike the breadfruit, the jakfruit does not produce its flowers and fruits on young leafy branches but on short twigs directly from the trunk and older branches. The barrel- or pear-shaped fruits, 1 to 3 feet long, and 10 to 20 inches in diameter, are golden yellow when ripe. They are the largest fruits known: specimens weighing ninety pounds have been recorded and others of forty or fifty pounds are not uncommon. Technically, each is a compound fruit. The jakfruit is used as food in the same manner as breadfruit, but is less highly regarded; its seeds are used in curries. Closely related to the jakfruit and often mistaken for it is the chempedak *(A. integer)* of Malaya, but its fruits are smaller and have a richer odor and its twigs are covered with long, brown, wiry hairs.

Broussonetia—Paper Mulberry

Here belong seven or eight eastern Asiatic and Polynesian deciduous trees and shrubs that contain milky juice and are chiefly noteworthy because their bark is used for making paper and tapa cloth. The inconspicuous male and female flowers are borne on separate plants, the males in cylindrical catkins, the females in globular heads. Best known is *B. papyrifera* of China, Japan, Taiwan and the Pacific Islands, which has a broad, rounded crown and grows up to 50 feet in height. The upper surfaces of its large leaves, ovate to lanceolate in shape and usually lobed, are distinctly sandpapery to the touch.

Cecropia

About a hundred species of tropical American

Above: Cecropia leaves. (National Audubon: V. R. Johnston) Right: Banyan tree. Ficus benghalensis (Andreas Feininger)

and West Indian trees comprise this genus. All grow rapidly, and have light soft wood, milky sap and large umbrella-like leaves that are conspicuously white-felted on their lower surfaces. The leaves are clustered near the ends of a few branches which form a candelabrum-like crown. The male and female flowers are very small and are borne on separate trees; they are without decorative appeal. The stems of cecropias are hollow and are usually inhabited by fierce ants which rush out and attack intruders if the branches are disturbed. The relationship between tree and insects is symbiotic, the ants protecting the tree from other leaf-cutting insects and the tree providing shelter and nourishment for the ants in the form of food bodies that develop near the base of the leaf stalks.

Natives use the bark of cecropias for making cordage and the latex for medicines. The best-known species is the trumpet tree (*C. peltata*), a native of the West Indies; its stems are used to make musical intruments, and the foliage provides forage for animals.

Ficus—Fig

The figs, which comprise the genus *Ficus*, number about eight hundred species, all natives of

Banyan-like fig, Australia. Ficus (Robin Smith)

Benjamin tree. Ficus benjamina (Max Hemple)

warm countries and most abundant in Indo-malaysia and Polynesia. Most are evergreen, but some, including the common orchard fig (*F. carica*), are deciduous. The flowers are morphologically remarkably similar throughout the genus, as are the fruits. The tiny flowers, lacking petals, are borne on the insides of hollow, globular or pear-shaped fleshy receptacles which, although not fruits in the botanical sense, are commonly called so and will here be referred to as such. The true fruits of figs are the seeds inside the swollen receptacles. Fig flowers are of three kinds, staminate (male), pistillate (female) and gall (sterile female). Some kinds of fig are monoecious or self-fertile; others are dioecious or self-sterile. In the former each receptacle or fruit contains all three types of flowers; in the latter male and gall flowers only are borne in the fruits of some trees and female flowers only in the fruits of others.

Fig flowers are pollinated in an extraordinary manner by gall wasps, and there is, apparently, a particular species of gall wasp for each species of *Ficus*. The gravid female gall wasp enters the fruit and lays eggs in the ovaries of the flowers. The grubs that hatch from the eggs feed upon the gall flowers and in time change into adult

Figs (Wlodzimierz Puchalski)

gall wasps, the females of which mate with males of the same brood. The males die shortly after mating but the females leave the fruits, becoming dusted with pollen as they emerge, and fly to other figs to deposit their eggs, at which time pollen is transferred to receptive female flowers inside the fruits they enter. Many kinds of *Ficus* bear their flowers and fruits on young shoots but some carry them on old branches and some gall wasps the females of which mate with males on stems or runners, up to 30 feet long, that grow from the lower part of the trunk and bury themselves a few inches underground.

In habit, figs vary widely from tiny-leaved creepers to trees of massive proportions. Some are epiphytes, that is to say they grow on other trees without taking sustenance from them; others are scrambling climbers. Of special interest are the strangling figs, which begin life from a seed dropped by a fruit-eating monkey, squirrel, bat or bird into a crotch or crevice of the branches of a tree. A bush that at first is epiphytic grows from the seed. Soon one or more perpendicular roots reach downward to the ground and side roots may grow from these and encircle the trunk. The trunk and branches of the host tree are soon enmeshed in a stout basketwork of roots of the strangler, and the host's crown is invaded by rapidly spreading branches and roots. As the roots and stems of the fig thicken they exert pressure on the bark of the supporting tree and crush it, interfering with the flow of sap and seriously weakening or killing it. The trunk of a tree killed in this way finally rots and leaves the fig supported by its own network of roots. Normally strangling figs do not develop a substantial trunk from the top of their basketwork of roots but only a wide-spreading crown of branches, the lower ones of which droop. Some strangling figs develop aerial roots from their branches. These are slender until they reach the ground but then they may thicken into trunklike supporting columns. This is the habit of the famous banyan tree (*F. benghalensis*); other figs that do this are also sometimes called banyans.

The fig of antiquity, to which Biblical reference is made, is *Ficus carica*, believed to be a native of Asia Minor. Attaining a maximum height of about 30 feet, this leaf-losing species has three- or five-lobed leaves and bears its fruits, an important food in many subtropical regions, on young shoots. Several cultivated types of this *Ficus* are grown. Common figs have no male flowers; their fruits, which are seedless, develop

Peepul. Ficus religiosa (M. Krishnan)

without pollination. Smyrna figs produce no male flowers but their fruits will not develop unless their flowers are pollinated (by the appropriate gall wasp) with pollen from caprifigs, a process called caprification. The caprifig is a primitive type of *Ficus carica*; its fruits have no commercial value but it is cultivated in fig-growing countries to ensure a supply of pollen for the caprification of Smyrna figs. San Pedro figs bear two crops of fruit each year; the first develops without pollination but the second only if the flowers are caprified.

Another fig of antiquity is the sycamore (*F. sycamoris*) of the Bible. This massive, widespreading tree, which occurs from North Africa to the Transvaal, is evergreen or deciduous depending upon climate. It has a yellowish trunk and forms a rounded head up to 80 feet in height. Its heart-shaped leaves grow up to 3 inches long. The globular fruits, about 1 inch in diameter, are borne in great clusters and are a favorite food of birds.

Many other figs are indigenous to Africa. One of the best known is the Cape fig (*F. capensis*), a species that reaches 80 feet in height and forms a stout trunk or sometimes several trunks, with bark at first white but darkening with age. Like the sycamore fig, it is sometimes deciduous, sometimes evergreen. The pointed-oval leaves, up to 6 inches long, have wavy margins; they are eaten by cattle. The edible round fruits, 1 to 1½ inches in diameter, are borne in large clusters from older parts of the branches and trunks.

Another interesting species is the wonderboom (*F. pretoriae*). One group in the vicinity of Pretoria represents the progeny of a single tree the branches of which bent to the ground, rooted and produced new trees; these repeated the process until the group now stands about 75 feet in height and has a spread of 165 feet. It can shelter about 1100 people. The wonderboom grows from the Transvaal and Natal into tropical Africa; it is usually evergreen and forms a spreading head. The bark cloth tree (*F. natalensis*), native to the Sudan and southward through most of tropical Africa to Natal, is a strangler fig. It may be 40 feet in height and has evergreen, obovate leaves up to 3½ inches long. Its small greenish white, yellow, or pink fruits are borne singly or in small groups in the

Jungle of fig trees (Paul Popper Limited)

leaf axils. The fibrous bark is macerated and beaten to form a kind of cloth which the natives stencil in various patterns and make into clothing and other equipment; they also make coarse cordage from the bark.

An interesting use is made of *F. exasperata*. The leaves contain appreciable amounts of silica and are employed by native carpenters like sandpaper to polish wood and calabashes. The tree, which grows up to 70 feet tall, has roundish or sometimes lobed leaves up to 5 inches long. The leaves are poisonous to livestock and are used by natives to make poisoned arrows; they are also employed medicinally for coughs, colic and eye disorders. The globose white fruits, mostly in pairs and borne near the ends of the twigs, are warty skinned and about one-half inch in diameter. *F. exasperata* is commonly found throughout tropical Africa and also occurs in Arabia.

The red kano rubber tree (*F. platyphylla*), a native from the Sudan and Abyssinia to Uganda and Somaliland, becomes 60 feet tall and spreads widely. Its major roots are often visible on the ground surface for a considerable distance from the trunk. Its leaves, although comparatively few, are large, up to 1 foot long by two-thirds as wide, broadly elliptic, and have heart-shaped bases and pinkish veins. The warty-skinned fruits, each 1 inch or less in diameter, are in clusters near the ends of the twigs. They are edible but not of very good quality. The white latex of this tree is boiled to form a rubber-like material, similar but inferior to gutta-percha, which has been used in the manufacture of chewing gum. Natives make cordage and cloth from the bark and use the wood as fuel.

There are other species of *Ficus* in Africa and many are important to the natives for a variety of purposes, such as shade trees in villages or in making bark cloth and cordage. The wood ashes of some are used in soapmaking; the latex of others is employed as glue and birdlime, and the bark of still others is used in tanning hides. The fruits of many kinds are eaten and medicines are prepared from fruits, leaves, bark and other parts.

Most famous, perhaps, of Asiatic figs is the banyan tree (*F. benghalensis*) of India. A handsome evergreen that begins life as an epiphyte but attains a height of 100 feet, its spreading horizontal branches send down roots which develop into secondary supporting trunks. Expanding in this way, a single banyan may occupy a large area. One specimen measured two thousand feet in circumference and could shelter twenty thousand people. This species is sacred to Hindus who believe that Brahma was transformed into a banyan tree. It has dark green, sparely veined, ovate leaves up to 8 inches long by 5 inches wide and pairs of edible rosered globose fruits about 1/2 inch in diameter. Seeds of the banyan, dropped by birds, germinate on walls and roofs of temples and other buildings which are often seriously damaged by the searching, penetrating roots. Of particular religious significance to both Hindus and Buddhists is the peepul or bo tree (*F. religiosa*). The Hindu divinity Vishnu is believed to have been born under a bo tree and it was under a bo tree that Gautama Buddha meditated for six years and received enlightenment. Hindus who desire children walk 108 times around a bo tree on Saturday mornings while repeating certain mantras or prayers. Bo trees are planted in front of houses to assure prosperity and happiness to the owners, and before temples. Like those of the banyan, the roots of the bo tree damage buildings by penetrating and eventually shattering masonry. Because of their sacred character, bo or peepul trees are allowed to do this without disturbance, for in India it is said that "it is better to die a leper than pluck a leaf of a peepul." The bo tree begins life as an epiphyte and attains a maximum height of 100 feet. Like the banyan, it branches indefinitely and supports its extended branches with thick prop roots that serve as additional trunks. The ovate leaves are handsome and distinctive, with their tips drawn out into long, slender tails and with stalks flattened so that even in the slightest breeze the foliage is always aflutter. When young, the leaves may be of various shades of pink and green, whereas at maturity they are a rich shining green above, paler beneath. The tree is usually deciduous but loses its leaves only for a short season. Its purple-black fruits, about a quarter of an inch in diameter, are borne in pairs on the twigs. They are eaten in times of famine and are a favorite food of birds.

The rubber tree (*F. elastica*) is as well known in temperate regions as a decorative pot plant as it is in the tropics as a tree. A native of India and Malaya, this sometimes gigantic evergreen begins life as an epiphyte and eventually anchors itself in the ground by adventitious roots. Its leathery, glossy green, pointed, elliptic leaves have their veins arranged differently from those of any other *Ficus;* from a prominent midvein fine, parallel lateral veins run nearly at right angles almost to the leaf margins. The leaves on young specimens are up to 1 foot long and half as broad, but on older trees they are usually much smaller. Another distinguishing characteristic is the large rosy pink stipules which sheathe the leaf buds and drop when the leaves unfold. The egg-shaped, half-inch-long, yellowish green fruits grow in pairs on the shorter twigs. The rubber tree is a strangler fig that in its native home envelops and destroys other trees. Growing 100 feet or more tall, it has a stout trunk, sometimes heavily buttressed at the base, and terrestrial roots that radiate over the ground for a considerable distance from the trunk. The rubber tree is so named because it is the original source of India rubber, first prepared and used by natives of Assam, and later introduced to Westerners and used by them chiefly for making erasers. In the last half of the nineteenth century the tree was cultivated in Assam and its white latex tapped as a source of India rubber. *Ficus elastica* is no longer cultivated for this purpose; essentially all commercial natural rubber comes from the South American *Hevea brasiliensis.*

One of the most beautiful evergreen figs is the benjamin tree *(F. benjamina)*, a banyan type native to most of the wetter parts of India, Burma, Sumatra, Timor, Celebes and the Philippines. The word *benjamina* is derived from the Sanskrit name for banyan. Because of its long, drooping branches this species is sometimes called the weeping fig. The benjamin tree develops a broad, spreading head up to 50 feet tall and has shining pointed, ovate leaves up to 5 inches long. The figs, in pairs in the leaf axils, are one-half to three-quarters of an inch in diameter and are orange, pink, red or purple. From the branches a few adventitious roots sometimes develop and occasionaly root into the ground and become subsidiary trunks. The root system is extensive and part of it snakes over the ground surface from the base of the trunk.

Easily distinguished from the benjamin tree by its blunt leaves, the species called Chinese or Malayan banyan *(F. retusa)* is native to the moister parts of India, Ceylon, Malaysia, China, the Philippines and New Caledonia. An evergreen, this kind grows up to 60 feet in height and has a wide-spreading crown. Its leaves, broadly elliptic, are up to 4 inches long. The paired fruits, borne in the leaf axils, are about one-third of an inch in diameter and when they

are ripe they are white or purplish. One of the most common of the evergreen figs, this species is planted in many warm countries as a shade tree. A strangler fig, *Ficus retusa* develops prominent surface roots and a few adventitious roots from its branches that often become secondary trunks. Its leaves, bark and aerial roots are used in native medicines to relieve toothache and headache and as a balm on bruises.

A large deciduous fig, epiphytic when young, is *F. infectoria*, a native of India, Malaya and China. This quick-growing, handsome species has a short and often knobbly trunk and spreading branches that support a dense crown of glossy green foliage. From the branches a few aerial roots sometimes develop. The leaves vary considerably in shape and size but most are narrowly ovate elliptic with wavy margins; they are 3 to 6 inches long. The fruits, usually in pairs, are about a quarter inch in diameter; they are whitish or reddish. A coarse fiber obtained from the bark is used to make cordage and the young shoots are used in curries. Cattle and elephants feed on the foliage. Various parts of the tree are used in native medicines and the wood is made into charcoal.

Many other species of *Ficus* inhabit tropical Asia. Notable among the strangler figs is *F. caulocarpa,* which is common in India and Malaya and develops an enormous crown of large, spreading branches with many aerial roots from their lower parts and from the trunk. The narrow, oblong, blunt leaves are on slender twigs and behind them, on older wood, small round figs are borne in clusters. The figs, at first whitish with pink spots, become grayish purple when ripe. This species bears a new crop of leaves three times a year and is leafless for a few days between crops. One of the largest stranglers is the Indian fig *(F. indica)*, a huge evergreen common in Malaya, India and the Philippines. It has a wide-spreading crown and an enormous basket of supporting roots but no pillar roots from its branches. The leaves are elliptic; the fruits, broader than long, become red or orange when mature. The Malayan *F. variegata,* which grows up to 90 feet in height, has a rounded crown and buttressed trunk. It develops a profusion of flowers and fruits directly on its trunk and branches. It is deciduous.

The remarkable earth-figs bear their fruits on running stems that originate from trunks and branch at various heights above ground. Most of the trees are less than 20 feet in height, but one of the most attractive and most useful, the gooseberry fig (F. cunia) of Malaya and Burma, grows up to 40 feet tall and bears clusters of edible fruits that have the flavor of gooseberries. Another, indigenous to Malaya and Borneo, is F. geocarpa, which sometimes becomes 25 feet tall and develops runners up to 30 feet long from up to a height of 4 feet on the trunk. It bears pubescent fruits that change from white to pink to reddish brown as they ripen.

Although the American tropics and subtropics are not as rich in Ficus species as similar regions in the Old World, probably a hundred kinds occur in the southern United States, the West Indies, Mexico, and Central and South America. Very few species, perhaps only one or two, are common to the West Indies and the mainland. One group or subgenus, the Pharmacosyce, which is characterized by its solitary, trilobed fruits and flowers with two stamens, is found only in the Americas. The figs have little or no commercial importance and foresters in the American tropics regard them as weed trees. The shortleaf fig (F. brevifolia) ranges as a native from Florida to Paraguay and the West Indies. It is the commonest fig in Puerto Rico and is there called jagüey blanco because of its whitish bark. It grows up to 60 feet in height with a trunk 2½ feet in diameter and has short-pointed, broadly elliptic leaves. The round fruits are about three-eighths of an inch in diameter and are borne on the younger twigs. They become brownish or reddish when ripe and are edible but rather tasteless. This species often begins existence as an epiphyte in the fork of a tree and sends down aerial roots which unite to form a cylinder around the trunk of the host tree and eventually kill it. The shortleaf fig is a good shade tree; its wood is used for fuel and for making guitars. Jagüey colorado is the Puerto Rican name for the native F. perforata, which is indigenous also in the Bahamas and Greater Antilles, and from Guatemala to Colombia. This becomes 65 feet tall with a trunk diameter of 1 foot. It has light gray bark, a spreading crown, and pointed, elliptic, thick leathery leaves. The small, stalked fruits are tinged pink or are reddish at maturity. The wood is used for posts and as fuel.

The strangling fig of Florida (F. aurea), like many of its kin, begins life as an epiphyte, sends down roots which anchor themselves in the ground and eventually surrounds and kills the host tree. This fig attains a height of 60 feet. Its oblong leaves are narrowed at both ends. The fruits, one-third inch in diameter, are yellow.

One of the commonest and most widely dispersed of the Mexican and Central American strangler figs is F. padifolia. Like its Asiatic relatives of the banyan type, it envelops its host, develops a large crown and sends aerial roots from its branches to the ground. Some of these develop into sturdy, supporting secondary trunks. Typically, the young plant starts life in the ground. As its ropelike stem elongates it attaches itself by aerial roots to the trunk of a nearby tree, often a palm. In time the host tree is killed. There is much variation in the shape of the leaves of F. padifolia, ranging from broadly ovate to lanceolate. The fruits are up to one-half inch in diameter.

The flora of the Philippines includes many native figs some of which have a much wider range, such as the benjamin tree and the Indian fig. Other kinds grow only in the archipelago. Among the most important endemics is F. nota, a small to medium sized tree with irregularly toothed oblong leaves that are heart-shaped at their bases and up to 10 inches long. The fruits are in dense masses on special branches that arise from the trunk and large branches. Another small- to medium-sized fig tree is the endemic Philippine F. odorata which has leaves so harsh that they are used for scouring. They are very unequally lobed at their bases and have obscurely toothed margins. The yellowish fruits are about 1 inch long. The designation odorata refers to the fact that the dried leaves are fragrant. Yet a third species that is found only as a native of the Philippines is the palmlike fig (F. pseudopalma). A small tree with a forked trunk, this kind has narrow, gracefully curved leaves, 2 to 3 feet long, crowded together at the top of the trunk.

Among figs from Australia are the Moreton Bay fig (F. macrophylla) and the Port Jackson fig (F. rubiginosa). The former, a native of Queensland and New South Wales, develops a large spreading crown and very extensive roots. It has oval, leathery leaves up to 10 inches long. When young they are rust-colored beneath and in the bud stage are enclosed in rose-pink sheaths. The tasteless spherical fruits, about 1 inch in diameter, are purple with lighter flecks. The Port Jackson fig, of New South Wales, is a large, heavy-crowned tree that develops aerial roots that sometimes become supporting trunks. The leaves, up to 4 inches long, are oval and are

Osage orange. Maclura pomifera (W. Rauh)

smooth above but more or less brown-hairy beneath. The globose fruits, borne in pairs, are warty and about one-third of an inch in diameter.

Maclura—Osage Orange

The only species of this genus, the osage orange (*M. pomifera*), has a very limited natural range centered in the Red River valley in Oklahoma but it is widely planted elsewhere and has been much used to form hedges, especially in prairie regions. It is a thorny tree with dark orange-colored bark, spreading branches that form an open, irregular crown, and attractive, deciduous, ovate to oblong leaves that are up to 6 inches long and turn yellow in fall. The minute flowers are without petals, the males forming pendulous racemes, the females globular heads. The latter, following pollination, develop into inedible orange-like compound fruits, irregular in shape, warty-skinned and up to 6 inches in diameter.

The very hardy, strong, tough wood of the osage orange is especially valued for wagon wheels, insulator pins and treenails as well as for posts and stakes. It is the most durable of all North American woods. The tree is also called bow wood and bodark, the latter being a corruption of bois d'arc and, like bow wood, a recognition of an Indian use for this wood.

Morus—Mulberry

About ten Northern Hemisphere deciduous, wind-pollinated trees with edible fleshy fruits that resemble blackberries but are morphologically quite different comprise this genus. The flowers, bisexual or unisexual, form short hanging catkins. Native throughout the eastern and central United States and southern Ontario, the red mulberry (*M. rubra*) sometimes is 70 feet tall and has a short trunk, 4 feet or less in diameter, covered with scaly brown bark and a dense rounded crown of stout, spreading branches. Its broad ovate, mostly unlobed, toothed leaves have rough upper surfaces and are pubescent beneath. They turn bright yellow in fall. The fruits, dark purple when ripe, provide food for hogs and poultry. The Mexican mulberry (*M. microphylla*) is rarely 25 feet tall and may have a trunk up to 15 inches in diameter. It occurs in the southwestern United States and Mexico and is perhaps a variety of *M. celtidifolia*, which ranges from Mexico to Peru and is a source of lumber for local building. As its name suggests, *M. microphylla* has small leaves; they are less than 3 inches long, ovate and often three-lobed. Rough above, their undersides are either smooth or pubescent.

Cultivated for thousands of years and probably originally a native of Persia and adjacent regions, the black mulberry (*M. nigra*) is planted in parts of Europe and Asia for its agreeably flavored, sub acid, dark red fruits. At maturity it is rugged and picturesque and has a short trunk and an irregular crown of wide-spreading branches. Its rather large, mostly unlobed, broad, ovate, toothed leaves, with deeply heart-shaped bases are a dull dark green and are rough above. Their undersides are lighter and are pubescent on the veins. Famous because it is the most important food of silkworms, the white mulberry (*M. alba*) of China grows up to 45 feet in height and has a trunk that may be 2 feet in diameter. This variable kind, which has been cultivated in the Orient and southern Europe since time immemorial, is round-topped and of rugged aspect when old. Its leaves, coarsely toothed and often conspicuously, variously and unevenly lobed, are smooth or only very slightly roughened above and are downy on their undersides. The white, pinkish or purplish fruits are insipidly sweet. The Russian mulberry (*M. a. tatarica*) has smaller much-lobed leaves and is hardier than the typical species.

CHAPTER 15

The Proteales

PROTEACEAE—PROTEA FAMILY

The order Proteales consists of only one family, the Proteaceae, composed almost entirely of trees and shrubs of South Africa, Australia and temperate South America. They are commonest where long dry seasons are usual and are xerophytic, that is, they are adapted to conserve moisture and to persist in regions of low rainfall. Their flowers, pollinated by birds and insects, contain abundant nectar. Their natural distribution is cited as support for the Wegener theory that all the continents once formed a single land mass which later split into smaller units and slowly drifted apart.

Banksia

Named after Sir Joseph Banks, the English botanist who accompanied Captain Cook on his voyage of discovery to Australia and other parts of the Pacific, this genus of about fifty species is almost entirely Australian but is also represented in New Guinea. Most kinds are shrubs but a few are trees. They have handsome foliage and flowers and in Australia are called honeysuckles. Most plentiful along the coast, they grow in all parts of the continent except the interior. The yellowish flowers, in pairs, are in spikes crowded with bracts. In fruit the spikes become woody and conelike. One of the best-known banksias is the red honeysuckle (*B. serrata*), a beautiful tree with saw-toothed elliptic leaves covered with gray pubescence on their undersides. The wood—its common name refers

to its color—is used for yokes, boat building, interior construction and turnery. This tree attains a height of 25 feet. The white honeysuckle (*B. integrifolia*) has smooth-edged oblanceolate leaves that are dark green above and silvery beneath. It grows to about 30 feet in height and is sometimes called beefwood because of its dark red wood which is strong and light and was once valued for airplane construction and is very suitable for decorative paneling. The largest flower spikes of the genus are those of *B. grandis*, a native of Western Australia that under favorable conditions becomes 40 feet tall. Its leaves, up to 1 foot long, are cut to the midrib and form many triangular lobes. The flower spikes are up to 1 foot long.

Embothrium

Of this group of small trees and shrubs of the Andes and Australia the best known are perhaps the South American *E. coccineum* and the Australian *E. wickamii pinnata*, the latter sometimes called waratah tree because of a fanciful resemblance of its flowers to those of the waratah shrub (*Telopea speciosissima*). In bloom, *E. coccineum* is truly gorgeous, its dense clusters of fiery scarlet flowers contrasting splendidly with its deep green persistent foliage. The leaves, leathery and elliptic, are paler on their lower than on their upper surfaces. This tree rarely attains a height of 40 feet. Not less lovely is *E. wickamii pinatta*, a small tree that has both simple and pinnate leaves and long-stalked red flowers crowded at the ends of the branchlets.

Faurea

This genus of eighteen African and Madagascan species includes the tallest proteaceous trees of South Africa. The terblans (*F. macnaughtonii*), which occurs in very widely separated small stands, is a handsome evergreen, up to 60 feet in height, and has lance-shaped or oval glossy green leaves. The sweetly-scented white or pinkish flowers are in 6-inch-long spikes. Its wood, beautifully grained, resembles that of the European beech. It has been described as the most beautiful furniture wood of South Africa. The African-beech or Transvaal boekenhout (*F. saligna*) grows almost as tall as the terblans. It is commoner and much more widely distributed, ranging from the Transvaal to the Nile. A graceful tree, this species attains a trunk diameter of 2 feet. Its long, leathery, dark green leaves, narrow and pointed, turn brilliant red in

Silky-oak. Grevillea robusta (Janet Finch)

fall. The yellowish white flowers are in spikes and are sweetly scented. The handsomely grained wood resembles that of the terblans and is used for wagons, furniture, waterwheels and other purposes; the wood is also the source of a red dye.

Grevillea

These trees and shrubs of Australia, New Caledonia, the New Hebrides and eastern Malaysia number 190 species. Their flowers, usually paired in the axils of the racemes, have styles which project from the flower bud in long loops, straightening only when pollen is shed on them. The best known is the silky-oak (*G. robusta*), a native of a very restricted area in coastal New South Wales and Queensland, but not commonly cultivated in other warm temperate regions as a street tree and ornamental. Of upright growth and attaining a height of 150 feet with a trunk diameter up to 3 feet, this tree has fernlike evergreen leaves with white silky hairs on their undersides. Its deep yellow flowers, in long comblike clusters, attract nectar-seeking birds and bees. The handsomely grained wood of the silky-oak is strong and durable and is excellent

for cabinetwork. The white silky-oak (*G. hilliana*) is so named because of its long, cylindrical racemes of white flowers. This species, which sometimes attains a height of 90 feet and is a native of New South Wales and Queensland, has beautifully grained rich red wood that takes a fine polish and is used for veneers and cabinetwork. A native of all Australian states except Victoria and Tasmania, the silvery-honeysuckle or turraie (*G. striata*) attains a maximum height of 80 feet and a trunk diameter of 20 inches. It has narrow, linear, often curved leaves from 6 to 18 inches long and slender racemes of flowers. Its excellent red, handsomely mottled wood polishes well and is used for cabinetwork and furniture.

Leucodendron—Silver Tree

Perhaps most famous of the Proteales is the silver tree (*Leucodendron argenteum*) of the Cape of Good Hope. Endemic to a small area at the southern tip of Africa, and quite abundant on Table Mountain, this species is remarkable for its persistently shining silvery leaves which are lance-shaped and up to 7 inches long by 1 inch wide. Both sides of the leaves are densely covered with fine silky hairs which in dry weather lie flat but at other times are raised at an angle of about thirty degrees. These hairs check excessive loss of moisture and are useful to a species that often grows in exposed dry and windy places. The silver tree grows rapidly when young, more slowly later; it occasionally attains a height of 50 feet. Male and female flowers are borne on separate trees. The silvery apricot males are in cone-shaped clusters at the branch ends, the females develop into silvery conical heads that remain decorative for a long time. The leaves have long been popular as bookmarks, and in South African colonial days the wood of this tree was used for construction, box-making and fuel.

Macadamia—Queensland Nut

One species of *Macadamia* inhabits Madagascar, the other nine Australia, New Caledonia and adjacent islands. By far the most notable is *M. ternifolia*, the only native plant of Australia that has attained any importance as a food producer; the hard-shelled nuts are nutritious and of excellent flavor. Orchards of macadamias are cultivated in Hawaii and elsewhere in the tropics and subtropics. The trees grow to a height of 60 feet and have their evergreen lanceolate, blunt-ended, usually toothed leaves in whorls of three. The spikes of small white flowers are succeeded by clusters of globular or hemispherical nuts, each 1 to 2 inches in diameter. The chocolate-colored, tough, strong wood of *M. ternifolia* is used for cabinetwork, shingles and heavy construction. Another Australian species, the opposum nut *(M. praealta),* which sometimes exceeds 60 feet in height, is of no importance as a nut bearer but produces prettily marked, close-grained, tough, strong, and durable red lumber useful for cabinetwork and tool handles.

Stenocarpus

This genus of twenty-five species of evergreens is native to Australia and New Caledonia. Especially interesting is the fire-wheel tree *(S. sinuatus),* which has brilliant scarlet-and-orange, 4-inch-wide flowers shaped like wheels with radiating spokes. The leaves are firm, deeply lobed and up to 1 foot long. The hard, durable wood of this native of New South Wales and Queensland is excellent for furniture and indoor trim. The red silky-oak, also called beefwood *(S. salignus),* a native of New South Wales and Queensland, forms a wide-spreading head and grows to a height of 80 feet. Its white or greenish white flowers, about 1 inch in diameter, are borne in fan-shaped clusters. Its leaves are ovate lanceolate. This decorative tree has deep red, close-grained hard wood that is excellent for furniture, cabinetwork, turnery, walking sticks and construction.

CHAPTER 16

The Santalales

SANTALACEAE—SANDALWOOD FAMILY

Only two out of seven families comprising the order Santales (distinguishable from related orders by flowers that are nearly always bisexual) are of importance or interest to man, including the mistletoe family (Loranthaceae), a group of mostly semiparasitic plants. The first of these two families, the sandalwoods (Santalaceae), contains about 400 trees, shrubs and herbaceous plants, many or perhaps all of which are semiparasitic on the roots of other plants.

Santalum—Sandalwood

The most important members of this group of evergreen trees and shrubs is the sandalwood *(S. album),* a native of India and other parts of southeastern Asia that is the source of a fragrant wood prized for making chests, boxes and incense and of an oil much used in perfumery and to some extent medicinally. Other species of *Santalum* with similar properties are indigenous to Pacific islands including Juan Fernandez and Hawaii. In the early part of the last century Hawaiian groves were the basis of such a considerable export trade to China that the Chinese knew the Hawaiian Islands as the Sandalwood Islands. The Indian *Santalum album* grows to a height of about 40 feet and has reddish wood that has no odor when newly cut but develops its characteristic scent upon drying. Its glabrous leaves, 2 inches long or less, are ovate to ovate-lanceolate. The flowers are at first straw-colored but later become bloodred.

CHAPTER 17

The Centrospermae

PHYTOLACCACEAE—POKEWEED FAMILY

This family belongs to the order Centrospermae, which has few trees and includes such familiar families as carnations, portulacas, four-o'clocks, cockscomb and bougainvillea. The pokeweeds are found chiefly in the American tropics. They have berry-like fruits with colored juices.

Phytolacca

To those familiar with the pokeweed *(P. americana)* it may come as a surprise to learn that it has relatives of tree size, the most notable of which is the ombú *(P. dioca)* of temperate South America. This remarkable species grows with amazing rapidity, withstands drought, heat and

Ombú. Phytolacca dioica (Ralph Cornell)

hurricanes, and repels ants, locusts, mosquitoes and other insects. The ombú becomes 60 feet tall with a branch spread of more than 100 feet. From the bottom of its very thick trunk it develops extraordinary irregular outgrowths that look like fantastic and bulky roots. These may occupy a circle 60 feet in diameter. They stand well above the ground and can serve as seats or benches for those who seek rest in the shade of the tree. The trunk is very unlike that of other trees. It consists of loose fibrous layers often with large voids in the interior. Structurally, it more closely resembles the stem of an herbaceous plant than a typical tree trunk and, like its branches, it contains 80 percent water. Because of this, the wood, when green, will not burn and the trees are highly resistant to grass fires. When thoroughly dried the loose fibrous wood burns like paper without producing much heat. The elliptic or ovate leaves of the ombú are evergreen and male and female flowers are on separate trees; the fruits are small and berry-like. The ombú is beloved in Argentina and other parts of South America and is the subject of many songs, legends and stories. Its especial value is the grateful shade it provides and for this it has been freely planted not only in its native lands but in southern Europe, Pacific North America and other such mild-climate regions.

CHAPTER 18

The Ranales

TROCHODENDRACEAE

Trochodendron Family

This genus, the only one in the family Trochodendraceae, belongs to the order Ranales, the plants of which have their parts in spirals, often with no clear distinction between sepals and petals.

Trochodendron consists of one species, *T. aralioides*, an evergreen tree of Japan and Taiwan, related to *Euptelea*. Attaining a height of up to 60 feet, *T. aralioides* has elliptic, lanceolate to obovate, lustrous green leaves and bisexual bright green flowers in erect terminal racemes but lacks petals. In Taiwan it forms pure stands at high elevations; it often grows near hot sulphur springs.

EUPTELEACEAE

Euptelea Family

Three deciduous trees of southeast Asia comprise *Euptelea*, the only genus of the family Eupteleaceae. By some botanists it has been included in the Trochodendraceae but recent investigations suggest no close affinity between the two families. Species of *Euptelea* become about 40 feet tall and have handsome foliage which colors attractively in fall. The long-stalked leaves are roundish ovate and toothed, those of *E. polyandra* of Japan are coarsely and unequally dentate, those of *E. franchetii* of China are more regularly doubly serrate, and those of *E. pleio-*

Right: Black oak. Quercus velutina (Irvin Oakes: National Audubon)
Overleaf left: Shingle oaks. Quercus imbricaria (John H. Gerard: National Audubon) Right: Cork oak. Quercus suber (Zentrale Farbbild Agentur)

sperma of China and the eastern Himalayas are simply serrate with tiny papillose projections on their somewhat glaucous undersurfaces. In the fall the flowers of *Euptelea* appear in clusters. They are without sepals or petals, have red anthers but are without decorative merit.

CERCIDIPHYLLACEA
CERCIDIPHYLLUM FAMILY

Cercidophyllum—Katsura Tree

The only species, *C. japonicum*, comprises the cercidophyllum family (Cercidiphyllaceae). Fossil evidence indicates that it is the sole surviving member of a group of many species that were widely distributed in ancient geological times. It differs markedly from any tree extant. The katsura tree forms a remarkably symmetrical rounded or pyramidal head that in the Chinese variety *(C. j. sinense)* may be 120 feet in height but in the typical Japanese form does not exceed 100 feet. In the open the tree may be almost as wide as high. The trunk usually divides low down into a number of secondary trunks. The dark bluish-green leaves are suborbicular or broad-ovate and are heart-shaped at their bases; their undersides are somewhat glaucous. The numerous unisexual flowers, both sexes on the same tree, develop from short woody spurs before the leaves appear in spring. They are without sepals or petals and have no decorative value. The winged seeds are borne in pods. The katsura tree is highly regarded as an ornamental and for its lumber. The wood is remarkable for the smoothness of its grain, which permits it to be tooled to sharp edges. Because of this it is especially useful for intricate moldings and carvings, and in the Orient it is used for wood engravings.

MAGNOLIACEAE—MAGNOLIA FAMILY

Here belong a group of deciduous and evergreen trees and shrubs, chiefly of North Temperate regions, that have alternate, undivided, usually smooth-edged leaves and usually solitary and often large and showy flowers. The family in-

Far left: Ficus variegata (Ivan Polunin) Left above: Tulip tree. Liriodendron tulipifera (Walter Chandoha) Left: Silky-oak flower. Grevillea (Emil Javorsky)

cludes a dozen genera and about 230 species. The parts of the flowers are arranged spirally. The family is considered to be one of the most primitive among the angiosperms.

Liriodendron—Tulip Tree

There are two species of tulip tree, one native to eastern North America, the other to China. They are alike except for minor botanical differences such as the filaments of the stamens in the American species *(L. tulipifera)* that are about twice as long as those of the Chinese kind *(L. chinense)*, which are about one-fifth of an inch long. The leaves of the Chinese tree are usually much more deeply lobed than those of its American relative. In preglacial times tulip trees had a wider distribution than now; they grew in Alaska, Greenland and in Europe as far south as Italy. The American tulip tree reaches a maximum height of almost 200 feet and has a straight, column-like trunk up to 10 feet in diameter. Under forest conditions the trunk may be free of branches for 100 feet from the ground and the branches above are short and the crown comparatively small. In the open the tree develops stout, spreading branches that form a broad, irregularly pyramidal open head. The leaves are unique in shape. About as long as broad, they are truncated and notched at the apex and have two to four lobes at the base; they have been described as saddle-shaped. The large greenish yellow flowers, tulip-like in overall appearance, are marked with bright orange blotches on the insides of their petals and are delicately fragrant. Ranking among the noblest trees of American forests, the tulip tree is a beautiful ornamental and an important timber tree. The lumber is known as whitewood and yellow poplar and is in demand for interior trim, shelving, plywood, furniture frames, boxes, crates and many other uses. The Chinese tulip tree attains a height of about 60 feet and a trunk diameter of 3 feet.

Magnolia

The magnolias are now natives only of eastern North America, eastern Asia and the Himalayas with outlying species in Mexico, the West Indies and the Philippines, but ample fossil evidence proves that until they were exterminated by glaciation at the end of the Tertiary Period they populated most of Canada, Greenland, Europe and Siberia. Botanists regard them as among the most primitive of living seed plants, almost as ancient as the ginkgo. They have bisexual flowers with stamens and pistils spiralled on an elongated central axis. Their sepals and petals are in three whorls or rings, the sepals sometimes resembling petals in color and appearance. When the flowers fade the developing seeds remain attached to the central axis to form a cone-like structure. At maturity the seeds fall away but remain suspended by a silky thread attached to the wall of the ovary. Birds eat the seeds, digest their fleshy outer coats and pass the viable parts through their bodies, thus aiding in the distribution of the species. The flowers of magnolias are pollinated by insects. Self-pollination does not occur because the flowers do not produce ripe pollen until after the stigma (female organ) has ceased to be receptive. All American and some Asiatic species bloom when the foliage is fully developed but many Asiatic kinds flower in spring before their leaves appear. Magnolias have the largest blooms and biggest leaves of all Temperate Region trees.

American magnolias include one magnificent evergreen, the bull bay (M. grandiflora), and one semi-evergreen, the sweet bay (M. virginiana). The latter is likely to be fully evergreen in the southernmost part of its range and deciduous in its northernmost localities; elsewhere it loses much of its foliage in winter but is never denuded. The bull bay may be 125 feet tall with a trunk diameter of 4½ feet. Its dark, glossy green, oval leaves, often rusty pubescent below, are often 8 or 9 inches long. Its flowers, from 6 to 12 inches in diameter, are creamy white and fragrant. The bull bay is native from North Carolina to Florida and Texas. The sweet bay reaches a maximum height of 60 feet and a trunk diameter of about 20 inches in its native coastal swamps from North Carolina to Florida and Louisiana. Its leaves, glaucous blue-gray on their undersides, are up to 6 inches long. The globose, fragrant, white flowers measure 2 to 3 inches across.

Growing to 100 feet high, the cucumber tree (M. acuminata) is the most stately of American deciduous magnolias. Its common name refers to its young fruits, shaped somewhat like cucumbers. Native from New York to Georgia and Arkansas, it sometimes develops a trunk 4 feet in diameter. Its leaves may be 10 inches long and its inconspicuous greenish flowers, the petals of which are erect, are up to 3½ inches long. This is a pyramidal tree, upright when young, wide-spreading at maturity. Similar to the cucumber tree, but having conspicuous creamy yellow flowers and twigs that are densely pubescent,

is M. cordata, a native of Georgia. This kind attains a maximum height of 50 feet. Originally discovered near Atlanta, Georgia, in the late eighteenth century and perpetuated in gardens since, truly wild plants were not again found by botanists until 1914, when specimens were found not far from Atlanta. The umbrella tree (M. tripetala) and the large-leaved cucumber tree (M. macrophylla) have deciduous leaves—those of the former up to 2 feet long, those of the latter up to 3 feet long. Their flowers, too, are impressive. Blooms of the umbrella tree are cup-shaped, white, from 8 to 10 inches across and have a disagreeable odor. From 10 to 12 inches wide, the flowers of the large-leaved cucumber tree are cup-shaped, fragrant and white with pink or purple areas at the bases of the petals. The umbrella tree, which ranges from Pennsylvania to Alabama and Mississippi, attains a height of 40 feet and a trunk diameter of 1½ feet. The large-leaved cucumber tree grows to a maximum of 50 feet and may have a trunk 20 inches in diameter. Its natural range is from Kentucky to Florida and Louisiana.

Magnolia fraseri and M. pyramidata are southeastern United States natives related to the large-leaved cucumber tree but considerably smaller, M. fraseri growing to about 45 feet tall with a wide-spreading open head and M. pyramidata up to 30 feet and forming a pyramidal specimen with spreading branches. Both are distinguishable from the large-leaved cucumber tree by their hairless leaf buds and branchlets; the leaves of M. fraseri are sharply pointed, those of M. pyramidata bluntly pointed. The fragrant white or pale yellow flowers of M. fraseri are 8 to 10 inches across; those of M. pyramidata are creamy white and about half as big.

Several evergreen magnolias allied to the bull bay and the sweet bay are native to Mexico, Central America and the West Indies, with the individual species restricted usually to comparatively small areas. Most noteworthy of the Mexican species is M. schiediana, which occurs in the southern part of the country and becomes a large tree. Its creamy white flowers, 4 inches or more in diameter, are used to prepare a decoction used locally to alleviate scorpion stings. The leaves, glabrous on both surfaces, are about twice as long as broad. In Costa Rica, M. poasana inhabits mountain slopes and attains large size but, like M. sororum of the mountains of Panama, which grows to a height of 70 feet, it is too inaccessible to be of other than local use for lumber. *Magnolia guatemalensis*, which takes its name from its native land, grows to about 25 feet high and has snow-white flowers 5 to 6 inches across. It is found in swamplands.

West Indian magnolias include the very handsome *M. splendens*, an endemic of Puerto Rico, known there as laurel sabino. Its ovate or elliptic leaves are used in its homeland as a condiment and its lumber is considered to be among the best produced in the island. Attaining a height of 80 feet or more, *M. splendens* has glossy leaves, silky hairy beneath and up to 6 inches long. The white flowers have petals about 4 inches in diameter. Native to the same island is *M. portoricensis*, a tree 80 feet tall with glossy, nearly orbicular, glabrous leaves and fragrant white flowers 4 inches or more in diameter. This tree is known by the vernacular names *mauricio* and *burro*. In the mountains of Cuba is *M. cubensis*, reported to become a fairly large tree. This native species, with much the habit of the sweet bay (*M. glauca*), has flowers that are white, fragrant and about 2 inches across.

Japan is the home of a number of fine magnolias. Largest is *M. obovata*, which blooms after its leaves appear and is similar to the American umbrella tree (*M. tripetala*). At its best it is 100 feet tall with a trunk diameter of 3 feet. Its leaves, up to 18 inches long, are green above and whitish beneath. The strongly scented creamy white flowers, decorated with bright purple-red stamens, become yellow as they fade and are 8 inches in diameter. The soft, light, smooth-grained wood of *M. obovata* is greatly valued by the Japanese as the base for lacquerwork.

Having pure white flowers which unfold before its leaves, *M. kobus* is another fine Japanese species. Sometimes reaching a height of 80 feet, its trunk may be almost 3 feet in diameter. Pyramidal when young it becomes more or less round-headed at maturity. Closely related to *M. kobus* is *M. salicifolia*, a species that does not exceed 30 feet in height and that occurs naturally most abundantly in the Mount Hakkoda region of Japan. It blooms when leafless in spring, bearing pure white flowers. The leaves of *M. salicifolia* are broadest below their middles, those of *M. kobus* above their

Above: Tulip tree. Liriodendron tulipifera
Right: Tulip tree leaf. (Both, Andreas Feininger)

Pawpaw. Asimina triloba (U.S.D.A.)

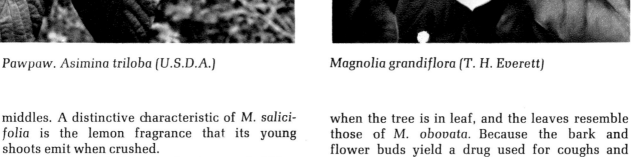

Magnolia grandiflora (T. H. Everett)

middles. A distinctive characteristic of *M. salicifolia* is the lemon fragrance that its young shoots emit when crushed.

The yulan (*M. denudata*) of central China grows up to 50 feet high and may have a trunk diameter of 2½ feet. It has spreading branches and pure white bell-shaped flowers, each 6 or 7 inches across; these appear before the leaves. The yulan is greatly admired by the Chinese, who have cultivated it for well over a thousand years. As a symbol of purity and candor it is frequently depicted in ancient paintings, porcelains and other art works of China. The yulan, hybridized with the shrubby *M. liliflora,* has given rise to a number of splendid hybrids known collectively as saucer magnolias (*M. soulangeana*). In western China *M. sargentiana* is native, grows to a height of 75 feet and forms a dense crown. Its trunk may be 2 feet in diameter. It differs from the yulan in having twelve or more petals, instead of nine and in leaves that are rounded, not abruptly pointed. Also, its flowers are pink. *Magnolia officinalis,* a close relative of the Japanese *M. ovata,* is another fine tree of western China, where it attains a height of 50 feet. Its bark, unlike that of *M. ovata* is yellowish, not purplish, and there are technical botanical differences between the two species. The fragrant flowers, which develop

when the tree is in leaf, and the leaves resemble those of *M. obovata.* Because the bark and flower buds yield a drug used for coughs and colds and as a stimulant and tonic, *M. officinalis* is commonly cultivated.

An evergreen species of note, *Magnolia delavayi,* related to the American bull bay (*M. grandiflora*), is a native of southwestern China. In that country this tree becomes 50 feet high and forms a somewhat flat-topped spreading tree with dull evergreen leaves up to 2 feet long. Its fragrant, creamy-white cup-shaped flowers measure as much as 8 inches in diameter, and its leaves may exceed a foot in length. Pyramidal in outline and sometimes 150 feet tall, and native at elevations from eight to ten thousand feet in the Himalayas, *M. campbellii* is an outstanding deciduous magnolia. Before its leaves unfold it bears 6- to 10-inch-wide, cup-shaped blooms that are delicate pink inside, heavily shaded with crimson outside and sweetly scented. The leaves of this very beautiful tree are often 1 foot long and are glaucous beneath. Considered to be possibly the most primitive of all flowering plants, *M. pterocarpa,* which grows at low elevations in the Himalayas, is a large evergreen tree with shining leaves and fragrant flowers that measure 3 to 4 inches across.

Michelia

A genus of deciduous and evergreen Asian trees and shrubs, *Michelia* differs from nearly related *Magnolia* in technical details. The flowers are much smaller and are mostly lateral rather than terminal on the twigs. Several species are important because of their lumber. One such is *M. formosana* of Taiwan, an evergreen that exceeds 50 feet in height. In Japan the evergreen *M. compressa* attains a height of 40 feet and has pale yellow flowers. Chinese species include *M. alba*, which has small white flowers and grows to 60 feet in height with a trunk diameter of 2 feet, and *M. champaea*, also an evergreen with white flowers that attains a maximum height of about 40 feet.

ANNONACEAE—CUSTARD-APPLE FAMILY

This family, which evolved from primitive magnoliaceous ancestors, consists of 120 genera and more than two thousand species, chiefly tropical and mostly natives of the Old World.

Annona—Sweetsop, Custard-Apple and Cherimoya

Among these tropical and subtropical natives of the Americas and Africa are several highly regarded for their delicious edible fruits. One of the best known is the soursop (*A. muricata*), an evergreen tree of tropical America that grows to a height of about 20 feet, has obovate to elliptic leaves and yellow flowers. Its ovoid fruits, up to 8 inches long and covered with short, fleshy spines, contain white, juicy but rather woolly flesh that tastes somewhat like pineapple. The sweetsop or sugar-apple (*A. squamosa*), also native to tropical America, is deciduous. About 20 feet tall, its leaves are oblong lanceolate to lanceolate. Its greenish yellow flowers are succeeded by globular or heart-shaped, glaucous yellowish green fruits covered with projecting scales and containing a sweet custard-like pulp. The custard-apple or bullock's heart (*A. reticulata*) of tropical America attains a height of 25 feet and is partially evergreen. Its leaves are lanceolate or oblong lanceolate, its flowers yellowish. The reddish yellow or brown fruits, heart-shaped or ovoid, are up to 5 inches in diameter and their outsides are marked with a reticulation of impressed lines. The pulp is sweet and custard-like. In the Andes of Ecuador and Peru the cherimoya (*A. cherimola*) is native. The fruits of this deciduous 25-foot-tall tree are considered the tastiest of the annonas. The pulp is white and somewhat acid. The leaves of the cherimoya are ovate to ovate lanceolate and velvety hairy on their undersides. The light green, spherical-to-conical fruits have skins that are smooth or covered with small knobs; they are about 5 inches long. The yellow or brownish flowers are fragrant.

Of the African species, *A. senegalensis* is of interest because of its great usefulness to the natives. It rarely exceeds 20 feet in height and occurs from the Cape Verde Islands to the Gambia, Nigeria and the Sudan. Its broadly elliptic, fragrant leaves are used for fodder and its flowers to flavor foods, and men eat both its fruits and its leaves. The wood is employed for building huts and for tool handles and its ashes to make snuff and soap. From the leaves and roots medicines are prepared and a perfume is obtained by boiling the leaves.

Asimina—Papaw

Only one of the eight species of this North American genus attains tree size; the papaw (*A. triloba*) under favorable conditions becomes 40 feet tall. It has large obovate leaves and bears edible, more or less cylindrical aromatic fruits that are sometimes 6 inches long. Its drooping, rich maroon flowers are almost 2 inches in diameter. This papaw, which must not be confused with the tropical papaw (*Carica papaya*), occurs throughout the eastern United States except in New England and eastern New York.

Cananga—Ylang-Ylang

There are only two species in this genus, which is native from Burma throughout the Malay Archipelago to New Guinea and northern Australia. By far the most important is the ylang-ylang or kenanga (*C. odoratum*), an evergreen tree that attains a height of 100 feet and is a familiar feature of villages throughout this area. Its fragrant, bell-shaped, yellowish green flowers are favorites for decoration and personal adornment. On the Philippines, Java and Reunion the tree is cultivated commercially for an oil distilled from its flowers that is used in perfumery and as an ingredient of Macassar oil—a hair dressing. Ylang-ylang or cananga oil, is one of the most important and valuable of essential oils. The ylang-ylang tree forms a narrow head and has drooping branches and pointed, oblong leaves.

Monodora

The most important of this group of twenty African and Madagascan species is the calabash nutmeg (*M. myristica*) of tropical Africa. It grows to a height of 80 feet and has a clean trunk and horizontal branches. Its obovate to elliptic leaves, with prominent midveins on their undersides, droop. The highly decorative fragrant flowers hang on long stalks from near the bases of the new shoots. They measure 6 inches or more across and are spotted yellow, red and green. The globose or oblong gourdlike fruits, which are suspended on stalks up to 2 feet long, may be 6 inches in diameter and contain numerous seeds embedded in fragrant pulp. The seeds are aromatic and are used as a condiment and in snuff, pomades and medicines. The wood is employed in carpentry, turnery and for walking sticks.

MYRISTICACEAE—NUTMEG FAMILY

This distinctive family is different from related families in having unisexual flowers with stamens united in one group and seeds that have a covering called an aril. It includes eighteen genera and three hundred species of tropical evergreen trees in Asia, Africa and America. The best known is the nutmeg (*Myristica fragrans*). From the seeds of some other species wax is obtained.

Myristica—Nutmeg

Two spices, mace and nutmeg, are products of one of the 120 species of *Myristica*. The nutmeg tree (*M. fragrans*) is a native of the Moluccas, formerly called the Spice Islands, where it thrives in the hot, humid climate, attains a height of about 60 feet, has dark brownish elliptic leaves and inconspicuous pale yellow flowers that have three sepals but no petals. Nutmeg trees bear heavy crops of golden yellow fruits that resemble apricots. Each fleshy fruit contains a single seed the kernel of which is the nutmeg of commerce. When completely ripe the fruits split to reveal the seeds and their surrounding red arils which are the source of the spice called mace. Nutmeg trees are handsome evergreens. From their seeds an essential oil is extracted that is

Above: Camphor tree. Cinnamomum camphora (U.S. Forest Service) Left: Avocado. Persea americana (G. J. H. Moon)

used in perfumery, in flavoring tobacco and in medicine; it also yields a yellow fat called nutmeg butter, which is used in ointments and for making candles. The seeds contain a toxic substance, myristicin; for this reason the spices nutmeg and mace should be used in moderation.

Nutmegs first became known to Europeans in the twelfth century, but not until the Portuguese discovered the Molucca Islands early in the sixteenth century was their natural habitat ascertained. About a hundred years later the Dutch obtained control of the Moluccas and monopolized the production of nutmeg and mace. They restricted cultivation of the trees to Amboina and Banda and transported convicts to work the plantations. An amusing instance of ignorance of botanical matters is revealed by the story that once, when nutmegs were plentiful but mace was in short supply, instructions were sent to planters to set out more mace-bearing trees and fewer nutmegs. By the end of the sixteenth century nutmeg trees had been planted in Mauritius and Penang; later they were introduced to the West Indies, and they are now cultivated in other tropical regions.

LAURACEAE—LAUREL FAMILY

This great tropical and subtropical family includes thirty-two genera and more than two thousand species of trees and shrubs, mostly with leathery, evergreen leaves; small, often unisexual, fragrant flowers borne in axillary panicles; and one-seeded berries or berry-like fruits that are enclosed at their bases by a persistent part of the flower tube that often suggests the cup of an acorn. Many species are aromatic and many are of commercial importance. The barks of some have irritating or poisonous qualities.

In the vast forests of tropical America and southeast tropical Asia there are numerous species belonging to so many genera that it would be impractical to deal with them all here. Not all are well understood or adequately known botanically; undoubtedly many undescribed kinds exist. Trees of the Lauraceae are so abundant in the lowlands of Malaya that it is said that one cannot walk half a mile without coming upon half a dozen species; they give character to mountain forests from the Himalayas to New Guinea.

Aniba

About forty tropical South and Central Ameri-

Leaves of Sassafras albidum (Andreas Feininger)

can trees are included in this genus; two occur in Trinidad and the West Indies. They are sources of useful lumbers, essential oils and medicinal materials. One of the most valuable is the bois de rose femelle (*A. rosaeodora*) of French Guiana, Surinam and the lower Amazon region, from the wood of which is distilled the fragrant, volatile oil called *essence de bois de rose*. This tree has a tall, straight, cylindrical trunk up to 3 feet in diameter and reaching a height of 100 feet. Its wood was used in France for fine furniture for more than a hundred years before the tree from which it came was identified botanically. Another good lumber is that of the comino or laurel comino (*A. perutilis*), an Andean species which attains 100 feet in height and ranges to Bolivia. An Amazonian native that grows as tall as the bois de rose femelle, has cinnamon-scented bark that is used as tea and for scenting linens, and is the source of hard blackish green or dark brown durable lumber, is *A. canelilla*.

Cinnamomum

The most important of this genus of 250 eastern Asiatic and Indomalaysian species are the camphor tree (*C. camphora*) and the cinnamon tree

155

(C. zeylanicum). The former is a native of Japan, China and Taiwan, the latter of Ceylon, India and Malaya. The camphor tree grows to a height of 90 feet and has a massive trunk with an enlarged base and dense, rounded head. It is a handsome ornamental that bears small yellow flowers and ovate elliptic leaves that are pinkish when young. Its highly aromatic, strong and durable wood, which is used for making clothes closets, chests, trunks, bookcases and interior trim, is markedly insect repellent. All parts of the tree contain the volatile colorless camphor oil that is of great value in medicine and industry. The cinnamon tree, which grows to a height of 40 feet, is a beautiful ornamental with short branches and very dark green, glossy, evergreen foliage. Its stiff leaves are elliptic with three to five prominent veins. The small, pale yellow malodorous flowers are succeeded by shiny, blue-black fruits. Commercial cinnamon is the bark of young sucker shoots peeled off and dried. Cassia bark, obtained from C. cassia, is an aromatic product used commercially in medicine and for flavoring. The tree is a handsome native of China and Sumatra that grows to a height of 40 feet and has stiff elliptic to lanceolate leaves that are conspicuously three-veined.

Laurus—Laurel

Two evergreen species comprise this genus, the true laurel or sweet bay (L. nobilis) of the Mediterranean region and L. canariensis of the Canary Islands. The former is the laurel of the ancients, sacred to Apollo and commonly planted in temple gardens. By the Romans it was fashioned into wreaths to crown victors, and doctors upon passing their final examinations were crowned with berried branches of this tree. From this custom our word baccalaureate (bacca, berry + laureus, of laurel) is derived, as also is the word bachelor. The title of poet laureate stems from the same source. Both species of Laurus grow to a maximum height of about 50 feet and commonly form crooked trees with inconspicuous bisexual or unisexual flowers which, unlike most members of the family, have their perianth parts in fours rather than in threes. The aromatic lanceolate or elliptic leaves of L. nobilis, known as bay leaves, are used for flavoring foods. The fruits resemble small plums.

Ocotea

Most of the more than three hundred members of Ocotea are natives of tropical and sub-tropical America; a few are South African. Notable among the latter is the stinkwood, a straight tree that grows up to 90 feet in height with a trunk that may be 6 feet in diameter. Its glossy, dark green leaves have small bubble-like swellings, which often harbor tiny insects, on both sides of the midvein toward their bases. The inconspicuous cream-colored flowers are succeeded by acorn-like fruits. The lumber of the stinkwood tree has a disagreeable odor when first cut but it is the most beautiful and most expensive furniture wood of South Africa. Lustrous and fine-grained, it varies from almost white through yellow and brown to nearly black. The wood called greenheart is obtained from the South American O. rodiaei and is strong, hard, heavy and highly resistant to marine borers, termites and decay. It is much used in Europe for bridges, piles, wharves and shipbuilding. The source of supply is north-eastern South America. The greenheart tree grows to a height of 80 feet and has glossy green, leathery leaves; it is one of the most handsome trees of the coastal forests.

Persea

Of the 150 species of this tropical and sub-tropical genus of evergreen trees, by far the most familiar is the avocado or alligator pear (P. americana). Probably originally a native of Mexico and Central America and cultivated there and elsewhere for centuries for its edible, highly nutritious fruits, this tree grows to a height of 60 feet and may have a trunk 1½ feet thick. Its leaves are elliptic to oval, its flowers small and greenish, its fruits large, fleshy and pear shaped, containing one large seed. Another species, with fruit very similar to that of the avocado, is P. scheideana, a native from Mexico to Panama. A large forest tree, its hard, coarse-grained lumber is used locally for interior construction. One of the most attractive woods of the genus is that of the Ecuadorian paracar (P. sericea), which grows in the forest to a height of 65 feet, with a trunk exceeding 3 feet in

Right: Tulip tree. (Gottscho-Schleisner)
Overleaf left: European mountain-ash. Sorbus aucuparia (G. Ohlstadt) Right above: Plums. Prunus domestica (Grant Heilman) Right below: American mountain-ash, fruits. Sorbus americana (Grant Heilman)

diameter, and forms a broad, flat-topped crown. Its wood, lustrous and pale reddish brown, is used for construction and interior trim.

The Chilean tree, cascara de lingue (P. lingue) has bark that is rich in tannin, for which product it is exploited locally; it also furnishes an attractive golden brown wood that is used for furniture and interior trim. The tree attains a height of 60 feet and a trunk diameter exceeding 3 feet. In some places it occurs in pure forest stands. The red bay or bull bay (P. borbonia) of the southern United States forms a narrow head up to 75 feet tall and may have a trunk 3 feet in diameter. Its bark is red. Its bright red lumber is used for interior construction and cabinetwork. The red bay is a handsome tree with elliptic to lanceolate leathery leaves, 2 to 3 inches long, which somewhat resemble those of the laurel (Laurus nobilis). The fruits are small and blue.

Sassafras

In addition to the well-known Sassafras albidum of the eastern United States and southern Ontario, one species, S. randaiense, occurs as a rare endemic in Taiwan, and another, S. tzumu, in China. All are very similar, handsome, pyramidal trees; unlike most members of the Lauraceae they are deciduous. The American species is sometimes 90 feet tall with a trunk 5 feet in diameter. Its branches are short and often crooked. Very characteristic of this and other species are their variable leaves, which are mitten-shaped, three-lobed or entirely unlobed, and assume beautiful orange and red autumn coloring. The flowers are inconspicuous, the fruits are like tiny dark blue plums surrounded at their bases by thickened red calyxes. All parts of sassafras trees are aromatic. From the bark of the roots of the American kind oil of sassafras, used commercially as a flavoring and fragrance, is extracted. The lumber is rather weak and coarse but is durable in contact with the ground and is resistant to insects. It is used for boxes, inexpensive furniture, posts, rails and fuel.

Umbellularia—California-Laurel

One species, the California-laurel (U. californica), constitutes Umbellularia. It is a green-barked evergreen tree that reaches an ultimate height of 175 feet and a trunk diameter of 6 feet.

Flowering cherry. Prunus (Gottlieb Hampfler)

Under forest conditions it develops a straight trunk, clear of branches for 30 to 40 feet from the ground, and a narrow head of upright branches; in the open it has a short, thick trunk and stout, long limbs that form a dense, wide, rounded head. The glossy, deep yellow-green leaves are elliptic to lanceolate and are up to 6 inches long. The flowers, small and yellowish, are followed by yellowish green fruits that resemble olives. California-laurel wood is one of the finest and most beautiful for cabinetwork and finishing work; it is hard, fine-grained, and rich yellowish brown. The bark and especially the leaves of this tree contain a volatile oil which, inhaled through the nostrils from crushed materials, induces sneezing and violent pain over the eyes. The California-laurel inhabits the Pacific slope of southwestern Oregon and California.

CHAPTER 19

The Rhoeadales

CAPPARIDACEAE—CAPER FAMILY

This family is a member of the order Rhoedales, which consists predominantly of herbaceous plants and includes such well known kinds as poppies, mignonette, spider flower (Cleome), cabbage, radish and sweet alyssum. The flowers are always bisexual.

Crateva

This is the only genus of the caper family, consisting mostly of shrubs and small trees, that we shall discuss, and only one of its nine species, all tropical, is of sufficient importance to be included here. Crateva religiosa, a native of southern India, Ceylon, Taiwan and Africa, is an attractive deciduous flowering tree that grows to a height of 25 feet and has a trunk about 1 foot in diameter. It forms a wide-spreading head furnished with trifoliate leaves and has clusters of creamy yellow to orange flowers, each with four long-clawed petals and long, protruding purple stamens. The globose, woody, yellow fruits contain numerous seeds. The species designation *religiosa* refers to the fact that this tree is revered in India; it is planted there for its bloom and for its bitter leaves. In Africa the leaves are used as a pot herb and are eaten as a vegetable. In Hong Kong *Crateva religiosa* is planted as a street tree.

MORINGACEAE—MORINGA FAMILY

Moringa

Of this family of one genus, *Moringa*, and twelve Asiatic, African and Madagascan species, the most important member is the horseradish tree *(M. oleifera)*, a native of India. The family represents a connecting link between the Capparidaceae and the Caesalpinioidae subfamily of the Leguminosae. The horseradish tree is so named because its roots taste like and are used like those of horseradish. It becomes about 25 feet tall and has fernlike leaves that are much divided and are sometimes 2 feet long. The white flowers, each about 1 inch in diameter, are in panicles and are succeeded by long, slender-angled pods that contain triangular-winged seeds. The young pods, rich in vitamin C, are used in curries and the seeds are fried and eaten. From the seeds is extracted oil of ben, used for lubrication, soap, perfume and salad oil. Various parts of the tree are used medicinally.

CHAPTER 20

The Rosales

The order Rosales includes many familiar families and genera. It is characterized by flower parts that generally occur in distinct layers or whorls rather than in spirals and typically in fives or multiples of five. The styles are usually separate, even when more than one carpel is united to form the ovary.

PITTOSPORACEAE—PITTOSPORUM FAMILY

The Pittosporaceae, a major family of the Rosales, comprises nine genera and two hundred species of trees, shrubs and woody vines ranging from Africa and eastern Asia through the islands of the Pacific to New Zealand and Australia. Its members are evergreen and have leathery, usually undivided leaves. The seeds are often glossy black and embedded in a sticky pulp.

Pittosporum

The 150 species of this genus have the same geographical distribution as the family, most of them being natives of the Southern Hemisphere. Several species are cultivated as ornamentals in warm climates. Ob the tree kinds, the lemonwood of New Zealand *(P. eugenioides)* is a beautiful example. It has masses of honey-scented, yellowish green flowers and leaves that emit a lemon-like odor when bruised. Another New Zealander, *P. crassifolium*, inhabits coastal areas and, like many other plants from such locations, has thick, fleshy leaves *(crassifolium* means thick-leaved), the better to withstand drying winds and sun. This species with black bark and deep purple flowers, reaches a maximum height of 30 feet. Of Australian kinds, the Victoria-box *(P. undulatum)* is of interest. Attaining a height of 40 feet, it is called mock-orange. The butterbush or willow pittosporum *(P. phillyraeoides)* is a very ornamental kind with pendulous branches and narrow willow-like leaves. It grows to a height of 20 feet and has yellow flowers. It is Australian. Another Australian, diamond-laurel or Queensland pittosporum *(P. rhombifolium)*, which attains a height of 80 feet, is one of the tallest species of the genus. It has rhomboid oval leaves that are coarsely toothed above their middles and clusters of small white flowers followed by bright orange-yellow berry-like fruits.

HAMAMELIDACEAE—WITCH-HAZEL FAMILY

Eighty species of deciduous and evergreen trees and shrubs are distributed among the twenty-three genera that comprise this chiefly subtropical family. They occur in North America, Asia, South Africa, Madagascar and Australia. None is native to Europe, although before the Ice Age, in the Tertiary Era, they were abundant there. Its wide distribution and the fact that the witch-hazel family is so diverse that eleven of its genera are monotypic (consist of a single species) strongly suggests that it is very old. Many of its members have stellate (starlike) branched hairs; all have simple, toothed or lobed leaves.

In addition to the genera discussed below, less well-known members of the witch-hazel family include *Exbucklandia,* also called *Bucklandia.* The Malayan-aspen *(E. populnea)* of India, Malaya, Sumatra and southern China is a handsome, massive-trunked tree with large glossy, long-stalked leaves, each with three prominent points; it becomes 100 feet tall and its lumber is of good quality. *Altingia* consists of seven large evergreen trees that range from Assam, southern China and the Malay Peninsula to Sumatra and Java. They are excellent timber trees. The evergreen genus *Sycopsis,* which is native from Assam and China to the Philippines and New Guinea, contains *S. formosana,* endemic to Taiwan where it forms pure stands of tall specimens, and *S. sinensis,* a 45-foot-tall tree of China. *Rhodeleia* consists of seven rhododendron-like evergreen trees and shrubs of southeastern Asia that have flowers pollinated by birds. *R. championii* grows up to 50 feet in height and has glaucous gray foliage and red flowers. *Distylium,* with twelve species in Asia and three in Mexico and Central America, includes a few small evergreen trees.

Hamamelis—Witch-Hazel

Here belong six species of trees and shrubs of North America and eastern Asia. Their flowers have narrow, strap-shaped yellow petals. An American species, sometimes of tree size, is *H. virginiana,* which is spontaneous from Canada to Florida and to Nebraska and Texas. Usually a crooked-branched shrub, it occasionally reaches a height of 25 feet. Its obovate or elliptic coarsely toothed leaves are 3 to 5 inches long. They persist well into the fall and then turn yellow, and at the same time bright yellow flowers bespangle the slender branches. The capsular fruits do not ripen until the following autumn; then they dry, contract and expel their solitary, slimy seeds, almost with the speed of an air-gun pellet, up to a distance of 40 feet. This witch-hazel is of considerable commercial importance; from its twigs, branches, and leaves is distilled an astringent extract. The largest American species is *H. macrophylla,* a native of the southeastern United States. It closely resembles *H. virginiana* but has smaller and more shallowly lobed leaves that are more symmetrical at their bases. Its maximum height is about 45 feet. Forked branches of American witch-hazels are favorites as water-divining rods.

The chief Asiatic species are the Japanese *H. japonica* and the Chinese *H. mollis.* The

Sweet gum. *Liquidambar styraciflua* (Gottscho-Schleisner)

leaves of the former are glabrous or very slightly pubescent on their undersides at maturity, whereas those of the latter are covered with gray hairs. Both grow up to 30 feet in height and have spreading branches. Their flowers appear in midwinter, the fragile-looking petals withstanding temperatures as low as 0° F without injury. The Chinese witch-hazel is decidedly the most beautiful and its flowers the most fragrant of all witch-hazels. It is of interest to note that the word "wich" in the name is akin to the word "weak," meaning pliant, and refers to the supple branchlets and twigs.

Liquidambar—Sweet Gum

Six species of North American and Asiatic deciduous trees compose this genus. In preglacial times liquidambars grew in Europe, but we have only fossil remains of these. Both the botanical and the common names of the genus refer to the fragrant balsamic resin, storax or styrax, obtained from all species, but chiefly from *L. orientalis.* It is used in perfumes, soaps, cosmetics, incense, lacquers, medicines and as a flavoring

London plane tree. Platanus acerifolia (Andreas Feininger)

for tobaccos. Liquidambars have unisexual flowers, without petals, in dense globose heads, and long-stalked, pendulous, spherical spiny fruits. Their palmate, five- to seven-lobed leaves somewhat resemble those of maples but are alternate rather than in pairs. On their undersides are tufts of hair in the axils of the main veins. The one American species, the sweet gum (*L. styraciflua*), is an important timber tree with a natural range from Connecticut to Illinois, and to Florida, Mexico, Guatemala, Venezuela and Honduras. It occasionally reaches a height of 150 feet with a bole 5 feet in diameter, and it forms a symmetrical, pyramidal tree. In fall its leaves turn brilliant crimson; its usually corky branches are conspicuous in winter. The wood of this sweet gum is used extensively for furniture, interior trim, veneers, boxes, barrels and baskets. As a source of storax this species is chiefly exploited in Central America. Storax was known and used in medicines and in perfumes by the ancient Mexicans.

Levant storax is obtained from *L. orientalis,*

a tree that grows up to 60 feet tall and is abundant along the coastal regions of Asia Minor. The gum accumulates in the inner bark as a result of bruising the outer bark and is recovered by boiling the interior layers in sea water. The leaves of this tree have usually five lobes and are completely hairless. In southern China and Taiwan *L. formosana* is native. It grows to a height of 130 feet and frequently has a stoutly buttressed trunk. Its usually three-lobed leaves turn rich red in fall.

EUCOMMIACEAE— EUCOMMIA FAMILY

Eucommia

One species of this genus, *Eucommia ulmoides,* is the only representative of the family. As *ulmoides* indicates, it resembles an elm, and some botanists think that it should be included in the same order as the elms, the Urticales, rather than in the Rosales.

Characterized by twigs that have a laminated pith and by the rubber latex found in all parts of the tree except the wood, *Eucommia ulmoides* attains a height of 60 feet and forms a broad, rounded head of ascending branches. Its deciduous, toothed leaves are ovate or elliptic. If a leaf is broken and the parts pulled an inch or two asunder, fine strands of rubber stretch between the two pieces of leaf; the same result is obtained by breaking and pulling apart a piece of inner bark or one of the winged fruits. First known from Western China, *Eucommia ulmoides* has never been found in a wild state; it is known only as a cultivated tree. It is hardy in southern New England, farther north than any other rubber-producing tree. Unfortunately its rubber content is too low—in the bark only three percent of the dry weight—to favor commercial extraction. The bark is employed medicinally in China.

PLATANACEAE—PLANE TREE FAMILY

Platanus—Plane Tree, Buttonwood

This genus, the only one in the family Platanaceae, consists of ten species of deciduous trees, which have maple-like leaves and bark that

American plane tree. Platanus occidentalis (Rutherford Platt)

flakes from the trunks in large irregular patches. The leaves, unlike those of maples, are alternate, with the base of each leaf stalk fitting like a cap over the axillary bud; not until the leaf falls or is pulled off is the bud revealed. The inconspicuous unisexual flowers of plane trees are borne in dense globular heads and appear with the unfolding leaves. Each head consists of blooms of one sex only, the males and females usually being suspended on separate stalks. The flower heads of both sexes look alike; following pollination, which is effected by wind, the females develop into globular seed heads which are conspicuous after leaf fall. The Platanaceae is most nearly related to the witch-hazel family, the Hamamelidaceae.

The American plane tree or buttonwood (*P. occidentalis*) is often called sycamore; this is somewhat confusing because a species of maple (*Acer pseudoplatanus*) is known in Great Britain as the sycamore and in North America as the sycamore-maple. The name sycamore was applied to the maple because it was deliberately selected to represent the fig (*Ficus sycamorous*) in religious dramas in the Middle Ages and the fig was the original sycamore.

The buttonwood is the most massive and probably the tallest deciduous tree of North America; at its best it may be 170 feet high with a trunk diameter of 14 feet and a massive irregular head as much as 100 feet in diameter. Identifying characteristics are the middle lobe of the leaf, which is broader than long, and fruiting heads that are usually solitary or, more rarely, in pairs. An inhabitant of moist bottomlands and watersides, this native from Maine to Florida and Texas supplies lumber for crates and boxes, furniture, woodenware, butchers' blocks, cooperage and plywood. Attractively figured samples are known to furniture manufacturers as lacewood. In the southwestern United States and northern Mexico are two other species called sycamores, *P. racemosa* and *P. wrightii*, which grow to a height of 80 or 90 feet, the former with a trunk diameter up to 9 feet, the latter with one up to 5 feet. Their trunks are often divided fairly close to the ground into several major branches, which may be contorted and inclined or prostrate for part of their length; but sometimes the trunks are solitary, erect and free of branches for a considerable height. Both *P. racemosa* and *P. wrightii* have several seedheads on each stalk, the former up to seven, the latter up to four. The leaves of *P. racemosa* have

three or five lobes, those of *P. wrightii* five to seven. The winter buds of *P. racemosa* are nearly one-half inch long while those of *P. wrightii* scarcely exceed one-eighth inch in length. There are five rather similar species of *Platanus* confined to Mexico and one, *P. chiapensis*, to Mexico and Guatemala. They have spreading crowns, grow to a height of about 125 feet with trunk diameters up to 6 feet and are most abundant near streams and lakes. Their lumber is used locally for woodenware, spoons and construction.

The Oriental plane (*P. orientalis*), a native of southeastern Europe and western Asia, grows to a height of 150 feet with a trunk diameter of 16 feet or more. It has more deeply lobed leaves than the American buttonwood and bears its seed heads mostly in strings of two to six. It attains a great age, probably living about a thousand years or more. This is the chinar tree of Asia Minor and Kashmir. In the Old Testament (*Genesis* 30:37 and *Ezekiel* 31:8) references are made to this plane tree, and the defeat of Xerxes in battle in 480 B. C. is said by Herodotus to have been caused by that king dallying too long with his army, enjoying the pleasant environment of a grove of plane trees.

Most widely cultivated is the London plane (*P. acerifolia*), which nowhere grows wild. It is believed to be a hybrid between the American buttonwood and the Oriental plane, but its origin is uncertain. It was known before 1700 and very likely originated in Spain as a chance seedling. It is a vigorous tree that thrives under adverse city conditions and stands pruning well. Because of this, it is freely planted as a street tree in major cities of the temperate regions including New York, London, Buenos Aires and many others. The London plane may exceed 100 feet in height and has a smooth, erect trunk. Its leaves have from three to five lobes and are intermediate in shape between those of its presumed parents. Its seed balls are usually in pairs; rarely they are solitary or in threes. Interestingly, the American buttonwood will not thrive in Europe nor does the Oriental plane prosper in the native home of the buttonwood, but the hybrid between these two, the London plane, luxuriates in both Europe and America — a good example of hybrid vigor.

ROSACEAE—ROSE FAMILY

One of the largest plant families, this contains

more than a hundred genera and three thousand or more species of trees, shrubs, vines and herbaceous plants. It is cosmopolitan in its distribution. Many of its members are cultivated for ornament. Comparatively few are exploited commercially but they include many popular fruits such as apples, pears, cherries, peaches, plums, quinces, raspberries, blackberries and strawberries. The flowers of the rose family are almost always bisexual and are usually five-petaled. The leaves generally have appendages called stipules at the bases of their leaf stalks.

Amelanchier—Service Berry or June Berry

This chiefly North American group of twenty-five deciduous trees and shrubs is confined naturally to the Northern Hemisphere; a few kinds inhabit Europe and Asia. All are handsome in bloom, and all have simple, toothed leaves. They differ from the nearly related apples and pears in technical characters of the ovaries, and, more obviously, in having fruits that are juicy and berry-like. Tallest of the species is *A. canadensis*, which inhabits the eastern United States and attains a maximum height of 65 feet and occasionally a trunk diameter of 1½ feet. In early spring its nodding racemes of white flowers make a pleasing display, followed shortly by a haze of grayish young foliage. The young leaves of this *Amelanchier*, unlike any others, are hairy on both sides. In fall the leaves turn yellow and red. The maroon-purple fruits are edible. Distinguishable from *A. canadensis* by its quite hairless and purplish young foliage, *A. laevis* is a very graceful kind. It ranges throughout the eastern United States and adjacent Canada and at its best is 40 feet tall. In fall its leaves become yellow and red. Its fruits are red and berry-like. The leaves of *A. florida*, which occasionally attains 30 feet in height and occurs from Michigan to Oregon and Washington, are much more coarsely toothed than those of the species discussed above. They are smooth on their upper sides and either smooth or sparsely hairy beneath. The flowers, in erect racemes, are white and are succeeded by deep red or purple edible berry-like fruits that are great favorites of birds and animals, especially bears. An interesting hybrid between *A. canadensis* and *A. laevis*, with larger flowers than either, is *A. grandiflora*. It has purplish young foliage that at first is pubescent but soon becomes glabrous. It has white or pale pink flowers and red to black edible fruits.

A beautiful flowering tree of Japan and Korea is *A. asiatica*, which grows to a height of 45 feet, has nodding racemes of white flowers and edible bluish-black fruits. It differs from *A. canadensis* in that its young leaves are glabrous on their upper surfaces and the tops of its ovaries are densely woolly. The leaves are toothed to their bases, a feature which distinguishes it from its variety *A. a. sinica*, a native of western China that has smaller leaves with teeth only above their middles. Rarely does the European *A. ovalis* attain a height of 20 feet. This kind is distinguished by having five styles that are separate right to their bases. Its white flowers, carried in erect racemes, are larger than those of most service berries. Its blue-black fruits are covered with a purplish bloom; they are edible but not very palatable. When the leaves are young their undersides are covered with pure white hairs but they lose these as they mature.

Crataegus—Hawthorn

Many hundreds of species have been described as belonging to this taxonomically bewildering genus but it seems probable that many represent hybrids. A conservative evaluation suggests that there are two hundred species, all native to the Northern Hemisphere. The hawthorns are dense, usually thorny, deciduous low trees or shrubs that bear flattish clusters of small, usually white five-petaled flowers in spring and small berry-like fruits in fall. Their thorns represent modified branches. The genus is most abundant in North America.

One particularly worthy of note is *Crateagus arnoldiana*, a native of New England and New York. This tree grows up to 30 feet in height and ripens its bright crimson fruits earlier than any other kind. It has zigzag branches and is dense and thorny. The cockspur thorn (*C. crusgallii*) is sometimes 35 feet tall. It grows throughout northeastern America, has widespreading branches and formidable thorns that are often several inches long. Its lustrous, handsome foliage turns orange and scarlet in fall. Its berries are bright red.

A species that has a range from the eastern seaboard to South Dakota and Kansas is the downy hawthorn (*C. mollis*). This tree has fruits so large that they resemble small crabapples, and leaves that are conspicuously bigger than those of most hawthorns. The fruits are pear-shaped and red. The Washington hawthorn (*C. phaenopyrum*) is one of the finest ornamentals.

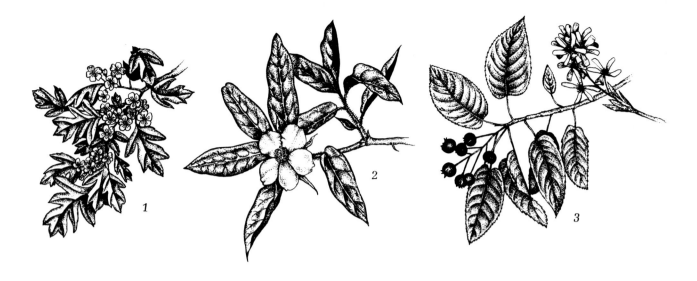

1. *Crataegus monogyna*   2. *Mespilus germanica*   3. *Amelanchier canadensis (Charles Fracé)*

Thorny and densely branched, it becomes 30 feet tall and forms a broad, columnar head. Its lustrous leaves change to orange and scarlet in fall. It blooms later than most kinds and has glossy bright red fruits that remain attractive throughout the winter. This hawthorn is a native of the southeastern United States. An inhabitant of the northeastern United States, the species C. *pruinosa* is handsome, especially in fruit. It attains a height of 30 feet, is thorny, densely branched and has bluish green leaves and orange or red fruits. Remarkable for being the only hawthorn with blue fruits, the pomette bleue (*C. branchyantha*) of the southern United States grows up to 50 feet in height with a trunk diameter exceeding 1½ feet. It has stout, spreading branches and many short spines. Its leaves are unlobed or scarcely lobed. The fruits, bright blue and bloomy, are borne in small clusters. The black haw (*C. douglasii*) of the Pacific Northwest sometimes becomes 30 feet tall and may have a trunk diameter of 20 inches. It has glossy black-purple or black fruits which are edible and palatable. This species has short spines or sometimes none.

The most familiar European species is the English hawthorn (*C. monogyna*), which grows up to 35 feet in height and has fragrant white flowers and red fruits. Despite its colloquial name, it is not restricted as a native to the British Isles but is found on the continent of Europe, in North Africa and western Asia. It is a picturesque, rugged tree with a trunk up to 2 feet in diameter and branches that droop at the ends. It is the hawthorn of which hedges of

Great Britain and northern France are formed and it is similar to the lower-growing C. *oxycantha*, also called English hawthorn, but it is distinct in that its flowers normally have one rather than two styles and its fruits one rather than two or three seeds. *Crataegus monogyna* has a number of distinct varieties one of which, C. *m. aurea*, has yellow fruits. Its most interesting variety is the Glastonbury thorn (*C. m. praecox*), which in favorable climates blooms in midwinter and again in May. Even around New York it bears flowers in November, in England often in December and January. Legend has it that after the crucifixion of Christ, Joseph of Arimathea came to England to introduce Christianity. On Christmas Day he preached at Glastonbury but failed to move the inhabitants until his prayers were answered by a miracle. He thrust his staff into the earth and God caused it to burst into foliage and flower immediately. Since then, the miracle of the Christmas blooming of the Glastonbury thorn has been repeated annually. The other English hawthorn (*C. oxycantha*) has also a number of excellent varieties, including kinds with double flowers, pink flowers, red flowers and one with yellow fruits. C. *oxycantha* is rarely 20 feet in height.

In southern Europe, North Africa and western Asia the azarole (*C. azarolus*) is native. A slightly thorny kind, it grows up to a height of 30 feet and produces an abundance of quite large, whitish, yellow or red, apple-flavored fruits. It is distinguished from the English hawthorns by having three to five seeds in each fruit

1. *Prunus mahaleb* 2. *Prunus avium* 3. *Prunus americana (Charles Fracé)*

and in the seeds, locking cavities on their inner surfaces. From the nearly related *C. orientalis* it can be told by its lustrous leaves. A variety of the azarole called *C. a. sinaica* is separately classified on the basis of its completely glabrous leaves. It grows in western Asia, including Sinai, and attains a maximum height of 40 feet.

One of the most beautiful hawthorns is *C. orientalis*, a dull-leaved tree which rarely exceeds 20 feet in height and is a native of southern Europe and western Asia; its pubescent fruits are coral red or orange-red. In China *C. pinnatifida major* is widely cultivated for its edible fruits, which are often seen candied and strung on little sticks in the markets. The fruits of the variety *major* are considerably larger than those of the species, the latter measuring about 1 inch in diameter. They are red and borne on trees that have a mature height of about 20 feet and have few or no thorns. Both the species and its variety are handsome trees. Asiatic hawthorns that have black fruits include *C. chlorosarca*, a native of Manchuria, and *C. dsungarica* of northern China and Siberia. They are closely related but the first has more shallowly lobed leaves with sharper points and finer teeth. They are small trees with purplish brown shoots

Cydonia—Quince

Ancient Greeks and Romans esteemed the quince as a symbol of happiness, love and fertility. They dedicated it to Venus and used its fruits in marriage ceremonies. The tree is a native of Per-

sia and adjacent lands and grows to a height of about 25 feet. It is rounded, broad-topped and low-branched. The flowers, pink or white, are solitary at the ends of short twigs. They are succeeded by very fragrant, pear-shaped fruits, 3 inches or more in diameter, that ripen a light yellow and are used for jelly. When raw they are astringent and inedible.

Eriobotrya—Loquat

About thirty species, all natives of the warmer parts of Asia, are included in this genus, but only one, the loquat (*E. japonica*), is of any considerable significance. This evergreen, with large, coarsely toothed leaves, has its home in southern China and Japan and is cultivated there and in many other warm-temperate climates for its pear-shaped edible fruits borne in clusters. The white, fragrant flowers are partly hidden among rusty woolly hairs. The tree grows as tall as 30 feet and is an attractive ornamental. Its leaves are glossy green above, rusty tomentose beneath and have conspicuous parallel veins running from the midrib to the marginal teeth.

Licania

This comprises a large group of shrubs and trees chiefly of the Americas. The wood is used for charcoal and construction but its resistance to decay in contact with the ground is poor. Species used in Central America for lumber are *L. arborea* and *L. hypoleuca*. There, too, the monkey-

169

apple (L. platypus) is esteemed for its yellow juicy fruits. The seeds of the oiticia (L. rigida) of Brazil contain a high percentage of an oil commercially important as an ingredient of varnishes and paints. In northeastern South America L. mollis and L. heteromorpha are exploited to some extent for their hard, strong, heavy lumber.

Malus—Apple and Crab-Apple

Thirty-five species of North Temperate region deciduous trees and tall shrubs comprise this well-known genus, some of which have provided food for man since prehistoric times, as remains of the Neolithic and Bronze Ages indicate. Apples have been cultivated for more than two thousand years. In the third century B. C. Cato recorded seven varieties, and apple trees were brought by Caesar to Great Britain. With the opening of the New World to Europeans they were transported across the Atlantic and soon became orchard fruits in North America.

Apples cultivated for their edible fruits fall into two main groups. The larger fruited varieties are derivatives of M. sylvestris, and the crab-apples are hybrids of the Siberian crab-apple (M. baccata) but it is possible that other species are also involved. The species mentioned are rugged, broad-headed trees with a maximum height of about 40 feet, the former a native of Europe and western Asia, the latter of Siberia, Manchuria and China. Other species and hybrids of Malus, grown chiefly for the beauty of their flowers and fruits, are called flowering crab-apples. Of nine species native to North America the most noteworthy are the prairie crab-apple (M. ionensis), the garland crab-apple (M. coronaria), the Oregon crab-apple (M. fusca) and the southern crab-apple (M. angustifolia). All grow from 25 to 30 feet in height and have more or less lobed and sharp-toothed leaves and pink or white flowers. The prairie crab-apple, a native of the north-central United States, has a double-flowered variety called Bechtel's crab that is often cultivated. The garland crab-apple ranges from Ontario and New York to Alabama and Missouri. The Oregon crab-apple occurs as a native from California to Alaska. The southern crab-apple, which has its home from Virginia to Florida and Missouri, is unusual because it is semi-evergreen. Its flowers are fragant.

Of great ornamental value are a group of Oriental crab-apples. Together with their many hybrids and varieties, these are the most popular of the genus for garden decoration. Without attempting any exhaustive treatment of the species, let alone the garden forms, mention must be made of the showy crab-apple (M. floribunda) which bears red fruits and a profusion of carmine red flowers that change to white. The tea crab (M. hupehensis) of China when in bloom resembles a cherry tree. Its fragrant flowers are white or pink, its fruits greenish yellow with red cheeks. Probably a native of Japan or China, it grows to a height of 25 feet. Malus spectabilis, which also hails from China, is about the same height and has showy pink flowers and yellowish fruits. From the same source comes M. toringoides, a handsome 25-foot tree with creamy white flowers and red-cheeked, yellow fruits.

The only Malus other than M. sylvestris that is native to Europe is M. florentina. A handsome, small, round-headed tree with white flowers and red fruits, it occurs in Italy.

Mespilus—Medlar

The only species of this genus, the medlar (M. germanica), is a sometimes thorny, usually crooked, 20-foot tree that has edible fruits and is native from Europe to central Asia. Its young twigs are very hairy, its flowers solitary and white or tinged pink. The brown apple-shaped fruits, up to 2 inches in diameter, have at the end opposite the stalk a conspicuous persistent calyx surrounding a broad opening. They are not suitable for eating until they are bordering on decay.

Photinia

Here belong sixty deciduous and evergreen simple-leaved shrubs and trees that are natives from the Himalayas to Japan and Sumatra. Their white flowers occur in rather dense clusters, each with five roundish petals, about twenty stamens and two styles. The small berry-like red fruits resemble those of hawthorns; each contains one to four seeds. The evergreen kinds include the Chinese P. davidsoniae and P. serrulata, which attain a maximum height of about 40 feet and have oblong to oval leathery leaves. Those of P. serrulata are rich brownish red when young, and form a lovely foil for the white flowers. The shorter-stalked leaves and downy flower stalks easily distinguish P. davidsoniae from P. serrulata. The leaf stalks of the former are one-half inch long or less, those of the latter three-quarters of an inch or more.

Deciduous photinias of tree size are *P. villosa* of Japan, China and Korea and the closely related *P. beauverdiana* of central and western China. They attain heights of 20 to 30 feet. The ovate oblong leaves of the former have five to seven pairs of veins, while those of the latter have eight to fourteen pairs. Their fruits are bright red.

Prunus

In the broad sense this genus consists of 430 deciduous and evergreen species of trees and shrubs mostly of the North Temperate zone. Some botanists split the group into several genera, placing the cherries in *Cerasus*, the almonds in *Amygadalus*, the cherry-laurels in *Laurocerasus* and so on. We follow the one-genus concept. *Prunus* includes all of the common temperate region stone fruits and many highly ornamental species. Their leaves are alternate and usually undivided, the flowers white or pink and normally bisexual, each with twenty or more stamens and a solitary pistil. Each fleshy fruit contains a single seed called a stone. Most deciduous species bloom normally before their leaves expand, but some bloom with their leaves.

American Prunus

American *Prunus* falls into four groups: plums, cherries, bird-cherries and cherry-laurels. The plums have fleshy fruits which are slightly bilobed, have flattened stones and are usually covered with a waxy bloom. The cherries have smaller fleshy fruits containing round stones and lack a waxy coating or bloom. The bird-cherries are similar to the cherries but have their flowers and fruits in spikelike racemes. The cherry-laurels are evergreen and have cherry-like fruits with little or no pulp, and thin-shelled stones.

The most noteworthy of the plums is *P. americana*, a species native through most of the eastern and central United States as far south as Georgia and New Mexico. A spreading tree, it grows up to 30 feet tall and has glabrous, pointed leaves. The fruits are red or yellowish. This species is the ancestor of many orchard plums. Closely related, but having a more southern distribution, is the big-tree plum (*P. mexicana*), which grows as a native from Tennessee and Oklahoma into Mexico; at its best it attains a height of 40 feet. From *P. americana* it differs in having downy undersides to its leaves and in not producing sprouts from its roots. Its fruits are purplish red. The hortulan plum (*P. hortulana*), a parent of a number of varieties culti-

vated for their fruits, has its home from Kentucky and Tennessee to Iowa and Oklahoma. About 30 feet tall, it has red to yellow fruits with little or no bloom. It does not produce sprouts from its roots. The wild goose plum *P. musoniana*) suckers profusely from its roots, has thinner leaves than *P. hortulana* and attains a height of about 25 feet. Its range extends from Kentucky and Tennessee to Kansas and Texas. It bears red or yellow fruits.

With a natural range extending from Newfoundland to North Carolina and westward to British Columbia and Colorado, the wild red cherry or pin cherry (*P. pensylvanica*) grows as a native from Newfoundland to British Columbia and southward to North Carolina and Colorado. A tree up to 40 feet tall with a trunk up to 20 inches in diameter, its flowers, four or five together in umbels, are succeeded by light red fruits about one-quarter of an inch in diameter. Differing from the wild red cherry in that they belong to the bird-cherry section of Prunus and have their many flowers bunched in terminal racemes, is the chokecherry (*P. virginiana*) and the wild black cherry (*P. serotina*). In the former the calyx is deciduous in fruit, in the latter persistent. The chokecherry is at home from Newfoundland to Saskatchewan and southward to North Carolina and Kansas. Its flowers are somewhat fragrant, and its fruits, which are dark red to nearly black or sometimes yellow, are one-quarter of an inch or slightly more in diameter. The chokecherry rarely grows taller than 25 feet.

The largest American *Prunus* is the wild black cherry, which attains an impressive 100 feet in height and a trunk diameter of 4 to 5 feet. It has a narrow, oblong crown and handsome foliage. Its agreeably flavored, dark red to almost black fruits are almost a half-inch in diameter. The wood of the wild black cherry is esteemed for interior trim and furniture and is the only American species exploited commercially for its lumber. The tree grows naturally from Nova Scotia to North Dakota and to Florida and Texas and, in slightly different form, extends through Mexico and tropical America into Peru and Chile. The southern type, called capulin, has been named *P. serotina salicifolia* and *P. capuli*. It has narrower leaves and larger fruits than the wild black cherry of the United States.

Evergreen *Prunus* or cherry-laurels that attain tree size are represented in North America by five species. Mostly in coastal regions from

North Carolina to Texas, *P. carolininia* is abundant and attains 40 feet in height. Known as wild-orange and mock-orange, it has creamy white flowers and glossy black fruits. The myrtle-leaved cherry-laurel *(P. myrtifolia)* differs from the above in having minute, sharp-pointed, rather than round, calyx lobes and orange-colored fruits. It occurs in southern Florida, the West Indies and from Mexico to Brazil. Similar, but with larger leaves, is the West Indian cherry-laurel *(P. occidentalis)*, a tree that is sometimes 50 feet tall and bears fragrant white flowers and 1-inch-long purple fruits. Very distinct is the islay *(P. ilicifolia)* of Pacific North America. Its leaves are conspicuously spiny-toothed and holly-like; the flowers are white and in slender racemes, and the fruits black-purple. This tree grows to a maximum height of about 30 feet. By some considered to be a form of *P. ilicifolia,* the Islands cherry *(P. lyonii)* differs chiefly in having only a few minute teeth on the margins of its leaves. It inhabits the islands off the coast of southern California.

European Prunus

The native *Prunus* of Europe include plums, cherries and cherry-laurels. With the exception of the Portugal-laurel, all range also into Asia. It is from these Eurasian kinds that almost all of our common orchard stone fruits are derived.

The common plum *(P. domestica)*, cultivated in many orchard varieties, is usually less than 40 feet tall and has white flowers and usually bloomy, bluish black, sweet freestone fruits. The undersides of its leaves are pubescent. The damson or bullace *(P. d. institita)* is a smaller tree with smaller leaves and fruits and young twigs that are pubescent. The sweet cherry, mazzard or gean *(P. avium)* has birchlike bark and a trunk that sometimes exceeds 2 feet in diameter. It is sometimes 100 feet in height, is pyramidal, has pure white flowers and blackish red, sweet or bitter, but not acid, fruits almost or quite 1 inch in diameter. Its leaves are coarsely hairy on the veins beneath. This is the parent of many orchard varieties, including the heart, bigarreau, and duke cherries. The sour cherry, *(P. cerasus),* unlike the sweet cherry, suckers freely from its roots; its leaves are glabrous beneath and it has red, acid fruits. It attains a height of about 30 feet. This is the ancestor of such orchard varieties as morello and Montmorency cherries. One variety, the All Saints' cherry *(P. c. semperflorens)*, blooms in summer and fall. A third

Eurasian species is the St. Lucie or mahaleb cherry *(P. mahaleb)*, a slender, round-topped, green-twigged tree up to 40 feet in height with small, fragrant white flowers which, unlike those of the sweet cherry and sour cherry, form in distinct racemes. The inedible fruits, less than one-quarter of an inch in diameter, are bright red. The fragrant wood is made into tobacco pipe-stems. The European bird cherry *(P. padus)* is very similar to the American chokecherry *(P. virginiana)*. Technical differences are that in *P. padus* the inside of the calyx tube is hairy, the stalks are longer and the fragrant flowers larger. Under favorable conditions *P. padus* attains a height of 50 feet. Its flowers, in drooping or spreading racemes 3 to 6 inches long, are a third- to a half-inch wide. The fruits, one-third inch or less in diameter, are black and bitter. This tree is native from western Europe to Japan.

Evergreen species of Europe include the Portugal-laurel *(P. lusitanica)* and the cherry-laurel *(P. laurocerasus)*. The leaves of the former are toothed and are shorter than the racemes of the flowers; the leaves of the latter are usually without teeth and longer than the flower racemes. The Portugal-laurel rarely exceeds 20 feet in height; the cherry-laurel is sometimes 60 feet tall. Both spread their branches widely and have handsome shining green ovate or oblong leaves, those of the Portugal-laurel being up to 5 inches in length and those of the cherry-laurel up to 6 inches or even more. The flowers of both are dull white, their fruits dark purple.

Asiatic Prunus

In addition to the Eurasian species discussed above under European *Prunus*, there are a large number of kinds endemic to Asia, so many in fact that only the more important can be considered here. The plum group includes the myrobalan or cherry plum *(P. cerasifera)* of southwestern Asia, a kind much used by orchardists as a stock upon which to graft superior varieties. A somewhat thorny, slender-branched tree up to 25 feet tall, it has solitary white flowers and slightly bloomy red fruits 1 inch or somewhat more in diameter. Its leaves have hairs only on their undersides along the midribs. A purple-leaved variety, *P. c. atropurpurea,* is often planted as an ornamental. The Japanese plum *(P. salicina)* is cultivated in several orchard varieties and as a result of hybridization with the apricot has produced the fruit known as the plumcot. The Japanese plum, about 30 feet in height, is cultivated in Japan but probably was originally a native of China. It differs from the cherry plum in having its flowers usually in threes and in having heart-shaped, yellow, red or green fruits 2 to 2½ inches in diameter. The apricot plum of China (P. simonii), a narrow, pyramidal tree up to 25 feet in height, has erect branches and peachlike foliage. Its white flowers, occurring singly or two or three together, are succeeded by aromatic, pleasantly flavored, brick red or maroon fruits that are up to 2 inches broad and are flattened at the top and bottom. The flesh is yellow and of the clingstone type.

Apricots, which are all Asiatic, differ from plums in having flowers that occur singly or in pairs instead of in cymes, fruits that are velvety, at least until they are nearly mature, stems that normally separate from the fruits when they are picked, and stones that usually have conspicuous longitudinal ridges and a groove along their margins. The common apricot (P. armeniaca), a round-crowned tree up to 30 feet tall, originated in western Asia and was early brought into cultivation. Many authorities believe that this is the "apple" referred to in Genesis, for the true apple was unknown in Bible lands. Its white or pale pink flowers are succeeded by palatable reddish-cheeked yellow fruits that contain smooth stones. The Japanese apricot (P. mume) has pitted stones and fragrant light pink flowers. Its greenish or yellow fruits are scarcely edible. This ornamental is a native of Japan and China.

The Oriental or Japanese cherries include some of the most charming small flowering trees of temperate regions. One of these is the Yoshina cherry (P. yedoensis), a kind much cultivated in Japan and perhaps of hybrid origin. It grows to a height of 45 feet, forms a flat-topped crown and has leaves that are hairy only on the veins beneath. Its white, slightly fragrant flowers are borne profusely. Its fruits are black. Another, P. serrulata, cultivated in Japan for hundreds of years, is the parent of well over a hundred named varieties of flowering Japanese cherries. Most of the kinds planted for ornament in Japan and China are of this kind. Their leaves are glabrous, the flowers single or double, white to pink, and range from ½ inch to 2½ inches in diameter; those of some varieties are fragrant. The fruits are black. Garden kinds are usually 25 feet tall or less but the wild species attains three times that height. It differs from the Yoshina cherry in having bell-shaped glabrous calyx tubes instead of cylindrical,

usually pubescent ones. A close relative, distinguishable by its densely pubescent leaves, also with single or double, white or pink flowers, is the Naden cherry (P. sieboldii). It is the earliest of the double-flowered cherries to bloom. The three flowering cherries discussed above leaf out when in bloom but the rose-bud cherry (P. subhirtella) produces its leaves after its flowers fade. The flowers are about three-quarters of an inch in diameter. One of the earliest Oriental cherries to bloom, it is 30 feet tall, has leaves pubescent on their veins beneath and black fruits.

Two varieties are of special interest, a weeping one with markedly pendulous branches (P. s. pendula) and a fall-blooming kind (P. s. autumnalis) which flowers in both fall and spring. Having glabrous leaves and decidedly thickened fruit stalks, the Taiwan cherry (P. campanulata) is a beautiful 25-foot tree with deep pink pendulous flowers 1 inch in diameter, and half-inch-long red fruits. It is a native of Taiwan and southern Japan. The bird cherries of Asia, which have elongated racemes of a dozen or more flowers, similar to those of the American P. virginiana and the European P. padus, include P. maackii of Manchuria and Korea, P. ssiori and P. buegeriana of northeast Asia and Japan, P. grayana of Japan and the Himalayan bird cherry (P. cornuta) of the Himalayas. Among bird cherries P. maackii is unique in bearing flowers on the shoots of the previous year instead of on those of the current season. It becomes 45 feet tall and has bright brownish red bark that peels like that of a birch. The Himalayan bird cherry is so similar to the European P. padus that some authorities regard it as simply a variation of that species. It grows to a height of 60 feet and has brownish purple fruits. Closely allied, but rarely exceeding 30 feet in height, P. grayana differs from P. padus chiefly in having no glands on its leaf stalks and in that its style is longer than the stamens. Its fruits are black. Distinguishable by its nearly white bark, P. ssiori attains a height of 75 feet and has black fruits. Its wood is used by the primitive Ainus of Japan for many domestic purposes.

Like plums, the fruits of peaches and almonds are furrowed down one side, but unlike plums, they have no bloom, that is, a waxy coating; except for the nectarine, they are pubescent. Three buds, the two lateral flower buds, are borne in each leaf axil. A native of China, the common peach (P. persica) was given its botanical name in the mistaken belief that it was a native of Persia. Cultivated since ancient times, it is about 25 feet tall, has pink flowers and fleshy, edible yellow and red fruits that contain hard, furrowed, deeply pitted stones. There are many horticultural varieties of which the nectarine (*P. p. nectarina*), with glabrous fruits, is one. The almond (*P. amygdalis*) is cultivated for its seeds, commonly called nuts. It differs from the peach in that its velvety fruits split as they dry to reveal the pitted stones. A native of western Asia and probably North Africa, this tree rarely exceeds 15 feet in height. The seeds of sweet almonds (*P. a. dulcis*) are eaten green or are roasted, salted, or made into paste. Those of the bitter almond (*P. a. amara*) contain the glucoside amygdalin which changes to prussic acid upon digestion; because of this, bitter almonds are unsuitable for food, although they are the source of oil of bitter almond. The poisonous principle is eliminated in the preparation from the oil of benzaldehyde, which is the flavoring principle of almond extract.

Pyrus — Pear

The chief differences between pears and apples are that the fruits of the former are decidedly gritty and are mostly pear-shaped rather than apple-shaped, and the styles of the flowers are not joined at their bases. A Eurasian genus, *Pyrus* consists of thirty deciduous species. By far the most important is the common pear (*P. communis*), cultivated in numerous varieties. This is a long-lived, broad-pyramidal tree indigenous to Europe and western Asia and old in cultivation, sometimes attaining a height of 60 feet with a trunk 3 feet in diameter. Its wood is of excellent quality but is not abundant enough to be of great commercial significance. Of even texture, it is excellent for carving and for making rules and drawing instruments. Other kinds worthy of notice include the Callery pear (*P. calleryana*), which was introduced from China by the great plant explorer E. H. Wilson. More resistant to fire-blight disease than other kinds, its foliage assumes beautiful shades of red in fall. Its tiny globular fruits have no value as food. The calyxes of this species are deciduous. The hardiest pear is *P. ussuriensis* of northeastern Asia, which attains 50 feet in height and is pyramidal in outline. Unlike most pears, its flowers in the bud stage are often pink, which adds to their attractiveness. Like the common pear, this kind has a persistent calyx. With foliage resembling that of a willow, as its names suggest, the willow-leaved pear (*P. salicifolia*) is the most ornamental of its genus. For several weeks after its leaves expand, they are a silky silvery gray and blend to advantage with the white flowers, which open at the same time as the expanding foliage. The leaves are up to 3½ inches long by more than one-half inch wide and they taper at both ends. The fruits, typically pear-shaped, are 1 inch long or a little more. This attractive species is a native of southeastern Europe and Asia Minor.

Sorbus — Mountain Ash

This is a group of about a hundred deciduous trees and shrubs of the North Temperate zone. They have simple, lobed or deeply pinnatified leaves, flatish clusters of creamy white flowers and, usually, red fruits, of which birds are inordinately fond. Although the fruits are berry-like in appearance, structurally they resemble apples and are highly decorative.

The American mountain-ash (*S. americana*) and the European mountain-ash or rowan (*S. aucuparia*) are very similar; a main difference is that the winter buds of the latter are not gummy and are covered with white tomentum, whereas those of the former are nearly hairless and are sticky. Closely related is another American species, *S. decora*, which has reddish pubescent, gummy winter buds and slightly pubescent and looser flower clusters than the hairless ones of *S. americana*. The flower clusters of the European mountain-ash vary from being hairy to nearly glabrous. The fruits of *S. decora*, which measure almost one-half inch in diameter, are almost twice as big as those of *S. americana*; those of *S. aucuparia* are one-third inch across. The two American kinds are tidy trees up to about 30 feet in height. *Sorbus americana* is indigenous from Newfoundland to North Carolina and Michigan, *S. decora* from Labrador to New York and Minnesota. The European mountain-ash, sometimes 60 feet tall, is spread widely through the cooler parts of Europe and Asia. It has smaller leaves and larger flowers than the American kinds. The mountain-ashes discussed above all have pinnate leaves and red fruits; a variety of *S. aucuparia*, called *xanthocarpa*, has orangle-yellow fruits. Of interest, too, is *S. a. edulis* which has larger fruits than typical rowans; they are especially suitable for making jellies.

The service tree (*S. domestica*), a species which occasionally reaches 60 feet in height, inhabits southern Europe, North Africa and western

Asia. It differs from the European mountain-ash in having rough, scaling bark, larger flowers and fruits, leaves conspicuously tomentose beneath and glutinous winter buds. Its red-tinged yellowish green or brownish fruits are apple- or pear-shaped and measure from ³/₄ to 1 inch in diameter. The service tree was well known to the ancient Greeks and Romans. In the fourth century B. C. Theophrastus described it as a cultivated tree and until well into the Middle Ages it was esteemed for its fruits. The development of more palatable kinds resulted in lessened interest in the service tree, although in Europe cider is still made from them. The fruits are not ready for eating until they have been frozen or have attained a state of incipient decay.

Eurasian species that have undivided leaves include the white beam (*S. aria*) and the wild service tree (*S. terminalis*). The white beam is especially partial to limestone and chalk soils. It has a rounded, rather open crown, white flowers in dense flat clusters and red berries speckled with brown. The undersides of its double-toothed leaves are completely covered with a dense felt of white hairs. This tree, which grows to a height of 70 feet, is indigenous through most of Europe and also in North Africa. The wild service tree differs from the white beam in having distinctly lobed leaves which at first have a thin tomentum on their undersurfaces but soon become glabrous and in its brown, bitter fruits. The tree, sometimes 70 feet tall, is very handsome; it is a native of much of Europe, North Africa and western Asia. Eastern Asia is the home of several excellent *Sorbus* species. *S. discolor* is noteworthy because of its white fruits. This native of northern China grows up to 30 feet in height. Remarkable for its unusual fruit color is *S. vilmorinii* of western China. This tree, scarcely 20 feet tall, has fruits that are pale rosy red. About 25 feet tall, *S. commixta* closely resembles the American mountain-ash but has smaller leaves and smaller and looser flowers and fruit clusters. It is a native of Japan and Korea. *S. folgeri*, native to central China, is a handsome tree with simple leaves that are white woolly beneath. It has arching, spreading branches and reaches a height of 25 feet. Another simple-leaved kind is *S. alnifolia*, a handsome native of Japan, Korea and China that develops a rounded crown up to

Right above: Acacia nilotica Right: Fruits of Acacia nilotica (Both, M. Krishnan)

Wattle trees. (Australian News and Information)

about 20 feet in height. Its leaves are glabrous or slightly pubescent beneath. Its fruits are orange or scarlet.

LEGUMINOSAE—PEA FAMILY

The third largest family of flowering plants, this group contains six hundred genera and twelve thousand species. Many are herbaceous, but a large number are trees and shrubs. Legumes live in every type of soil and climate. Most develop on their roots tubercles containing nitrogen-fixing bacteria, which enable plants to avail themselves of atmospheric nitrogen and actually enrich the soils in which they grow. The most characteristic feature of the Leguminosae is the fruit, called a legume. This is a dry pod, the product of a single ovary, that splits along two longitudinal sutures or (in a modified form) breaks apart between the seeds at transverse constrictions of the pod. The family is divided into three subfamilies which some botanists regard as distinct families, the Mimosoideae with quite regular, symmetrical flowers, the Caesalpinioideae with more or less irregular flowers, and the Papilionoideae with usually markedly asymmetrical flowers.

Acacia

The genus *Acacia,* consisting of more than 750 species of trees and shrubs, is widely dispersed in the tropics and subtropics and has a few representatives in temperate regions; most of them are trees. They belong to two groups, those with feathery bipinnate leaves, each consisting of many small leaflets, and those with apparently undivided leaves. The latter, however, are not true leaves but phyllodes, expanded petioles (leaf stalks) which serve the purposes of leaves. The morphology of the phyllodes is apparent in young seedlings, the first leaves of which are bipinnate with only a tendency to have flattened and broadened petioles. In successive leaves the leaf blades are reduced and finally disappear as the petioles become broader and more obviously phyllodes. Adult plants occasionally revert in part to the more primitive type and some of their phyllodes develop bipinnate leaf blades. With very few exceptions the phyllodine acacias are natives of Australia and islands of the Pacific; they are one of the most characteristic features of the flora of Australia and are there called wattles. Chiefly, acacias are natives of dry climates and are characteristically xerophytic, adapted to conserve water and to withstand drought. Lower growing kinds often form extensive scrub in semidesert and desert regions and are usually thorny. The thorns, which in some kinds are formidable, are modified stipules (appendages at the bases of leaves). The flowers of acacias are showy because of their numerous stamens, yellow, orange or white; they occur in globular or cylindrical heads, singly, paired or in clusters. Many acacias are sources of valuable commercial products, notably cutch, gum arabic, tanbark, perfumes and lumber. From them also are derived dyes and fibers. The shittam wood of which the Ark of the Covenant and furnishings of the Tabernacle were made was *A. seyal;* the same wood was used in burial caskets for

Above: Cootamundra wattle. Acacia baileyana (Ralph Cornell) Right: Woman's tongue. Albizzia lebbeck (Harriet Burkhart) Far right: Sweet thorn flowers. Acacia karroo (D. C. H. Plowes)

Overleaf left above: Golden shower. Cassia fistula (Ivan Polunin) Left: Golden shower flowers. (M. Krishnan) Right above: Flame of the forest. Butea frondosa (Janet Finch) Right: Powderpuff tree. Calliandra (Emil Javorsky). Far right: Flame of the forest flowers (Janet Finch)

ancient Egyptian kings. The genus *Acacia* includes many splendid ornamentals.

North American acacias of tree size, all small, include five or six species in the Southwest. The most important is the cassie (*A. farnesiana*) which, although now widely distributed in tropical and subtropical regions throughout the world, is believed to be indigenous from Texas to Chile. Rarely 30 feet in height or with a trunk as much as 1½ feet in diameter, the cassie is a small thorny tree or shrub that forms a rounded head of more or less pendulous branches. Its globular, very fragrant clusters of bright yellow flowers are borne singly, paired or in threes. Its finely divided foliage is deciduous. The cassie is cultivated in southern Europe for its flowers, used in making perfume. In South America its flowers and seed pods are used medicinally. The pods are used for tanning, dyeing and in the manufacture of ink. In warm countries it is planted as an ornamental but in Hawaii and some other areas it has become something of a weed. In West Africa its durable wood is used for making plows and the pods are employed to dye leather black and to make ink.

A native Hawaiian acacia of importance is the koa (*A. koa*), which is considered to be a monarch of the island forests. Common on mountain slopes, it attains a height of 70 feet and develops a broad, rounded crown of dark green foliage; its trunk diameter may be 10 feet. This species has sickle-shaped phyllodes in place of leaves. Its pale yellow flowers are borne in globular clusters in spring. The red, beautifully figured wood of the koa takes a high polish and, under the name of Hawaiian mahogany, is used for interior trim, furniture and musical instruments. The native Hawaiians have made war clubs, surfboards and canoes of koa.

Most of the "thorn trees" of the drier parts of Africa are acacias, thorny natives with fine feathery foliage. They are important as sources of shade and shelter and of fodder for wild and domestic animals. Most conspicuous in the drier parts of East Africa and South Africa is the camel thorn (*A. giraffe*), which is sometimes 40 feet tall. It has an umbrella-shaped, widespreading head and in spring small balls of yellow flowers. The big thorns, often inflated at

their bases, are in pairs. The pods, up to 5 inches long aer oval or half-moon-shaped. They are a favorite food of livestock but, like the foliage, under some conditions they contain dangerous amounts of hydrocyanic acid and have proved deadly. The camel thorn grows slowly and, unlike many acacies, is long-lived; specimens several hundreds of years old are known. Like most dry-country trees, its roots spread deeply, in mature specimens even to a depth of 80 feet. Camel thorn wood is good fuel and large numbers of trees have been felled to supply this need; this is especially true near Kimberley. Natives make domestic utensils and other articles from the wood. The name camel thorn refers to the fondness of giraffes (once called camelopard) for the pods and foliage; the botanical name *Acacia giraffe* has the same derivation.

The gum arabic tree (*Acacia nilotica*) is a close relative of the American cassie from which it can be distinguished by its scentless flowers, almost straight twigs and marked constrictions of the seed pods between individual seeds. Native to Africa, southern Europe, the Near East and India, this thorny species is one of the most widespread trees of India, where it is known as black babool, and of parts of Africa, where it is called redheart. Often shrubby but sometimes 40 feet tall, it may have a trunk diameter of 1½ feet. The tiny yellow flowers are in globular heads. The usually grayish or bluish leaves are bipinnate. In India, Africa, and elsewhere its hard, heavy wood, resistant to water and insects, is used for such purposes as wheels, oil and sugar presses, tool handles, and curbs around wells. It is an excellent fuel. The astringent bark and pods have been used for tanning since the time of the ancient Egyptians; ink is prepared from the pods, which, like the foliage, provide fodder for domestic animals. Bark and pods are employed medicinally and the edible gum secreted by this tree is made into sweetmeats. The original source of gum arabic and still tapped to some extent for this harvest, *A. nilotica* has been superseded by *A. senegal*, which yields a superior product, as the chief commercial source of gum arabic.

The sweet thorn (*A. karroo*) is often the only tree over large areas of the karroo and highveld regions of South Africa. It is the most widely distributed of South African trees, occurring fom the Cape to the Kalahari Desert, the Transvaal and Natal into Rhodesia and Nyasaland. It sometimes exceeds 40 feet in height and has a

Umbrella thorn. Acacia tortilis (Eve Palmer)

wide spread. The leaflets are tiny so that the tree produces only light shade. Where steady supplies of water are available, the sweet thorn may be evergreen, but the foliage is dropped during droughts and cold periods and under extreme dry conditions the trees may remain leafless for successive years. The sweet thorn in summer is decked with small fluffy balls of fragrant yellow flowers which attract great numbers of insects. The flowers are succeeded by slender straight or curved pods up to 5 inches long. The thorns, which are white and from 1/2 to 7 inches long, are in pairs; they are used by the natives as pins and needles. The sweet thorn has many uses. Its foliage and pods are excellent forage, its wood good fuel. In colonial times the wood was made into furniture, wheels, yokes, poles and agricultural implements, and its bark was used for tanning and, by the natives, for making cordage and mats. The bark and roots are also used medicinally. This tree lives to a considerable age; a specimen 320 years old is recorded. In South Africa the sweet thorn is often called mimosa.

One of the largest trees of northern Transvaal and extending northward into tropical Africa, the ana tree (*A. albida*) grows to a height of 90 feet or even more. It has a gray-barked trunk and a noble head of bluish green foliage. The thorns, 1 inch or less in length, are white with red tips and are straight, a characteristic which distinguishes the tree from near relatives. The

ana tree is the only *Acacia* which has both straight thorns and flowers in cylindrical spikes. The flowers are cream colored and are succeeded by twisted pods about 4 inches long which, like the foliage, are good fodder and are avidly eaten by elephants and baboons as well as by sheep, goats, cattle and camels. In Rhodesia a fish poison is prepared from the pods, and decoctions of the bark are used medicinally by the natives of tropical Africa.

The graceful kaffir thorn (*A. caffra*), common in many parts of South Africa, is highly ornamental. It grows up to 30 feet high and has feathery deciduous foliage. Its pale yellow flowers, which become deeper in color as they age, are borne in spring in spikes 2 or 3 inches long. The pods are 3 to 4 inches in length, straight and slender and, like the foliage, are eaten by game and domestic livestock. The tree has fewer small, hooked, sharp thorns than most other African acacias. The wood is used for fence posts and fuel and, by the natives, for making pipes. The natives use the bark medicinally.

The apiesdoring (*A. galpinii*) is one of the noblest of Sorth African trees, rivaling the ana tree in size. It has a wide-spreading head, usually up to 80 feet in height, but specimens much taller have been reported. Its corklike, flaky bark, whitish yellow at first, darkens as it ages. The light green leaves are large and finely dissected. Honey-scented, the flowers, which occur in branched inflorescences, are maroon in bud but open a creamy yellow; they are great favorites of bees. The flat pods, up to 8 inches long and 1 inch broad, are eaten by animals. The glossy brown thorns of the apiesdoring give a clue to its identity; unlike those of most acacies, they are short and strongly curved. The wood of this tree is excellent for cabinetwork.

Occurring in several forms as a native from Arabia to South Africa, the umbrella thorn (*A. tortilis*) is one of the most widespread of African acacias. Rarely exceeding 30 feet in height, it assumes a flat-topped form and tends to favor alkaline soils, and is very drought-resistant. Its leaves, rarely more than 1 inch long, are finely divided into numerous tiny leaflets. The fragrant, white to pale yellow flowers are in round clusters and are followed by flat, spirally twisted seed pods 3 to 4 inches long. These highly nutritious pods are great favorites of cattle and other animals. In South Africa this tree is called haak-en-steek (hook-and-prick) in reference to the thorns, which are of two kinds, one long,

Acacia with weaver bird nests (Weldon King)

straight and white, the other small, curved and brown.

Differing from most other acacias in having thorns arising from conspicuous swollen structures or knobs that grow along the stems, the knob thorn (A. nigrescens) becomes 50 feet tall and may have a trunk up to 20 inches in diameter. It is common in many parts of South Africa and East Africa, sometimes forming a single-species forest. The flower spikes, reddish brown at first, develop their creamy flowers in early spring and are followed by pods about 5 inches long by 1 inch broad that are browsed by animals. The leaves are bipinnate but each lateral subdivision consists of one pair of leaves only. Especially troublesome are the small curved thorns which upon contact easily penetrate clothing or flesh. Knob thorn wood, durable, termite-resistant and hard, is used for mine props and fence posts.

Blooming before the new leaves appear or while they are yet quite tiny, the enkeldoring (A. robusta) is a beautiful native of South Africa more than 30 feet tall and is distinguished by its very thick branches and branchlets and its rough, dark trunk and branches. The thorns are straight and from 1/4 to 3 inches long. Just above each pair is a swelling out of which the leaves and flowers grow in bunches. The latter, deliciously fragrant, whitish to butter yellow and in globular heads, are followed by straight or slightly curved pods 2 to 5 inches long.

The paperbark thorn (A. woodii), which has a wide-spreading, flat-topped crown very characteristic of the species is native from tropical Africa to Natal. Its common name refers to the fact that its corky bark sheds in papery strips. It has finely divided leaves up to 4 inches long, white or pale yellow flowers in small balls, and is an attractive ornamental. Both its foliage and large pods are readily eaten by livestock but under some circumstances the leaves contain enough hydrocyanic acid to result in poisoning.

183

The unusual greenish yellow color of the trunk and branches serves to distinguish the fever tree (A. xanthophloea) from other African acacias. Its common name was given it because it is believed locally that the tree causes malaria; in some places it is said that the trunk becomes moist in fall when malaria is most prevalent. Occurring in South Africa, Rhodesia and tropical east Africa and northward, usually in swampy locations, the fever tree, tall and graceful, has leaves about 1½ inches long, each consisting of many tiny leaflets, and fragrant balls of yellow flowers. The pods are small and flat, the thorns straight and white. The heavy hard wood of this tree is used for many purposes.

The most important commercial source of gum arabic is Acacia senegal, a native of the drier savannas of tropical and North Africa and parts of Asia. This tree, which grows up to 30 feet or sometimes more in height, has a short trunk, much divided leaves and fragrant cream-colored flowers in spikes usually longer than the leaves. Its small pods are densely hairy and its thorns are strongly hooked. The gum, collected in the Sudan from cultivated trees and elsewhere from wild specimens, is used for making mucilage, polishes, ink, pottery pigments, for textile finishing, and in pharmacy. Locally the root fibers are used for making very strong ropes and fishnets.

Second in importance only to Eucalyptus among Australian trees are the acacies or wattles. They are ubiquitous, occurring in a wide range of habitats and over even more of the continent than the eucalypts. They are so typical of the Australian flora that scarcely a landscape is without some representative of the genus. Not all are trees; most are shrubby. Among the trees are some valued for their lumber and other commercial products; many are prized ornamentals. The Australian acacias belong in two groups, those with bipinnate ferny leaves and those in which phyllodes (expanded, flattened leaf stalks) serve as leaves. Among the former the green wattle (A. decurrens) and its varieties, the silver wattle (A. d. dealbata) and the black wattle (A. d. mollis), are handsome ornamentals. They grow up to 50 feet or more in height, the silver wattle occasionally up to 100 feet. All have fine feathery foliage and slender strings of globular golden yellow flower heads. The green wattle, a native of New South Wales, has green foliage; that of the silver wattle is a beautiful silvery gray. The silver wattle is common in Tasmania, South Australia and eastern Australia. Having darker foliage than the green wattle and dark gray to nearly black bark, the black wattle is a native of Victoria. The cedar wattle (A. elata) of New South Wales is one of the most decorative kinds. It has feathery, dark green foliage and, in spring and summer, large trusses of creamy yellow globular flower heads in racemes about 6 inches long. Its young shoots are covered with a yellow pubescence. The bark of this tree, which grows up to 90 feet in height, is rich in tannic acid. Differing from the cedar wattle in having leaflets less than 1½ inches long and in rarely exceeding 20 feet in height, the Cootamundra wattle (A. baileyana) is a favorite ornamental. At blooming time its finely divided, silvery gray foliage is completely hidden with masses of small globular heads of yellow flowers. The Cootamundra wattle forms an attractive round-headed specimen. In nature confined to a small area of New South Wales, it sometimes has a trunk diameter of 12 inches. This is one of the earliest acacias to bloom in spring. The mealy-barked wattle (A. pruinosa), a native of New South Wales, is a graceful small- to medium-sized tree with delicate fernlike foliage. It has an open crown and is distinguished by the mealy appearance of its branches. Its pale yellow flowers form ball-like heads.

The biggest Australian acacias belong in the group that have phyllodes instead of leaves. Especially noteworthy are A. bakeri and the blackwood (A. melanoxylon). The former, which sometimes reaches a height of 200 feet with a trunk diameter of up to 4 feet, is the largest species. A native of New South Wales and Queensland, it is valued for its strong, hard, handsome lumber, which is used for turnery, furniture and decorative purposes and for a transparent, adhesive gum which it yields. The blackwood also is the source of fine lumber; in fact its wood is the most ornamental of all Australian acacia woods for furniture, cabinet-making and paneling and is also used for boat-building and parts of musical instruments. The blackwood occurs over a large territory in Tasmania, Victoria, New South Wales and Queensland. It attains a height of 110 feet with a trunk up to 4 feet in diameter and forms a wide-spreading, round-topped crown. Its lanceolate phyllodes, usually curved along one side, are up to 6 inches long. Its cream-colored flowers form short racemes. The blackwood is an excellent ornamental shade tree.

The durable, dark-colored wood of the coast myall or mountain brigalow (A. glaucescens) has been likened to that of English walnut. Close-grained and handsomely marked, it is in demand for furniture and cabinetwork. This species is also the source of an adhesive gum of excellent quality. The coast myall is one of the most beautiful acacias. Native to Queensland and New South Wales, it grows to a height of 50 feet and has ash-gray phyllodes that are straight or curved and up to 6 inches long. The bright golden yellow flowers, in spikes up to 2 inches long, are succeeded by twisted pods. A close relative of the coast myall, and sometimes confused with it, is A. maidenii, which is about the same height and has similar dark-colored, rough bark. It is less pubescent than the coast myall, its flower spikes are 1 inch long and its seed pods are very much twisted, even forming bowknots.

Another tall grower is the lightwood tree (A. implexa), which at its best is 50 feet tall. This kind, a native of eastern Australia, has very rough bark, phyllodes that are usually conspicuously curved and pale yellow flowers that are 6 inches long or more, and occur in short racemes. Its slender pods are constricted between the seeds and are much twisted. The wood of the lightwood tree resembles that of the blackwood. Known as the mountain hickory, A. penninervis grows to a height of 40 feet or sometimes considerably more and has bark that is very rich in tannic acid and is used for processing leather and also for paper pulp. This tree has curved lanceolate phyllodes up to 5 inches long. Its pale yellow flowers are in short racemes. It is a native of Tasmania, Victoria, New South Wales and Queensland.

Known as the raspberry jam tree because of the odor of its freshly cut wood, A. acuminata is plentiful in western Australia, where it attains a height of 40 feet. It has gray, fibrous bark and reddish brown wood resistant to borers and other insects. The wood is very durable and is used for fence posts, tobacco pipes and other small articles and for cabinetwork. It also makes excellent charcoal. The phyllodes of the raspberry jam tree are up to 10 inches long and are dark green. Its flowers, in spikes, are succeeded by slender pods that are somewhat contracted between the seeds. A native of New South Wales and Queensland, the two-veined-hickory (A. binervata) attains a height of 40 feet and a trunk diameter of 12 inches and has pale pink wood that is light and strong and is used for

bullock yokes and tool handles. Its phyllodes are curved and have two, or sometimes three, conspicuous veins. The flower heads are in racemes. The green casha bush (A. sentis) is a somewhat thorny species from central and eastern Australia that occasionally becomes 30 or even 40 feet tall. It provides good forage and is conspicuous because of its bright green foliage, which contrasts sharply with the prevailing hoary or glaucous blue leaves of the desert species with which it associates. Naturally drought-resistant, this wattle has yellow flowers in solitary or paired globular heads. Its roots are extensive and have been found as much as 80 feet below the ground surface.

One of the most popular acacias is the Sydney golden wattle (A. longifolia), which in many variations is a native of all states except Western Australia. It has fairly broad phyllodes, each with a few prominent longitudinal veins. Its golden yellow flowers, in cylindrical spikes 1 to 2 inches or more long, are borne in spring. This is a good street tree and its bark is useful for tanning. The bark of the burra (A. falcata) contains so much tannic acid that it is used by the natives to stupefy fish. A small tree, its trunk may be 12 inches in diameter and its hard, tough wood can be bent into sharp curves. Its grayish green phyllodes are markedly curved and have a prominent midvein. Its pale yellow flowers are in spikes.

Among the smaller wattles that reach ultimate heights of 20 or 25 feet are many that are highly decorative. The best include the weeping myall (A. pendula) which has stiff silvery gray phyllodes on more or less pendulous branchlets and flower heads in pairs or clusters. The flowers are sparse and less decorative than those of many wattles so that the ornamental value of the tree lies in its lovely drooping habit rather than in its floral display. The foliage is excellent fodder and the wood, which is almost as dense and heavy as lignum vitae, is dark colored and has the odor of violets. It is greatly valued for turnery. The weeping myall is a native of the drier interior parts of Queensland and New South Wales.

Two other ornamental species with branchlets that droop are the golden or broad-leaved wattle (A. pycnantha) and the golden wreath or golden hickory wattle (A. saligna). The former is a native of south Australia, the latter of western Australia. Both have long, fairly broad phyllodes and bear an abundance of large globular golden yellow flower heads. Both yield valuable tanbark, that of the golden wreath wattle containing the highest percentage of tannin of any species. The golden hickory wattle can be distinguished from the golden wattle by its straight, as opposed to sickle-shaped, phyllodes. The phyllodes of both species have one conspicuous vein, which is often to one side of the center of the phyllode.

Adenanthera—Bead Tree

Here belong eight more or less deciduous trees of Asia, Australia and the Pacific Islands, all of which have hard red or red and black seeds. The best known is the red sandalwood tree (A. pavonina), a deciduous native of the Old World Tropics. Of slender growth and attaining a maximum height of about 80 feet, it has twice-pinnate blue-green leaves and small, yellow, fragrant flowers in slender, dense racemes. Its seeds, the circassian seeds of commerce, are lens-shaped and scarlet. They are so uniform in weight (nearly four grains) that they were for long employed as weights in the Orient by goldsmiths and silversmiths. They are commonly used as beads and for making other articles of adornment. When the pods shed their seeds they become much coiled and twisted. The strong and durable wood is used as a substitute for true sandalwood (Santalum). Another species, A. bicolor, from Ceylon, has seeds that are half red and half black. It grows up to 50 feet tall and has smaller leaves than the red sandalwood.

Albizzia

More than a hundred species in the warmer parts of the Old World constitute Albizzia. The woman's tongue or siris tree (A. lebbeck) of North Africa, Indo-Malaysia, and northern Australia, becomes 100 feet in height and forms an umbrella-shaped crown of spreading branches and feathery bipinnate foliage. The pale green or white or yellowish fragrant flowers are clustered in tassel-like heads. Very conspicuous are its large, flat, tan-colored, papery pods which hang for several months and rattle in every breeze like, the Filipinos say, the tongues of women. The wood of this species, which resembles walnut, is excellent for cabinetwork. One of the fastest growing of all trees is A. falcata, a native of eastern Malaysia. Under favorable conditions it reaches 50 feet in height in three years and 100 feet in 10 years; then its crown spreads to form a large umbrella-shaped canopy.

This tree eventually reaches a height of about 150 feet. Its leaves are twice-pinnate, its flowers are creamy white and slightly fragrant. Because of its rapid growth the wood of A. falcata is soft and lacks strength. It is used for matches and paper. The tree, which is sometimes called A. moluccana, provides shade for coffee and tea plantations. The hardiest Albizzia is the one called mimosa in the southern United States. This species (A. julibrissin) survives winters outdoors in New York and even in New England. Often called the silk tree, it grows as a native from Persia to Japan and under favorable conditions attains a height of 45 feet and a trunk diameter of 1½ feet. Its elegant, finely divided foliage is light green, and its flowers, in large pink or pink and white pompons, are in evidence for several weeks during the summer. They are succeeded by light brown, papery, flat pods which hang on the branches for a long time.

Amherstia

A tree described as the most beautiful in the entire vegetable kingdom surely merits attention. Such is Amherstia nobilis, of Burma. This spectacular legume grows to a height of 60 feet and has long pendent sprays of red, rose pink and yellow flowers displayed to fine advantage below handsome foliage. The leaves, 1 to 2 feet long, are pinnate, with four to seven pairs of leaflets but no terminal leaflet, and are whitish on their undersides. Young leaves are flaccid, drooping and a beautiful pinkish copper; gradually they change to rich bronze and finally green as they stiffen and become capable of holding themselves horizontally. The flat pods contain several seeds. The name Amherstia commemorates the Countess Amherst, the wife of a governor of Burma, and her daughter Lady Sarah Amherst, an artist and botanical collector who died in 1838. Amherstia nobilis, the only species of the genus, is successfully cultivated for its singular beauty in India, Ceylon and Jamaica, but in many tropical regions, including Hawaii and Malaya, it does not thrive.

Andira

The most important of this genus of thirty-five tropical American and tropical African trees is the partridge wood (A. inermis), an evergreen that becomes 100 feet tall in its native South America and has ragged, malodorous bark. Its pinnate leaves are large and have an uneven number of leaflets. The flowers, in terminal panicles, are rosy purple and fragrant. The chief uses of partridge wood are for small articles such as umbrella handles, canes and turnery. Locally the lumber is used for heavy construction.

Bauhinia

The name of this genus of three hundred species of tropical and subtropical trees, shrubs and lianas commemorates two sixteenth century brothers, the Swiss herbalists John and Casper Bauhin. To the botanist Plumier, who named *Bauhinia*, the paired leaflets (in some species joined to form one deeply lobed entity) suggested the relationship of the men he wished to honor. The lobed leaves commonly fold along their middles and in outline are shaped like the hoof mark of a deer or goat; the veins of the leaves spread palmately from their bases. Among the most attractive of flowering trees, bauhinias are commonly planted as ornamentals in warm regions. Their lovely orchid-like or pelargonium-like flowers, which range from white to purple and yellow, are in clusters. Each has five somewhat unequal petals, conspicuously narrowed toward their bases, and up to ten stamens. The number of fertile stamens is of significance in the identification of the species. The pods are long and flat.

Among the most popular species is the orchid tree or mountain-ebony (*B. variegata*). This deciduous native of India and China reaches a maximum height of about 20 feet, has broader than long leaves lobed to one-third of their length, and beautiful rose-colored, magenta pink or pinkish violet flowers variegated with red and yellow. The petals are broadly spoon-shaped, the lower one somewhat longer than the others. The flowers measure 3 to 4 inches across, have five fertile stamens and are fragrant. Similar to *B. variegata*, but almost or quite evergreen, is *B. purpurea* of India, Burma and China. This species reaches a maximum height of 50 feet, has deeply lobed leaves up to 5 inches in diameter and fragrant red flowers that are streaked with white on the claws (slender bases) of their narrow petals. The flowers range from almost white through pink and red to rich purple and are variously streaked and shaded. They have three or four fertile stamens.

The butterfly flower or Jerusalem-date (*B. monandra*), as its botanical name indicates, has flowers with only one fertile stamen. A native of southeastern Asia, this species has naturalized itself in the West Indies and other tropical areas.

Woman's tongue. Albizzia lebbeck (M. Krishnan)

It grows up to 30 feet tall, has leaves lobed to about one-third of their length and shaped like the wings of a butterfly. It has pink flowers with darker markings. The flowers are 3 to 4 inches wide.

Brownea

Endemic to South America and the West Indies, this group of twenty-five small evergreen trees and shrubs includes some that are very beautiful in bloom. Their pinnate leaves have one to several pairs of leathery leaflets and their flowers form globular rhododendron-like heads or dense short racemes which grow from the branchlets, branches or even the trunk, according to species. When new leaves first develop they are pink, brown or red, often spangled with white and they dangle from the branches limply like slender tassels of seaweed. Soon they stiffen and straighten and change to the green of the mature foliage. The most important kinds are *B. ariza*, a small spreading tree with drooping heads of scarlet flowers from the ends of its branches and leaves of four to nine pairs of leaflets; the rose-of-Venezuela (*B. grandiceps*), which becomes 40 feet tall and has large heads of bright red flowers from its branch ends and leaves with twelve to eighteen pairs of leaflets; *B. rosa-de-monte*, which has scarlet blooms and

187

two or three pairs of leaflets to each leaf; and *Brownea macrophylla*, which grows in dense forest and has erect trunks or stems almost completely hidden by its red flowers. Commonly its trunk is hollow and inhabited by black ants.

Butea

The flame of the forest *(B. frondosa)* is a very beautiful member of a genus of thirty Indo-Malaysian and Chinese trees and vines. Of erect habit and deciduous, it grows to a height of 50 feet and bears masses of showy-2-inch-long, orange-crimson flowers which have nine stamens united and one free. The flowers are chiefly pollinated by birds. Hairy, broad and leathery, the pods, each about 8 inches long, contain near their tips a solitary seed. The leaves consist of three roundish leaflets pubescent on their undersides. A native of Ceylon, India and Burma, the flame of the forest is the source of an astringent red resin called Bengal kino and is one of the most important hosts of the lac insect. From its inner bark a fiber used for rough cordage and for caulking boats is obtained and the flowers yield a yellow or orange-red dye. Hindus consider the flame of the forest sacred to Brahma and use its wood in religious ceremonies and for sacred utensils. The three leaflets are regarded as emblematic of the Hindu trinity.

Caesalpinia

A hundred tropical and subtropical species comprise this genus. Many are vinelike; others are shrubs or trees. They have bipinnate leaves and racemes of yellow, yellow and red, red or whitish flowers. Many kinds are thorny. One of the most important is the divi-divi *(C. coriaria)*, a spreading tree, 25 to 30 feet in height with a short trunk sometimes 16 inches in diameter. A native of semi-arid parts of Mexico, Central America, South America and the West Indies, this species is cultivated in other places in the tropics for its pods; these contain a high percentage of good-quality tannin, which is used commercially for preparing leather and a black dye. The flint-hard wood has no practical use except that a red dye is sometimes made from it. The flowers of the divi-divi are greenish white and fragrant, its leaves feathery and finely divided.

Brazil was named after a *Caesalpinia*. In the Middle Ages a bright red dye called brésil (the word, akin to braise, means live coals or fire and refers to the dye color) was an important product of the sappanwood *(C. sappan)*, a na-tive of India and Malaya. Its wood was then called brésil wood. Early in the sixteenth century the Portuguese discovered a similar wood in South America, called it brésil wood and gave the country from which it came the name Brésil. The New World tree was *C. echinata* and its wood and that of related American species is still known as brazilwood. The commercial exploitation of these Brazilian kinds was of such importance that from 1623 until the middle of the nineteenth century it was preserved as a monopoly of the Portuguese crown. Because the colors imparted by sappanwood and brazilwood are fugitive, as dyes they have largely been replaced by synthetics and are no longer of significant commercial importance. Now, the chief value of *C. echinata* is for its wood, which is greatly valued for violin bows and is known in the trade as pernambuco after the name of the Brazilian state from which the finest grades come. The brazilwood *(C. echinata)* attains 100 feet in height and may have a trunk 3 feet in diameter and free of branches for 50 or 60 feet. It has bipinnate leaves; its flowers are small and yellow. Very different is the sappanwood *(C. sappan)*. It is more often a shrub than a tree, although occasionally it is 20 feet tall. It has evergreen, twice-pinnate leaves and has sulphur yellow fragrant flowers marked with orange-red lines. Its wood is very hard.

Calliandra

One hundred species comprise this genus, all natives of the warmer parts of America and Asia and of Madagascar. Many are shrubs a few are small trees. All have bipinnate leaves and flowers massed in dense pompons and with long protruding stamens. Their pods are flat and straight. Best known is the powder puff tree *(C. haematocephala)*, a native of Bolivia which has handsome, brilliant crimson flower heads that resemble powder puffs and are up to 3½ inches in diameter. This tree, usually less than 20 feet tall, is often cultivated under the name *C. inae-*

Right above: Royal poinciana. Delonix regia (Josef Muench) Right: Poinciana gilliesii (T. H. Everett)
Overleaf left: Palo Verde. Cercidium torreyanum (Floyd R. Getsinger) Right above: Umbrella thorn. Acacia tortilis (James R. Simon) Right below: Candelabra tree. Euphorbia ingens (Janet Finch)

quilatera. Another kind, *C. portoricensis* of the West Indies, becomes 25 feet high and has white flowers or white flowers with the stamens tipped with red.

Cassia

Represented by native species in most tropical and warm temperate regions except Europe, *Cassia* numbers between five hundred and six hundred species of trees, shrubs and herbaceous plants. They have asymmetrical flowers with petals of nearly equal size and usually seven, but sometimes ten, fertile stamens. Most commonly the two lower stamens are long and protruding, the five upper ones shorter. In many kinds the pollen produced by the short stamens serves as food for insect visitors while that of the long ones is carried away on their bodies to pollinate other flowers. Several kinds are cultivated for their leaves, which are dried and used as a drug.

The horse cassia (*C. grandis*) is a deciduous tree that occurs from southern Mexico to Brazil and in the West Indies. In the open it is a spreading tree of medium height but under forest conditions it may become 100 feet tall. When in bloom it has the appearance of an apple tree; its abundant flowers are delicate pink. The leaves have ten to twenty pairs of leaflets. The four-angled pods are up to 2 feet long and contain seeds embedded in an ill-scented pulp with laxative properties. Another tall grower is *C. apoucouita,* which occurs from French Guiana to Rio de Janeiro. The blackish heartwood of this tree, which is sometimes 100 feet in height with a trunk diameter of 3 feet, is excellent for cabinetmaking. Its flowers are yellow.

The golden shower, Indian laburnum, or pudding pipe tree (*C. fistula*) is an extraordinarily beautiful yellow-flowered deciduous native of India. When in bloom it resembles the golden chain (*Laburnum*). The flowers hang from the branches in great racemes and are succeeded by straight, slender, cylindrical pods up to 2½ feet long. Each contains up to a hundred seeds embedded in a sweet sticky pulp that is used as a laxative and, in India, for mixing with smoking tobacco. The flowers are used in temple offerings. This tree grows up to 50 feet in height. Its leaves have from four to eight pairs of leaflets.

The pink-and-white shower (*C. javanica*), as its name suggests, is indigenous in Java; it is also native to Sumatra and the Philippines. A moderate-sized tree, it differs from the nearly related *C. nodosa* of southeastern Asia in having spurlike spines on its trunk and branches. *Cassia nodosa* is recorded as growing up to 80 feet in height in Malaya, but it is usually smaller. Both species are very beautiful in bloom and their floral displays last for a long time. Their sweetly scented flowers are pink or pink and white. The cylindrical pods, up to 2 feet in length, are without sticky pulp. When crushed, pods, bark and twigs give off a fetid odor. Both species are deciduous and each of their leaves have five to fifteen pairs of leaflets. The kassod tree (*C. siamea*) is an evergreen native to India and Malaysia that forms a rounded crown up to 60 feet in height. Its leaves have seven to ten pairs of leaflets, each with a bristle point. The bright yellow flowers open a few at a time and form erect pyramidal clusters. The pods, up to 9 inches long, are often curved. The African laburnum (*C. sieberiana*) resembles *C. fistulosa* and grows to a height of 50 feet. It is a common native through much of tropical Africa and has leaves that are often purplish and hairy when young. The pods contain but little pulp; the pulp is laxative. Bark, leaves, roots and other parts are used in native medicines.

Castanospermum—Moreton Bay-chestnut or Black Bean

A native of Queensland and New South Wales, this ornamental Australian evergreen has a compact head of glossy dark green foliage. It has 6-inch racemes of showy yellow, orange and red pea-shaped, long-stemmed flowers succeeded by pods 6 to 9 inches long, each containing about six large chestnut-like seeds which are edible after they are well cooked. The pinnate leaves are 1 foot or more in length and consist of eleven to fifteen leaflets. Very handsome lumber, resembling walnut and esteemed for cabinetwork and furniture, is obtained from the Moreton Bay-chestnut It is the only species of the genus.

Ceratonia—Carob

The only species of *Ceratonia*, the carob or St. John's bread (*C. siliqua*), is a native of the eastern Mediterranean region, especially, perhaps, of Arabia. Old in cultivation, it was familiar to the ancient Greeks who undoubtedly aided its dissemination. According to legend, its pods were the "locusts" which John the Baptist ate

Left: Sugar maple. Acer saccharum (Winston Pote)

Golden shower. Cassia fistula (M. Krishnan)

while in the wilderness and for centuries the fruits have been called locusts. When early settlers in North America first saw *Robinia* and *Gymnocladus*, they marked the resemblance of their pods to those of the carob and named them respectively locust and honey-locust. The carob is an evergreen tree with a broad crown up to 50 feet in height and pinnate leaves of four or six rounded glossy leaflets. The reddish flowers occur in dense racemes and may be bisexual or unisexual. Carob pods vary somewhat in size and shape. Up to 1 foot long, they are broad and flat, and contain a number of very hard seeds embedded in sweet, mealy nutritious pulp. They are readily eaten by animals and are palatable to humans. The seeds have been used as weights by jewelers and apothecaries and there is good reason to believe that they were the original carat weights.

Cercis—Redbud

There are seven species of *Cercis*, all natives of the North Temperate zone and all small deciduous trees or shrubs that bear pea-shaped flowers either just before or as their leaves unfold. With the exception of those of *C. racemosa*, they are in stemless clusters and, most unusual among trees of temperate regions, they grow from thick branches and sometimes from the trunk as well as from young twigs. This phenomenon, called cauliflory, is more common among tropical trees, examples of which are the chocolate tree, jakfruit and cannon ball tree. The leaves of redbuds are rounded or kidney-shaped, are undivided and have heart-shaped bases, untoothed margins and veins that spread like the fingers of a hand.

Most famous is the Judas tree (*C. siliquastrum*). According to legend it was from a specimen of this native of southern Europe and adjacent Asia that Judas Iscariot hanged himself. At its best 40 feet tall, the Judas tree may have a trunk 20 inches in diameter. Its flowers, normally bright purplish rose but in variety *alba* pure white, are eaten in salads. They have a sweet-acid flavor. The redbud of eastern North America differs from the Judas tree in having smaller flowers, and leaves tipped with a short point. It also has a white-flowered variety called *alba*. The redbud is spontaneous from New Jersey to Missouri, northern Florida, New Mexico and Texas. It has a maximum height of about 40 feet. Transparent cartilaginous margins to the leaves serve to distinguish the Chinese redbud (*C. chinensis*) from *C. canadensis*. Also, its leaves when young are glossy green beneath, and its flowers are somewhat larger than those of its eastern American relative. The Chinese redbud, largest of the genus, grows up to a height of 50 feet and sometimes attains a trunk diameter of 4 feet. Another Asiatic species, *C. racemosa*, is distinguished from all other redbuds by its flowers being in pendulous racemes, 3 to 4 inches long. Each raceme has up to thirty or forty rosy pink blooms. This is the handsomest kind in bloom. It is a native of central and western China and is up to 30 feet tall.

Cladrastis—Yellow-wood

Of the five species of *Cladrastis*, a genus closely related to *Maackia*, four are natives of eastern Asia and one of eastern North America. All are deciduous trees with pinnate leaves having an uneven number of leaflets that are not in opposite pairs but are alternate, and racemes of fragrant creamy white or pinkish, pea-shaped flowers. They are unusual in having hollow bases of the leaf stalks cover the buds so that the latter are not visible until the leaves drop or are pulled off. In fall the foliage turns bright yellow. The American yellow-wood (*C. lutea*), indigenous to a limited area in North Carolina, Kentucky and Tennessee but nowhere abundant, is occasionally 60 feet tall and has a short smooth-barked trunk up to 3 feet in diameter. Its crown is wide-spreading and its branchlets are slender and somewhat zigzag. The white or creamy white flowers form pendulous, wisteria-like panicles. From the roots of *C. lutea* a yellow dye is obtained. Quite different is the flowering habit of the Chinese yellow-wood *(C. sinensis)*. Its white or pinkish blooms are in upright branched panicles. This somewhat rare native of western China grows to a height of 80 feet and may have a trunk 3 feet in diameter. The Japanese yellow-wood *(C. platycarpa)*, endemic to Japan, differs from the American and Chinese kinds in that its leaflets have tiny appendages called stipels at their bases and its pods are winged. It attains a height of 60 feet and has erect panicles of white flowers with a yellow spot at the bottom of each standard petal.

Copaifera

Members of this genus of twenty-five tropical American and five tropical African trees have pinnate, leathery leaves, small, usually white flowers in panicles and pods that each contain one seed. Their woods are permeated by canals containing oleoresins for which some kinds are exploited commercially. Copaiba balsam, used in medicines and varnishes, is obtained by tapping into the heartwood of several South American species. One of these, *C. reticulata*, is very widely distributed in the Amazon region. Its balsam is a thick, yellowish brown and has a disagreeable smell. A clearer, more fluid, less odorous product is obtained from *C. multijuga*, also a native of tropical Brazil. Other American species include *C. langsdorfii*, *C. officinalis* and *C. chiriquensis;* the last, which extends into Panama, is the most northern kind. *Copaifera officinalis*, a native of northern South America, is cultivated in the West Indies. Its balsam, called Maracaibo copaiba, is rather thick. Para copaiba, obtained from *C. langsdorfii*, is much more fluid.

The wood of *C. chiriquensis*, a species found native in the region of São Paulo, Brazil, provides lumber for the local production of furniture and for turnery and shipbuilding. West African species of *Copaifera* are sources of copals, resins that contain little or no oil and are used in the manufacture of hard, elastic varnishes. The copal is obtained from living trees and in a semifossilized state from the ground where trees are growing or have grown. Im-portant African species include *C. ehie*, a tree which grows up to 150 feet high, and *C. guibourtiana*, which rarely exceeds 80 feet in height. Others are *C. demeusii* and *C. mopane*.

Dalbergia

Many lianas and shrubs as well as trees are included in this tropical and subtropical group of three hundred species. Some yield valuable lumber; all true rosewoods belong here. Dalbergias have pinnate leaves with an uneven number of leaflets, or, rarely, only one leaflet, and panicles of small purple, yellow or white pealike flowers. Brazilian rosewood or jacarandá *(D. nigra)*, a native of tropical South America, grows up to a height of 125 feet and has leaves which consist of a multitude of small oval leaflets. Its flowers are yellow and its pods often contain more than one seed. The rose-scented heartwood is brown or violet, streaked irregularly with black. This beautiful wood is used for cabinetmaking, brush backs, knife handles and carpenters'-plane handles.

A rosewood (the name refers to their scent) of the American tropics is Honduras rosewood *(D. stevensonii)*, which grows up to a height of 100 feet. Its wood is used for making musical instruments, particularly the bars of xylophones. A native of the lower Amazon region, jacarandá do Para *(D. spruceana)* produces mildly fragrant lumber of good quality. The tree is usually of small to medium size, its leaflets considerably larger and fewer than those of the Brazilian rosewood. Other South American dalbergias that are exploited commercially include two rather small trees, the Brazilian kingwood *(D. cearensis)* and Brazilian tulipwood *(D. variabilis)*. Wood of the latter has long been a favorite of French furniture builders and is greatly esteemed for marquetry, turnery, brush backs and other small articles. Brazilian kingwood has some similar uses but because of its small size is of little value for furniture. *Dalbergia caerensis* has leaves similar to those of jacarandá do Para but those of the Brazilian tulipwood have only about seven leaflets. Other species, *D. retusa* and closely allied kinds from Mexico and Central and South America, provide a beautifully grained lumber called cocoloba which withstands prolonged immersion in hot, soapy water without damage and polishes well and is therefore much used for knife handles, inlays, turnery and umbrella handles.

Among the best known of the Asiatic rosewood

Indian rosewood. Dalbergia latifolia (M. Krishnan)

poinciana is one of the showiest of flowering trees. It is wide-spreading, up to 50 feet tall, and has lacy, twice-pinnate leaves. At blooming time its great sprays of dazzling red or red and yellow flowers turn the tree into a fiery parasol that lights up the landscape with its brilliant display. The pods, up to 15 inches long and 1½ inches wide, at first are green but gradually change to brown and then to black. They hang on the tree thoughout the year. The royal poinciana is normally deciduous, at least for a short season. Its wood contains a gum that does not dissolve but forms an opalescent mucilage when put into water.

Enterolobium

Ten New World species comprise this genus. The best known are the timbó or timboúba (*E. contortisiliquum*) and the guanacaste or elephant's ear (*E. cyclocarpum*) of northern South America, Central America, Mexico and the West Indies. Both are tall, wide-spreading, bipinnate-leaved trees with yellowish or greenish flowers in large clusters. Their pods coil backward, those of the first named species forming two-thirds or less of a circle, those of the latter making a complete circle. Their woods are durable and are used for carpentry, cabinetwork and dugout canoes. Both species are good shade trees; the timbó is used as a street tree in Buenos Aires. The pods of the elephant's ear are employed as cattle feed and as a substitute for soap; when young they are sometimes cooked for human food.

Erythrina—Coral tree

About a hundred species of deciduous trees, shrubs and a few herbaceous plants are included in the genus *Erythrina*, which is widely distributed throughout tropical and subtropical regions. Their leaves are trifoliate and they usually have spiny trunks and branches. Their showy red or orange-red pea-shaped flowers, with usually erect or spreading standard petals and keel petals that are often curved like a scimitar, occur in dense racemes. The flowers are pollinated by birds, the American species usually by hummingbirds, the African kinds by honeysuckers, and the Asiatics by bulbuls and other fowl. The seed pods are markedly constricted between the seeds.

Of the New World species the bucare (*E. poeppigiana*), a native probably of Peru, is one of the best known and is frequently planted to give shade to coffee trees. Up to 70 feet in height and with a trunk diameter up to 4 feet, it

species are the sissoo (*D. sissoo*) and the Indian rosewood or blackwood (*D. latifolia*). The former is a deciduous Indian tree, with leaves of three or five leaflets and white flowers, that grows to a height of 80 feet. Its durable, elastic lumber is much esteemed for construction and boatbuilding and can be carved to greater depth and more intricately than perhaps any other wood. The Indian rosewood, a native of Ceylon and India, is one of the most important timber trees of India; its fragrant wood is one of the chief furniture woods of India, Ceylon and Burma and is much esteemed for patternmaking because it does not shrink.

Delonix

Few who have visited the tropics can have failed to admire the royal poinciana or flamboyant (*D. regia*), the only well-known member of a genus of three African and Madagascan species. A native of Madagascar, but freely planted as an ornamental in most warm climates, the royal has cinnabar-red flowers in short horizontal racemes. Its parchment-like pods open at only one suture to release several brown, kidney-shaped, poisonous seeds. From tropical America comes the *E. glauca,* 60 feet tall and prickly when young but often unarmed later. Its flowers, in 8-inch racemes, have orange-red standards and crimson-tipped, brown wings. Its leaves are pale or glaucous on their undersides. Much smaller and sometimes without spines is *E. corallodendrum,* also of tropical America. Its scarlet flowers, with standard petals that never open or spread, occur in loose racemes and are succeeded by scarlet seeds. This species is about 20 feet tall. The cockspur coral tree *(E. crista-galli),* a native of Brazil, attains 30 feet in height. One of the handsomest in bloom, both the petioles and midribs of its shiny, dark green leaves are usually spiny. The standards of its brilliant crimson flowers are 1¹⁄₂ inches long and curve backward. Very similar but of more southerly distribution is the mulungú *(E. falcata),* the national flower of Argentina. It differs from *E. crista-galli* in having larger flowers, pods and seeds and racemes that are leafless and lateral rather than leafy and terminal on the branchlets.

The tiger's claw or Indian coral tree *(E. indica)* is a seashore species that occurs spontaneously from India through Polynesia. Up to 45 feet tall, its thick branches are furnished with short, black thorns and its foot-long racemes of scarlet blooms spread horizontally from the ends of the branches. Its dark carmine seeds are contained in black pods; although poisonous when raw they are edible after they have been cooked. In Hawaii they are used in the garlands called leis. This tree is planted in India to provide shade for coffee. Its bark is the source of an excellent fiber and its wood is used as a base for lacquerware. The wiliwili *(E. sandwicensis)* is a native Hawaiian tree that grows in dry regions on the lee side of the larger islands. Occasionally reaching 30 feet in height, it is somewhat spiny and has wide-spreading branches. The flowers range in color from white through yellow and orange to pale red. Its hairy pods each contain two bright red seeds. This tree produces the lightest of native woods, which the natives used for fishnet floats, surfboards and canoe outriggers. In South Africa erythrinas are called kafferbooms and have the most brilliant flowers of all native trees. One of the commonest is *E. caffra,* which attains a maximum height of 70 feet and has clusters of bright red or orange-red flow-

ers with conspicuously protruding stamens. Its bright coral-red poisonous seeds, each with a black spot, are called lucky beans and are made into necklaces. Its wood is used to float fishnets and for brake blocks. Another kafferboom, *E. lyistemon,* is very similar, differing chiefly in that its stamens do not protrude.

Tropical Africa is the home of *E. senegalensis,* a common savanna tree. Sometimes as tall as 50 feet, but usually much smaller, it has lax racemes of scarlet flowers that have scarlet seeds and standards that are folded flat rather than erect. Its roots, bark and wood are used in native medicines. Unusual because its flowers are pink and generally in threes, the tropical African *E. altissima* is a spiny tree that grows up to 100 feet in height. Its roots are chewed by natives to relieve toothache. Four species of *Erythrina* are natives of Australia. The one called cork tree or bat's-wing coral tree *(E. vespertilio)* grows up to 40 feet tall and has erect racemes of pendulous scarlet flowers. The wood of this kind, which ranges over a large part of Australia, was used by the aborigines for making shields.

Gleditsia—Honey-Locust

The living species of this genus are but remnants of much larger populations that flourished over vast areas during the Tertiary Era. One kind now survives in South America, two in North America and eight in the tropics of Africa and Asia and in temperate Asia. All are large deciduous trees usually with clusters of vicious and often branched spines growing from the trunks and branches. Their finely divided leaves are pinnate or bipinnate, with both types often on the same tree. Both unisexual and bisexual flowers, in racemes or panicles, are also borne on the same tree. The flowers are not pea-shaped but have petals of nearly equal size and are usually greenish. The large, flattened pods contain one to many seeds, often embedded in sweet pulp.

The familiar honey-locust *(G. triacanthos* of North America has a stout trunk forked into secondary trunks and furrowed bark that is commonly armed with firmly attached three-branched thorns up to 1 foot long. The thorns occasionally bear small leaves, which indicates that morphologically they are modified branches. A maximum height of 150 feet is attained by this tree, and its more or less flat-topped crown spreads widely. Its trunk may be 6 feet in diameter. The greenish flowers, in slender, pendulous racemes, appear in early summer. Thorn-

Honey-locust. Gleditsia triacanthos (Jeanne White)

less forms of this honey-locust, grouped under the name *G. t. inermis,* are much used as shade trees and for street trees. The tough, strong, reasonably durable wood is suitable for furniture and other purposes but is too scarce to be commercially important; from it the Cherokees made their bows. The pods, which are 1 to 1½ feet long and at maturity become markedly twisted, contain sweet pulp and are eaten eagerly by cattle and other animals. *Gleditsia triacanthos* is native from Pennsylvania to Nebraska, Missouri and Texas. The water-locust (*G. aquatica*), which ranges from South Carolina to Kentucky, Florida and Texas, differs from the honey-locust in having obliquely diamond-shaped pods not more than 2 inches long that contain three or fewer seeds. It rarely exceeds 60 feet in height. Like the honey-locust, its trunk branches low and carries formidable spines, and its crown tends to be flat-topped. Its wood remains very durable, even when in contact with moist soil.

Of the Asiatic species the most important are the Chinese honey-locust (*G. sinensis*) and the Japanese honey-locust (*G. japonica*). The former occurs only in eastern China, the latter in mainland Asia as well as in Japan. The Chinese honey-locust differs from the American and Japanese species in that its spines are not compressed, its leaves are very rarely bipinnate and its pods are not twisted. It grows up to 50 feet tall. *Gleditsia macrantha* from western China is very similar but has larger spines and leaves with pedicels one-third of an inch long; those of *sinensis* are a tenth of an inch long. The Japanese honey-locust becomes 75 feet tall and has somewhat compressed thorns, pods that become twisted, and mostly bipinnate leaves. From the American honey-locust it differs in having obtuse rather than pointed leaflets and usually less than twenty to each leaf. The Caspian honey-locust (*G. caspica*) is closely allied to the Japanese species. It grows up to 40 feet in height and is the most dangerously spined of all honey-locusts. Its pods are about 8 inches long. This species is native in the region of the Caspian Sea.

The only species native south of the equator is the coronilla or espinho de Cristo (*G. amorphoides*) of Argentina, Bolivia and southern Brazil. This normally very thorny kind is sometimes 75 feet tall with a bole 2½ feet in diameter. Its pods are no longer than 4 inches. The wood of the coronilla is used for fence posts and fuel.

Gymnocladus

One North American and three Asiatic species constitute this genus. The Kentucky-coffee tree (*G. dioica*), native from New York to Nebraska and southward, sometimes attains a height of 120 feet and a trunk diameter of 4 feet. Usually the trunk is divided some ten or twelve feet from the ground into a few secondary trunks. The branches are stout and have few branchlets. The leaves are bipinnate; the greenish white flowers are not pea-shaped but are symmetrical. They are borne in early summer in large terminal panicles and may be unisexual or bisexual. The pods, 6 to 8 inches long and up to 2 inches wide, each contain several seeds embedded in sweet, dark pulp. They hang on the branches throughout the winter. When roasted the seeds are edible and were used by pioneers as a substitute for coffee. The wood of the Kentucky-coffee tree is durable and takes a high polish but the tree is not abundant enough to be of commercial importance for lumber. The Chinese *G. chi-*

198

Logwood. *Haematoxylon campechianum (Lorus and Margery Milne)*

nensis has leaflets that are smaller than those of the Kentucky-coffee tree and are pubescent on both sides; those of the American species are pubescent only beneath and only when they are young. Also, the Chinese kind has purplish or white flowers that appear before the leaves. A native of southern China, it grows up to 60 feet in height. In its native country its pods are used as a soap substitute.

Haemotoxylum

The two tropical American species of *Haemotoxylum* were once important sources of dyes. In addition to these, other species have been described from southwest Africa. The logwood (*H. campechianum*) is a native of the West Indies and Central and South America. It grows up to 50 feet tall, has pinnate leaves with two to four pairs of blunt leaflets and has racemes of small bright yellow fragrant flowers. Its pods are flat and about 1¼ inches long. British privateers at one time cruised the Spanish Main especially to capture Spanish ships carrying cargoes of logwood. During the latter half of the nineteenth century the logwood exports reached enormous tonnages but the development of synthetic dyes sharply reduced their importance and much less logwood is shipped than formerly although it is still an important natural dye. The dye, which is purplish red, reacts with iron salts to produce a black that is the most lasting obtainable. The other tropical American species, the brazilette (*H. braziletto*) is the source of a bright red dye. The brazilette is a tree that grows up to 35 feet high and inhabits the Pacific coast from Baja California to Nicaragua, Columbia and Venezuela.

Laburnum—Golden Chain

Here belong three deciduous species, two trees and a shrub, which have trifoliate leaves, showy racemes of yellow pea-shaped flowers—those of the tree kinds pendulous—and narrow pods. All parts of these plants are poisonous, particularly

199

the young fruits; children have died from eating them. Laburnums are natives of southern Europe and central Asia. They are so commonly planted in Great Britain that they there provide one of the most glorious of spring floral displays. Both the Scotch laburnum (L. alpinum) and the common laburnum (L. anagyroides) are occasionally 30 feet tall. The former produces racemes of bloom up to 15 inches long; those of the common laburnum are not more than 8 inches long. The lower sides of the leaves and the pods of the Scotch laburnum are nearly glabrous whereas those of the common laburnum are silky, pubescent.

Leucaena

This group of about fifty shrubs and trees is primarily American with its center of distribution in Mexico. One American species, L. glauca, is planted and naturalized almost throughout the tropics and subtropics and is a frequent roadside small tree. It has feathery foliage and pompon-like clusters of whitish flowers. Its pods, which hang in clusters, contain seeds that are eaten with rice in the West Indies and are used in leis in Hawaii. In Hawaii, too, this species is grown for its stems, leaves and pods, which are used for cattle fodder. Curiously, these have no ill effects on cattle or goats but reports from South America indicate that they cause loss of hair on hogs, horses or mules that eat them. Leucaena glauca is planted to provide shade for tea, coffee and other crops, to control soil erosion and to supply fuel and charcoal. Other species are used locally for fuel and lumber, notably L. pulverulerta of northern Mexico and Texas, which grows up to 60 feet in height and may have a trunk diameter of 20 inches, and L. esculenta of southern Mexico, a somewhat similar kind that bears edible fruits.

Maackia

The ten deciduous species of this genus, all eastern Asiatic, are closely related to the yellow-woods (Cladrastis). They are easily distinguished, however, by the fact that their buds are not concealed by hollow-based petioles, and by leaflets that are opposite rather than alternate. The white flowers occur in dense, erect, usually panicled racemes. The compressed, slender pods contain one to five seeds. Maackia amurensis, a native of Manchuria and China, is 45 feet tall and has glabrous leaves of seven to eleven leaflets. A variety, M. a. buergeri, with leaflets that

are pubescent beneath, inhabits Japan. Maackia chinensis, a native of central China, attains a height of 70 feet and has leaves of eleven to thirteen leaflets which are pubescent on their undersides. The wood of these trees is used locally for construction, furniture, railroad ties and agricultural implements. Their bark yields a yellow dye.

Parkinsonia

One species of this small genus is now widely dispersed in most warm-climate regions. Despite its common name, the Jerusalem thorn or palo verde (P. aculeata) is not an Old World native but is indigenous from Texas to Argentina. It is a thorny evergreen with slender, bright green branches and racemes of charming fragrant yellow flowers, each with five spreading petals of nearly equal size. The narrow pods are constricted between the oblong seeds. Often the Jerusalem thorn is shrublike but occasionally it attains a height of 30 feet. Its leaves are bipinnate, but because of the extremely short main axis they appear to be only once-pinnate with a slender striplike main axis and very tiny ultimate leaflets. These ultimate leaflets are deciduous. The wood is of no value except as fuel.

Peltophorum

Twelve species of this genus inhabit warm regions of the New World and of Asia and Africa. They have bipinnate leaves, showy clusters of yellow flowers and flat pods. The most noteworthy American kinds are P. adnatum of the West Indies, which is often 100 feet tall and has glossy, fernlike leaves, and the canafístula (P. vogelianum) of Argentina, Paraguay and Brazil, a wide-crowned tree that sometimes attains 125 feet in height and has lustrous leaves, and pods with one or two seeds. Their lumber is used for construction, furniture and turnery. One of the most attractive species is the yellow flame or yellow poinciana (P. pterocarpum), a tree 80 feet in height that is native from Malaya, Viet Nam, southern India and Ceylon to Australia. It is a splendid shade tree with a straight trunk and dense crown. Its leaves are dark green on their upper sides, paler beneath. Displays of delightfully fragrant flowers in large erect, pyramidal panicles are, in many regions, borne twice yearly. The wood is good for furniture and fuel. Widely dispersed in the southern half of Africa is the lovely huilboom or African-wattle (P. africanum), a deciduous thornless native of dry bush country that grows up to 50 feet tall. It has silvery gray, acacia-like foliage and bears great masses of brilliant yellow flowers. Its trunk is often gnarled and crooked or forked.

Pithecellobium

Here belong two hundred species of tropical trees and shrubs, many of which are thorny. Their pods of many kinds coil to form complete circles. The best known is the guaymochil or Manila tamarind (*P. dulce*), a spiny species attaining up to 50 feet in height. It is a native in Mexico, Central America and northern South America and is naturalized and freely planted for shade and ornament elsewhere in the tropics. A wide-topped evergreen, this species is notably drought-resistant. Its leaves consist of four leathery, pale green leaflets. The whitish flowers, in small, globular heads three-eighths of an inch across are favorites of bees. The red or brown curved or coiled pods contain a sweet pulp in which are embedded flat, black seeds. The pods are used as fodder and a lemonade-like beverage is made from the pulp. From the trunk, bark, leaves and roots a yellow dye, an adhesive mucilage as well as tannin are extracted. The durable, strong, wood is used for construction, posts and fuel.

Pongamia—Pongam Oil Tree

One Indo-Malaysian species comprises this genus. It is a deciduous or semideciduous tree of seashores and riverbanks that sometimes is 75 feet tall and has pink, or occasionally white, blooms that hang in racemes much like those of wisteria. The shining green foliage is fairly dense, and when the leaves first expand they are pink. Pongam oil or poona oil, which is extracted from the seeds, is used in India medicinally and for illumination. From the roots of this species a fish poison similar to derris is obtained.

Prosopis—Mesquite

Most members of this genus, about forty species, are natives of the New World but one is tropical African and two range from the Caucasus to India. Many are arid-country plants, and some have no leaves, which helps to conserve scanty supplies of water. Many are thorny. Characteristically the leaves are bipinnate and consist of numerous leaflets; the small, greenish·flowers are in cylindrical or globular axillary spikes.

Probably the best known is the mesquite

Guaymochil. Pithecellobium dulce (M. Krishnan)

(*P. juliflora*), a native of the southwestern United States, Mexico, Central America and the West Indies. In dry locations it is shrubby and often has enormous underground stems and wide-ranging roots but where water is more abundant it develops as a tree up to 60 feet in height with a trunk up to 4 feet in diameter. The wood is esteemed as fuel and for fence posts and paving blocks. The outer bark is used for tanning and the inner bark serves in medicines. The pods provide excellent feed for livestock and also food for humans. In Mexico, meal produced from the pods is used to make cakes and in the preparation of a kind of beer. The bark has been used for tanning. The flowers are great favorites of bees, and honey derived from them is of good quality. Another species of interest is the screw bean or tornillo (*P. pubescens*) of the southwestern United States and Mexico. Occasionally attaining a height of 35 feet, this kind has much-spiraled pods that are extraordinarily sweet and may be eaten out of hand or made into syrup, flour or a fermented drink.

Two native species of Argentina and Uruguay called algarrobo (*P. alba* and *P. nigra*) are important. With twisted trunks, up to 2 feet in diameter, and umbrella-like crowns, they are usually between 25 and 40 feet tall. Their pods are eaten by livestock and by the Indians. Algorrobo wood is extremely resistant to moisture and abrasion and for this reason has been much used as paving blocks to surface streets in Buenos Aires; it is considered to be one of the best woods for window frames and doors. Several other species occur in South America, of which one, *P. chilensis*, which is closely related to the North American mesquite, is used for posts, stakes, fuel and food for man and beasts in desert areas remote from other sources of lumber. A very closely related kind, *P. pallida*, of Peru, has been introduced into Hawaii and has been declared to be the commonest and most valuable non-native tree growing there. It is sometimes 60 feet in height and its roots may reach as deeply into the ground as its crown does into the air. This species has long, slender, pliable branches with or without thorns and leaves of eighty or more tiny leaflets. The flowers, in spikes, are pale yellow, and provide abundant nectar for bees. Both honey and beeswax from this source are exploited commercially. The seeds, which are embedded in a sugar-rich pulp, are an important cattle food.

Prosopis africana, which inhabits savanna forest in tropical Africa, is a spreading open-crowned tree up to 60 feet tall with dense racemes of fragrant yellowish flowers and pods up to 6 inches long. Its blooms, which contain abundant nectar and pollen, are much visited by bees. Its seeds serve as food and in the Sudan its pods are pounded, boiled and used as fish poison. The durable, termite-proof wood of this species is made into many domestic articles such as mortars and pestles and tool handles and is employed in cabinetmaking and boatbuilding. The bark is used for tanning. Because the pods contain a high percentage of tannin, cattle do not eat them.

Pterocarpus

A hundred species belong in this widely dispersed tropical genus, the members of which, as the generic name indicates, have winged seeds. Several Old World species yield useful woods, one of the best known being the narra, padauk or angsane (*P. indicus*) of Malaysia and the Philippines. This handsome, lofty, large-crowned, deciduous or evergreen tree has leaves up to 12 inches long, each consisting of seven to eleven pointed leaflets. It bears panicles of fragrant, pealike, half-inch-long, ocher-yellow blooms and flat, beaked pods that contain one or two seeds. Narra wood has a roselike fragrance and is used for good-quality furniture. A kino type of gum that is exuded from the trunk is used medicinally. A native of India and Ceylon, the gammalu (*P. marsupium*) grows up to 80 feet in height and has leathery leaves indented at the tips of the leaflets. Its winged, flat, circular pods contain one seed. When cut, the trunk exudes a red gum. The nodding, bright yellow flowers attract bees. Another Indian kind is the red-sandalwood (*P. santalinus*), which grows to medium size and has a fragrant red heartwood that resembles that of the true sandalwood (*Santalum*). The red-sandalwood is the source of a reddish brown dye.

Robinia—False-Acacia, Black Locust

This group of twenty American species consists mostly of shrubs, but a few are trees. They have lacy, pinnate leaves and fragrant pealike flowers, usually in drooping clusters. The flowers are followed by flat seed pods. The most important tree species is the white-flowered false acacia, black acacia or yellow acacia (*R. pseudoacacia*). A native of the eastern and central United States, this species attains a height of 80 feet and a trunk diameter of 4 feet. It has a narrow head of usually erect, brittle branches and dark, deeply furrowed bark. The lumber of the false acacia is extremely resistant to decay and is valued for fence posts, pergolas and other garden construction. Because of its toughness and resistance to shrinkage it was used for treenails in the days of wooden ships and today is in demand for making the pins that hold glass insulators for telegraph and telephone wires. A variety called shipmast locust (*R. p. rectissima*) forms a narrower specimen and is said to have more durable wood. The false acacia has been naturalized in many parts of Europe and Asia and trees reproduced spontaneously are frequent; sometimes they are so numerous that they drive out native vegetation. In Rumania and Hungary the false acacia is the most important lumber tree. The clammy locust (*R. viscosa*) has pink flowers and grows to a height of about 40 feet with a trunk 1 foot in diameter. It has slender, spreading branches and branchlets covered with sticky, glandular hairs. This species is native in the region from North Carolina to Alabama.

Samanea

Of the twenty species of this tropical genus only one is well known. This is the rain tree, monkey pod or saman *(S. saman)*, an evergreen or deciduous native of the West Indies and Central America now planted in many other tropical regions. It has a wide-spreading, dome-shaped crown and grows up to 100 feet in height with a trunk up to 7 feet in diameter. Its bipinnate leaves have blunt leaflets that are velvety beneath; the outer leaflets are conspicuously bigger than those near the center of the leaf. The pinkish flowers form powder-puff heads about 2¹/₂ inches in diameter; the stamens form the showy part of the blossoms. The long-persistent blackish pods, 4 to 8 inches in length, contain a sweetish pulp between the seeds. This species is prized for shade for man and animals and as a source of nutritious seed pods relished by cattle, hogs and goats and eaten by those who like a licorice flavor. The flowers are attractive to bees. The wood is used locally for a variety of purposes but is not of commercial importance. The name rain tree refers to the honeydew that often drips copiously from the tree; at one time thought to be exuded by the tree, it is now known to be an excretion of sap-sucking insects that feed on the foliage.

Saraca

Twenty species, all Asiatic, are in this genus and are among the most beautiful of tropical trees. In the open most do not exceed 30 feet in height but under forest conditions they may be twice as tall. They have large, dark green leaves with pointed leaflets. Like those of *Amherstia* and *Brownea*, the leaves at first hang in limp grayish pink or purplish red tassels but soon stiffen, straighten and become green. The fragrant yellow, orange or red flowers, without petals and usually with dark centers, appear in compact clusters from the trunk, branches or twigs. The purple-black pods are large, flat and leathery; each contains several flat seeds. Most famous of the genus is the asoka or sorrowless tree *(S. indica)*, held sacred by Buddhists as the tree under which the Buddha is believed to have been born. It is evergreen and up to 30 feet in height. It has stalkless clusters of flowers that change from yellow to orange to red. The asoka is a native of India. The red saraca *(S. declinata)* of Malaya, Thailand, Sumatra and Java is very similar to the asoka, but differs in having a distinct stalk to its larger leaves, longer stalks to the leaflets and darker eyes to its deeper, richly colored flowers. The showiest species is the yellow saraca *(S. thaipingensis)* of Malaya. It is distinguished from the others discussed above by the fact that its basal leaflets do not clasp the twigs. It is strictly cauliflorous, which means that the flower clusters arise only from the trunks and major branches. The flowers of the yellow saraca open yellow, change to apricot yellow and finally to deep yellow with a blood-red eye.

Schizolobium

Of the five species of this genus from Mexico to Brazil and Peru that have been described *S. parahybrum* is the most important. This species sometimes exceeds 100 feet in height and has a buttressed trunk that above the flared base may be 2¹/₂ feet in diameter. Its deciduous bipinnate leaves consist of numerous leaflets and resemble in appearance the fronds of tree ferns. They may be 3 feet long. When the tree is leafless it bears great masses of beautiful golden flowers in erect, foot-long clusters. Each bloom is about 1 inch in diameter and has five petals and ten stamens. The pods, spoon-shaped and about 4 inches long, contain one long-winged seed.

Sesbania

Some twenty species, mostly shrubs, are included in this tropical and subtropical genus. One Asiatic kind, *S. grandiflora*, is sometimes called *Agati grandiflora*. Quick growing, short-lived and evergreen or deciduous, it attains 30 feet in height and a trunk diameter of 1 foot. Its pinnate leaves are swollen at their bases and have leaflets with short, hairy stalks. Two to five blooms comprise each short, pendulous flower cluster. They are white, pink or red, unpleasantly scented and 2¹/₂ to 4 inches long. The slender, four-angled pods, a foot or more long, contain many elliptical brown seeds. *Sesbania grandiflora* is an attractive ornamental. Its flowers, young pods and young leaves are used in salads, curries and soups; they are also fried and eaten, and are used as cattle fodder. The astringent bark is used medicinally.

Sophora

Chiefly native of subtropical and warm-temperate areas, *Sophora* includes about fifty evergreen and deciduous trees, shrubs and herbaceous plants. Their leaves are pinnate with an odd number of leaflets, their flowers pealike in

racemes or panicles, their pods cylindrical or angled, sometimes winged, and much constricted between the seeds. The tree members of the genus are all handsome. The hardiest is the Japanese pagoda tree *(S. japonica)*, a deciduous species which, despite its common name, is a native of China and Korea. It is round-headed, up to 90 feet in height and 6 feet in trunk diameter, and bears large terminal pyramidal clusters of yellowish white flowers in midsummer. This species withstands city conditions well. From its flower buds and bark a yellow dye is extracted and from its leaves and pods an adulterant of opium. Its wood closely resembles that of chestnut *(Castanea)* and has similar uses.

The mamane *(S. chrysophylla)* is a native of nearly all of the Hawaiian Islands and is sometimes 40 feet tall. An evergreen, this kind has small axillary clusters of pale yellow flowers that are up to 1 inch long and quadrangular, four-winged pods that contain yellow seeds. The foliage and young shoots are favorite foods of grazing animals. Its durable, hard wood is used for fence posts. Similar to the mamane but a native of New Zealand, Chile and some Pacific islands is the yellow kowhai *(S. tetraptera)*, a species that attains a height of 40 feet and may be evergreen or deciduous depending upon local conditions. Its flowers are sulphur yellow with deeper colored calyxes and are 1 to $1^{1}/_{2}$ inches long. They contain large quantities of nectar which is eagerly sought by parson birds, the birds tearing the flowers apart to obtain the sweet liquid. The wood of the yellow kowhai is extraordinarily durable under moist conditions and is very beautiful. In Chile it is used by wheelwrights for implement handles, cabinetwork and turnery. Two sophoras of tree size are natives of the United States, the coral-bean *(S. secundiflora)* and *S. affinis*. The flowers of the former are blue and occur in terminal racemes; those of the latter occur in axillary racemes and are white. The coral-bean is evergreen, narrow-headed, and up to 35 feet tall. It has a straight trunk as much as 8 inches in diameter and bright red seeds which contain a poisonous alkaloid. The heavy wood is orange-colored streaked with red. This tree is a native of Texas and New Mexico. *Sophora affinis* is a deciduous, round-topped kind, about 20 feet tall,

Rain tree. Samanea saman (Lorus and Margery Milne)

Yellow kowhai. Sophora tetraptea (Robin Smith)

that ranges from Louisiana to Arkansas, Oklahoma and Texas. Its blooms appear in spring with the young leaves.

Tamarindus—Tamarind

The native origin of the only species of this genus is not surely known but presumably it is tropical Asia or Africa. The tamarind *(T. indica)* has been cultivated for centuries, chiefly for its fruits, which are edible and have medicinal qualities, but also as a shade tree and for its lumber, which is used for fuel, charcoal, furniture and small articles. The tamarind is evergreen or deciduous, much branched, reaches a height of 80 feet, and has a massive trunk and branches, the trunk often fluted. The leaves are pinnate and have ten to twenty pairs of leaflets which are minutely notched at their tips. The rose red flower buds open to asymmetrical pale yellowish blooms that are marked with pink veins and are about 1 inch in diameter. They occur in short racemes. The brown pods, slightly constricted between the seeds, contain a sweet-acid pulp used in beverages, chutneys and medicines.

CHAPTER 21

The Geraniales

Differences of opinion exist among botanists as to the limits of this order; some feel that the group as accepted here should be split into three or more orders. Members usually have twice as many stamens as sepals, in two whorls or circles or with the outer whorl lacking.

ZYGOPHYLLACEAE—CALTROP FAMILY

This chiefly pantropical family of nearly two hundred species consists mostly of shrubs and herbaceous plants; only a few are trees.

Guaiacum—Lignum Vitae

The most important of the six species of this New World genus, the wood of which is known as lignum vitae, is *G. officinale,* which is common in the West Indies, Central America and northern South America. A handsome evergreen tree up to 30 feet in height, with a short trunk up to 1½ feet in diameter, it has leaves about 3 inches long, each of four to six leaflets. The delicately fragrant flowers have five spreading pale blue petals about a half inch long and ten stamens. Lignum vitae, the hardest of commercial woods, is abrasion-resistant, resinous and self-lubricating. It is esteemed for bushings, pulley sheaves, bearings, and propellor shafts for steamships, for which last-mentioned purpose it is unequaled, as well as for furniture casters, bowling balls and turnery. Other species of *Guaiacum,* all similar to *G. officinalis,* are *G. coulteri* of Mexico, the durable wood of which is used locally for construction and fuel, *G. guatemalense* of Central America and *G. sanctum,* which occurs in Mexico, the West Indies and the Florida Keys. The wood of *G. sanctum* is second in commercial importance to that of *G. officinale.*

RUTACEAE—RUE FAMILY

Distinguishing characteristics of this family are translucent dots in the foliage, clearly evident when the leaves are held up to light, and the presence of glands that secrete aromatic oils. The family includes about 150 genera and about nine hundred species, mostly trees and shrubs of tropical and temperate regions throughout the world. Many are of commercial importance.

Calodendrum

The Cape-chestnut (*C. capense*) and one other African species constitute this genus. Beautiful in bloom, the Cape-Chestnut is sometimes 60 feet tall and spreads its branches widely; frequently its trunk is buttressed. Its opposite, undivided, pointed-oval, glossy leaves have prominent midveins with lateral veins almost at right angles to them. The foliage is deciduous or evergreen according to local climate; when deciduous the leaves become bright yellow before they fall. The fragrant, five-petaled flowers, light rose pink with purple markings, are in loose terminal clusters. They are succeeded by dry, knobbly fruits up to 2½ inches in diameter that contain about ten glossy, black, inedible, bitter seeds that yield an oil suitable for soap making. The wood of the Cape-chestnut is used for furniture, planking, tool handles and other purposes.

Citrus

Here belong a dozen or so evergreen small trees or shrubs of southern China and southeast Asia. Their leaves, usually undivided, are jointed where the stalk meets the blade, which indicates that the group has developed from compound-leaved ancestors. Their white or purple-tinged flowers are fragrant. Technically the fruits are berries, which may surprise non-botanists unused to applying this term to oranges, lemons and grapefruit. Present-day *Citrus* represents the end development of an evolutionary line that started perhaps twenty million years ago, certainly before Australia was isolated by water from New Guinea and Asia. Citruses are of great commercial importance and many kinds are cultivated in warm countries, especially in those with Mediterranean climates, for their fruits, which are rich in vitamin C. The British early learned that drinking lime juice controlled the dreaded scurvy that was the bane of sailors and they issued rations of it to men in their navy many years before vitamins were discovered. The nickname "limey," still sometimes applied to Englishmen, refers to this custom. The genus is divided into two subgenera, *Eucitrus,* which includes all of the kinds with edible fruits, and *Papeda,* which has inedible fruits that contain an acrid oil.

With the exception of the citron *(C. medica),* all of the *Eucitrus* group have winged leaf stalks. The leaves of the citron are serrated and have short solitary spines in their axils. Their fragrant blooms, in few-flowered clusters and purplish in bud, are large and predominantly white, with the outsides of their petals pinkish; they have numerous stamens. The large oblong or oval fruits are often rough and bumpy. This, the oldest citrus fruit in cultivation in Mediterranean lands, was introduced there by the armies of Alexander the Great about 300 B. C. Theophrastus described the fruit and called it the Median (Persian) apple. The chief product of the *Citron* is the peel of the fruits, which is candied and used in cakes and confectionery.

The lemon *(C. limonia)* has narrowly winged leaf stalks and differs from other *Citrus* with winged leaf stalks in having more than four times as many stamens as petals and in having flowers of two kinds, some with functioning stamens and ovaries and others with fertile stamens but abortive ovaries. The young foliage and flower buds are reddish, the leaves are pointed and more or less serrate, the petals are white inside and purplish on their undersides, the stamens number from twenty to forty, and the nippled, oval fruits are yellow when ripe. Lemons are used for flavoring in beverages and for other culinary purposes. Lemon trees are thorny. Their origin is unknown, possibly they are derivatives of the citron. They were introduced by the Arabs to the Mediterranean region between A. D. 1000 and 1200 and soon became important medicinal plants. Other edible species discussed here usually have four times as many stamens as petals and all their flowers with functioning stamens and ovaries; their leaf stalks are winged. They may be divided into two groups, those with fruits with loose peel and those in which the rind adheres rather firmly to the fruit segments. Best known of the former is the king orange *(C. nobilis),* which includes mandarin and tangerine oranges, and the satsuma orange *(C. n. unshiu). Citrus nobilis* is a native of southwest Asia and the Philippines. It has white flowers that are solitary or are in small clusters, globose fruits flattened or depressed at their poles, and very narrowly winged leaf stalks.

Two *Citrus* species that have adherent peel have extraordinarily large fruits, usually more than 4 inches in diameter. They are the grapefruit *(C. paradisi)* and the shaddock or pummelo *(C. maxima).* The former bears its fruits close together in clusters, whereas those of the shaddock are solitary. The shaddock is probably a native of Malaysia and Polynesia; the origin of the grapefruit is not known but it probably developed under cultivation in the West Indies. Both are comparatively large, round-topped trees with angular twigs and broadly winged leaf stalks, with those of the pummelo wider than those of the grapefruit, and both have large flowers borne singly or in clusters. The fruits of the shaddock are esteemed in Asia, but elsewhere the grapefruit is of far greater importance. The pulp vesicles of shaddocks are larger than those of grapefruit and they fall apart easily.

Limes *(C. aurantifolia),* sweet oranges *(C. sinensis)* and sour oranges *(C. aurantium)* all have fruits with adherent peel and are usually less than 4 inches in diameter. Those of the lime rarely exceed 2¹/₂ inches in length and have greenish, usually very acid pulp and a thin rind which, when the fruit is ripe, is greenish yellow. These trees, indigenous to the East Indies, have sharp spines and small leaves with narrowly winged stalks. The juice of limes, taken internally in quantity or applied externally, has the curious effect of sensitizing the human skin to strong sunlight with the result that exposed areas turn dark brown. The effect wears off after a few days. The flowers, white in bud, are small and are usually in clusters of a few individuals. The sweet orange differs from the sour orange in having fruits that are smoother and sweet rather than bitter and are orange-colored rather than scarlet-orange, in having a central core of fully ripe fruit that is solid rather than hollow, and in leaf stalks that are more narrowly winged. The fruits of the sour orange are used for marmalade, beverages, candied peel and in the preparation of the liqueur curaçao; from the flower comes oil of neroli, an important ingredient of eau de cologne. The fruits of the sweet orange are chiefly eaten or are used for juice.

The calamondin *(C. mitis)* is a small, dense, somewhat prickly tree that bears from the ends of its branches ellipsoid or globose fruits about 1¹/₂ inches in diameter and with loose skins. It has narrowly winged leaf stalks, and small white flowers. Its fruits are used for the same purposes as lemons and limes. In all probability the calamondin is of hybrid origin. It is one of the hardiest of *Citrus*.

Evodia

Here are forty-five deciduous and evergreen trees and shrubs of tropical Africa, Asia, Australia and the Pacific Islands. They are closely related to *Zanthoxylum*, from which they can be distinguished by their opposite leaves. They differ from *Phellodendron* in having neither berry-like fruits nor axillary buds covered by the bases of the leaf stalks. The most familiar kinds have large deciduous pinnate aromatic leaves, broad clusters of small yellowish white flowers, and dry fruit capsules which open to reveal glossy black seeds. *Evodia danielli* of Korea and northern China, about 25 feet tall, bears its flowers in summer. Its leaflets are almost stalkless and its fruits have short beaks. In these respects it differs from *E. hupehensis*, which has distinctly stalked leaflets and long-beaked fruits. *Evodia hupehensis* attains a height of about 60 feet.

Phellodendron—Cork-tree

Ten species of eastern Asiatic deciduous, aromatic trees constitute the genus *Phellodendron*. In general appearance they resemble walnuts, although they belong—as an examination of their flowers and fruits quickly reveals—to a quite different family. The flowers are unisexual, with the sexes on separate trees, and form terminal clusters. They are small and yellowish green. The black, berry-like fruits taste strongly of turpentine and contain five one-seeded stones. The leaves, each consisting of an odd number of leaflets, have stalks with bases that are swollen and fit over and conceal the axillary buds. The name cork-tree refers to the thick corklike bark of the Amur cork-tree *(P. amurense)*. This broad-headed species attains a height of 50 feet and has leaves that are hairless beneath, except sometimes for a few hairs on the midribs, and leaflets fringed with fine hairs. This cork-tree is a native of northern China and Manchuria. Similar except for its thinner bark and leaflets that are scarcely fringed with hairs or have no fringe at all is *P. sachalinense* of China, Korea and Japan. *Phellodendron lavallei*, *P. japonicum*, and *P. chinense* have leaves that are pubescent beneath or at least quite hairy along the veins. The first named has thick corky bark but that of the other two is comparatively thin. *Phellodendron japonicum* differs from *P. chinense* in having glabrous rather than pubescent ovaries and looser flower clusters that are broader than they are tall.

The cork-trees are handsome decorative forms that withstand dryness and city conditions. They are well adapted for landscape planting. This is especially true of *P. amurense*. The wood of *P. amurense* is used for furniture, gun stocks and domestic articles.

Ptelia—Hop Tree

The hop tree or wafer-ash *(P. trifoliata)* is the best known of the three deciduous North American trees or shrubs in this genus. A native from Ontario and New York to Minnesota and Florida, it reaches a maximum height of about 25 feet and has trifoliate leaves. Its greenish white flowers, about one-half inch across, form clusters and the females are succeeded by compressed suborbicular, broadly winged fruits almost or quite 1 inch in diameter and containing two seeds. Both unisexual and bisexual flowers occur on the same tree.

Zanthoxylum

Twenty to thirty temperate and subtropical prickly trees and shrubs of eastern Asia, Malaysia, the Philippines and North America belong here. They have pinnate leaves that in most species are aromatic, and clusters of small flowers, either all unisexual or with bisexual and unisexual flowers in the same cluster. The Hercules club or toothache tree *(Z. clava-herculis)*, a native from southern Virginia to southern Florida and Texas, rarely attains a height of 50 feet and a trunk diameter of 1½ feet. A round-headed, deciduous species, it branches horizontally. Its leaves have an odd number of leaflets, pubescent or spiny stalks, and hang on the twigs until late winter. The flowers appear in early spring, with the male and female on different trees. They are greenish and form terminal panicles. The fruits are in dense, nearly globular clusters. The bark and fruits were popular for the treatment of toothache and rheumatism.

The prickly-ash *(Z. americanum)*, which is also sometimes called toothache tree, ranges from Quebec to Nebraska and Virginia. Usually shrubby, its maximum height is 25 feet. A prickly-branched, deciduous species, its leaves have an odd number of leaflets, and its small greenish flowers are in nearly stalkless axillary clusters. Male and female flowers are usually on separate trees. Its red fruits, the size of small peas, have a distinct bitter-lemon odor; they open to reveal shining black seeds. The wild-lime (*Z. fagara*) of Florida, Mexico, the West Indies and Central and South America is an evergreen species that grows up to 30 feet in height, has upright branches and glossy foliage. Its branchlets are armed with hooked spines. Its flowers form axillary clusters, the males and females on separate trees. Differing in having stems without prickles and fragrant flowers clustered at the ends of the shoots is the West Indian satinwood (*Z. flavum*), a native of the West Indies, Bermuda and the Florida Keys. This species is up to 50 feet in height and has a trunk up to 20 inches in diameter. Its hard, heavy, fine-textured and beautifully grained wood when newly cut has an odor of coconuts. Used for turnery and backs of brushes, it is prized for inlays and cabinetwork. The leaves, bark and fruits of the Chinese and Japanese *Z. piperitum* are popular in the Orient for flavoring; the hard wood is used for utensils. This is a small tree or shrub that has leaves with toothed leaflets and clusters of greenish flowers.

SIMAROUBACEAE—QUASSIA FAMILY

Twenty genera totaling 120 species of alternate-leaved trees and shrubs comprise the quassia family. Their leaves lack the translucent dots characteristic of the closely related Rutaceae. Most have pinnate leaves and unisexual flowers, the sexes ordinarily on separate plants. The family is primarily pantropical with minor extensions into temperate regions. Its members contain a bitter principle for which some are exploited commercially.

Aeschrion—Bitter-ash

The five tropical American species of this genus are sometimes named *Picrasma*. The most important is the Jamaica-quassia or bitterwood (*A. excelsa*) which occasionally reaches a height of 80 feet. It has a smooth whitish trunk, leaves with an odd number of leaflets, clusters of small greenish flowers, and berry-like fruits that are solitary or in twos or threes. The extremely bitter wood is used medicinally and as an insecticide. At one time cups turned from it were sold in pharmacies; they were filled with water which, after being allowed to stand for a few minutes, was drunk for its tonic properties. Jamaica-quassia is a native of the islands of the West Indies.

Tree-of-heaven. Ailanthus altissima (T. H. Everett)

Ailanthus

Ten Asiatic and Australian deciduous trees belong in this group. All have the peculiarity that the leaflets usually fall from the midrib of the leaf before the midrib falls from the tree. By far the best known is the tree-of-heaven (*A. altissima*), a native of China, freely naturalized in North America, Europe and Asia but quite rare as a wild tree in its native country. So accommodating is the tree-of-heaven that even in metropolitan areas it is often a weed. In downtown New York this immigrant flourishes wherever there is a little poor earth to support it and even crops up in crevices between paving blocks and in other unlikely places, apparently unharmed by soot and smog. This is the species made famous by the novel *A Tree Grows in Brooklyn*. No other introduced tree competes as aggressively with native American forest trees.

The tree-of-heaven is open-topped and casts minimum shade. It sometimes attains a height of 90 feet and has pinnate leaves up to 2 feet long, or sometimes more, with leaflets that have one or two pairs of coarse teeth near their bases. Each tooth usually has on its underside a conspiciuous gland. Male and female flowers are normally on separate trees but rare individuals produce flowers of both sexes. The tiny greenish

Ailanthus leaves (Andreas Feininger)

yellow flowers, in terminal clusters, are without decorative merit; the males are malodorous. The fruits, borne in large, prominent bunches, are quite ornamental; they are winged, much like those of ashes, but with a single seed near the center of the wing rather than close to its end. Those of some trees become brilliant red.

Quassia

Of forty tropical species in this genus the most important is the South American bitterwood (*Q. amara*), the source of Surinam quassia used in medicine and as an insecticide. Rarely more than 25 feet in height, this tree has leaves with winged stalks and five leaflets, terminal racemes of crimson flowers, each 1 to 2 inches long, and dark purple, ovoid, berry-like fruits, one-half inch long, that may form star-shaped clusters of five.

BURSERACEAE—BURSERA FAMILY

This family of sixteen genera and five hundred tropical species consists of alternate-leaved trees and shrubs with small, usually unisexual flowers. Many kinds supply balsams and resins.

Canarium

Of the hundred species that inhabit Africa, Asia, northern Australia and islands of the Pacific, the Java-almond or pili nut (*C. commune*) is most notable. This native of Malaysia grows up to 90 feet in height and has planklike buttresses supporting the lower part of its trunk; slender aerial roots often hang from the trunk. The leaves are of seven to eleven leaflets. The small, yellowish white, three-parted fragrant flowers, bisexual or unisexual, are in loose panicles and are succeeded by ovoid, somewhat three-angled, bluish-black nuts containing single kernels which have an almond-like flavor. The kernels are eaten raw or roasted. From the nuts a cooking oil is obtained. The Java-almond is a first-class shade tree. There is a magnificent avenue of it in Bogor, Java. The Ceylon-almond (*C. javanicum*) is endemic to the island from which it takes its name. It has a buttressed trunk and apple green, deciduous, pinnate leaves. The seeds of the ovoid fruits are edible and from them is expressed an oil used for illuminating. A gum resin exudes copiously from the trunks. Another species worthy of mention is the Chinese white-olive (*C. album*), which grows up to 60 feet in height and has leaves with eleven to thirteen leaflets. This species has egg-shaped fruits that are greenish white when ripe and are esteemed for their edible pulp.

MELIACEAE—MAHOGANY FAMILY

Fifty genera, embracing 1400 species, are included in this chiefly pantropical family of trees and shrubs. With few exceptions their leaves are pinnate and alternate; they lack translucent dots. The flowers are in panicles. Only rarely do unisexual flowers occur, and then interspersed with bisexual ones. The stamens are joined to form a tube that surrounds the pistil. The seeds are usually winged.

Azadirachta—Neem Tree; Margosa Tree

There are two species of *Azadirachta*, both natives of Indomalaysia. The neem or nim tree (*A. indica*), common in India and Ceylon, is greatly valued for its bitter, antiseptic resin, which is used in medicines, soaps, lotions and toothpaste. From its seeds margosa oil, used medicinally and to some extent as an illuminant, is extracted; its twigs are used as toothbrushes. The leaves of this tree, placed between the pages of books and among clothes, are said to deter insects. To Hindus the neem tree is sacred and idols are made from its wood. The wood is also used for furniture, agricultural implements and shipbuilding. The neem tree is a graceful evergreen, up to 50 feet tall; it thrives in dry climates. Its pinnate leaves have an odd number of curved, pointed, toothed, shiny leaflets. The numerous small, fragrant, white flowers occur in loose panicles usually partially concealed by the foliage; they are followed by small yellow berries that are great favorites of birds.

Cedrela

The six or seven species of *Cedrela* are very similar to each other; they are deciduous natives of Mexico, the West Indies and tropical Central and South America. The most important is the West-Indian-cedar (*C. odorata*), which is indigenous from the West Indies to the Amazon basin. Attaining a height of 100 feet and a trunk diameter of 3¹/₂ feet above its substantially buttressed base, this tree has small yellowish flowers in panicles and leaves with eight pairs of leaflets. The principal South American species is *C. fissilis,* which differs in having leaves with nine or more pairs of leaflets. The lumber of all species is similar and provides the most important domestic wood of South America; it is used for fine furniture, interior trim and many other purposes. A principle use in countries other than where it is native is for making cigar boxes; the volatile oil responsible for the fragrance of the wood is said to impart a desirable aroma to cigars stored in the boxes.

Khaya

Eight species of tall tropical African and Madagascan trees are included here. Several yield woods marketed as mahoganies. They resemble true mahogany (*Swietenia*) in that they contain oleoresins and are durable and resistant to insects. An important species is the 200-foot-tall African mahogany (*K. ivorensis*), which may have a trunk diameter of 5 feet above its prominent buttresses and a trunk clear of branches for 90 feet above the ground. The glabrous, leathery leaves, crowded at the ends of the twigs, have four or five pairs of leaflets. The small white flowers form small clusters. The wood of the African mahogany is esteemed for interior trim, furniture, plywood and veneers.

Melia—Bead Tree

This small group of tropical and subtropical trees is not well defined as a species. The best known is the Persian-lilac, pride-of-India, or China-berry (*M. azedarach*), a deciduous native of tropical Asia that has naturalized itself in many warm regions including Hawaii and the southern United States. It is a quick-growing, useful shade tree that attains a height of 60 feet, with a wide-spreading crown and delicate, fern-like foliage. Its bipinnate, toothed leaves may be 20 inches long or more. Its clusters of small, fragrant, lilac flowers are succeeded by glossy golden yellow berry-like fruits that remain long after the leaves fall. They are said to be poisonous to man, to some animals, and to poultry but are reported not to harm cattle and most birds. There is no doubt that many parts of this tree are poisonous to a greater or lesser extent. Its dried leaves are used to deter insects from attacking books, clothing, and pulses in storage. Its wood is used for furniture and other purposes, and its seeds as beads and rosaries. A variety called the Texas umbrella tree (*M. a. umbraculiformis*) has radiating branches and drooping foliage that give the crown an umbrella-like appearance.

Swietenia—Mahogany

True mahogany, the premier cabinet wood of the world, is a product of members of this genus of seven or eight trees of the New World tropics. The two most important species are the West Indian mahogany (*S. mahagonii*) and the Honduras mahogany (*S. macrophylla*). Obvious differences between them are the much larger leaves, flowers, fruits and seeds of the latter. West Indian mahogany reaches a maximum height of 60 feet with a short, swollen or buttressed trunk up to 4¹/₂ feet in diameter. It has a spreading top and deciduous, pinnate leaves up to 7 inches long that have an even number of untoothed leaflets. The flowers, small and greenish, occur in lateral clusters. The fruits, up to 4 inches long, split into five parts by opening upward from their bases. The astringent bark has been used in medicine. The West Indian mahogany, a native of southern Florida as well as the West Indies, is an attractive ornamental shade tree. Its wood, considered to be superior to that of Honduras mahogany, is used for veneers, furniture, cabinetmaking and interior trim.

The Honduras mahogany occasionally exceeds 60 feet in height. It has a buttressed base, deciduous leaves, 8 to 16 inches long, fragrant,

Candlenut tree. Aleurites moluccana (Tad Nichols)

greenish yellow flowers each almost one-half an inch in diameter, and fruits 4½ to 7 inches long that split upward from the base into five parts. Wood of this species is used for the same purposes as West Indian mahogany; it is much more important commercially. The Honduras mahogany is native from southern Mexico and Central America to Peru, Bolivia and Brazil.

EUPHORBIACEAE—SPURGE FAMILY

Five thousand species distributed among three hundred genera comprise this nearly cosmopolitan family that is considered to be most closely related to the Sterculiaceae and the Flacourtiaceae. Tremendous variation in plant form occurs in the Euphorbiaceae; many kinds are cactuslike, others are tropical trees, some are lowly lawn weeds; and the Christmas poinsettia and the house plant called crown-of-thorns belong here. In the spurge family the flowers are unisexual and nearly all members have a milky sap.

Aleurites

The candlenut tree (*A. moluccana*) and the tung

oil tree (*A. fordii*) are important members of a small group of Asiatic trees. The first named, an evergreen native of Malaysia and the Pacific Islands that is common in Hawaii, is easily recognized by the frosted appearance of its younger foliage (*Aleurites* is Greek for "flourlike"). It is a large tree with an irregular crown and mostly spearhead-shaped leaves; on young trees and often on lower branches of older ones the leaves are three- or five-lobed. The twigs, flower clusters, branches and younger leaves are covered with a whitish scurf. The panicles of small, yellowish flowers are succeeded by small clusters of olive-green fruits 2 to 2½ inches in diameter, each containing one or two large seeds. These, eaten raw, are violently purgative but this property is destroyed by cooking and they are baked and eaten. Candlewood oil, used extensively in paints, varnishes, linoleum and soft soap, is expressed from the seeds. The residual oil cake is poisonous and unsuitable for stock feed but is used as a fertilizer. The name candlenut reflects a former use of the seeds; they were dried, strung on the midribs of coconut leaves and used for illumination.

The tung oil tree (*A. fordii*), native to China, is the source of a very important commercial oil used in paints and quick-drying varnishes. Flattopped and up to 25 feet in height, this species has heart-shaped leaves and showy white flowers, marked with red and yellow, that are about 2 inches in diameter. The poisonous, slightly pointed fruits, 2 to 3 inches in diameter, contain three to five seeds, and from these the oil is expressed. In China, tung oil is used for illumination and is burned for its soot, an important ingredient in Chinese ink. A very similar species, the mu tree (*A. montana*), which has egg-shaped fruits with three longitudinal and numerous transverse ridges, is the source of a similar oil. It is a native of southern China. The Japanese wood oil tree (*A. cordata*), also a native of southern China, is much cultivated in Japan. Its somewhat flattened, warty fruits have flattened seeds the size of castor beans and pointed, broadly ovate leaves that are lobed or toothed. Its oil is used for illumination.

Euphorbia

Most of the 2,000 species of *Euphorbia* are herbaceous plants or shrubs. Many inhabit desert and semidesert regions and are cactus-like in appearance, but they are easily separated from cactuses by their milky sap and the fact that

Candelabra tree. Euphorbia ingens (Emil Schulthess)

when they have spines, such spines are solitary or in pairs. Only a few species are trees and of these, *E. cooperi, E. excelsa, E. grandidens, E. ingens, E. tetragona* and *E. triangularis* are grotesque, cactus-like plants of South Africa. These species, all commonly known as nabooms, are so much alike that it is difficult to separate them except by technical botanical characters. The tallest attain heights of 40 feet. They have thick green branches and stems that function as leaves (the true leaves are rudimentary and soon drop). Typical of the group is the candelabra tree *(E. ingens)*, which rarely exceeds 30 feet in height and forms a dense broad head of mostly vertical, strongly angled, leafless branches. Its flowers are small, fleshy and reddish. The sap is acrid and will blister the skin; it is reported that the natives used it dried as a poison and threw cut branches into ponds and streams to stupefy fish. A native Canary Island tree, *E. canariensis,* is similar in appearance to the nabooms of South Africa. It attains a maximum height of 20 feet.

The tiru-calli or milk bush *(Euphorbia tirucalli)* is a succulent native of the southern half of Africa that was first described botanically from plants growing in India. Apparently their ancestors had been taken there by early Portuguese travelers and natives of Malabar gave to the plant the name tiru-calli. Sometimes called the rubber euphorbia because its sap is richer in rubber than that of most species that contain rubber, this unisexual tree attains a height of 30 feet and has a dense rounded head of branches and very numerous green cylindrical pencil-thick branchlets. Its rudimentary leaves are soon deciduous. The tiru-calli is commonly cultivated in many warm climates.

Hevea—Rubber Tree

A dozen tropical American trees, by far the most important of which is the rubber tree *(H. braziliensis)*, belong in this genus. The rubber tree must not be confused with the rubber plant *(Ficus elastica)* popular for growing in pots. The rubber tree is a deciduous native of the Amazon Basin that is cultivated extensively in tropical Asia and tropical Africa and is the source of almost all commercial natural rubber. *Hevea braziliensis* attains a maximum height of about 100 feet. Its long-stalked leaves each have three narrow, pointed leaflets. The tiny fragrant yellowish white flowers are in clusters with a few female blooms in the center and many males surrounding them; they have no petals. The three-lobed fruits explode when they are ripe and release three large seeds. The young foliage is purplish bronze; old leaves before they drop turn bright orange, brown, or red. Until late in the nineteenth century all *Hevea* rubber was collected from wild trees, and exportation of trees or seeds from South America was forbidden. Despite this, seeds were smuggled from Brazil to England, germinated in greenhouses at the Royal Botanic Gardens at Kew, and the young plants raised were transported in miniature greenhouses by ship to Ceylon, Singapore and Java. From this modest beginning the great rubber plantations of Java, Sumatra, Malaya and Liberia were developed. Rubber is obtained by making incisions in the bark, collecting the latex that flows from the cuts and coagulating it with acid. Rubber latex in liquid form, stabilized by adding ammonia, is also exported as a commercial product.

Hura—Sand Box Tree

Of the two species of *Hura* the most familiar is the sand box tree (*H. crepitans*) of Central and tropical South America and the West Indies. Differing scarcely at all except in the structure of its stamens, and having similar properties, is *H. polyandra* of Mexico. These deciduous trees attain heights of 200 feet. Their buttressed trunks and branches are usually furnished with sharp spines. They have more or less heart-shaped, toothed leaves, deep red male flowers in dense, stalked spikes and solitary red female flowers nearby. The flattened fruits, about 3 inches in diameter, are furrowed like small pumpkins. When ripe they explode with a loud noise and with considerable force discharge their many, flattened seeds. All parts of *Hura* trees are poisonous and their caustic milky sap inflames the skin and is especially irritating to the eyes; it may temporarily cause blindness. The wood is used for general carpentry, interior construction and for crates and boxes.

Sapium

Here belong 120 species of trees and shrubs of the tropics of both hemispheres. They have terminal spikes of small petalless flowers, the males in threes on the upper parts of the spikes, the females singly below. The most noteworthy is the Chinese tallow tree (*S. sebiferum*), a native of China, Taiwan and Japan that attains a maximum height of about 40 feet. It contains a poisonous milky sap and its black seeds are covered with a thick layer of hard white fat used for making soap and candles. Other products of this species are a drying oil which is expressed from the seeds and used for waterproofing hats and umbrellas, and a black dye obtained from the leaves. The white wood is used for printing blocks and other purposes. The Chinese tallow tree is up to 45 feet tall. It has long-stalked triangular leaves that turn brilliant red before they drop in fall. The ellipsoid fruits contain three seeds. The Puerto Rican tabaiba (*S. laurocerasus*) is an evergreen species up to 60 feet in height with a columnar crown and ovate-elliptic leaves. The flower clusters are green. The globular fruits, three-eighths of an inch in diameter, contain three white seeds. The sap is irritating and poisonous. Some South American species of *Sapium* exceed 100 feet in height and have trunks 3 feet in diameter. Among them are *S. giganteum* and *S. jenmanii*.

CHAPTER 22

The Sapindales

BUXACEAE—BOXWOOD FAMILY

This ancient group of four genera and one hundred species belongs to the order Sapindales, an order differing from the Geraniales in the arrangement of the ovules within the ovaries. Buxaceae exhibits a close relationship with the Euphorbiaceae but lacks a milky sap. It includes but few trees.

Buxus—Boxwood

Seventy species belong in this widely distributed tropical, subtropical and temperate region genus of evergreens. Their flowers, without petals, form clusters of one female surrounded by a number of males. The small fruits explode when ripe to expel six glossy black seeds. Most species are shrubs; a few are trees. Of the trees the best known is the English or common boxwood (*B. sempervirens*), which rarely is 30 feet tall. This native of Europe, North Africa and western Asia has glossy ovate leaves, usually notched at their tips, ¹/₂ to 1¹/₄ inch long, dark green above and paler on their undersides. Quite similar to the English boxwood is the Balearic boxwood (*B. balearica*). A native of Spain and the Balearic Islands, it has larger and duller leaves than *B. sempervirens* and sometimes attains a height of 80 feet. A species formerly called *B. macowanii* but now named *Notobuxus macowanii*, is the Cape-boxwood, a native of South Africa. It closely resembles the English boxwood and is used for the same purposes. The hard, bony or ivory-like woods of the boxwood and of the Cape-boxwood do not split easily and can be turned and planed to fine surfaces. They are especially esteemed for engraving blocks, rulers, woodwind instruments and inlay work.

ANACARDIACEAE—CASHEW FAMILY

This family, chiefly tropical, is represented also in temperate North America, eastern temperate Asia and the Mediterranean region. It consists chiefly of trees and shrubs.

Anacardium

The most important of this tropical American group of fifteen species is the cashew nut (*A. occidentale*), an evergreen tree native to the Caribbean region that has a dense, irregular crown about 20 feet high, and dull, bluish green elliptic or obovate leathery leaves up to 6 inches long and about half as wide; the lateral veins of the leaves are at nearly right angles to the midrib. The small, fragrant, pinkish, five-petaled flowers form broad terminal clusters. The apparent fruits are quite remarkable, each consisting of an enlarged stalk, pear-shaped, juicy, yellowish or reddish and fruitlike, up to 3 inches long by 2 inches broad. To the end of this, outside the apparent fruit, is attached a kidney-shaped body up to 1¹/₄ inches long, which is the true fruit. It consists of a seed enclosed in a hard shell containing cardol oil that blisters the skin in the same way that poison-ivy (*Rhus*) does. The fruits are roasted to destroy the poisonous oil and prevent contamination of the seed inside, which is the edible cashew nut of commerce. The enlarged fruitlike stalks are spongy and juicy and have a pleasant acid

Cashew nuts. Anacardium occidentalis (Paul Popper Limited)

flavor. Other species of *Anacardium* are trees up to 150 feet in height, including *A. excelsum*, *A. giganteum* and *A. spruceanum*. The wood of these larger kinds is used locally in South America for making household utensils, furniture and dugout canoes and for construction.

Mangifera—Mango

The mango (*M. indica*) is the best known and most important of the forty Indo-Malaysian deciduous and evergreen trees that comprise this genus. All have undivided leaves and flowers with four or five petals and the same number of stamens; only one or two of the stamens are fertile. The fleshy fruits contain a single stone. The mango, a native of India and, possibly, Malaya that has been cultivated since time immemorial and now exists in countless varieties, is one of the most important tropical fruits. Occasionally more than 75 feet tall and with a trunk up to 3 feet in diameter, it forms a rounded crown of spreading branches and dense evergreen foliage. Its pointed, elliptic leaves are leathery, up to 1 foot long, and often have wavy margins; when bruised they emit a sweet resinous odor. The young

215

Mango. Mangifera indica (U.S.D.A.)

leaves are pink or reddish and hang limply. The strongly scented unisexual or bisexual flowers, small and yellowish and with three minute orange-colored ridges on the inner face of each petal, are in stiff, erect, terminal clusters. The smooth-skinned fruits vary considerably in shape and size and when ripe are yellow, red or green according to variety; usually they are more or less egg-shaped and 3 to 4½ inches long. Each contains a large, flattened seed covered with coarse fibers and surrounded by juicy yellow or or orange pulp that in the best varieties is deliciously flavored; inferior fruits taste strongly of turpentine. Mangoes are eaten raw and are used in curries, preserves, desserts and other ways. Some people are sensitive to the raw fruits and many suffer from a poison-ivy-like rash about the lips and face as a result of eating them. Mango wood is used for doors, window frames, packing cases, boatbuilding and plywood. Cattle eat the foliage greedily and a yellow dye is obtained from the leaves and bark. Hindoos regard mango leaves as symbols of happiness and prosperity and use them on festive and religious occasions.

Other species of *Mangifera* are common in Malaya. Chief among these are the kwini (*M. odorata*), the bachang (*M. foetida*), the binjai (*M. caesia*) and the lanjut (*M. laginifera*), all cultivated for their fruits. Unlike the common or Indian mango, they have tall, columnar, undivided trunks and conical crowns. The kwini and the bachang seldom exceed 80 feet in height; the others often attain 100 feet. The saps of the binjai and lanjub are especially likely to cause severe dermatitis. The binjai and, under some conditions, the lanjut are deciduous. The former has violet flowers with five fertile stamens. The flowers of the binjai are pink or reddish with one fertile and four sterile stamens; their leaves have flattened stalks. The pink flowers of the kwini are fragrant; the stalks of their pointed leaves are not flattened. The bachang has blunt leaves without flattened stalks, and scentless flowers.

Pistacia—Pistache

Ten species constitute *Pistacia*, which is native from the Mediterranean region to southeastern Asia, the Canary Islands, and Central and North America. Its most familiar member is the pistachio (*P. vera*), a deciduous tree about 30 feet in height that ranges as a native from southern Europe and North Africa to the Orient. Its seeds, commonly called nuts, after steeping in brine are used for flavoring confectionery and ice cream. *Pistacia vera* has leaves of three to eleven or more leaflets. Its small, unisexual flowers, without petals, are brownish green, with the sexes on separate trees. The males have a five-part calyx and from three to five stamens, the females a three- or four-part calyx and a three-part style. The leaves have up to five pairs of leaflets. The ovoid, reddish fruit, dryish and wrinkled, contains one seed.

Pistacia lentiscus, of the Mediterranean region that is usually less than 20 feet tall, is the source of mastic, a resin that exudes from the bark and is used in varnishes, oil and water-color paints, in medicine and as cement in dental work. It was much used in Turkish and Arabian harems to perfume the breath and whiten the teeth. This species has an even number of leaflets, three to five pairs to each leaf, and winged leaf stalks. Other kinds exploited for their resins include *P. terebinthus* of the Mediterranean region, a deciduous small tree that has flowers with purplish stamens, leaves of nine to thirteen leaflets and dark purple, wrinkled fruits. On warm evenings this kind gives off a penetrating, resinous odor. The North African *P. atlantica,* also a source of resin, is deciduous, up to 60 feet in height, and has leaves with seven to eleven leaflets. Its lumber is similar to walnut.

The Chinese *P. chinensis* is deciduous, may be up to 45 feet tall, and has foliage that turns orange and red in fall. Its leaves have an odd number of leaflets. Its small fruits, at first scarlet, turn purplish or blue as they ripen. In China the young shoots and leaves of this species are eaten.

The *P. mexicana* is an evergreen tree up to 30 feet tall that has a short trunk up to 1¹/₂ feet in diameter and an uneven number of nearly stalkless leaflets to its leaves. Its small, dry purplish fruits contain edible seeds. A resin exudes from the branches. This is a native of Mexico and the southwestern United States.

Rhus—Sumac

The subtropical and temperate regions of both hemispheres provide homes for this genus of 250 species of evergreen and deciduous trees, shrubs and vines that contain milky or resinous juices. Contact with some, including poison ivy, causes severe dermatitis. Their small flowers are in clusters, their fruits are small and berry-like.

Of the more than a dozen species that inhabit the New World the commonest of those that attain tree size are the shining sumac (*R. copallina*), the smooth sumac (*R. glabra*) and the staghorn sumac (*R. typhina*). All three have handsome large, pinnate leaves that change to brilliant red or reddish purple before they drop in fall, greenish flowers in terminal panicles and great, dense clusters of crimson fruits that remain attractive for a long time. Maximum heights of about 30 feet are reached by the staghorn sumac and the shining sumac, but the smooth sumac rarely attains 20 feet; all are often shrubby. Both the branches and fruits of the staghorn sumac, a native from Quebec to Ontario, Georgia, Indiana and Iowa, are densely velvety hairy. The smooth sumac, which ranges from Maine to British Columbia, Florida and Mexico, has glabrous, glaucous branches and sticky-hairy fruits. Quite distinct is the glossy-leaved, shining sumac, which has smooth-margined or few-toothed leaflets attached to winged midribs. Its branches are covered with short, fine hairs. It is a native from Ontario to Minnesota, Florida and Texas. Differing from the above species in having axillary flower clusters and whitish or yellowish gray fruits is the poison sumac (*R. vernix*)

Pistache. Pistacia atlantica (A. Brosset)

which grows in swamps from Ontario to Minnesota to Florida and Louisiana. Its branches are glabrous, and its leaves, quite glabrous at maturity, turn brilliant scarlet in fall. All parts of this 20-foot-tall tree are extremely poisonous to the touch. A native of southern California, the sourberry (*R. integrifolia*) is an evergreen that is sometimes 30 feet tall. Its oval leaves, which are about 2 inches long, are not divided. White or pinkish flowers in pubescent panicles are succeeded by dark red, hairy fruits.

Several Asiatic sumacs are important, notably the varnish tree or lacquer tree (*R. verniciflua*) of China and Japan. Occasionally reaching 100 feet in height, this handsome deciduous tree has branches that are pubescent when young but later are glabrous. It has large, pinnate leaves and axillary, pendulous clusters of yellowish white flowers succeeded by straw yellow fruits. Its leaves are pubescent beneath, at least on the veins. This very poisonous species is the source of a natural varnish called Japanese or Chinese lacquer, which is collected as a syrupy white liquid that flows from incisions made in the trunk; the varnish darkens upon exposure to the

217

air. From the seeds is expressed an oil used as an illuminant and sometimes as an adulterant of tung oil. The wax tree (R. succedanea) of Japan, China and Taiwan is the source of a commercial wax expressed from the berries. This poisonous species is 30 feet tall, has glabrous, pinnate leaves with glossy, untoothed leaflets, axillary clusters of flowers and yellowish white fruits.

Rhus coriaria, a native of the Mediterranean region and western Asia, grows up to 20 feet in height. Its leaves differ from those of the American staghorn and smooth sumacs in that the midribs between the leaflets are winged. In this respect it resembles the southeastern Asian R. javanica, which differs from it, however, in having larger and pointed rather than blunt leaflets. Rhus javanica has showy terminal panicles of creamy white flowers in late summer. The flowers of R. coriaria are greenish and in loose terminal clusters. Both species have red fruits. The leaves of sumacs contain tannin, for which those of R. glabra, R. typhina, R. copallina and R. coriaria are exploited commercially.

Schinopsis—Red Quebracho

Of seven species, all South American, two are chief sources of the extremely important tanwood, red quebracho. Schinopsis lorentzii has pinnate leaves with numerous narrow leaflets and S. balansae undivided or slightly divided leaves. The former is deciduous, the latter partly so. Both have inconspicuous flowers and winged fruits. They attain heights of up to 50 feet. Quebracho means ax-breaker and refers to the flinty hard wood. In addition to its chief use as a source of tannin, red quebracho wood, which is extremely durable, is used for fuel and also for posts, heavy construction and wood paving.

Schinus

Entirely American, this group of thirty species of resinous, pinnate-leaved trees ranges from Mexico to Argentina. Their small whitish flowers occur in terminal panicles; their fruits are berry-like. Two species are common, the California pepper tree or Peruvian mastic tree (S. molle) and the Brazilian pepper tree or Christmas-berry (S. terebinthifolius). The former is a native of Peru, the latter of Brazil. Both are commonly planted as shade trees in warm temperate climates. The California pepper tree attains a height of 50 feet and has a graceful, rounded crown with rather pendulous branchlets. Its fernlike leaves, composed of fifteen to thirty narrow leaflets up to 2 inches long, are evergreen. The flowers are in lax, pyramidal clusters at the ends of the branches, the sexes normally on separate trees. The fruits, about the size of peppercorns, are rose red and contain a single seed; in Mexico they are used to prepare beverages and the bark for tanning. The Christmas-berry differs from the California pepper tree in having leaves of five to nine leaflets up to 3 inches long, and scarlet fruits. It is sturdier than S. molle and its branchlets are not pendent. When they are in fruit the female trees are highly ornamental.

Spondias

Natives of tropical Asia and America are ten or twelve species of Spondias, a few of which are commonly cultivated for their edible fruits. The hog-plum (S. mombin) is cosmopolitan in the tropics. It grows up to 60 feet in height and may have a trunk 2 1/2 feet in diameter with many spinelike projections up to three-fourths of an inch long. Its crown spreads widely and its few branches are usually nearly horizontal. The yellowish green leaves have nine to nineteen leaflets. The fragrant, yellowish, five-petaled flowers, in terminal clusters, are followed by yellow or purple fruits about 1 inch long. The Otaheite apple (S. cytherea) is a native of the Society Islands grown for its thick-skinned, juicy fruits. These have an apple-like flavor, are globular or egg-shaped and are up to 4 inches long. This tree attains a height of about 40 feet and a trunk diameter of 1 1/2 feet. Its pinnate leaves, up to 1 foot long, have eleven to twenty-three leaflets. Its small greenish white flowers form terminal clusters. Each tree bears male or female and bisexual flowers. The purple mombin (S. purpurea) is up to 30 feet in height with a trunk up to 1 foot in diameter. A native of tropical America, it has heavy, brittle branches, stout twigs, and leaves with nine to twenty-five yellow-green leaflets. Its small red or pink flowers are in small lateral clusters on older shoots. They are succeeded by slightly sour yellow or purplish red, plumlike fruits up to 1 1/4 inches long. Each tree bears male or female as well as bisexual blooms. This is one of the most important fruits in parts of Mexico and Central America. Its foliage provides fodder for animals and is sometimes cooked and eaten by human beings.

AQUIFOLIACEAE— HOLLY FAMILY

The holly family includes three genera and five hundred species of tropical and temperate region trees and shrubs with undivided leaves.

Ilex—Holly

To most people of the temperate world holly means a prickly-leaved evergreen with red berries that is popular at Christmas. But the genus *Ilex* includes many kinds that do not fit this concept —about four hundred species of trees and shrubs, evergreen and deciduous, with red, black, or yellow berries, according to kind, and with leaves either prickly or smooth-edged. Many hollies are decidedly unholly-like! Most have alternate leaves, but those of a few species in Borneo are in pairs. The flowers are normally unisexual, and usually individual plants have flowers of only one sex, but occasionally bisexual flowers and bisexual trees occur and then individual trees may bear berries without a tree of the opposite sex being nearby.

The holly of tradition is the English holly (*Ilex aquifolium*), a native of Europe, western Asia and China that sometimes attains a height of 80 feet and forms a handsome, pyramidal tree. This kind typically has dense clusters of bright red berries, but yellow-berried variants are among its numerous horticultural forms and hybrids. Its highly glossy leaves are characteristically spiny but those on the upper branches of tall specimens are often more or less smooth-edged, and there are smooth-edged horticultural varieties. The spines serve as strong deterrents to browsing animals. Closely related to the English holly is *I. perado* of the Canary Islands, Madeira and the Azores. The most obvious difference is that the leaf stalks of the island kind, which grows to a height of 30 feet, are winged. Another closely allied species, by some botanists regarded as merely a variety of *I. perado*, is *I. platyphylla*, of the Canary Islands. Thirty feet high or more, this species has larger, duller, and smaller-toothed leaves than the English holly. Both *I. perado* and *I. platyphylla* have hybridized with *I. aquifolium* to provide a number of splendid horticultural hollies.

The American equivalent of the English holly is *I. opaca*, a native from Massachusetts to Florida and Texas. This is commonly called American holly, although there are other species

that so far as distribution is concerned would be equally entitled to that designation. Forming a pyramidal specimen up to 50 feet high, it has spiny-margined leaves that are duller than those of the English holly and its flowers and berries are solitary or few together so that it does not produce the dense clusters of berries that are so characteristic of *Ilex aquifolium*. Ordinarily the berries of the American holly are red but there is a yellow-fruited variety called *I. o. xanthocarpa*. Berried branches are much used for Christmas decorations.

The dahoon (*I. cassine*) sometimes attains 30 feet in height but is often shrubby. A native of coastal regions from Virginia to Florida and Louisiana, it has dull red or rarely yellow berries and smooth-edged or shallowly toothed evergreen leaves. Its trunk occasionally has a diameter of 1½ feet but usually is smaller. Its flowers and berries are borne on shoots of the current season's growth. The dahoon must not be confused with the yaupon or cassena (*I. vomitoria*), another evergreen kind with approximately the same geographical distribution, but which extends also into Texas. The yaupon is about the same size as the dahoon; its leaves are distinctly crenated at their edges. Its flowers and berries are borne on shoots that grew during the previous season. *Ilex vomitoria* takes its name from a use made of it by the Indians; each spring they visited coastal regions to drink an infusion of its leaves as an emetic and purgative.

Two deciduous hollies of tree size are North American, the possum haw (*I. decidua*) and *I. montana*. The possum haw, which occurs in swamps from Virginia to Florida and Texas, is 30 feet tall with a slender trunk and spreading branches. Its orange-red berries often remain on its branches until spring. *Ilex decidua*, which is up to 40 feet tall, is found from New York to South Carolina and Alabama. It has a short trunk up to a foot in diameter, a slender, pyramidal head, and bright red berries. The leaves of *Ilex decidua* are sharply serrated; those of the possum haw have blunter, more rounded teeth, spaced farther apart.

Although tropical America has many species of holly, few are well known or have significant commercial values. The most important, *I. paraguariensis*, barely warrants inclusion as a tree for only rarely does it become 20 feet high. A native of Brazil, this evergreen is cultivated widely for its wavy-toothed leaves which, dried, are called maté and are infused to make a tea

that is used daily by millions of South Americans. Maté is an important article of commerce. One of the largest hollies is *I. guianensis* of northern South America and Central America. This evergreen tree attains a maximum height of 130 feet and a trunk diameter of 20 inches.

Asiatic hollies include several evergreen Japanese natives. One of the largest and most beautiful is the tarago (*I. latifolia*), which attains a height of 60 feet and has large, glossy, serrated but not spiny leaves and dense clusters of red berries. This species was described by Charles Sprague Sargent of the Arnold Arboretum as "probably the handsomest evergreen tree that grows in Japan." Differing from the tarago in having leaf margins that are not toothed or at most have a very few scattered teeth, are *I. integra* and *I. pedunculosa*. The former becomes 40 feet tall and forms a narrow, pyramidal tree that is often planted in temple gardens in Japan. *Ilex pedunculosa* is easily recognized by the long stalks of its bright red berries. These are 1 to 2 inches long; those of *I. integra* are about a quarter of an inch long. The leaves of *I. pedunculosa* are glossy and usually lighter green than those of *I. integra*. Similar to *I. pedunculosa*, but having larger leaves and shorter stalks to the flowers and berries, is *I. rotunda*, which occurs in Japan, Korea, China and Taiwan.

Among native Chinese evergreen hollies two are especially worthy of notice, *I. corallina* and *I. pernyi*. Both grow to a maximum height of about 30 feet. *Ilex corallina* has tiny red berries and leaves with spines that point in several different directions, some even backward. *Ilex pernyi* is of compact growth and has dark green, somewhat quadrangular leaves, 1 to $1^{1}/_{2}$ inches long, with five to seven stout spines and nearly stalkless red berries. Another fine Asiatic species is the Himalayan *I. dipyrena* which grows to 40 feet and has short-stalked elliptic leaves with distantly spaced teeth or spines. Its foliage is glossy green, the berries red.

ACERACEAE—MAPLE FAMILY

Consisting of two genera, this family is confined to the North Temperate zone and to mountains in the tropics. Fossil records reveal that it was prominent in Tertiary floras.

1. *Acer platanoides* 2. *Acer palmatus* 3. *Acer pseudoplatanus* 4. *Acer negundo (Charles Fracé)*

Acer—Maple

Of approximately two hundred species of maples known, the greatest number are natives of China and Japan, but the genus is also well represented in North America and Europe. The giants of the tribe are Americans and Europeans; most of the orientals are small trees or sometimes shrubs. Many maples are excellent ornamentals; some are of considerable commercial importance as lumber. All have opposite leaves, and their fruits consist of two winged nutlets joined at the bases to form the well-known and distinctive maple "keys." Their flowers are borne before or after the leaves expand, according to species. Best known, perhaps, of American species is the sugar maple *(A. saccharum)*. This is not the only kind that has a sweet sap but its sugar content is higher than that of others. Before cane and beet sugars became plentiful, maple sugar was of considerable commercial importance; even now it is prepared in significant amounts in the northern United States and Canada, as it was when the early settlers first learned the art from the Indians. The sugar maple grows to a height of 120 feet with a trunk almost 4 feet in diameter and an oval or bell-shaped head. Its pale yellow blooms appear at about the same time as its leaves. In fall it is the most colorful of American trees; its foliage then assumes a wide range of glowing yellows, oranges, reds and scarlets, and forest and countryside are set aflame with the brilliance of the display. Its wood, called hard maple, is valued for flooring, furniture and vehicles; sometimes it is beautifully figured, as in bird's-eye and fiddleback maples. The sugar maple is native over most of the forest areas of eastern North America. The black maple *(A. nigrum)*, distinguished from the sugar maple by leaves pubescent on their undersides and black rather than gray bark, grows to 120 feet tall and has a natural distribution from Canada to South Dakota, Missouri, West Virginia and Kentucky. Its lumber is practically identical with that of the sugar maple and it too is called hard maple.

The most important American soft maples are the red or swamp maple *(A. rubrum)* and the silver maple *(A. saccharinum)*. Their lumber is less attractive in appearance and not as resistant to wear as hard maple; nevertheless, it

1. Acer campestre 2. Acer saccharinum 3. Acer macrophyllum 4. Acer saccharum (Charles Fracé)

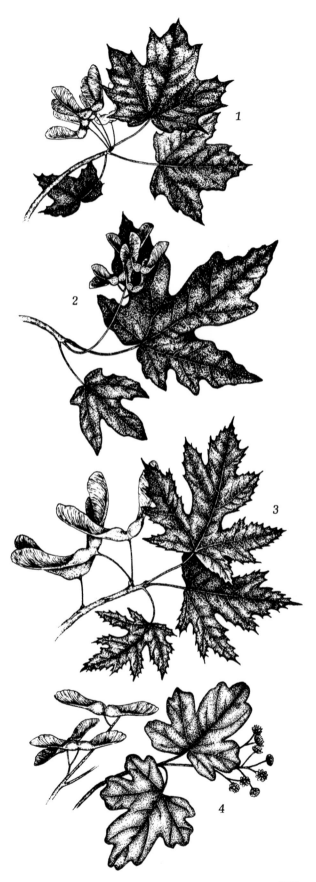

Silver maple. Acer saccharinum (T. H. Everett)

is much used for furniture, flooring, interior trim, cooperage and other purposes. The red maple, abundant throughout eastern North America, especially in meadows and swamps, forms an open, somewhat irregular, rounded crown, has steel gray bark and attains a maximum height of about 120 feet. Its crimson flowers, the males with conspicuous yellow anthers, make an attractive display in earliest spring, long before its leaves unfold. In early autumn its foliage turns brilliant red. The silver maple grows as tall as the red maple and has a wide-spreading oval or rounded head. Its long-stalked, deeply lobed, coarsely toothed leaves are green above and grayish white on their undersides. Its flowers, which appear long before the leaves, are greenish yellow. In fall its foliage turns clear yellow. This fast-growing species has brittle wood and is much subject to storm damage. It grows over most of eastern North America.

The big-leaf maple (*A. macrophyllum*) is a round-headed tree that grows up to 100 feet

high and inhabits coastal areas from Alaska to California. It has fragrant yellow flowers and its leaves, which measure up to a foot across, are the largest of any maple; they turn bright yellow in fall. Its wood is of the soft maple type and is used for the same purposes as that of the red maple. A maple so distinct that some authorities consider placing it in the separate genus *Negundo* is the box-elder (*A. negundo*). Conservative botanists classify it as *Acer negundo*, a true maple. This tree, which occurs through much of Canada and the United States and the mountains of Mexico and Guatemala, has leaves consisting of three to five separate leaflets and is therefore sometimes called the ash-leaved maple. Attaining a height of 70 feet and forming a wide-spreading, open head, this fast-growing species is planted for shelter belts in regions of extremely hot dry summers and cold winters, but its weak wood is much subject to storm damage and it has little to recommend it where better trees thrive.

Smaller American maples also include the vine maple (*A. circinatum*) of the Pacific coast, a 25-footer with red fruits and white and purple flowers that are the most decorative of all maples. Its wide-spreading branches originate close to the ground. Its wood is extremely hard and it is believed to have been used by the Indians for making fishhooks. In fall its foliage becomes orange and red. Conspicuous in winter because of its white-striped bark, the moosewood (*A. pensylvanicum*) inhabits open woods throughout eastern North America. Its large, coarse leaves, trilobed at their ends, turn yellow in fall. It grows to a height of about 35 feet. Similar in size and also favoring shaded locations through much of eastern and central North America is the mountain maple (*A. spicatum*); it has greenish yellow flowers, bright red fruits and foliage that changes to orange and scarlet in fall.

Native European maples lack the splendid autumn coloring that is such a striking feature of many American and Oriental kinds. The two largest, up to 100 feet tall, are the sycamore maple (*A. pseudoplatanus*) and Norway maple (*A. platanoides*). Both species inhabit Europe and western Asia and have been cultivated for centuries. The sycamore maple is one of the most satisfactory trees for planting near the sea. Its lumber is smooth, white and greatly valued for wood carving and furniture. The Norway maple is easily distinguished from the sycamore maple by the fact that its leaf stalks, when broken, exude a milky sap; this also readily differentiates it from the sugar maple. The hedge maple (A. campestre) of Europe and western Asia rarely exceeds thirty-five feet in height. Its name derives from the fact that it is popular for planting to form sheared hedges. Like the Norway maple, its leaf stalks contain a milky juice but its leaf lobes are obtuse, not sharply pointed like those of the Norway maple. From southern and central Europe hails one of the most attractive kinds in bloom, the Italian maple (A. opalus), a round-headed tree that rarely is 50 feet tall and in early spring bears an abundance of clear yellow flowers well before the foliage. It has the general appearance of a small-leaved sycamore maple.

Best known of the orientals is the Japanese maple (A. palmatum), a kind cultivated in numerous horticultural varieties varying in stature, habit, leaf dissection and leaf color. Many are scarcely more than shrubs; others may become 25 feet high or more and are highly ornamental. Typically, this kind is round-headed and green-foliaged, the leaves turning scarlet in fall, but there are varieties with leaves that are red in spring and green later and others that retain their red coloring throughout the season. The full-moon maple (A. japonicum) of Japan is somewhat similar, but its leaves are lobed to below their middles, whereas the leaf lobes of another Japanese species, the Japanese maple, are much shallower. Another native of the Japanese islands is the hornbeam maple (A. carpinifolia), which develops several trunks from the base and has bright green, unlobed leaves resembling those of hornbeam. This species attains a height of 30 feet. Another Japanese kind is the round-headed, painted maple (A. mono), which attains a height of about 60 feet and has bright green leaves with five to seven triangular lobes and clusters of yellow flowers. Some varieties of this maple have variegated foliage.

The paperbark maple (A. griseum) of western China is remarkable for its beautiful rich cinnamon brown bark which peels in broad paper-thin strips and remains attached to the trunk in curled sheets. It has a rather open round head that grows up to about 25 feet high and blunt-toothed, trilobed leaves. White-striped bark, resembling that of A. pensylvanicum, is an attractive characteristic of A. davidii, a Chinese maple that sometimes is 50 feet tall. It has unlobed leaves that turn yellow and purple in fall. The coliseum maple (A. cappadocicum),

native from the Himalayas to the Caucasus, is a handsome tree up to 60 feet high. Its young branches are lustrous green. This species closely resembles the Norway maple but differs from that tree in that the lobes of its leaves are not toothed.

HORSECHESTNUT FAMILY— HIPPOCASTANACEAE

Closely related to the soapberry family (Sapindanceae) and sometimes combined with it, the horsechestnut family consists of two genera, Aesculus and Billia. The latter consists of two species of evergreen trees, native from southern Mexico to Colombia, readily distinguished from Aesculus by the fact that their leaves have only three leaflets.

Aesculus—Horsechestnut, Buckeye

These are easily recognized deciduous trees and shrubs—nine in North America, one in Europe, and five in Asia. Their opposite leaves have five to nine leaflets, spread like the fingers of a hand. Their showy panicles of flowers arise from the ends of the branchlets and open before or when the trees are in full leaf. They are succeeded by large fruits, each containing one or two chestnut-like, inedible seeds. Large and conspicuous scars on the branchlets mark the places from which leaves have fallen.

Giant of the genus, and probably the best known, is the common horsechestnut (A. hippocastanum). This is the "chestnut" planted so commonly in Paris, France, and at Hampton Court, England. The most probable explanation of the name horsechestnut is that Matthioli, physician to Emperor Maximilian II, received a specimen from Constantinople in 1565 with information that the Turks fed their horses meal prepared from the seeds. Matthioli gave the tree the Latin name of Castanea equina. Later this was translated into Greek as Hippocastanum, and Linnaeus adopted this form in the name he gave to the tree, Aesculus hippocastanum. Both the Latin and Greek names mean horsechestnut. The tree was introduced into North America in 1746 by means of seeds sent by Peter Collinson of London to the distinguished Pennsylvania botanist John Bartram. In 1763 Collinson wrote to Bartram, "But what delights me is to hear that our horsechestnut has flowered"—the first record of this splendid exotic blooming in the New World.

Although cultivated widely throughout the temperate world for hundreds of years, it was not until the end of the nineteenth century that naturalists discovered that the native home of this tree was the Balkans, rather than the Himalayas or other parts of Asia. The common horsechestnut has a rounded, wide-spreading head that may exceed 100 feet in height and a trunk up to 7 feet in diameter. Its large winter buds, conspicuously coated with sticky resin, open in early spring to produce leaves, each of five to seven obovate leaflets, smooth on their upper surfaces but with hairs beneath. The pyramidal flower clusters soon follow and may be a foot long. The petals are typically white with a patch of yellow that turns red as the flowers age. They are succeeded by very spiny, globular fruits. Horticulturists cultivate pink- and red-flowered variants as well as a double-flowered one which does not produce fruits. The latter is preferred in places where the fruits may attract the attention of boys, who go to great efforts to obtain the seeds, frequently damaging the trees by bombarding them with sticks and stones. The seeds are eaten by deer, squirrels and some other animals, but not by horses. The lumber of the common horsechestnut is weak, soft and not durable, therefore it is of little commercial importance.

Blooming at least a month later than the common horsechestnut, the Indian horsechestnut (A. indica) is nearly as massive and, like its European relative, is one of the most magnificent of temperate region trees. It differs from the common horsechestnut in having stalked leaflets, four instead of five petals, and smooth pear-shaped fruits. About as tall as the preceding kinds, the Japanese horsechestnut (A. turbinata) also has sticky winter buds. Its leaves are larger than those of the common horsechestnut but its flower clusters are smaller and not as handsome. Its flowers are yellowish with a red spot. Its pear-shaped fruits are warty. The wood of this kind is employed for making articles for domestic use. Other Asiatics include two closely related Chinese horsechestnuts, A. chinensis and A. wilsonii; both are about 80 feet high and have sticky winter buds.

The American species are commonly called buckeyes. Only one, A. californica, has sticky winter buds; the others belong to the Pavia section of the genus which characteristically has winter buds without resinous coverings. A. californica rarely attains 40 feet in height and usually has a short trunk 6 inches or less in diameter, and stout spreading branches. Its white or pale pink four-petaled flowers are in dense clusters. This kind is restricted in its natural distribution to California. The largest of the Americans is the sweet or yellow buckeye (A. octandra). It is native from Pennsylvania to Georgia and Illinois, grows up to 90 feet tall and develops a straight trunk up to 3 feet in diameter. Its branches tend to be pendulous. The yellow flowers, with petals of unequal size and stamens shorter than the petals, borne in 6-inch-long panicles, open in the spring when the leaves are about half-grown. The fruits of this buckeye lack prickles.

Occupying the same geographical areas and extending also west of the Mississippi River is the Ohio buckeye (A. glabra), distinguished by petals that are of nearly equal size and shorter than the stamens and prickly fruits. This tree sometimes is 70 feet high, its trunk up to 2 feet in diameter. The red buckeye (A. pavia), which rarely attains 40 feet in height or a trunk diameter of 10 inches, is a native of the southeastern United States occurring most commonly near the coast. Its flowers are dark red to purplish with petals of very unequal size. Its fruits are smooth. Aesculus neglecta of North Carolina, which grows to a maximum height of 60 feet, has yellow flowers with red veinings toward the bases of the petals. It is closely related to the sweet buckeye from which it may be distinguished by the absence of sticky hairs on the flower stalks and sepals. The woolly buckeye (A. discolor), found from Georgia to Texas, has red or yellow and red flowers with very unequal petals that are shorter than the stamens, and leaves that are whitish and hairy on their undersurfaces. It attains a height of 30 feet. The fruits are smooth.

As sources of even-textured, fairly wear-resistant lumber for interior trim and for making packing cases, boxes, pails, piano keys and other articles, the buckeyes have considerable importance.

Right: Akee fruits. Blighia sapida (Harriet Burkhart)
Overleaf left above: Litchi chinensis (Werner Stoy: Camera Hawaii) Left below: Mango. Mangifera indica (Emil Javorsky) Right above: Baobab. Adansonia digitata (James R. Simon) Right below: Baobab fruits (Pierre Pittet) Far right: Baobab flowers (D. C. H. Plowes)

SAPINDACEAE—SOAPBERRY FAMILY

Two thousand species distributed among 150 genera of chiefly tropical trees, shrubs and vines are members of this family. All have tiny flowers that are functionally unisexual; the apparently well-developed stamens of the females do not produce viable pollen. The leaves are usually pinnate and the tissues of most kinds contain latex or resinous sap.

Blighia—Akee

The name of this genus of seven species of tropical African trees commemorates Captain Bligh of the *Bounty*. Its most important member is the akee *(B. sapida)*, which is cultivated in the tropics for its edible, somewhat pear-shaped fruits that are yellow to red, about 3 inches long, and contain three shiny black seeds surrounded by white, nut-flavored pulp. Only when quite ripe are the fruits safe to eat; both unripe and overripe fruits are poisonous; fatal cases of akee poisoning are recorded. The fruits are eaten raw, roasted, fried and in soups; in West Africa they are pounded and used to stupefy fish. When rubbed in water the fruits lather and are used by natives to wash clothes. The akee attains a height of 60 feet and a trunk diameter of about 2 feet. Its leaves have three to five pairs of light green leaflets, of which the largest are near the tip of the leaf. The fragrant flowers, in slender racemes, are greenish yellow and have conspicuous stamens. The akee is a very handsome shade tree.

Euphoria—Longan

The longan *(Euphoria longan)* closely resembles the litchi. A native of China, it is cultivated for its edible, reddish fruits which are up to three-quarters of an inch in diameter. They are not as rough-surfaced as those of the litchi and the pulp separates from the solitary seed. The leaves of the longan have two to five pairs of leaflets. Its flowers have five sepals and five petals.

Koelreuteria

Here belong eight native deciduous trees of Japan, China, Taiwan and Fiji. They have large, terminal panicles of asymmetrical yellow flowers and inflated, bladder-like fruits. Their leaves are pinnate or bipinnate with lobed or toothed

Tamarisk in bloom. Tamarix (Gottlieb Hampfler)

Litchi chinensis (Anna Riwkin: Full Hand)

leaflets. The best known is the golden-rain tree *(K. paniculata)* of China, Korea and Japan. This species, sometimes 60 feet tall, has a flattish crown and pinnate or partially bipinnate leaves. Its attractive blooms, borne in summer, are followed by large clusters of three-sided fruits which remain decorative for a long period. The golden-rain tree withstands well the winters of New England and the hot, dry summers of the American Middle West. In China it was often planted to mark the tombs of feudal princes. From it is obtained a yellow dye and its flowers are used in Chinese medicine. Endemic to Taiwan is the beautiful *K. formosana*, which may be 60 feet tall and has bipinnate leaves. Its large flower panicles and fruits are conspicuously ornamental.

Litchi

Botanists recognize two species of this genus, which is a native of China and the Philippines. The most important, variously known as the litchi, litchee, leechee, or lychee *(L. chinensis)*, is widely cultivated in the warmer parts of the Orient for its edible fruits. The litchi is a dense-foliaged, broad-topped tree up to 40 feet in height. Its glossy, leathery leaves have two to four pairs of leaflets. The flowers are without petals but have five greenish or yellowish sepals. They are in panicles up to 1 foot long. The red fruits, globular and 1½ inches in diameter are covered with rough tubercles; their flesh separates readily from the seeds. The fruits are dried and sold as litchi nuts. The flesh of the dried fruits is raisin-like, whereas that of fresh fruits has the consistency of grapes.

Melicoccus

This genus (sometimes spelled *Melicocca*) consists of two South American species with edible fruits that are much planted for ornament and shade. The more tropical is the Spanish-lime or genip, a native of northern South America that is now naturalized elsewhere in the New World tropics. In northern Argentina, Bolivia and Paraguay the timbó or arbol de la lecheguana *(M. lepidopetala)* is native. This species attains a height of about 35 feet and a trunk diameter of 20 inches. The Spanish-lime is sometimes 60 feet tall and may have a trunk 2 feet in diameter. It has a dense, globular crown and evergreen leaves of four leaflets attached to a winged midrib. Its small greenish white fragrant flowers provide pasture for bees and are succeeded by clusters of round or elliptic, sweet-acid, grapelike fruits up to 1¼ inches in diameter. Each contains one or two large seeds which are roasted and eaten.

Nephelium

This genus of thirty-five natives of the Asiatic tropics is very closely related to *Euphoria* and *Litchi*; indeed these last named were once included in *Nephelium*. It differs in that the flesh of its fruits adheres to the seeds. The rambutan *(N. lappaceum)*, native to Malaya, is well known for its ornamental, edible fruits, which are 1¼ inches long, are orange or red and are covered with fleshy, curling spines. It forms a wide-topped crown and attains a height of 60 feet. Its evergreen leaves have an even number of leaflets from 3 to 8 inches long and 1½ to 3½ inches in width. The flowers, male and female on separate trees, are fragrant. Another Malayan species, the pulasan *(N. mutabile)*, is similar to the rambutan but has narrower leaflets that are glaucous or greenish white beneath and less than 2 inches in width, and crimson fruits 2 inches long and covered with blunt fleshy spinelike or knoblike protuberances.

Sapindus—Soapberry; Soapnut

Thirteen species of tropical and subtropical trees belong in this group. Only one, the soapberry *(S. saponaria)*, is a native of the New World; it is spontaneous from the southern United States to Argentina and in Hawaii. Attaining a maximum height of 80 feet, this species is somewhat variable and is deciduous or evergreen depending upon local climate. The soapberry has a broad, dense crown and leaves of four to twelve leaflets attached to more or less winged midribs. The white flowers, occurring in terminal panicles, are succeeded by shining brown fruits, each three-quarters-inch in diameter and containing a single large seed and yellowish, soft pulp that has a high percentage of saponin and is excellent for washing fabrics and hair. The fruits of the soapnut *(S. muskorossi)*, a native of Japan, China and the Himalayan region, are used for the same purposes. It is an evergreen that becomes 70 feet tall and has feathery leaves with twelve to twenty-two leaflets. Its white flowers form terminal panicles and the fruits, from ¾ to 1 inch in diameter, are yellow, orange or greenish gray.

Ungnadia—Mexican-buckeye

This genus, containing only one species, is a native of Texas and northern Mexico. The Mexican-buckeye *(U. speciosa)* is a shrub or tree that grows up to 30 feet in height and has pinnate leaves of five to nine toothed, lustrous leaflets and clusters of 1-inch-wide sweetly scented flowers. Both unisexual and bisexual flowers occur on the same plant. The broadly pear-shaped fruits are 2 inches in diameter.

Xanthoceras

Two northern Chinese deciduous trees belong here. The best known is X. *sorbifolia*, which is sometimes 20 feet tall and has a rather stiff, erect crown. Its handsome, glossy, pinnate leaves consist of nine to seventeen narrow and conspicuously sharp-toothed leaflets. Its beautiful flowers, which appear at the same time as the new leaves, are carried in erect terminal and lateral racemes. The flowers are 1 to 1¼ inches in diameter and each of their five white petals are marked at the base with a blotch that at first is yellow but changes to crimson. Both unisexual and bisexual flowers are borne on the same plant. The fruits, containing many seeds resembling small chestnuts, are triangular and about 2 inches in diameter.

CHAPTER 23

The Rhamnales

RHAMNACEAE— BUCKTHORN FAMILY

Of the two families in the order Rhamnales, one, the Vitaceae, consists mostly of vines, whereas the other, the Rhamnaceae, is made up chiefly of trees and shrubs. Many of the shrubs are more or less climbers. The Rhamnales differ from the Geraniales and Sapindales in having a single whorl or circle of stamens which equal the sepals in number and are alternate with them. The buckthorn family has undivided, usually alternate leaves and generally small, greenish, bisexual flowers; its fruits are small and berry-like. Cosmopolitan in distribution, it includes fifty-eight genera and nine hundred species.

Hovenia—Raisin Tree

The fruits of this genus of five Asiatic species have swollen edible stalks. The raisin tree (H. dulcis) is generally less than 75 feet tall. Deciduous and round-headed, it has long-stalked, pointed-ovate, usually toothed leaves that are rounded or heart-shaped at their bases. Its three-seeded, globular fruits, about one-third of an inch in diameter, have swollen red stems that taste like pears; it is for these stems that this handsome tree is cultivated in the Orient.

Paliurus

Eight species belong in this genus, which has a natural range from southern Europe to Japan. By far the best known is the Christ-thorn or Jerusalem-thorn (P. spina-christi), a 20-foot tree or shrub with finely toothed ovate leaves up to 1½ inches long. At the base of each leaf stalk are two spines, one straight and pointing upward, the other curved and pointing downward. The clusters of many small, five-petaled, yellowish green, bisexual flowers are succeeded by curious fruits, each about 1 inch in diameter and consisting of a three-celled, roundish chamber surrounded by a flat wing. The fruits are shaped like Chinese cymbals or broad-brimmed, low-crowned hats; each contains three seeds. According to one legend, the crown of thorns Christ wore was made of branches of this tree. How-ever, another legend describes the crown as made of branches of Zizyphus spina-christi.

Rhamnus—Buckthorn

This genus numbers 160 deciduous and ever-green species; a few of these attain tree size but most are shrubs. It is represented in the Old and New Worlds and north and south of the equator. The best-known American species is the deciduous cascara sagrada (R. purshiana), source of a medicinal laxative and native of the northwestern United States and British Columbia. This tree reaches a maximum height of 40 feet; its trunk usually divides into several stout branches ten or fifteen feet from the ground. The leaves are finely toothed, oblong and up to 8 inches long. Its fruits change from red to purplish black as they ripen. The drug is obtained from the bark, which is stripped from the trees, dried and marketed. The name cascara sagrada—sacred bark—was given to it by Spanish pioneers. The Indian-cherry (R. crocea), also deciduous, ranges from New York to Florida and westward to Nebraska and Texas. It grows up to 30 feet in height and has lustrous leaves. Unlike the cascara sagrada, the stalks of its leaves are usually longer than those of the flower clusters. Its sweet fruits, at first red, become black when fully ripe. The red berry (R. californica) is an evergreen shrub about 6 feet tall, but its variety, R. c. illicifolia, occasionally attains a height of 20 feet. It has stout branches and spiny-toothed, ovate or round leaves which are shiny dark green above and are often golden on their undersides. The fruits, bright red, are a quarter-inch long. Differing from the red berry in having naked rather than scaly winter buds, R. alternatus is an evergreen native of the Mediterranean region that reaches a maximum height of about 20 feet. Its elliptic to ovate leaves, lustrous dark green above and yellowish green beneath, have edges that are widely toothed or quite smooth. Its yellowish green flowers, in small clusters, are tiny and inconspicuous. The fruits of this species are black and a quarter of an inch long.

The common buckthorn (R. cathartica) is a deciduous shrub or tree up to 20 feet in height with broad elliptic or ovate, finely toothed dull leaves and small clusters of inconspicuous flowers in the axils of the lower leaves. Its black fruits are about a quarter of an inch across. A native of Europe and Asia, it is closely allied to the Dahurian buckthorn (R. davurica), which, how-

Chinese jujube. Zizyphus jujuba (E. Aubert de la Rue)

Indian jujube. Zizyphus mauritania (M. Krishnan)

ever, has decidedly narrower glossy leaves. The Dahurian buckthorn, a native of northern China, Manchuria and Korea, attains a maximum height of 30 feet.

Zizyphus

This genus of a hundred species of deciduous shrubs and trees is represented in all continents. Its members are often thorny, and the thorns, like those of *Paliurus*, are sometimes solitary but more frequently in pairs with one recurved and the other straight. The small, whitish, greenish or yellow flowers, occurring in axillary clusters, are succeeded by single-stoned, datelike fruits; in many kinds these fruits are edible. Chinese jujube (*Z. jujuba*) has fleshy orange-red fruits $1/2$ to $3/4$ inch long which are eaten fresh or cooked and are dried or preserved in other ways and used in confectionery. This is a native from the Mediterranean Region to China. It is deciduous, reaches a maximum height of about 40 feet, has leaves that are green on both sides and is usually spiny. Three or four hundred horticultural varieties of the Chinese jujube are cultivated in the Orient. The Indian jujube (*Z. mauritania*) is an evergreen shrub or tree up to 40 feet in height, a native of India now extensively cultivated in warm countries. It differs from the Chinese jujube in that its twigs

and the undersides of its leaves are covered with whitish hairs. Its fruits are edible and its leaves are used for tanning. *Zizyphus spina-christi* a small, thorny tree of North Africa and Arabia, shares with *Paliuris spina-christi* the distinction, according to legend, of being the species used for Christ's crown of thorns.

CHAPTER 24

The Malvales

The Malvales consist predominantly of tropical and subtropical trees and shrubs usually having bisexual flowers. Star-shaped hairs are frequently present on the leaves and stems. Often the tissues are mucilaginous.

MALVALACEAE—MALLOW FAMILY

Of nearly worldwide distribution, the mallow family consists of seventy-five genera and a thousand species of trees, shrubs and herbaceous plants. Its leaves are usually palmately lobed and its bisexual flowers have five parts. Familiar non-woody plants that belong here include the holly-hock, cotton and mallow.

TILIACEAE—LINDEN FAMILY

Composed almost entirely of trees and shrubs, the linden family embraces fifty genera and 450 species in the tropics and temperate regions of both hemispheres. Its leaves are usually in two distinct ranks; often they are asymmetrical. The flowers are symmetrical, have four or five sepals and petals and are usually bisexual.

Berrya

Here belong six species of Indomalaysia and Polynesia. One, *B. cordifolia,* the source of trin-comali wood, is important. A native of Burma, India and Ceylon, it attains a height of 80 feet and has linden-like, heart-shaped, deciduous leaves and large terminal and axillary panicles of five-petaled flowers. Its fruits have six wings and contain seeds covered with irritant hairs. Trincomali wood is tough and flexible; it is much used for construction, building, and agricultural implements.

Tilia—Linden; Basswood; Lime

The lindens include eighty species of North Temperate zone deciduous trees that in summer bear on young shoots clusters of small, fragrant yellow flowers that secrete abundant nectar and are great favorites of bees and other pollinating insects; unfortunately, the nectars of *T. tomentosa* and *T. petiolaris* are poisonous to bees. The flower clusters are attached to conspicuous strap-shaped membranous bracts and are succeeded by ovoid nutlike fruits about the size of peas. Because of their attractive shapes and hand-some, usually heart-shaped leaves, lindens are commonly planted as shade and street trees; for these purposes they were used in both ancient Greece and ancient Rome. Differences between species of *Tilia* are often slight, and this, together with the variability that occurs within species and the fact that hybrids are common, renders correct identification often difficult. The flowers of some lindens have sterile stamen-like parts called staminodes as well as functional stamens, a feature that is useful in identification. In North America lindens are often called basswoods and in Great Britain, limes, although

they are not related to the citrus that produces the fruits called limes.

The wood of all species of lindens is remarkably similar. It is light, strong, attractive in appearance and free of odor so that it is useful for boxes, tubs, pails and other containers for foods. It is also used extensively for excelsior, for interior finish and for wood carving. The tough inner bark or bast (from which is derived the name basswood) is used, especially in Russia and in China, as tying material and for making ropes, mats, shoes and other articles.

The European lindens are most important for landscape planting. Even in America they thrive better than Asiatic species, a reversal of a situation that exists with most genera that are natives throughout the Northern Hemisphere; in America, European kinds are more commonly planted than are native species. Outstanding European kinds are the silver linden *(T. tomentosa)* and the pendent silver linden *(T. petiolaris).* The former attains a height of 100 feet, the latter of about 80 feet. The flowers of both have staminodes and their leaves are covered with silvery white felty pubescence. The pendent silver linden may be recognized by its comparatively narrow crown of drooping branches and by leaf stalks that are more than half as long as the blades of the leaves; the silver linden typically develops a broad, pyramidal head of upright branches and has leaf stalks less than half the length of its leaf blades. Another fine European species is the small-leaved linden *(T. cordata),* which, except for tufts of hair at the junctions of veins, is quite glabrous on its underleaf surfaces. It grows to about 100 feet in height and has dark green leaves that are distinctly paler beneath. This is the latest linden to bloom and, like the next mentioned kind, its flowers are without staminodes. Tallest of the Europeans is the large-leaved linden *(T. platyphyllos),* which sometimes becomes 120 feet tall. This, the earliest linden to bloom, is round or pyramidal in outline and has large, rather coarse, markedly asymmetrical leaves that are usually pubescent beneath and often above. From southeast Europe and western Asia comes the 100-feet-tall *T. dasystyla,* which has red twigs, flowers without staminodes, and lustrous dark green leaves that are bright green below with axillary tufts of whitish hairs and bristle-tipped marginal teeth, distinct from merely sharply pointed teeth.

In North America lindens are not native west

Crimean linden. Tilia euchlora (T. H. Everett)

Linden. Tilia moltkei (T. H. Everett)

of the Rockies. The flowers of all American species have staminodes. Most impressive is the American linden (T. americana), which occurs from Canada to North Dakota, Virginia, Alabama and Texas. Attaining a height of 120 feet, it forms an open head and has large, coarsely toothed leaves that are usually green on their undersides and are without hairs except for tufts in the vein axils on their undersides. The branchlets of the American linden are green; which differentiates it from T. neglecta, which has red branchlets. Tilia neglecta, native from Canada to North Carolina and Minnesota, has leaves with a thin grayish pubescence over their lower surfaces, and tufts of hairs at the vein junctions. Two smaller Americans are T. heterophylla and T. monticola, both about 60 feet high. The former is closely related to the American linden, but differs from it in having reddish or yellowish brown twigs and a covering of white or brownish hair on the undersurface of its leaves. It is native throughout the southeastern United States. T. monticola of the southern Appalachian Mountains has leaf undersides that are covered with densely matted white hairs and leaf stalks 2½ to 3 inches long. about twice as long as those of T. heterophylla.

The Japanese linden (T. japonica) is very similar to the European little-leaved linden but differs from it in that its flowers have staminodes; it grows up to a height of 60 feet. The very distinct and graceful Mongolian linden (T. mongolica), which also has flowers with staminodes, rarely exceeds 30 feet in height and has small, birchlike, often three-lobed leaves that are distinctly red when they expand in spring. T. maximowicziana of Japan grows 100 feet high. Its leaves, without axillary tufts of hair, are dark green above and gray-hairy beneath.

Outstanding hybrid lindens are the Crimean linden (T. euchlora), the common linden (T. europaea) and T. moltkei. The Crimean linden is one of the best for landscape uses. Of graceful habit and with slightly pendulous branches, it grows up to 60 feet tall and has bright green glossy leaves that are glabrous except for tufts of brown hair at the junctions of the veins beneath. Its flowers have no staminodes. The parentage of this hybrid is probably T. cordata crossed with T. dasystyla. The common linden, a hybrid of T. cordata and T. platyphyllos, is the kind that is used along nearly all of the avenues and in other large plantings in Europe.

234

Its flowers are without staminodes and its dull green leaves are hairless except for axillary tufts at the vein junctions on their undersides. This tree becomes 120 feet high. *T. moltkei*, a hybrid between *T. americana* and *T. petiolaris*, is a vigorous tree with somewhat pendent branches. Its leaves are smooth above and grayish pubescent beneath without axillary tufts of hair; its flowers have staminodes.

Gaya—Mountain Ribbonwood; Lacebark

The mountain ribbonwood or lacebark (*Gaya lyalli*), sometimes identified as *Hoheria lyallii* and *Plagianthus lallii*, is a New Zealand representative of a genus that occurs also in tropical America. It is a handsome, deciduous shrub or tree that grows up to 30 feet in height. Its ovate leaves are deeply toothed and are downy on their undersides, at least along the veins. The handsome white flowers, 1 inch in diameter, are sometimes solitary but more often are in clusters of three to five. The inner bark has the lacelike appearance of that of *Hoheria*.

Hibiscus

Three hundred mostly tropical and subtropical trees, shrubs and herbaceous plants belong in this group. Characteristically they have large, attractive flowers with their stamens united and their style branches spreading at maturity so that their stigmas are separate. The fruit is a capsule that splits into five parts. Some species are pollinated by birds. The sea hibiscus or mahoe (*H. tiliaceus*), probably a native of the Old World, is common near the coasts in many tropical countries. It attains a maximum height of about 40 feet and has a spreading crown of many branches. Its evergreen, heart-shaped leaves, up to 6 inches long, are about as wide as they are long; their margins are slightly toothed and their undersides are finely downy and whitish. The 4-inch-wide flowers are bright yellow with maroon centers and crimson-purple stigmas. Each flower opens for only a few hours and, unlike those of *Thespesia*, falls the same day or the next morning; after they fall they fade to dull pink. The bark yields an excellent fiber used for fishnets, caulking and other purposes. A form or variety of the mahoe called Cuban bast, distinguished by some botanists as *H. elatus*, attains a maximum height of 80 feet and a trunk diameter of 1½ feet.

Somewhat resembling the mahoe but with larger leaves, *H. macrophyllus*, a native of lowland forests of tropical Asia, is sometimes 80 feet high. Its heart-shaped leaves are up to 14 inches long and it has clear yellow flowers, about 4 inches in diameter, with maroon centers. From the mahoe this species differs in having twigs covered with long, bristly yellow hairs; those of *H. tiliaceus* are finely downy.

The orange hibiscus (*H. floccosus*) of Malaya is a deciduous kind attaining a height of 80 feet that forms a narrow crown of many spirelike branches. Its heart-shaped, often shortly lobed leaves are up to 8 inches across and are rough hairy on both sides. The flowers, a reddish orange streaked with red, are 4 to 5 inches wide; their petals are up to 4½ inches long; they retain their color for several days after they have fallen and have shriveled. The white hibiscus of Hawaii (*H. arnottianus*) is sometimes 25 feet in height. It forms a dense head and has smooth, ovate leaves up to 4 inches long, usually with red veins and stalks. Its very fragrant white flowers, 3 to 4 inches long, have a white or red staminal column from which the free parts of the stamens diverge. This species is a parent of many horticultural varieties. Best known of tropical kinds is the Chinese hibiscus or rose-of-China (*H. rosa-sinensis*). A native of the warmer parts of Asia, this species is cultivated in many varieties and hybrids throughout the tropics and subtropics. It attains a maximum height of 30 feet and has ovate, usually toothed leaves and single or double flowers in a wide range of colors according to variety. The typical kind has red, bell-shaped flowers about 4 inches in diameter. When crushed they change to purplish black and are used for dyeing and, in India, for blacking shoes. Chinese women use them to color their hair and eyebrows. The flowers are eaten raw pickled.

Hoheria—Ribbonwood; Lacebark

Endemic to New Zealand, this genus of five species consists of trees that grow up to 40 feet in height. Their leaves vary considerably in shape even on the same tree and they have beautiful white flowers in dense axillary clusters. These ribbonwoods or lacewoods are so called because their tough inner barks resemble ribbons of lace and are used decoratively for basketwork, trimming hats and other ornamental purposes. *Hoheria populnea*, an evergreen with snow-white blooms, is one of the best known of the genus. Its flowers are from ¾ to 1 inch in diameter. Its leaves, up to 5 inches long by half as wide, are coarsely toothed. This kind is na-

tive chiefly to the North Island. Predominantly native to the South Island, *H. angustifolia* differs in having leaves that are smaller and proportionately much narrower and flowers one-third of an inch in diameter. Also with smaller and narrower leaves is *H. sexstylosa*. The flowers of this species are three-fourths-inch in diameter and have pink styles.

Lagunaria

This monotypic genus of eastern Australia, Norfolk Island and Lord Howe Island, is one of the tallest, if not the tallest, members of the mallow family. A tree up to 80 feet in height with a trunk that may be 5 feet in diameter, the white wood or white-oak *(L. patersonii)* has leathery, oblong evergreen leaves with pale undersides, up to 4 inches long, and handsome pink to purple flowers about 2¹/₂ inches in diameter. Fine barbed hairs that grow inside the fruit capsule irritate the skin in the same way as do those of some cactuses. The bark of this tree is the source of a handsome fiber; its lumber is used for building.

Montezuma — Maga

One species endemic to Puerto Rico and one to Cuba comprise the genus *Montezuma*, which differs from *Hibiscus* in having its styles united and from *Thespesia* in its deciduous calyx and seeds that are not pubescent. The Puerto Rican maga *(M. speciosissima)* is a handsome tree that grows in humid forest regions and limestone soils. It grows up to 50 feet tall with a trunk 1¹/₂ feet in diameter and has long-stalked, heart-shaped leaves with blades up to 9 inches long by two-thirds as broad. Its solitary, long stalked, hibiscus-like red flowers, 3¹/₂ to 5 inches across, have spreading petals that overlap at the bases. The podlike fruits, which do not split like those of *Hibiscus*, contain a few half-inch-long brown seeds. The chocolate brown heartwood is hard, excellent for furniture, musical instruments, turnery and for posts and poles. The Cuban species, *M. cubensis*, is a medium-sized tree that provides lumber used locally.

Plagianthus—Lowland Ribbonwood

Is this category belong fifteen New Zealand and Australian species of trees, shrubs and herbaceous plants. Of particular interest is the low-

Giant bombax trees, Panama (Lorus and Margery Milne)

land ribbonwood (*P. betulinus*) which is ever-green to a great extent in its native New Zealand, although in most of the South Island it loses its leaves in winter. The lowland ribbonwood attains a height of 60 feet; its trunk is sometimes 3 feet in diameter. It has coarsely toothed or lobed, broadly ovate leaves and large trusses of flow-ers, each 1 to 1½ inches across. The flowers are unisexual, the females greenish, the males yellow-ish white. Like *Hoheria* and *Gaya*, it has ribbon-like, lacelike inner bark; this the Maoris use for making ropes and fishing nets.

Thespesia — Portia Tree

The most important of this genus of fifteen tropical species is the Portia tree (*T. populnea*). Common along the coasts of tropical Asia and the Pacific Islands, this evergreen attains a height of 60 feet and a trunk diameter of 2 feet. It has a rather dense crown and long-stemmed, yellow-veined, triangular heart-shaped, glossy, thick leaves up to 7½ inches long by two thirds as broad. The bell-shaped flowers, 2 to 3 inches long and about as wide, are pale yellow with maroon centers when they first open but within a few hours they fade to pink; they remain on the tree for several days before they fall. The styles of the flowers are united; their calyxes are persistent. The fruits, flattened spheres about 1 to 1½ inches in diameter, contain a bright yellow gum. The attractive wood of the Portia tree is used for furniture and other purposes.

BOMBACACEAE—BOMBAX FAMILY

Twenty genera of tropical trees, mostly of the New World and often very large, comprise this family of 180 species. Many have thick, barrel-shaped trunks which contain considerable water-storage tissues. Their leaves are palmate or un-lobed and many kinds have large blooms. The flowers are bisexual.

Adansonia — Baobab

The baobabs, totaling about a dozen species, are natives of hot dry savannas in Africa, Mada-gascar and northern Australia. Of grotesque appearance, they have grossly obese trunks, com-paratively short, stubby branches and sparse fo-liage. Typical of the group and one of the best known is the African baobab or monkey bread

Kapok. Ceiba pentandra (H. Wilhelmy)

237

tree (*A. digitata*). Attaining a maximum height of 75 feet, this strange tree has an enormous, swollen, barrel-shaped trunk that contains little wood but a great amount of water-storage tissue. The tapering branches when leafless look somewhat like roots; understandably, some African natives believe that the baobab grows upside down. The leaves of this baobab are palmate with three to seven glossy leaflets, each about 5 inches long. The attractive, sweet-scented flowers, suspended on long stalks and facing downward, are 5 to 7 inches in diameter and have five pure white petals that soon curl backward and a projecting staminal tube ending in a spherical mass of numerous purplish stamens. Beyond these the long style, tipped with a ten-pointed stigma, extends. The fruits, shaped like fat sausages narrowed toward their ends, are velvety, 6 to 10 inches long and up to 4 inches wide. They contain a mealy, acid pulp and about thirty seeds. The African baobab grows slowly and lives to an immense age, certainly up to a thousand years or more; some observers have calculated it lives more than five thousand years but this is probably an exaggeration. The maximum girth of the trunk is usually about 60 feet, but one specimen is recorded as having a trunk 85 feet in diameter three feet above ground level. Trunks of old baobabs are often hollow or are hollowed by natives who use them for shelter, storing grain and as water reservoirs. The most important product of this tree is an excellent fiber obtained from its bark and used for fish-nets, cordage, sacking and rough clothing. The fruits and seeds are eaten by men and animals; the pulp of the fruit, dried and mixed with water, provides a pleasant lemonade-like beverage. The leaves are used by natives as a vegetable and some parts of the tree are used medicinally.

The Australian baobab, also called the bottle tree (*A. gregori*), is similar to the African kind. It usually does not exceed 40 feet in height and may have a trunk 60 feet or so in circumference a few feet above the ground. The aborigines use the fiber obtained from it for cordage and eat its fruits and seeds. A white gum that the tree exudes is diluted with hot water to make an agreeable beverage; when fermented this is

Left above: Kapok fruits. Ceiba pentandra (M. Krishnan). Left: Silk-cotton trees, Cambodia (Paolo Koch)

highly intoxicating. Seven species of baobab occur in Madagascar but, curiously, they are less closely allied to the African kind than to the Australian baobabs. The Madagascan baobabs have symmetrical, bottle-shaped trunks and short-stalked flowers and fruits.

Bombax

This small genus of New World and Old World trees is closely related to *Pachira* but differs in having its small pealike seeds embedded in silky kapok-like fibers after the fashion of *Ceiba*. The red silk-cotton tree (*B. malabaricum*), a native of India, Malaysia and Australia, has a spiny, conspicuously buttressed trunk and spiny branches. Its digitate leaves are deciduous and its numerous red or white flowers are clustered at the ends of the branches; their five petals curl back to expose the tufts of long, pink stamens, joined only at their bases. The pods, 4 to 7 inches long, contain a reddish floss, inferior to that of the kapok tree but used similarly. The red silk-cotton tree attains a height of 150 feet or more. *Bombax ellipticum* or, as it is named by some botanists, *Pseudobombax ellipticum,* is a Mexican kind, a large deciduous tree with handsome flowers. Its long-stalked palmate leaves usually have five oval leaflets 4 to 9 inches long. Its petals are white and downy inside and are purple on their outsides; they curl backward to expose the mass of long, pink stamens. The pods, about 4 inches long contain brownish floss. Several African species of *Bombax* are of local importance. The trunks of *B. brevicuspe*, a deciduous tree up to 100 feet tall, are used for dugout canoes, a reddish-brown dye is obtained from the bark, and the floss is used in pillows. Another species, *B. buonopozense*, which attains 120 feet in height, has a buttressed trunk, and branches furnished with black-tipped spines, is put to similar uses; in addition, its wood serves for water troughs, domestic utensils and drums and its spines are carved with little figures or letters and used for embossing.

Ceiba — Kapok

Ten tropical American trees constitute the genus *Ceiba*. By far the most important is the kapok (*C. pentandra*), a massive deciduous species 120 feet tall or more with a branch spread of up to 150 feet. Its cylindrical trunk, spiny when young, is often supported by flangelike buttresses; above the buttress it may have a diameter of 8 feet or more. Its horizontal, usually spiny

Kapok, open pods. Ceiba pentandra (Paolo Koch)

branches are in widely spaced tiers and its long-stemmed, palmate leaves have five to nine pointed elliptic leaflets up to 8 inches long. The whitish or pinkish flowers, about 1½ inches wide, have five petals that on their outsides are densely covered with silky hairs, and five stamens united by their bases to form a column divided above into five or ten parts. The flowers form axillary clusters; each flower remains open for only a few hours. The pods, 3 to 6 inches long, burst to release masses of white, grayish or brownish floss with small seeds embedded in it. This floss, called kapok, it the most important commercial product of the tree. It is harvested chiefly from cultivated specimens in Java, Ceylon, Africa and the Philippines. Kapok is extremely elastic, light in weight and impervious to water. It is used in pillows, sleeping bags, upholstery and life preservers; it is the most valuable of all natural stuffing materials. From the seeds a bright red oil used in soaps and margarine is expressed.

Chorisia

Entirely South American, this genus of five species of trees is chiefly confined to the southern portion of the continent. The most important

239

kinds are the floss-silk tree or paineira (*C. speciosa*) of southern Brazil and Argentina and the Argentinian palo borracho (*C. insignis*). Both have palmately divided leaves of five to seven leaflets which, unlike those of the other species of silk-cotton-producing trees, *Bombax* and *Ceiba*, discussed here, are toothed at their margins. The floss-silk tree attains a large size; its trunk and branches are spiny, its leaves glabrous. Appearing with the new leaves, the flowers have five pink, purple or red petals that are yellowish and dark-striped at their bases and 3 inches in diameter. The pear-shaped fruits contain an abundance of white floss that is used for the same purposes as kapok. Because of its bottle-shaped trunk, the palo borracho is often called palo botella. It is smaller than the floss-silk tree, rarely more than 50 feet tall or with a trunk diameter greater than 6 feet at the widest part, which is a few feet above the ground. The floss that surrounds its seeds is used for stuffing, its trunks for dugouts and its inner bark for cordage.

Durio — Durian

The durian, one of the most celebrated fruits of the tropics, is the product of *D. zibethinus*, a member of a genus of twenty-seven species, all natives of tropical Asia. At least one, *D. testudinarium* of Malaya and Borneo, bears its flowers and fruits directly from its trunk. The durian grows to a height of 100 feet or more. Its short-stalked, undivided, oblong leaves are covered on their undersides with silvery or coppery scales. The flowers, borne in clusters on the branches, are white, cream, yellow, or in one variety, rose-red. They are about 2 inches long, have five petals and numerous stamens joined at their bases into a column. Durian fruits are spherical to ovoid, green or yellowish, thickly set with sharp spines; they may weigh up to 100 pounds and contain a few large edible seeds surrounded by a white, custard-like pulp that has an extremely offensive odor (the specific designation *zibethinus* is derived from the Italian *zibetto*, civet). Despite this, its flavor is considered delicious by those who have acquired a taste for it. It can, perhaps, best be likened to that of Limburger cheese; one European sampler compared it to "French custard passed through a sewer pipe," but Alfred Russel Wallace said "the sensation of eating durians is worth a voyage to the East."

Ochroma — Balsa Wood

The only species of this genus, the balsa wood (*O. pyramidale*), is the source of the lightest commercial lumber. It occurs as a native over the greater part of tropical America and the West Indies and is a fast-growing evergreen tree up to 80 feet tall with an open crown of a few spreading branches. Its trunk, slightly buttressed when large, may be 2½ feet or more in diameter above the buttresses. The leaves have reddish stalks and nearly round, heart-shaped blades that are 8 to 16 inches across. The whitish or greenish bell-shaped flowers have five petals and are 5 to 6 inches long. The ten-angled seed pods, 6 to 12 inches long and 1 to 1½ inches in diameter, contain numerous tiny seeds embedded in brown floss. Under cultivation the trees when six years old may be 60 feet tall and have a trunk diameter of 2½ feet. Lumber from such fast-grown trees weighs six to eight pounds a cubic foot when dry, whereas that from trees of slower growth may be three times as heavy. The famous raft Kon-Tiki which Thor Heyerdahl sailed to Easter Island, was constructed of balsa logs. In the first World War the wood was used for rafts, life preservers and floats for the 250-mile mine barrier in the North Sea. The peace time uses of balsa wood are chiefly for insulation, floats for fish nets, model airplanes and novelties. The floss that surrounds the seeds is sometimes used for the same purposes as kapok.

Pachira

This group of two trees differs from other genera of the bombax family treated here in that its fruits contain comparatively large seeds not surrounded by floss or pulp. The Guiana-chestnut (*P. aquatica*) is a big tree with palmate leaves of five to seven tertiary, oblong leaflets, up to eight inches long. Its flowers have slender, greenish or pinkish petals up to six inches long that soon drop, leaving a cluster of many white stamens joined at their bases into a tube that divides and subdivides into the final anther-tipped filaments. The fruits, 4 to 12 inches long and up to 5 inches in diameter, contain seeds one-half inch in diameter that are eaten raw or roasted. The Guiana-chestnut is a native of northern South America. *Pachira macrocarpa*, a smaller tree with ovoid or nearly spherical fruits about 9 inches long, is native from Costa Rica to Mexico.

STERCULIACEAE — STERCULIA FAMILY

This chiefly tropical and subtropical family includes sixty genera and seven hundred species of trees, shrubs, lianas and herbaceous plants. Its flowers, bisexual or unisexual, are usually symmetrical with the parts in fives; the stamens are generally joined in one group. The family is related to the Euphorbiaceae as well as to the Tiliaceae, Malvaceae and Bombaceae.

Brachychiton — Bottle Tree; Kurrajong

This Australian genus consists of eleven species. The kurrajong (*B. populneum*) ranges as a native from Victoria to Queensland. Growing up to 60 feet in height, it has a heavy oval crown. Even in droughts that parch the countryside, the foliage of this deep-rooted species retains its greenness. Its long-stalked leaves vary considerably in shape, from broad ovate to variously lobed or pronged; they are about 3 inches long. The creamy bell-shaped flowers are speckled pink or red on their insides and are borne in axillary clusters succeeded by fruits 1 to 3 inches long. The foliage of the kurrajong is excellent fodder for livestock. The flame tree (*B. acerifolium*), a deciduous or semideciduous species up to 60 feet tall, may have a trunk 3 feet in diameter. A native of New South Wales and Queensland, it bears loose panicles of rich red, bell-shaped flowes more than one-half inch long and is lovely when in bloom. The long-stemmed leaves of the flame tree are somewhat maple-like, five- or seven-lobed and up to 10 inches in diameter. The inner bark furnishes material suitable for cordage, mats, hats, bags and baskets. Having a trunk usually sharply constricted at the top and bottom and up to 6 feet in diameter at its base, the barrel tree (*B. rupestris*) well deserves its common name. Semideciduous, this kind is endemic to the dryer parts of Queensland. It attains a maximum height of about 50 feet and has a dense crown. Its leaves are narrow and undivided or are cut into five to nine narrow leaflets, each up to 4 inches long. The trunk of this species contains a sweet edible jelly-like material as well as an abundance of water between the inner bark and the wood.

Cola

This tropical African group of 125 species is chiefly known as the source of cola nuts, the

Above: Floss-silk tree. Chorisia speciosa (Studio Editoriale Fotografico) Right: Barrel tree. Brachychiton rupestris (Janet Finch)

Chocolate tree fruit. Theobroma cacao (U.S.D.A.)

seeds of certain species. These have a high content of caffeine and other stimulants and are chewed to delay fatigue. One of the chief sources of the nuts is *C. nitida*, a tree that grows up to 80 feet tall with dense foliage and a trunk usually unbranched for several feet from its base. Its elliptic leaves, variable in shape and size, are often obovate; they average 8 inches long by 3 inches wide. The flowers are whitish or yellowish with dark red stripes. The star-shaped fruits have five recurved podlike divisions containing many seeds. The other prime source of cola nuts is *C. acuminata*, a slender tree about 60 feet in height which usually branches from its base and forms a broad, sparsely foliaged top. Its leaves, smaller than those of *C. nitida*, are elliptic or slightly obovate. Its flowers, yellowish with a red blotch on each bloom, form small clusters. The five divisions of the fruits spread at right angles. Cola nuts are used in the preparation of beverages and medicines. From the dried cotyledons of *C. nitida* comes a drug that acts on the central nervous system.

Dombeya

More than 350 species are included in this African, Madagascan and Seychelles Islands genus; most are shrubs but a few are small trees. Most notable is *D. wallichii*, a native of east Africa and Madagascar that is sometimes 30 feet in height. It has large, usually shallowly lobed leaves with heart-shaped bases and large globular heads of tightly packed, 2-inch-wide, five-petaled, pink or red flowers that are suspended from the branches on long stalks. Like the undersides of the leaves, the flowers are hairy.

Firmiana

This group of fifteen species is limited in its natural distribution to eastern Africa, Indo-Malaysia, and eastern Asia. Its most notable member is the Chinese parasol tree or phoenix tree *(F. simplex)*, a deciduous native of China, Taiwan and Japan that grows up to 50 feet in height, has a rounded crown and three- to five-lobed leaves that are shaped like those of the sycamore *(Platanus)* and are up to 1 foot in diameter. The flowers, small, greenish and without petals, have no decorative appeal but the tree is handsome and is planted for shade.

Fremontia

One member of this small group of Californian and Mexican natives is familiar as a shrub or small tree planted as a garden ornamental. The slippery-elm *(Fremontia californica)* occasionally attains a height of 30 feet and a trunk diameter of 14 inches. It has evergreen, short-stalked, roundish ovate, and sometimes 3- to 5-lobed leaves that are whitish pubescent beneath. Its flowers are without petals but the sepals are so large, showy and petal-like that the non-botanist can easily mistake them for petals. They are bright yellow and, inside, hairy at their bases, cup-shaped at first but becoming shallower as they age, and 1¹/₂ to 3 inches in diameter.

Theobroma — Cacao; Chocolate Tree

This group of about thirty species of small trees are all natives of tropical South and Central America. The principal species, the cacao or chocolate tree *(T. cacao)*, is the source of chocolate and cocoa, both of which are prepared from its roasted, pulverized seeds. The seeds contain much fat and the mildly stimulating alkaloid, theobromine. Cocoa is obtained by removing most of the fat, called cocoa butter; chocolate results when most of the fat is retained. Cocoa butter is an important ingredient of pharmaceutical and cosmetic preparations. The chocolate tree is evergreen and up to 40 feet tall.

Its leathery, pointed oblong, short-stalked leaves, up to 1 foot long, hang limply and are coppery red when they first appear but soon stiffen and become green. The small, fragrant, yellowish flowers form clusters on the branches and trunk. They give rise to woody, ribbed, pointed ellipsoid, reddish fruits, 10 to 12 inches long, that contain about fifty flat, inch-wide seeds surrounded by whitish, mucilaginous pulp. The chocolate tree was exploited by the Incas both as the source of a beverage and for its seeds, which were used as currency and as the basis of the Peruvian financial system. Several other species of *Theobroma*, such as *T. bicolor, T. glauca, T. pentagona,* and *T. speciosa* (the last is called cacao de Sonusco), are used locally like *T. cacao.*

CHAPTER 25

The Parietales

This large order contains many dissimilar families. Further study will probably result in its being divided into several orders.

EUCRYPHIACEAE—EUCRYPHIA FAMILY

The botanical affinities of this family, which contains only one genus, are puzzling, and botanists formerly included it with the Rosaceae and with the Saxifragaceae.

Eucryphia

Here belong five or six evergreen trees and shrubs of Australia, Tasmania and southern South America. Their four-petaled, white, bisexual flowers have conspicuous masses of stamens and are borne singly in the leaf axils. The fruits are dry, woody or leathery capsules that contain a number of winged seeds. The leatherwood or pinkwood (*E. billardieri*) of Tasmania attains a height of 60 feet and is the source of a fairly hard and strong pinkish brown lumber used in building and cabinetwork. The undivided narrowly oblong leaves are up to 3 inches long;

the flowers are 1 inch across or more. Also known as pinkwood and as coachwood and white sally, *E. moorei* of Victoria and New South Wales rarely exceeds 30 feet in height. It has handsome, pinnate leaves that are dark green above and grayish beneath, and large white flowers. Its light brown wood is useful for cabinetwork and building. Tannic acid is extracted from its bark. The ulmo (*E. cordifolia*) of Chile is sometimes 130 feet in height with a trunk 2 feet in diameter. It is one of the handsomest of flowering trees and has been compared, in its effect, to the flowering dogwood of North America. It has individed leaves.

THEACEAE — TEA FAMILY

Five hundred species of trees and shrubs with undivided, leathery leaves, distributed among sixteen genera, belong in the tea family. Their flowers are usually bisexual and mostly have five sepals, five petals, and fifteen or more stamens in several whorls. Frequently the stamens are in distinct bundles joined to the bases of the petals.

Camellia

About eighty Indo-Malaysian, Chinese, Taiwanian and Japanese evergreen trees and shrubs constitute *Camellia*. One, the tea plant (*C. thea*), is of commercial importance as the source of tea. This species and others are also exploited for the oil contained in their seeds, which is used in the textile industry, soap manufacture and for other purposes. Undoubtedly the most familiar camellia to Westerners is *C. japonica,* a native of China and Japan cultivated in numerous horticultural varieties that have stemless, single or double, white, pink or red flowers of remarkable beauty and 2 to 5 inches in diameter. These are the camellias planted most abundantly in gardens in the warmer parts of the United States, Europe and elsewhere. *Camellia japonica* attains 45 feet in height and has shining dark green, serrated leaves. Its seeds are the source of Tsubaki oil, an ingredient of hair oils. The tea plant (*C. thea*), together with other species that have nodding, stalked flowers, is considered by some botanists to belong to a separate genus and is then named *Thea sinensis*. It grows to a maximum height of 30 feet but under cultivation is kept low and bushlike by the frequent picking of its young shoots and leaves which, when dried, form the tea of commerce. The flowers of this species are white, fragrant and about 1¹/₂ inches in diameter. Green tea results from leaves that are picked and dried promptly; to obtain black tea the newly picked leaves are fermented before they are dried. Tea contains the alkaloid theine, a stimulant, an astringent, and a nervine. It also contains tannin, which is responsible for the bitter taste of the beverage if the tea is brewed too long.

Franklinia — Franklin Tree

Only one species of this remarkable genus exists and since it has not been found in the wild since 1803, it is presumed that it is extinct insofar as present native flora is concerned. Fortunately, it has been preserved in cultivation and is not uncommon in gardens. The franklin tree, named in honor of Benjamin Franklin, was discovered in Georgia by John Bartram in 1765 and all plants now known to exist are descendants of specimens obtained by Bartram a few years later and planted in his botanical garden in Philadelphia.

The franklin tree is much like *Gordonia* but its leaves are deciduous, its stamens are separate and its seeds are angled but not winged. From *Stewartia* it differs in having fruits that split from both top and bottom and have a persistent central taxis. This attractive species attains a maximum height of about 30 feet, is of upright habit and has foliage that turns brilliant tones of orange and red in fall. Its beautiful, white, cup-shaped flowers, borne over a long period in summer, have many conspicuous yellow stamens and are 3 inches across. The globose fruits, about three-quarters of an inch in diameter, do not mature until the year following flowering.

Gordonia

Except for one native of North America, the forty species of this genus of trees and shrubs are all indigenous to Indo-Malaysia and Taiwan. They are evergreen, summer-blooming trees and shrubs with handsome flowers that have stamens united at their bases to form fleshy pads, fruits bases and winged seeds. The loblolly-bay (*G. lasianthus*) of the southeastern United States reaches a maximum height of about 80 feet and a trunk diameter of 20 inches; it has a dense, narrow crown and finely toothed, obovate or oblanceolate leathery leaves that are glossy and about 6 inches long. Its white, pungently fragrant, solitary, long-stalked flowers are 2¹/₂ inches in diameter. A native of forests in southeast Asia

and Taiwan, *G. axillaris* has almost stalkless, creamy white flowers, 2 to 3 inches in diameter, that are solitary or in pairs. This kind attains a maximum height of about 25 feet and has short-stalked, usually serrated, glossy, oblanceolate leaves up to 6 inches long.

Stewartia

Ten species of this genus are distributed in the eastern United States and eastern Asia. They are summer-blooming deciduous shrubs and trees with smooth, flaky bark and short-stalked, undivided, toothed leaves. Their solitary, bisexual, cup-shaped flowers have numerous stamens and five to eight white petals that are more or less silky and hairy on their outsides. The fruits are woody capsules that mature in their first season and split open from the top but not from the base. The American species *S. malacodendron* and *S. ovata* do not attain tree stature. One of the largest species is *S. pseudo-camellia* of Japan, which may be 60 feet or somewhat more in height. It has erect branches, reddish bark and cup-shaped flowers that look like those of single camellias and are 2 to 2¹/₂ inches across. Its elliptic or obovate bright green leaves assume purplish hues in fall. Like the shoots, the leaves are glabrous or have a few scattered hairs beneath. The Japanese *S. monadelpha*, which attains a height of 75 feet, differs from *S. pseudo-camellia* in that its young shoots and leaves are at first hairy but they lose much of this quality as they mature. Its fragrant flowers are 1 to 1¹/₂ inches across. *Stewartia koreana* differs from *S. pseudo-camellia* in having zigzag rather than straight branchlets and nearly flat flowers, 3 inches in diameter, that are densely pubescent on the outsides of the petals. It has a maximum height of about 45 feet; in fall its foliage becomes orange-red. This species is a native of Korea. Sometimes attaining 40 feet in height, *S. sinensis*, which has its home in central China, is distinct from other species dealt with here in that it has leafy bracts that are located

Right: Red silk-cotton tree. Bombax malabaricum (M. Krishnan)

Overleaf left: Flame tree. Brachychiton acerifolium (Ralph Cornell) Above right: Kurrajong. Brachychiton populneum (Janet Finch) Above far right: Palo borracho flower. Chorisia insignis (Ralph Cornell) Right below: Copey, flower. Clusia rosea (Werner Stoy: Camera Hawaii)

just below the flowers and are almost as long as or longer than the sepals. Its cup-shaped flowers, 2 inches in diameter, unlike those of most stewartias, are almost hairless on their outsides.

GUTTIFERAE — GARCINIA FAMILY

Mostly tropical trees and shrubs with resinous sap and oil glands, which often show on the leaves as translucent dots, constitute the Guttiferae. Their flowers are predominantly unisexual. The group includes forty genera and about a thousand species. The presence of oil glands differentiates members of this family from those of the closely related Theaceae.

Calophyllum

Here we have more than a hundred species distributed in the tropics, and most abundantly in Asia. One of the best known is the Alexandrian-laurel (C. ionophyllum), which inhabits the shores of lands bounded by the Indian and western Pacific oceans. An evergreen up to 60 feet tall, this species has usually a short, crooked, leaning trunk and many branches that form an irregular crown. Its blunt, elliptic to obovate glossy leaves are up to 7 inches long by about half as wide; they have prominent midveins with numerous fine lateral veins at nearly right angles to the midveins. The short-lived, sweetly scented flowers, 1 inch wide and in erect racemes, are white with pink ovaries. Green, globose and about 1 inch in diameter, the fruits contain seeds, called punnai nuts, that are the source of a strong-scented oil called dilo or domba that is used in medicine and for burning. The wood of the Alexandrian-laurel, hard, elastic, close-grained and durable, takes a fine polish and is esteemed for cabinetwork, boat-building, and railroad ties; it is known as Borneo mahogany. The Alexandrian-laurel is commonly planted as an ornamental and shade tree.

Calophyllum tomentosum is a huge straight-trunked tree of India, Malaya and Ceylon with quadrangular twigs and white flowers up to 1 inch wide. Its cedar-red wood is used for building and its seeds yield an orange-colored oil, called keena-tel, used for illumination and in medicine. Valued for its reddish lumber that is

Sour gum. Nyssa sylvatica (Irvin Oakes: National Audubon)

much employed for interior trim, and for the medicinal qualities of its bark, C. soulattri is a native of Ceylon, Malaya, Java and Fiji. The leaves of the two last-mentioned species have prominent midveins with numerous lateral veins diverging almost at right angles. The chief New World Calophyllum is the maria (C. braziliense), which ranges over vast areas of tropical America and is sometimes 150 feet high with a trunk 6 feet in diameter. It has opposite, undivided leaves up to 5 inches long by half as wide, with numerous side veins at nearly right angles to the midrib and fragrant white flowers, a half inch or less across, in clusters. Each fruit contains a single seed from which an oil used for illuminating is obtained. A yellow gum resin extracted from the bark is used medicinally. The handsome, strong lumber is used locally for ship-building, construction and furniture. This tree is widely planted.

Clusia

Like the strangling figs (Ficus species), most of the 145 members of this genus are epiphytes or partial epiphytes, that is to say, they live, at least for a time, on other plants without taking sustenance from them; they are, in other words, roomers but not boarders. Abundant in the American tropics, the genus is also represented in Madagascar and New Caledonia. One of the best-known New World kinds is the copey (C. rosea), which has a broad, speading, evergreen crown up to 60 feet in height and a trunk up to 2 feet in diameter. Its thick, leathery leaves are more or less triangular with the apex of the triangle joined to the stem. The outermost end of the leaf is flat or slightly convex or concave. Male and female flowers occur on separate trees, singly or a few together at the branch tips. They face downward, are 2 inches in diameter and have pink-tinged, white petals. The female flowers are succeeded by globular fruits about 3 inches in diameter, at first green but at maturity brown; these contain a scarlet pulp and small seeds. The copey commonly begins life as a seed deposited by a bat or bird on a branch of a tree. This develops into a young plant that after a while sends roots down into the ground. These nourish the copey and as it grows it slowly strangles, kills and replaces the host plant. Spanish conquistadores made playing cards from copey leaves by scratching representations of kings, queens, jacks and other card symbols on them. The wood of this tree is used for fuel,

Tamarisk, desert region. Tamarix (Paul Popper Limited)

fences, construction and other purposes. A resin obtained from the bark, fruit and other parts is used for caulking boats. The copey is an attractive ornamental especially well adapted for planting near the sea.

Garcinia — Mangosteen

Four hundred tropical species of the Old World are included in *Garcinia;* most of them are Asiatic. They are leathery-leaved evergreen trees and shrubs with unisexual flowers on separate trees and fruits that technically are berries. By far the most important, the mangosteen *(G. mangostana)* bears one of the most delicious and highly prized tropical fruits; unfortunately, it rarely succeeds in cultivation outside southeast Asia. The mangosteen is about 30 feet tall, its foliage is lustrous and it bears 2-inch-wide, four-petaled, buff yellow flowers suffused with pink around their edges; their inner pair of sepals are light red on the inside. In most regions where the mangosteen grows there are no male trees

and, as females have no pollen, the fruits which contain fertile seeds, develop parthenogenetically. They are purple, globose, about 3 inches across, and have five to eight red-veined white segments resembling those of an orange, each containing one or no seeds and a snow-white juicy pulp which partakes of the flavor of strawberries and grapes. Other species cultivated to some extent in tropical Asia for their edible fruits include the gelugor *(G. atroviridis),* a lofty, narrow-crowned tree that has red flowers and fluted fruits that ripen orange-yellow. They are sliced before they are fully ripe, dried like apple rings, and used in curries and in the preparation of other foods, especially fish. From *G. hanburyi* and other nearly related species is obtained a gum resin which is the basis of the yellow dye gamboge.

Mammea — Mammee-apple

With the exception of one species in the tropics of the New World and one in Africa, all of the approximately fifty members of this genus are natives of Indo-Malaysia, the Pacific islands and Madagascar. The American kind, the mammee-apple *(M. americana),* of the West Indies and northern South America, is an oval-crowned evergreen up to 60 feet in height with a short trunk up to 2 feet in diameter. Its opposite, glossy, short-stalked, broad elliptic leaves up to 6 inches long have numerous parallel lateral veins at nearly right angles to the midrib. The unisexual or bisexual white flowers, 1½ to 2 inches across and fragrant, have usually six petals. The globular fruits, 3 to 10 inches in diameter, have thick skins and red or yellowish apricot-flavored pulp surrounding the few large seeds; they are eaten raw and made into preserves. From the flowers the liqueur called eau or crème de creole is made; the seeds are said to be poisonous. The African mammee-apple *(M. africana),* a tropical African species 100 feet tall, bears showy white flowers 1½ inches in diameter on red stalks and has egg-shaped fruits 4 inches long that contain fragrant, peach-flavored, yellowish pulp and three or four seeds. The oblong elliptic glossy leaves are up to 1 foot long by 4 inches wide. The wood of the African mammee-apple is of good quality and is used locally for furniture and interior trim.

Pentadesma—Butter Tree; Tallow Tree

Of four species native to Africa and the Seychelles Islands the most notable is the butter tree or tallow tree *(P. butyracea)*, the seeds of which yield an oil or fat that is used as butter and for making soap and candles. The butter tree has a buttressed trunk and is up to 100 feet in height; it has tiers of horizontal branches. Its evergreen leaves are up to 1 foot long by 3 inches wide. The yellowish, fragrant, bell-shaped flowers are 3 inches long and about the same width. The egg-shaped fruits, about 4 inches long, contain three to ten seeds embedded in a yellowish pulp. The lumber of the butter tree is used for mine timbers, building, fuel and other purposes.

TAMARICACEAE—TAMARIX FAMILY

Four genera of desert, steppe and seashore shrubs and small trees—in all 120 temperate and subtropical species—constitute this family. They are generally adapted to withstand dry and saline soils and wind; their reduced scalelike leaves are suited to these environments.

Tamarix — Tamarisk

Most of the ninety species of this genus are shrubs and only a few attain tree size; they are native from the Mediterranean region to China. Their leaves are tiny, and their small flowers occur in racemes or panicles with four or five petals. Their seeds are hairy. The French tamarisk *(T. gallica)* occurs spontaneously from western Europe to the Himalayas and attains a height of 30 feet. Its slender branches and fine bluish-gray foliage produce a light, feathery effect. In early summer it is veiled with a profusion of white or pinkish blooms. The athel tamarisk *(T. aphylla)*, a 30-foot inhabitant of western Asia, has tiny leaves that encircle the twigs like those of *Casurina*. Its pink flowers form terminal panicles.

BIXACEAE—BIXA FAMILY

This tropical American and West Indian family of trees and shrubs consists of one genus with four species. They have reddish sap, undivided, alternate leaves, bisexual flowers with five or, rarely, four petals, and seeds with bright red fleshy outer coats.

Bixa — Anatto

The anatto *(B. orellana)* yields an orange dye that is obtained from its seeds and is used for coloring butter, cheese, candy, rice and other foods as well as soaps and varnishes; the Carib Indians used it to paint their bodies. It is a fast-growing evergreen, about 20 feet tall, with long-stemmed, thin, ovate or heart-shaped leaves up to 7 inches long and panicles of pink flowers, each 2 inches wide, that resemble wild roses. The somewhat flattened seed capsules are covered with prominent soft bristles. They are about 1½ to 2 inches long and split into two parts to reveal the numerous brilliant orange-red angular seeds. Anatto dye is flavorless and harmless and is obtained by boiling the seeds or their coverings in cooking oil or fat. The tree is an attractive ornamental and is now planted in many parts of the tropics. Its flowers are favorites of honey bees.

FLACOURTIACEAE—FLACOURTIA FAMILY

This family of trees, shrubs and a few climbers, pantropical and subtropical in its distribution, includes a thousand species in ninety-three genera. Its usually bisexual flowers have numerous stamens which distinguish it from its most closely related groups.

Dovyalis—Kei-apple; Ceylon-gooseberry

These shrubs and trees of African and Ceylon number thirty species. They have inconspicuous unisexual flowers, with the sexes on separate trees, and undivided leaves. The kei-apple *(D. caffra)*, often spiny and shrubby, is sometimes a more or less spineless tree up to 30 feet in height. Its quite variable leaves are most often egg-shaped, up to 2 inches long and prominently veined. The apple-shaped, acid fruits, up to 1½ inches in diameter and containing about a dozen seeds, are excellent for jelly. The Ceylon-gooseberry *(D. herbacea)*, a native of Ceylon, is often a shrub but is sometimes a small tree. It has oval, somewhat hairy leaves and velvety purplish fruits 1 inch in diameter; the fruits are eaten out of hand.

Flacourtia—Ramontchi; Governors-plum

The most important of this Old World genus of tropical and subtropical trees and shrubs is the ramontchi or governors plum *(F. indica)*, a deciduous tree up to 40 feet tall, of southern Asia and Madagascar. It has fragrant yellowish flowers and deep maroon berry-like fruits about one-half inch in diameter from which excellent jelly is made. Its ovate leaves are about 2 inches long.

A similar tree of India and Malaya, *F. cata-phracta*, has pleasantly flavored, cherry-like, deep maroon fruits.

Hydnocarpus

This genus of forty Indo-Malaysian species is most noteworthy because one of its members, *H. kurzii*, is the source of chaulmoogra oil, at one time much used in the treatment of leprosy. A native of Burma and Thailand, it is an ever-green up to 50 feet tall, with narrow, leathery leaves up to 10 inches long. Its flowers have four sepals and eight stamens; the sexes are on sep-arate trees. The smooth, velvety fruits, as large as oranges, contain a pulp with many seeds that are said to render the flesh of animals that eat them poisonous to human beings. Other species of *Hydnocarpus* yield oils similar to chaul-moogra and they also have been used in treating leprosy. Among these are *H. anthelminticus* and *H. wightiana*, the former of Thailand and adja-cent lands, the latter a native of India. The fruits of *H. venerata*, an endemic of Ceylon, are used there as a fish poison.

Idesia

There is only one species of this Chinese and Japanese genus, *I. polycarpa*, a deciduous tree that is 50 feet tall and bears small, fragrant, greenish, mostly unisexual flowers without pet-als and with the sexes on separate trees. They form drooping panicles up to 10 inches long; after pollination the females produce an abun-dance of bright orange-red berries. The widely toothed leaves are more or less heart-shaped and up to 10 inches long. This tree is an attractive ornamental.

CHAPTER 26

The Opuntiales

CACTACEAE—CACTUS FAMILY

The order Opuntiales contains only one family, the Cactaceae, the cactus family, and this entire family of perhaps two thousand species, except for one species of *Rhipsalis* that occurs in Africa,

Madagascar, the Seychelles, Mauritius and Cey-lon, is native to the New World. Some kinds, especially prickly-pears (*Opuntia*), are now freely naturalized in warm, dry regions elsewhere, and many plants that superficially look like cactuses—for example, many euphorbias—are natives of the Old World. Botanists differ as to the number of genera into which cactuses should be grouped, but the range is between 50 and 150.

The Cactaceae includes comparatively few trees. While a few cactuses have regular leaves, the vast majority, including those dealt with here, do not; their leaves are reduced to insig-nificant scales or are entirely absent, photosyn-thesis and other normal leaf functions being assumed by the stems. Most cactuses have clus-ters of spines arising from specialized portions of the stem called areoles and nearly all have watery juice in contrast to the nearly always milky juice of euphorbias. Generally the flowers are solitary with sepals and petals not well differ-entiated. In addition to the genera discussed below, cactuses of tree size occur in other genera, including *Cephalocereus*, *Pilocereus* and *Trich-ocereus*.

Carnegiea — Saguaro; Giant Cactus

This cactus, the most massive, consists of one species, the saguaro or giant cactus (*C. gigantea*) of the southeastern United States and adjacent Mexico. It has a columnar trunk up to 2 feet in diameter and 70 feet in height and sometimes a few erect branches. Trunk and branches are con-spicuously ribbed. Like most cactuses, it is leaf-less. Its 4-inch-long white flowers are succeeded by pale red edible fruits.

Cereus

This group of fifty South American and West Indian leafless species includes some of the tallest cactuses. Characteristically, they have erect, columnar and usually branching stems, strongly ribbed and furnished with clusters of sharp spines. The flowers, which open at night, are long, funnel-shaped and mostly white. One of the largest is *C. argentinensis*, a native of Argentina that has branches that are 6 inches thick and attains a height of 70 feet. Another species from Argentina, *C. dayamii*, is reported to grow up to 80 feet tall and to have stems 8 inches in diameter. Still another tree type, *C. peruviana*, from southeastern South America, is much branched and up to 40 feet tall. Brazil is the home of *C. jamacaru*, a thirty-footer with stems that are very glaucous blue when they are young. *Cereus hexagonus* occurs in the West Indies and in northern South America. This kind has usually six-ribbed stems; its trunk may be 1 foot in diameter.

Lemaireocereus

These day bloomers number about twenty-five leafless species that range from Arizona to northern South America; most are large and columnar. They differ from *Cereus* in that their ovaries have scales with felt in their axils. One of the best known is the organ pipe cactus (*L. marginatus*) of Mexico, which branches freely from its base and has many vertical stems, each with five or six ribs, and attains a height of 25 feet. In central Mexico *L. dumortieri* sometimes becomes 50 feet tall; it has bluish, usually six-ribbed branches. There are other treelike species including two fairly common Mexicans, *L. pruinosus* and *L. weberi;* the former becomes 25 feet tall and the latter grows up to 30 feet or more.

CHAPTER 27

The Myrtiflorae

The order Myrtiflorae is composed of families that exhibit transitional characters between orders with perigynous flower parts (that is, arising from around the ovary but not beneath it) and orders that have epigynous flowers (that is, arising from the top of the ovary). Usually the leaves of this order are opposite.

ELAEAGNACEAE—OLEASTER FAMILY

The oleaster family, natives of the Northern Hemisphere, consists of three genera of trees and shrubs numbering fifty species. They are primarily seashore and steppe plants that have undivided, leathery leaves and, like the stems and other parts, are covered with scaly hairs; often they are thorny. The flowers, bisexual or unisexual and without petals, have as many or twice the number of stamens as sepals. The fruits are berry-like.

Cannon ball tree. *Couroupita guianensis* (G. Tomsich)

Elaeagnus — Oleaster

This circumboreal genus of forty-five species consists chiefly of evergreen and deciduous shrubs. The only common one that sometimes is of tree size is the Russian-olive (*E. angustifolia*). This beautiful willow-like tree has silvery gray leaves, tiny fragrant flowers and, on the female trees, yellow berries coated with silver scales. It has a rather loose, wide-spreading head and is extremely hardy and tolerant of seaside conditions. It is native from southern Europe to western Asia.

Hippophaë—Sea-buckthorn

Three spiny species belong in this Eurasian genus. They have alternate, willow-like, scaly leaves and inconspicuous flowers that appear before the foliage; the males and females are on separate trees. *Hippophaë rhamnoides* of Europe and Asia attains a height of 30 feet; its variety, *procera,* has hairy young branches and becomes 50 feet tall. *Hippophaë salicifolia* of the Himalayan region also reaches 50 feet in height. It has pendulous branchlets and is less spiny than

253

Red mangrove. Rhizophora mangle (Kurt Severin)

H. *rhamnoides;* also its leaves are broader and not silvery, and its fruits are yellow and duller.

LYTHRACEAE—LOOSESTRIFE FAMILY

Herbaceous plants, shrubs and trees are represented in this family of twenty-five genera and 550 species. It occurs in all regions but is most abundant in the American tropics. The leaves are opposite or in whorls and are undivided. The flowers are bisexual.

Lagerstroemia—Crape-myrtle; Pride-of-India

The best-known member of this group of fifty trees and shrubs is the crape-myrtle *(L. indica).* This is more often shrubby than treelike but it sometimes reaches a height of 20 feet. A native of China, it has slender, four-angled stems, de-

ciduous elliptic to oblong leaves up to 2 inches in length and, in summer, panicles of white, pink, red or purplish flowers. It is a favorite ornamental in warmer temperate and in tropical regions.

The queen crape-myrtle or pride-of-India *(L. speciosa)* is one of the most important lumber trees of India; its wood is used for railroad ties and general construction and is considered second only to teak in quality. This deciduous species, which occurs as a native from India to Australia, attains a height of 60 feet and has beautiful pink, mauve or purple flowers in panicles up to 1½ feet long. Its leathery leaves are oblong and 4 to 12 inches long.

LECYTHIDACEAE—LECYTHIS FAMILY

Four hundred and fifty tropical trees and shrubs representing twenty-four genera constitute this family. Their large, undivided leaves are often concentrated near the ends of the twigs. Their bisexual flowers are solitary or clustered and have numerous stamens. The fruits of many kinds are large woody capsules that usually open by a lid.

Barringtonia

A hundred evergreen Old World species belong here; many, such as the handsome *B. asiatica,* which attains a height of 70 feet and has obovate leaves up to 1½ feet long by half as wide, are characteristic of shoreline jungles. The flowers of this kind are up to 7 inches in diameter and have large central bunches of stamens that measure up to 6 inches across. The fragrant, four-petaled blooms, which are white except for the stamens, which are tipped with pink, occur in more or less upright racemes; they open in the evening and fall the following morning. The heart-shaped fruits, 3 to 4 inches long, are strongly four-angled and retain at their tips the persistent calyxes; each fruit contains a single poisonous seed. The spongy, fibrous husk surrounding the seed is so light that the fruits are buoyant; they float for great distances in the ocean without impairing the seed. *Barringonia asiatica* is common in Ceylon, India and the Philippines and on some islands of the Pacific.

Bertholletia — Brazil Nut

Two species are admitted in this South American and West Indian genus. The Brazil nut *(B.*

excelsa) is of great importance in the Amazon Basin as the source of nutritious seeds, the Brazil nuts of commerce. These nuts are produced inside a thick-walled spherical capsule, 4 to 6 inches in diameter and so hard that it must be broken with an ax or other tool to release large three-sided seeds fitted together so exactly that no spaces exist between them. Unlike the seed containers of most genera in the Lecythidaceae, those of *Bertholletia* do not open to liberate their seeds; when the seeds germinate their growing parts extrude through an opening in the shell and develop roots, stems and leaves outside of it. The Brazil nut has leathery undivided leaves up to 2 feet long and 6 inches wide and cream yellow flowers with their stamens united into a hood-shaped mass; the upper stamens are sterile. This tree, which attains a height of 100 feet or more, forms extensive forests along the Amazon and the Rio Nigro. From its seeds an oil is obtained and its bark is used locally for caulking boats.

Couroupita — Cannon Ball Tree

By far the best known of this group of twenty natives of tropical America and the West Indies is the cannon ball tree (*C. guianensis*), which attains a height of 80 feet and bears its blooms on short, tangled branches that spring directly from the trunk. This tree has large, globular woody fruits, 6 to 8 inches in diameter, that take about eighteen months to mature. Its curious, fragrant, six-petaled flowers are about 5 inches wide and orchid-like. They have a curved central column that bears fertile stamens at its apex and base and fleshy petals tinged yellow on their outsides and pink or crimson within. The deciduous oblong leaves, up to 1 foot long, are grouped near the tips of the slender branchlets. Fallen fruits that litter the ground beneath give off what has been described as a putrid odor. This species occurs as a native throughout northern South and Central America and in the Lesser Antilles.

Gustavia

All forty-five species of this genus are trees and shrubs native to Central and South America. *Gustavia speciosa* of Panama attains a height of about 50 feet and has thick, toothed, narrow oblong leaves up to 3 feet long clustered at the ends of its few branches and clusters of beautiful fragrant flowers, each about 4 inches across. The six white petals have yellow bases and red outsides; the stamens are white. The wood is fetid and of no commercial importance.

Lecythis

All tropical American, the fifty species of this genus are similar to the *Couroupita* but the stamens at the top of the central column of the flower are sterile. The fruits are large, lidded, woody capsules called monkey pots because they are used as traps for those animals. Sugar is placed in the pot and is seized by the monkey; the animal cannot withdraw its clenched paw, and since it will not release the sugar, it cannot escape. There is some confusion as to the identification of the various species. The common monkey pot or wodaduri of British Guiana is probably *L. davisii*; a variety, the kwattapot (*L. d. gracilipes*), is prevalent in Surinam. These trees attain a height of about 100 feet and produce durable lumber of high quality. The guatecare (*L. laevifolia*), a massive evergreen of Trinidad, also produces good lumber. In Venezuela, Colombia and Panama the woods of *L. curranii*, *L. elliptica* and other species, known locally as coco do mono and olla do mono, are exploited for their wood. Several Brazilian species of *Lecythis* are known as sapucaias and their seeds, about the size of Brazil nuts, enter trade under the name of paradise nuts or sapucaia nuts. One of the best known of these, *L. ollaria*, has a trunk up to 6 feet in diameter that is free of branches up to 50 or 60 feet from the ground. The inner bark of these trees is used for caulking and for making cigarette papers and the trees also supply materials for tanning. Monkey pot fruits are employed for various domestic and ornamental purposes and the lumber is used for railroad ties, construction and cabinetwork.

RHIZOPHORACEAE — MANGROVE FAMILY

This family of sixteen genera and 120 species is found chiefly in the Old World and is most abundant along tropical shores. Its members, all trees and shrubs, are characteristically evergreen, usually with opposite leaves, stems swollen at their nodes and flowers that are nearly always bisexual. Most kinds are mangroves; they spread out from the land as far as the tidal low-water mark and in most cases develop great tangles of stiltlike, interlacing aerial roots that collect sediments, weeds and debris that wash among them; in this way they stabilize mud flats and

build land so that the shoreline gradually advances into the ocean. Some kinds, such as the Old World genus *Bruguiera*, produce numerous kneelike aerating roots, analogous to those of the swamp-cypress *(Taxodium)*; these develop from underwater roots, stand well above the surface of the water and supply the submerged roots with needed oxygen. *Bruguiera* does not have aerial roots from its higher branches, but its knee roots serve the same purpose in stabilizing mud and building land. A characteristic of mangroves of the Rhizophoraceae is that their fruits, which usually have only one seed, are viviparous. That is to say, the seed germinates inside the fruit while it hangs on the tree, developing a considerable rudimentary root system and, oftentimes, leaves before the fruit and its attached seedling—or the seedling separated from the fruit—finally drops, bomblike, and either embeds itself in the mud or floats until it is washed up on the strand. If conditions on the shore are at all favorable, it roots into the mud and soon becomes established.

Rhizophora — Mangrove

About seven species constitute this genus. The red mangrove *(R. mangle)*, which occurs from southern Florida to South America as well as along the Atlantic shore of Africa, is according to some authorities identical with mangroves found elsewhere in the tropics; other botanists consider it distinct. The red mangrove attains a maximum height of 100 feet and may develop trunks up to 3 feet in diameter that are devoid of branches for the lower 35 or 40 feet. The trunks form several feet above the ground and are supported by the great tangles of aerial roots that are anchored in the mud flats below. The name red mangrove refers to the color of its hard wood which is so heavy that it sinks in water. The wood can be made into high-quality charcoal and, as it is impervious to teredo worms and other borers and is durable under water, it is excellent for piles and other submerged construction. It is excellent fuel, producing great heat when burned. The bark is used for tanning and the flowers are a source of good honey. Along the east coast of Africa and in tropical Asia *R. mucronata* replaces *R. mangle* as the most common species.

Mangrove tree, Galapagos Islands. *Rhizophora* (Rolf Blomberg: Full Hand)

Davidia—Dove Tree

The dove tree *(D. involucrata)* is the only member of this Chinese genus. Handsome, deciduous and growing up to 60 feet in height, it forms a wide, pyramidal crown and has alternate, broad ovate, toothed leaves up to 6 inches long and tiny, bisexual, yellow flowers that form globular clusters 1 inch through. A remarkable showy feature is the pair of unequal-sized large, creamy white bracts that accompany each flower cluster; the largest of these may be 7 inches long. When festooned with these blooms the tree is very ornamental; because of its showy bracts it is sometimes called the ladies' handkerchief tree. The plum-size fruits are hard and green.

NYSSACEAE—NYSSA FAMILY

This family of three genera and about a dozen species of trees and shrubs of eastern North America and eastern Asia, is closely related to the Cornaceae, from which the Nyssaceae is believed to have evolved.

Nyssa—Pepperidge; Black Gum; Tupelo

Ten American and Asiatic species are credited to this genus. They have undivided leaves, minute, greenish white flowers, and small berry-like fruits that usually contain a single, hard, ribbed or winged seed. Here belong some of the most handsome of North American trees; unfortunately, their use in landscaping is limited because they are difficult to transplant. The pepperidge, black gum, or tupelo *(N. sylvatica)* of eastern North America ranges from Maine to Michigan, Florida and Texas. Up to 100 feet in height, it forms a flat-topped columnar or pyramidal head of usually somewhat pendulous branches and has blunt, obovate or elliptic, lustrous leaves that turn brilliant scarlet to orange in fall. Male and female flowers are borne on separate trees. The ovoid fruits are dark blue and $1/3$ to $2/3$ inch long. This species, which commonly inhabits moist soils, is one of the most handsome of American trees.

Abundant in swamplands from Virginia to Florida and Texas is another species called tupelo or cotton gum *(N. aquatica)*. Attaining a height of 100 feet and a trunk diameter of 4 feet, this kind has its natural northern limit from Virginia to Illinois and extends to Florida and Texas. It differs from *N. sylvatica* in having sharp-pointed leaves and solitary female flowers; the flowers of *N. sylvatica* occur in groups of two or more. The fruits of the cotton

Terminalia arjuna (M. Krishnan)

gum are purple and about 1 inch long. The above species supply tupelo lumber which is used chiefly for boxes, crates, plywood, paper, pulp, flooring and other purposes. The Ogeechee-lime (*N. ogeche*) is a native of swamplands from South Carolina to Florida. It grows up to 60 feet in height, has blunt leaves and a bushy crown with twigs that when young are covered with silky red hairs; its female flowers are solitary. In late summer and fall the red fruits hang in clusters and often remain long after they are ripe and the leaves have fallen. Sour and juicy, and 1 to 1¹/₂ inches long, the fruits are used to make delicious preserves. The Chinese tupelo (*N. sinensis*) is a rare tree of central China that is up to 60 feet tall with a trunk 2 feet in diameter. It has narrow, oval leaves and female flowers in clusters of twos or threes. Its bluish fruits are one-half inch long.

COMBRETACEAE—COMBRETUM FAMILY

This family consists of trees, shrubs and vines with usually alternate leaves and mostly bisexual flowers; eighteen genera and five hundred species are included, all tropical or subtropical.

Terminalia

About 250 species of this pantropical genus are recognized. They are trees and shrubs with leaves often crowded toward the ends of their branchlets, flowers that lack petals and are usually in elongated spikes, and fruits that generally are winged. The Indian-almond, tropical-almond, or almendro (*T. catappa*) is one of the best-known kinds. A native of the seashores of Malaya, this deciduous or partially evergreen tree is up to 80 feet in height and has a stout, often leaning trunk and a spreading crown. Its thick, obovate leaves, up to 1 foot long by 7 inches broad, turn vivid red or yellow before they fall. The greenish white flowers, about one-fourth of an inch across and in spikes up to 5 inches long, are ill-scented. Often all the flowers of a spike are males; sometimes most are males and the few lowermost are females or are bisexual. The fruits of the tropical-almond are ovoid, somewhat flattened and two-edged, and 1 to 2 inches long. Their tough rind encloses a tough shell containing one or two delicately flavored seeds that can be eaten raw or roasted. The tropical-almond is commonly cultivated in warm regions as a shade tree. Its wood, strong and elastic, is esteemed for construction and boatbuilding; its bark is used for tanning; a dye and ink are prepared from its fruits; and parts of the plant are employed medicinally. *Terminalia belerica*, a large tree of Malaya, the East Indies and the Philippines has dark red fruits that resemble small plums; unripe they are called myrobalan nuts and are used, often mixed with the fruits of *T. chebula*, for tanning leather. They are also used to produce inks and dyes and in medicines. The fruits of *T. chebula*, of India and Burma, are also called myrobalan nuts and are used for tanning. The last two species have unpleasantly scented white or yellowish flowers. The Indian *T. arjuna* differs from the Indian-almond in that it has smaller leaves and fruits and yellow, bisexual flowers.

MYRTACEAE—MYRTLE FAMILY

In this family are about a hundred genera and three thousand species of trees and shrubs varying in size from forest giants to small creepers. Almost all are tropical or subtropical; they are most abundant in Australia and South America. Their usually opposite leaves have translucent dots visible to the naked eye or through a hand lens when the leaf is held to the light. The flowers are bisexual and usually in clusters; they have numerous stamens and, generally, four or five petals.

Agonis

Fifteen Australian species constitute this genus which, unlike most members of the myrtle family, has alternate leaves. Most notable is the Western Australian-peppermint or willow-myrtle (*A. flexuosa*), an evergreen ornamental tree about 40 feet tall that has alternate, 6-inch-long, narrow, drooping, three-veined leaves and such a profusion of small, white, velvety flowers, grouped in stemless, globular heads, one-half-inch wide, in the leaf axils that when in bloom it looks as if it were spattered with snow. The fruits are leathery capsules.

Backhousia

This eastern Australian group comprises seven species of trees and shrubs closely related to *Meterosideros*. The sweet-verbena-myrtle of Queensland (*B. citriodora*) has evergreen, ovate lanceolate, leathery leaves up to 6 inches long that when crushed emit a strong citron odor. Its small white flowers are in umbel-like clusters. This species attains a height of about 25 feet. The gray-myrtle or scrub-myrtle (*B. myrtifolia*) has clusters of larger white flowers and ovate or broad lanceolate evergreen leaves. It becomes 40 feet tall. Its tough, strong wood is used for construction and tool handles.

Callistemon — Bottle Brush

Here belong twenty-five species of evergreen shrubs and small trees of Australia, Tasmania and New Caledonia. A characteristic of the group is that the stem that forms the central axis of the flower cluster continues to grow and bear leaves beyond the blooms. The flowers, commonly pollinated by birds, have conspicuous stamens which, unlike those of *Melaleuca* are not joined together; the cylindrical flower clusters resemble bottle brushes. The leaves of *Callistemon* do not occur in pairs but are scattered along the stems. *Callistemon viminalis* is occasionally 60 feet in height; it has pendulous branches, linear oblong leaves and dense spikes of bright red flowers. *Callistemon salignus* attains a height of 40 feet, has lanceolate, willow-like leaves up to 3 inches long, and pale yellow or slightly pink-tinged blooms. *Callistemon lanceolatus* is sometimes 30 feet in height. It has lanceolate leaves up to 3 inches long and rather loose clusters of red flowers. The woods of the above species are hard, tough and resistant to decay; they are used for fence posts and other purposes.

Eucalyptus

Except for two or three natives of Indo-Malaysia, all five hundred species of eucalypts are Australian or Tasmanian. They dominate the flora of Australia to the extent that they comprise about seventy-five percent of the natural forest. Among them are some of the tallest trees of the world as well as some kinds, called mallees, that are scarcely taller than a man. A distinguishing characteristic of members of the genus *Eucalyptus* is that the flower bud has an operculum or lid consisting of united petals, sepals or bracts that, when the bud opens, falls off and exposes the stamens and other parts beneath. The closely

related genus *Angophora* differs in having opposite leaves and no operculum.

The shape of the operculum is often a guide to the identification of species. All eucalypts develop distinct types of leaves at different stages of their lives. There may be as many as five recognizable types, including cotyledon, seedling and intermediate leaves, but by far the most important are the juvenile and the adult leaves; these are usually very dissimilar and are important diagnostic features. Juvenile leaves, like those of most trees, usually spread horizontally, but mature foliage nearly always hangs vertically. Except for a very few tropical species that lose their leaves in summer, eucalypts are evergreens, but individual leaves are on the average retained for no more than eighteen months and often for much shorter periods; sometimes they do remain for three or four years.

The leaves, especially the juvenile ones, of most eucalypts are glaucous; they have a bluish or whitish appearance caused by the structure of the tissues or by a waxy surface covering. The flowers lack petals but are often highly decorative; their color is provided chiefly by the filaments of the numerous stamens, which may be white, cream, pink, red or yellow, according to kind. They are pollinated by insects or, occasionally, by birds. The woody fruits consist of capsules enclosed or partly enclosed by an adherent calyx tube. The numerous seeds are tiny and usually angular. Although often very tall, the trunks of eucalypts are usually comparatively slender. The bark is smooth, tessellated or fissured according to kind. The botanical classification of eucalypts is complex and sometimes confusing. Primarily the genus is divided into groups distinguished by differences in the anthers of their flowers, and these groups are split into series and subseries, the members of which generally resemble each other more than they do the other eucalypts in bark, wood, foliage, fruits and other characteristics. Foresters and lumbermen classify the kinds that yield commercial lumbers into groups distinguished by such vernacular names as bloodwoods, boxes, gums, ironbarks, messmates, peppermints and stringybarks, chiefly on the basis of their bark types; they call some kinds ashes, mahoganies,

Above: Relative of eucalyptus. Angophora intermedia Left: Angophora intermedia flower (Both, Janet Finch)

and oaks, because of resemblances their woods bear to those of true ashes, mahoganies and oaks.

As producers of commercial products eucalypts rank high. They are probably the world's most valuable source of hardwood lumber. Their woods include some of the hardest, heaviest and most durable; and most are excellent fuel. Because of this and their rapid growth and ability to reseed themselves, eucalypts are widely planted in warm temperate regions of the world outside of their native lands. All kinds contain volatile oil in their leaves, and some kinds in their bark; oils commercially distilled from the foliage of about twenty species are used in industry as disinfectants and deodorants and in medicine and perfumery. *Eucalyptus* flowers secrete abundant nectar and are the chief bee pasture in Australia. The honey derived from many kinds is of very high quality. Other commercial uses of eucalypts include the production of paper pulp, fiberboard, veneers, plywood and tanning materials, and as fodder.

Essentially tropical, the ghost gum (*E. papuana*) extends over most of the northern half of Australia excepting only the westernmost part; it is also native in New Guinea. In the central part of the continent it often is the only tree; elsewhere it occurs in company with other species. The ghost gum grows up to 60 feet in height; it has a short trunk up to 1½ feet in diameter and a comparatively large crown. The bark is smooth and white except toward the base of the trunk, where it is gray. The pointed, lanceolate adult leaves are thin, dull or shiny and light or dark green. Lumber of this tree, which is not of high quality, is used locally for construction; it is subject to attacks by termites.

The Sydney blue gum (*E. saligna*) grows up to a height of 160 feet and has a tall, straight trunk that may be 6 feet in diameter; it is often unbranched for half to two-thirds the height of the tree. The bark is smooth and white or blue-gray except for sections of rough gray or brown persistent bark on the lower part of the trunk. The adult leaves are lanceolate and taper to long points; they are dark green above, paler beneath. The cylindrical or slightly bell-shaped fruits mostly have short stalks. A handsome ornamental, this fast-growing kind produces abundant nectar and is commercially important for its lumber, which is used for general construction and, because of its non-greasy character, is particularly useful for steps and flooring.

The southern mahogany or bangalay (*E. botryoides*) inhabits coastal strips from New South Wales to Victoria. Often it grows in somewhat saline soils, rarely in dense stands. At its best it is 140 feet tall with a trunk diameter of 4 feet but in open locations it is usually considerably lower and may be branched to the ground. Its bark is mostly persistent and dark brown. The adult leaves are lanceolate and have long points. The stalkless fruits are cylindrical. A beautiful shade tree, the southern mahogany withstands exposure to sea wind better than most eucalypts, and it is well adapted for coastal landscaping. Its reddish brown lumber is strong, hard and durable. The swamp mahogany (*E. robusta*) is occasionally 90 feet tall and may have a trunk diameter of 4 feet. Characteristically, its straight trunk is without branches for about half the height of the tree, and its well-foliaged spreading branches form a head that provides good shade. This is essentially a subtropical species that occupies a very narrow coastal strip in Queensland and New South Wales; it usually grows in wet soils. Its adult leaves are broad lanceolate, glossy dark green above, lighter colored beneath. Able to withstand shade better than most eucalypts, the red mahogany or red messmate (*E. resinifera*) produces a strong, durable, easy-to-work, red lumber that is valued for construction, interior trim, shipbuilding and railroad ties. The tree forms a well-branched compact crown and grows up to 100 feet in height and has a trunk that may be 5 feet in diameter. Its rough, stringy, reddish bark is persistent. Its leaves are thick, lanceolate, glossy dark green above and dull and paler beneath. The fruits, hemispherical or egg-shaped, usually have distinct stalks. The red mahogany occurs in mixture with other species and in small pure stands. It is native along the coasts of Queensland and New South Wales.

The source of one of the best Australian lumbers for construction purposes, the gray gum (*E. propinqua*) is fairly abundant in a coastal area of Queensland and New South Wales. Usually it grows in mixture with other species and may be 130 feet tall and have a trunk diameter of 3½ feet, with the trunk branchless for half the height of the tree. The bark, which sheds in large irregular patches, is mottled pink and gray. The thick, dull green, lanceolate adult leaves are paler on their undersides than above. The short-stalked fruits are hemispherical to conical. The wood is red or

River red gum. Eucalytus camaldulensis (Janet Finch)

red-brown and very hard, strong and durable.

A native chiefly of New South Wales and Victoria, the woollybutt *(E. longifolia)* grows in a coastal strip not more than forty miles wide. It attains a height of 130 feet and a trunk diameter of 3½ feet. The trunk is rarely half the height of the tree and supports a large, irregularly branched crown. The furrowed gray bark is persistent on the trunk and large branches, but elsewhere it sheds and exposes smooth, light tan or greenish areas. The adult leaves are narrowly lanceolate, usually curved and dull green or gray-green. This species, which grows rather slowly, produces durable lumber used in heavy construction and for poles, posts and railroad ties. It is a good bee tree. Notable for the strength and hardness of its lumber, which is said to equal that of wrought iron, the yate *(E. cornuta)* inhabits the extreme southwestern corner of Australia, where it grows to a height of 70 feet with a trunk diameter of 3 feet. The dark gray bark is persistent on the trunk and larger branches but elsewhere sheds to reveal smooth grayish brown surfaces. Both sides of its lanceolate adult leaves are glossy dark green. The lumber is used to the greatest extent

by wheelwrights; although one of the hardest and strongest woods in the world, it is not very durable. The tuart *(E. gomphocephala)* is remarkable because its strong, heavy, durable wood does not corrode metals; it is chiefly used in the construction of railroad cars. The best, nearly pure stand of tuart does not extend over more than 6000 acres and its natural range is a narrow belt, often not more than a mile wide, along the coast of Western Australia. The tree grows to a height of 130 feet with a trunk that grows up to 7 feet in diameter and is covered with persistent, deeply fissured, light gray bark. The crown usually occupies half to two-thirds of the height of the tree. The thick, gray-green adult leaves are narrowly lanceolate, long-pointed and usually curved.

Because its bark has the highest tannin content of any commercial tanbark, the brown mallet *(E. astringens)* is cultivated in Australia, and natural stands of it are exploited for this product; it is also cultivated in South Africa. The brown mallet is a native of southwestern Australia, where it attains a height of about 80 feet and a trunk diameter of 2½ feet. Its straight trunk, half or more as tall as the tree, supports a fairly dense-foliaged crown; its bark is smooth and brown. The slightly curved adult leaves, thick and lanceolate, are shining dark green on both sides. The wood, brown with reddish streaks, is hard, strong and tough. The wandoo *(E. wandoo)* is a drought-resistant native of southwestern Australia that occasionally becomes 100 feet tall with a trunk diameter of 4 feet. The trunk occupies about one-third the height of the tree, which branches to form a large, rounded open crown. The bark is smooth, creamy white or yellowish with patches of red; sometimes the lower part of the trunk is clothed with persistent yellow-brown bark. The narrowly lanceolate mature leaves are dull green or grayish green. Only rarely does the wandoo occur in forests; more often it forms sparse savanna woodland. The wood, durable and heavy, is used for flooring and general carpentry; it is also excellent for posts and heavy construction. Both its wood and bark are of considerable commercial importance as sources of tannin. Honey from the flowers of this tree is of high quality.

Because of its value as a source of poles, posts and for farm construction as well as for its ornamental qualities, the sugar gum *(E. clado-calyx)* has been planted extensively in

Australia; it is also cultivated in California, North Africa, Spain and other places. Under good conditions this tree becomes 100 feet high and may have a trunk 5 feet in diameter that is unbranched for a third to one-half the height of the tree. The foliage, clustered at the ends of the branches, results in a distinctive open crown. The lanceolate adult leaves are slightly paler beneath than on their upper sides. A peculiarity of the foliage is that under some circumstances it accumulates so much hydrocyanic acid that it poisons animals that eat it; this is especially true of young stems and leaves. The bark of the sugar gum sheds in large irregular patches, leaving trunk and branches mottled with yellowish brown, light gray and white. This tree is a native of South Australia. Having a greater natural range than any other eucalypt, the river red gum (E. camaldulensis) occurs in pure forest stands and in savanna woodlands over about half of Australia; it is a native to every state except Tasmania. Characteristically, it occupies land adjacent to watercourses and flood plains. At its best the river red gum becomes 150 feet tall and may have a trunk more than 3 feet in diameter. It forms a spreading, open top and has a trunk that is usually unbranched for about one-third the height of the tree. The bark is white, light gray, or yellowish marked with patches of red; it sheds in long strips or flakes but is sometimes persistent toward the base of the trunk. The adult leaves are thin, dull pale green and lanceolate. The red river gum is a fast grower and produces hard, red, durable lumber that is much used for railroad ties and construction. It is a good tree for planting for shelter and windbreaks. Its nectar makes high quality honey.

Native only in Tasmania, the cider gum (E. gunnii) has proved to be the hardiest species for cultivating in the Northern Hemisphere. In the British Isles it succeeds better than any other eucalypt. A specimen planted at Wittinghame Castle in 1846 was 90 feet tall and had a trunk diameter of more than 6 feet a hundred years later. The cider gum is so named because good quality cider is prepared from its sap. A native of subalpine regions, this species reaches a maximum height of 100 feet; its smooth bark is green and white, and deciduous. Its adult leaves are lanceolate to ovate, and are green or glaucous gray-green. A good ornamental shade tree, the cider gum produces hard, easily worked lumber.

Probably the best-known eucalypt is the blue gum (E. globulus), a native of Tasmania that attains a height of 180 feet and a trunk diameter of 7 feet. It is one of a group of closely related species that dominate extensive forests in southern Australia. All have dense crowns and gray bark that peels in coarse strands to reveal streaks and blotches of paler blue-gray. The mature leaves have stalks and are dark green.

Juvenile foliage of young trees is especially beautiful; it is glaucous blue and feels waxy. Juvenile leaves lack stalks and on the lower parts of the shoots are opposite. The twigs on which they grow are winged or quadrangular. The fruits of the blue gum are large and warty and have four ribs. Of all eucalypts this species has been most widely planted outside of Australia for ornament and commercial use. It was the first kind to be exported, seeds having been sent to France in 1804. It is now cultivated in South America, Africa, Portugal, Spain, California, China and many other areas. It is a splendid shade tree and is useful for windbreaks. In Ecuador it flourishes in windswept locations up to ten thousand feet above sea level; it is the chief source of industrial lumber in Peru Its lumber makes excellent fuel and is also used for construction, boatbuilding, piles, poles, railroad ties, fencing, paper pulp and a variety of other purposes. The introduction of the blue gum into Ethiopia was responsible for stabilizing a nomadic population and for the development and preservation of its capital, Addis Ababa. The original forests over large areas of the country had been practically destroyed about a century ago and it would soon have been necessary for the population to move southward to find the fuel essential to life in the harsh climate of that mountainous country. Then a French forester introduced Eucalyptus globulus. It is now grown by fifteen million farmers, every village has its groves, and there are great plantations near Addis Ababa.

The manna gum (E. viminalis) is widely distributed throughout southeastern Australia and Tasmania. Usually growing in company with other eucalypts, it sometimes attains a height of 150 feet and a trunk diameter of 4 feet. It forms a spreading, open head, and has drooping branchlets. Its rough gray bark is persistent on the lower part of the trunk; elsewhere it sheds in long strips and exposes yellowish or white undersurfaces. The adult leaves are thin and pale green on both surfaces. The wood of the manna gum is tough but lacks durability and has a marked tendency to warp. The tree is a worthwhile

ornamental. The Argyle-apple (*E. cineria*) is one of the most ornamental species. A wide-spreading tree, it has beautiful, silvery blue adult leaves that are ovate or rounded and soft, fibrous brown bark on its trunk and major branches. Up to 50 feet tall, it grows naturally on poor soils in a very restricted area in southeastern Australia. Its wood is inferior.

An important wood tree of Australia, the jarrah (*E. marginata*) is a native of the southwestern corner of the continent. This species accounts for at least three-quarters of the lumber produced in Western Australia; it is used for construction of all kinds, for posts, piles, railroad ties, road paving blocks, interior trim, furniture, fiberboard and densified wood. Jarrah wood is resistant to fire and termites but does not make good fuel. The tree grows up to 130 feet high with a trunk diameter of 6 feet and has an open crown. The bark is persistent, brown and stringy. The adult leaves are lanceolate, darker green on their upper surface.

Blackbutt (*E. pilularis*), which is one of the most important Australian hardwoods, attains a height of 200 feet and a trunk diameter of 7 feet. Its straight trunk, unbranched for half to two-thirds the height of the tree, supports an open, spreading crown. The dark, glossy green adult leaves are paler on their undersurfaces. Blackbutt is the principal lumber tree of southeastern Queensland and the coastal region of New South Wales, where it naturally forms pure stands or grows associated with other eucalypts. The wood is used for all kinds of construction and for poles, posts and railroad ties. Tallowwood (*E. microcorys*), a native of coastal areas in southern Queensland and northern New South Wales, reaches a height of 150 feet with a trunk diameter of 7 feet or more. Its straight trunk is usually unbranched for two thirds the total height of the tree and, like the branches, is covered with persistent, brown, soft, fibrous bark. The adult leaves are thin, pointed lanceolate and green, paler below than above. This species produces abundant pollen and nectar. Its wood, which has great strength and durability and is easily worked, has a smooth, greasy quality which makes it particularly useful for dance floors; it is also used for poles, posts, railroad ties and heavy construction. One of the

Alpine-ash. Eucalyptus delegatensis (Michael Sharland)

White sallee. Eucalyptus pauciflora (Michael Sharland)

most important hardwoods of Australia, the messmate stringybark (*E. obliqua*) is widely distributed through the cooler regions of southern and eastern Australia and Tasmania. It occurs in pure stands and intermixed with other species. It grows to 225 feet or more in height with trunk diameters up to 10 feet. Its tall, straight trunk occupies up to two-thirds of the height of the tree and, like the branches, is covered with a persistent, furrowed, stringy brown bark. The adult leaves are asymmetrically lanceolate, thick and dark green on both surfaces. The wood of the messmate stringybark is fairly hard, strong and durable and is used for construction, interior trim and pulping.

Exceeded in height only by the redwoods of California, the Australian mountain-ash (*E. regnans*) is the tallest non-coniferous tree in the world. The biggest specimen reliably recorded was 374 feet high; taller ones have been reported. Ordinarily, their heights are from 175 to 250 feet, occasionally up to 300 feet. Trunk diameters

can be impressive, up to 20 feet or more, but 6 to 9 feet is more usual. The straight trunk, commonly unbranched for two-thirds the height of the tree, is covered with persistent rough bark for up to 50 feet from its base but is smooth and white or greenish gray above; the bark sheds in long strips. The thin, smooth, broadly lanceolate adult leaves are glossy green on both surfaces. The Australian mountain-ash is a native of Tasmania and Victoria, usually occurring in pure stands in regions of cool summers and fairly cold winters; in its native home it is exposed to frosts and snowfall. One of the most important lumber trees of the continent, its wood is easily worked and takes a good finish. Light in weight and pale-colored, it is used for furniture, interior trim and general carpentry as well as for veneer, plywood and paper pulp. For the latter it is the most important Australian tree.

The alpine-ash (E. delegatensis) is a native of Tasmania and southern Australia where in pure stands it attains heights of 225 feet and two-thirds the height of the tree and on its lower portion is covered with persistent, brown, fibrous bark. Above, the bark peels to exhibit smooth white or bluish gray under-surfaces. The adult leaves are lanceolate and usually curved, and are dull green or bluish green on both sides. As a lumber tree the alpine-ash is important; its beautifully grained wood is light and is easy to work and is much used for interior trim, furniture, construction and paper pulp.

The name snow gum is applied to a small group of species and their variants that occur at high elevations and are more frost-tolerant than most eucalypts. Most are shrubs or small trees, others are medium-sized trees. None yields high-quality lumber but their woods make useful fuel. The most important snow gums are E. pauciflora and E. stellulata. The former, also called white sallee, has a picturesque crooked trunk and rarely grows as tall as 75 feet. It ranges widely through the mountains of southeastern Australia and Tasmania. At the highest elevations at which it grows frosts are common and snow may lie for several weeks of the year. Its bark sheds, leaving the trunks and branches mottled gray. The adult leaves, thick,

Above: White sallee. Eucalyptus pauciflora Left: Coolabah tree. Eucalyptus microtheca (Both, Australian News and Information Bureau)

Tasmanian snow gum. Eucalyptus coccifera (Michael Sharland)

lanceolate and usually curved, are gray-green. Very similar to the white sallee and by some considered to be only an alpine form of it is *E. niphophila,* a white-barked crooked tree or mallee up to 20 feet tall that at an altitude over six thousand feet forms the limit of tree growth in Australia. It differs from *E. stellulata* in having very glaucous foliage. The black sallee (*E. stellulata*) forms a spreading specimen up to 50 feet tall. Its bark is greenish and smooth except at the base of the trunk, where it is rough. Its adult leaves are broadly lanceolate to elliptical. The Tasmanian snow gum (*E. coccifera*) is confined to Tasmania. There it inhabits high mountains up to the limits at which trees grow and endures subalpine conditions with frosts occurring up to 150 nights of the year and snowfall on thirty to forty days. The rainfall may be 50 to 100 inches a year. In exposed locations it becomes, like other snow gums, stunted and shrublike, but in more favored places it grows up to 70 feet tall with a trunk diameter of 1¹/₂ feet; its trunk and branches are white, and the bark sheds in long strips. The

adult leaves are lanceolate and finely pointed; they are thick and green or gray-green. The snow gums serve usefully as shelter trees at high elevations, affording protection to birds and animals.

The narrow-leaved peppermint gum (*E. radiata*) is one of the most important oil-producing eucalypts. It is found in several forms, one of which, often known as *E. phellandra,* is the source of an oil of especial value in the manufacture of deodorants and disinfectants; another form is the one sometimes called *E. robertsonii.* This gum grows to 80 feet in height and has fibrous bark that persists on trunk and branches. Its linear to lanceolate adult leaves are thin and dark green. *Eucalyptus radiata* is a shapely ornamental and produces lumber that is used for making fiberboard; it is native to southeastern Australia.

Immortalized in the Australian song "Waltzing Matilda," the coolabah tree (*E. microtheca*) is known at least by name throughout the English-speaking world. Usually having a crooked trunk and spreading branches, it is rarely

267

more than 50 feet tall. Its gray bark is more or less persistent and usually deeply fissured near the bottom of the trunk. The adult leaves are dull green, lanceolate and often curved. The coolabah tree grows in moist flatlands and along the banks of watercourses from southern Queensland northward. Its wood is brown to nearly black, hard, tough and very durable. The broad-leaved peppermint gum (*E. dives*) and its physiological forms are important sources of medicinal and industrial oils. The oil is the chief commercial source of piperitone which is used in the production of synthetic menthol and thymol. The wood, although not of highest quality, is used for light construction. The broad-leaved peppermint gum is a handsome shade tree. It grows to a height of 80 feet with a trunk diameter of 2½ feet and has persistent bark on its trunk and main branches. The trunk may be clear of branches for up to one-third the height of the tree or it may be branched to the ground. The adult leaves are lanceolate to ovate and are dark and glossy green on both sides. A native of Victoria and New South Wales, this species usually occurs in association with other eucalypts.

Especially striking because of its persistent, deeply furrowed black or dark brown bark, the red ironbark (*E. sideroxylon*) enjoys a wide distribution in New South Wales and Victoria and is of a limited occurrence in Queensland. It occurs in pure stands and as individuals scattered among other species. Its lanceolate adult leaves are dull green or glaucous gray-green on both surfaces; the flowers are white, pink or red. Attaining a height of 100 feet and a trunk diameter of 4 feet, this species has an irregular crown and a trunk that is rarely longer than half the height of the tree. The wood of the red ironbark is red, hard, strong and durable. It is used for railroad ties and construction. Its bark contains tannin and the tree is a source of high-grade medicinal oil. The red ironbark, a good shade and shelter tree, is drought-resistant.

A distinctly ornamental tree is the white ironbark or yellow gum (*E. leucoxylon*), a native of Victoria and South Australia. This tree becomes 90 feet tall and has a trunk up to 3 feet in diameter that is about half the height of the

Above: Salmon gum. Eucalyptus salmonophloia
Left: Karri gum. Eucalyptus diversicolor (Both, Australian News and Information Bureau)

tree. Its crown is irregular and ofen rather open. The bark sheds from the trunk and branches in sheets to reveal a mottled yellow, white and blue-gray surface beneath. The adult leaves are lanceolate and dark green on both surfaces. The hard, tough, durable wood is used as posts and piles and for mining timbers, railroad ties and heavy construction. The tree is a source of high quality medicinal oil.

The yellow-box (E. mellidora) is native to Victoria, New South Wales and southern Queensland. It attains 100 feet in height and a trunk diameter up to 3 feet. Its large rounded crown accounts for one half to two-thirds of the height of the tree. The bark, yellowish or brown, is persistent on portions of the trunk. The adult leaves are dull bluish or grayish green and are lanceolate. They provide useful fodder for sheep, cattle and horses. The yellow-box is a handsome ornamental that grows quickly and is useful for shade and shelter. It is the best bee tree of all eucalypts, the honey produced from its flowers ranking with the finest in the world. The wood is used for heavy construction and for posts and poles; it is splendid firewood.

The drought-resistant salmon gum (E. salmonophloia), is a native of southwestern Australia. Sometimes this species is 100 feet tall with a trunk diameter of 3 feet. It branches comparatively low so that a clear trunk accounts for about one-third of its height. Its branches spread into a large rather open crown with most of the foliage near the branch extremities. An attractive feature of the salmon gum is its bark, which sheds in large patches, leaving smooth salmon pink trunk and branch surfaces that sometimes exhibit expanses of pale gray. This is a valuable ornamental shade tree for dry areas. Its dark, red wood is good fuel and is also used for mine props; although heavy and very strong, it is susceptible to termites. Honey produced from its flowers is excellent. The marri or red gum (E. calophylla) has its home in southwestern Australia. It becomes 150 feet tall with a trunk 5 feet in diameter and has a dense, well-branched crown. The adult leaves are lanceolate, dark green on the upper surfaces, paler beneath. Its flowers, in large decorative terminal clusters, are cream-colored or pink; they produce abundant nectar. This is a good ornamental and shade tree. Its lumber is used for boxes and light construction. Quite distinct is the red flowering gum (E. ficifolia) which occurs naturally only in a narrow coastal belt about fifty miles long in

Spotted gum. Eucalyptus maculata (U. S. Forest Service)

Western Australia. Rarely exceeding 35 feet in height or a trunk diameter of 2 feet, the chief value of this species is as an ornamental. Its red flowers are very attractive.

The red bloodwood (E. gummifera) grows along a coastal strip of New South Wales, Queensland and Victoria. Attaining a height of 120 feet and a trunk diameter of 4 feet, it generally has a trunk about half as tall as the height of the tree. Its bark is brown and persistent. This species forms a rather dense, compact head. Its mature leaves are lanceolate, dark glossy green above, paler below. The strong, heavy, durable wood is dark red to pink and is resistant to termites. The red bloodwood is a desirable shade tree.

Graceful, with a shaftlike trunk up to 4 feet in diameter and an open, rather sparsely foliaged crown, the lemon-scented gum (E. citriodora), native to subtropical Queensland, grows up to a height of 130 feet. It is a favorite ornamental and produces easily worked lumber with a wide range of uses, including both light and heavy construction. Its smooth bark, white or pinkish, sheds in thin plates. The adult leaves are lanceolate and have wavy margins. The foliage when crushed is strongly lemon-scented. Closely related to the lemon-scented gum, but lacking the characteristic odor, the spotted gum (E. maculata) is a native of New South Wales and Queensland. It becomes 150 feet tall with a trunk diameter of 5 feet. Its bark, thick, smooth and pinkish or bluish, is fire-resistant. The adult leaves are lanceolate. The tough, heavy lumber of this tree is exploited commercially for construction, flooring and tool handles. The tallest native tree of Western Australia, the karri gum (E. diversicolor), is one of the most important lumber producers of that region and excellent honey is obtained from its flowers. It sometimes attains a height of 250 feet and has a straight, clean trunk up to 9 feet in diameter. Its bark sheds in irregular patches, leaving yellowish, white or blue-gray places. Karri wood, red, strong, hard and heavy, is available in large sizes and is valued for heavy construction, shipbuilding and plywood. The bark is rich in tannin.

Eugenia

A thousand to fifteen hundred species of evergreen trees and shrubs belong in *Eugenia*, a genus of wide distribution. They have opposite, usually glossy leaves and clustered, or sometimes solitary, usually white flowers with conspicuous stamens. The fruits are berry-like. Many kinds are sources of useful products. One such is the clove tree (E. aromatica), a 40-foot-tall handsome native of the Molucca Islands. It has ovate oblong, evergreen leaves and terminal clusters of small, pale purple flowers. The dried flower buds are the cloves of commerce. Clove is an adaptation of the French *clou* (nail) and refers to the shape of the flower buds. When the Dutch took the Moluccas from the Portuguese early in the seventeenth century they attempted to maintain a high price for cloves by restricting their cultivation; trees on all islands except Amboina were destroyed. This was resented by the natives who were accustomed to plant a clove tree upon the birth of each child to serve as an approximate record of the age of the individual. The Dutch monopoly was ended in 1770 when the French succeeded in introducing cloves into Mauritius and later into Zanzibar and Cayenne. In addition to their culinary uses, cloves are the source of an essential oil used medicinally and for flavoring and perfumery. The rose-apple or jambos (E. jambos) is a broad-topped tropical Asiatic native that is now naturalized in many warm regions. It is up to 30 feet in height and has handsome, short-stalked, pointed elliptic leaves up to 8 inches long by 2 inches wide. Its brushlike, fragrant, whitish flowers, up to 3 inches across, usually occur in small terminal groups and are succeeded by crisp, edible, apple-shaped fruits about 2 inches in diameter and with a distinct rose perfume. This tree is a good honey plant. Another Asiatic species, the Malay-apple or pomerack (E. malaccensis), has edible pear-shaped fruits, 2 to 3 inches long, red, pink or whitish, that have an apple-like flavor and are eaten raw, cooked or preserved, and are also made into wine. This tree reaches a height of about 60 feet and has scentless, almost stalkless, purplish red flowers that are 2 inches wide and form clusters 4 to 5 inches across. Highly ornamental, it has much larger leaves than most eugenias; they are from 8 to 14 inches long by about half as broad. The sea-apple (E. grandis), of Malaya, Thailand and Borneo exceeds 100 feet in height and may have a branch spread of 150 feet. Its leaves are up to 9 inches long by about half as wide; they have down-turned tips. The white flowers, which have a rather sickly odor, are up to 1½ inches in diameter and form clusters up to 6 inches wide. Green and edible when ripe, the fruits are about 1 inch long.

Native to the Philippines, E. curranii is sometimes cultivated for its pleasantly flavored, dark red to black, acid fruits about three-quarters of an inch in diameter; they are eaten raw or made into jelly and wine. The tree attains a height of about 50 feet, has oblong elliptic leaves up to 1 foot long and flowers in panicles. The Australian lilly-pilly (E. smithii) is often shrubby although under optimum conditions it may be 100 feet tall. Its bronzy green leaves, ovate to ovate-lanceolate, are up to 3 inches long. The small white flowers, in terminal panicles, are succeeded by an abundance of globular, purple or whitish and quite decorative fruits, ¼ to ½ inch in diameter. The wood of this kind is suitable for veneers, golf sticks and cabinetwork. Another Australian species is the weeping tree-myrtle (E. ventenattii), which becomes 100 feet tall with a trunk diameter of 2 feet. Its glossy, dark green leaves are up to 5 inches long and about a quarter as wide. Its branches are pendulous. This tree has white flowers and globular fruits. Another Australian that attains 100 feet in height is the sour-cherry (E. crynantha) of New South Wales and

Queensland. This tree has red, very acid fruits.

Two South African species that by some authorities are segregated in the genus *Syzygium* are the water berry *(E. cordatum)* and the water-pear *(E. gerradii).* The former reaches a height of 60 feet and has four-angled twigs, blue-green, leathery, ovate leaves and creamy white flowers in terminal clusters, followed by agreeably fla-vored purplish black fruits about one-half inch long. The durable wood of this tree is used for construction. The water-pear is sometimes 80 feet tall with a trunk diameter up to 5 feet. Its leaves are slenderer and more closely veined than those of the water berry and it has inconspicuous, small flowers that are succeeded by small purple fruits esteemed by monkeys. The wood is used for furniture. Among New World species the grumixameira *(E. dombeyi)* of Brazil produces fruits about as large as cherries that at first are red but ripen black; they are eaten raw or candied. This tree attains a height of 50 feet; unlike those of most species, its white flowers are solitary. Also native of Brazil, the jaboticaba *(E. cauliflora),* which is about 40 feet tall and branches from near the ground, bears its small white flowers directly on the trunk and branches. They are followed by spherical purple fruits, 1 to 1½ inches in diameter, that are much esteemed for eating. Scarcely 20 feet in height, the Surinam-cherry or pitanga *(E. uniflora)* has small solitary or clustered, white four-petaled flowers and edible bright orange-red to dark red, acid-sweet fruits, ½ to 1 inch in diameter and with eight ribs; they resemble tiny tomatoes. The aromatic, ovate leaves are 1 to 2 inches long.

The jambolana or Java-plum *(E. cuminii)* often has many branches, the smaller ones drooping. It attains a height of 80 feet and has oblong to ovate-pointed leaves up to 8 inches long. Its white flowers, about a third of an inch across, are in branched clusters. The edible, purplish red fruits are about 2 inches in diameter. This species, which is sometimes named *Syzygium cuminii,* is a native of the East Indies and Burma. Its wood is used locally for construction, carts, imple-ments, wells and other purposes. Hindus use the fruits and foliage in the worship of the elephant-headed god Vinayaka or Ganesa; the tree is sacred to Buddhists.

Above: New Zealand Christmas tree. Metroside-ros excelsa   Right: New Zealand Christmas tree, blooms (Both, Robin Smith)

Leptospermum—Australian Tea-Tree; Manuka Tea-Tree

Fifty species of Malaysia, Australia, New Zealand and the Caroline Islands constitute this genus. Most are shrubs but a few are small trees with alternate leaves and five-petaled flowers that are solitary or occur in twos or threes in the leaf axils or at the ends of short branchlets. The Australian tea-tree (*L. laevigatum*) is well known. It is used extensively for stabilizing and reclaiming moving sands. This white-flowered tree is up to 30 feet tall and has blunt leaves, 1 inch long by about half as broad. Its flowers are three-quarters inch across. The manuka tea-tree (*L. scoparium*) of Australia and New Zealand occasionally is 30 feet tall but is often shorter. It has narrow, sharp-pointed leaves, one-half inch long or less, and solitary white or pinkish flowers one-half inch in diameter. Early colonists in New Zealand and Australia made tea from the leaves. The wood of the manuka tea-tree has been used for fences, spears and paddles. The tree manuka (*L. ericoides*), of New Zealand, sometimes attains a height of 60 feet and a trunk diameter of 3 feet. The leaves of this kind are one-half inch long or less and occur in clusters. Its very fragrant white flowers are one-third of an inch across.

Melaleuca—Bottle Brush; Paper-Bark Tree

Of about a hundred species of *Melaleuca* all except one are endemic to Australia and the Pacific Islands; the exception, *M. leucadendra*, extends into Indo-Malaysia. The genus differs from *Calistemon* in that its stamens are united in five bundles. The flower clusters resemble bottle brushes with the numerous long stamens representing bristles. The cajeput tree or punk tree (*M. leucadendra*) is notable because its thick, light-colored, spongy bark shreds in broad strips. It has a rather narrow, dense crown up to 100 feet in height, and spirally arranged, lanceolate, grayish green leaves up to 5 inches long. The fuzzy, creamy white, fragrant flowers form spikes up to 6 inches long; as with *Calistemon*, the branch lengthens beyond the flower cluster. This tree thrives in waterlogged soils. Its wood is good fuel and is used for posts and shipbuilding; its bark is used for caulking and packing. From the foliage is distilled cajeput oil which has a camphor-like odor and is used in medicine. The prickly-leaved paper-bark tree (*M. styphelioides*), of New South Wales and Queensland, is a rather narrow-crowned species, 30 feet in height, with sharp-pointed, oval leaves up to three-quarters of an inch long, and flower clusters 2 to 8 inches long. It grows in saline, wet soils. Because its wood resists attack by teredo worms and other borers, it is used for marine work. The bark is used for packing and caulking. The flax-leaf paper-bark tree of New South Wales and Queensland (*M. linariifolia*) attains a height of 50 feet, has slender branches, linear to linear-lanceolate leaves up to 1½ inches long and flowers in distinct pairs arranged in dense spikes up to 2 inches long. Its wood is excellent for piles and fuel.

Metrosideros—Rata; New Zealand Christmas Tree

Sixty species of trees, shrubs and vines of this wide-ranging genus occur in New Zealand, Australia, Malaysia, Polynesia, South America and South Africa. They include shrubs, trees and climbers that differ from the nearly related *Callistemon* and *Melaleuca* in having opposite leaves and flowers clustered at the branch ends but not in bottle brush fashion. One of the most interesting is the North Island rata (*M. robusta*) of New Zealand, which usually starts life as an epiphyte from a seed deposited by winds high in the forked branch of another tree. The young rata sends many roots to the ground; as these thicken, they join to form a strong corset around the trunk of the host, which is usually eventually killed. The North Island rata grows up to 100 feet tall and may have a trunk 10 feet in diameter. Its blunt, oblong leaves, up to 1½ inches long, are leathery and glossy. The flowers, conspicuous because of their many stamens, are scarlet. The wood is hard and durable and makes excellent fuel. As its name suggests, this species is most abundant on the North Island of New Zealand, but it occurs in the South Island also. The southern rata or ironwood (*M. umbellata*), a native of the South Island, the North Island and the Auckland Islands, attains a height of 60 feet.

Right: A tall eucalypt and acacias in bloom (Douglass Baglin) Overleaf left above: Ghost gum. Eucalyptus papuana (Robin Smith) Below far left: Woollybutt. Eucalyptus longifolia (Zentrale Farbbild Agentur) Below left: Malay-apple. Eugenia malaccensis (Ivan Polunin) Right: A flowering rata. Metrosideros (John H. Johns: New Zealand Forest Service)

Its lustrous leaves, pointed at both ends, are from 1 to 3½ inches long. The flowers, in short terminal clusters, are brilliant scarlet. The wood of this tree is extremely hard. The New Zealand Christmas tree *(M. excelsa)* is one of the most glorious elements of the flora of New Zealand. Up to 70 feet tall, with spreading branches and variably shaped leaves from 1 to 3 inches long that have their undersides covered with dense white hairs, this kind bears terminal clusters of brilliant scarlet flowers in December and January; its flower buds are covered with snow-white woolly hairs. The New Zealand Christmas tree rarely grows far from the sea or a lake; it produces hard, durable lumber.

Pimenta—Allspice; Bay Rum Tree

Eighteen species of the New World tropics make up this genus. Two are important, the allspice or pimento *(P. officinalis)* and the bay rum tree *(P. acris)*. They have opposite, leathery leaves, small white flowers in clusters and berry-like fruits. The allspice, a native of the West Indies, Mexico and Central America, attains a height of 40 feet; all parts of the tree are strongly aromatic. Its oblong leaves are up to 7 inches long. The flowers have four sepals, four petals and many stamens. The spicy brown fruits, one-quarter inch in diameter are gathered while green and are dried and used as a condiment, and in medicine and perfumery. They are thought to combine the fragrances and flavors of cinnamon, nutmeg and cloves; hence the name allspice. The wood of this species is used for walking sticks and cart shafts. The bay rum tree is a native of the West Indies and northeastern South America. It differs from the allspice in that its small white flowers have five sepals and five petals. A columnar tree up to 45 feet in height, its evergreen leaves vary in size and shape; usually they are elliptic or obovate and up to 6 inches long. The fleshy fruits, almost a half an inch long, are black. All parts of the tree are aromatic when crushed. The chief product of this species is bay oil or myrcia oil, the critical ingredient of bay rum. The wood is used for posts and general carpentry; it is excellent fuel.

Psidium—Guava

This genus consists of 140 species of trees and

Coolabah tree. Eucalyptus microtheca (Douglass Baglin)

Quaresmeira. Tibouchina granulosa (T. H. Everett)

shrubs of tropical America and the West Indies. They have opposite, undivided leaves, comparatively large, white flowers with numerous stamens and berry-like fruits to which remain attached the persistent calyx lobes. The common guava *(P. guajava)* is a tree up to 30 feet tall with four-angled twigs and blunt, oval, prominently veined leaves, hairy on their undersides and up to 6 inches long. The 1-inch-wide, fragrant flowers, solitary or in small clusters, have four to six petals. The yellow fruits are up to 4 inches long; they have white, pink or yellow pleasantly acid flesh and are eaten raw and in preserves. The strawberry guava *(P. cattleianum)*, a native of Brazil that grows to a height of 25 feet, has quite glabrous, glossy leaves up to 3 inches long. Its flowers are solitary and 1 inch or less in diameter. The nearly round, purplish red, white-fleshed fruits are up to 1½ inches long. A variety of this species, named *lucidum,* has yellow flowers and fruits. The fruits are eaten raw and made into preserves.

Syncarpia—Turpentine Tree

The most notable of this genus of five Australian trees is the red turpentine tree *(S. glomulifera)*

277

of coastal Queensland and New South Wales. In exceptional cases it attains a height of 200 feet and may have a trunk over 8 feet in diameter. Characteristically it is unbranched for up to two-thirds of its height. Its leaves are opposite, those of the adult type oval oblong, 2 to 3 inches long and densely hairy on their undersides and with edges that tend to curl downward. The juvenile leaves are smaller and are elliptic. The creamy flowers, each with four or five petals, form dense, globular heads. The fruits are hard, woody, three-celled capsules containing numerous, small, wedge-shaped seeds. Red turpentine lumber is highly durable and is resistant to fire and to attack by termites and borers; it is the finest Australian wood for salt-water piling and is used for building, shipbuilding, heavy construction and poles. Other species that provide good lumber are the giant ironwood (*S. subargentea*), a Queensland endemic that attains a height of 120 feet and a trunk diameter of 3 feet, and *S. leptopetala*, which does not exceed 60 feet in height or a trunk diameter of 2 feet.

Tristania—Brisbane-box; Kanuka-box

Fifty species are accommodated in this genus, which ranges from Malaysia to Fiji, New Caledonia and Australia. They have undivided, alternate or whorled leaves and axillary clusters of small flowers. Most notable is the Brisbane-box or brush-box (*T. conferta*), a native of eastern Australia that sometimes is 200 feet tall with a trunk up to 7 feet in diameter, although on poor ground it is often little bigger than a shrub. It has reddish twigs, bright green, whorled leaves that are hairy on their undersides and white flowers about 1 inch in diameter. This species produces good lumber and is popular as a shade and street tree. The kanuka-box or water gum (*T. laurina*) is highly ornamental; it has white bark and a profusion of small, golden yellow flowers. At its best it is 100 feet in height with a trunk diameter of 7 feet; usually it is smaller. The lumber of this native of New South Wales and Queensland is used for boat building, handles, tobacco pipes and other purposes.

MELASTOMACEAE—MELASTOMA FAMILY

Some three thousand species of 240 genera constitute this mostly pantropical family which consists chiefly of herbaceous plants, shrubs and climbers, but only a few trees; some kinds are epiphytes. The undivided leaves, commonly paired, often have one member of the pair distinctly smaller than the other and characteristically have a few prominent longitudinal veins that diverge from the base and converge near the top of the leaf. The flowers are usually bisexual. In addition to *Tibouchina*, a few other genera of the West Indies and tropical America are represented by small trees. Among these are the endemic jusillo (*Calycogonium squamulosum*) of Puerto Rico, the camasey (*Miconia prasina*) of Puerto Rico and Tortola and the verdiseco (*Tetrazygia elaeagnoides*) of Hispaniola, Puerto Rico and the Virgin Islands. The woods of these kinds are used for fencing and fuel.

Tibouchina

This tropical American group includes among its more than 200 species a few small ornamental, trees. The quaresmeira (*T. granulosa*) of Brazil, up to 40 feet tall, has quadrangular twigs and short-stalked, oblong-lanceolate, hairy leaves up to 5 inches long by one third as wide. The violet-purple or pink flowers, in terminal panicles, are 2 to 2¹/₂ inches across.

CHAPTER 28

The Umbelliflorae

The flowers in the three families of the order Umbelliflorae tend to form clusters in which the central bloom opens first and the outer ones last.

ARALIACEAE—ARALIA FAMILY

The aralia family includes trees, shrubs, and vines of seven hundred species in fifty-five genera. Its distribution is chiefly tropical and subtropical; it is especially well represented in the warmer parts of the New World and in Indo-Malaysia. The flowers are usually five-petaled, with males and females on separate plants. Often the stems are prickly. The leaves are usually alternate and generally lobed or composed of separate leaflets. The fruits are berries.

Aralia—Hercules Club; Prickly-Ash; Angelica Tree

Here belong thirty-five Indo-Malaysian, eastern

Asiatic and North American trees, shrubs and herbaceous plants. The best-known American tree is the Hercules club, devil's walking stick or prickly-ash *(A. spinosa)*, which is native from New York to Florida and Texas. This deciduous species attains a height of 30 feet or sometimes more. It has twice-pinnate leaves up to 4 feet long clustered at the ends of its thick, very spiny branches and numerous, tiny creamy flowers in umbels that form huge terminal panicles. The berries are black. The Chinese angelica tree *(A. chinensis)* is similar, but is less prickly and, unlike the Hercules club, it has leaflets that are almost without stalks. It is a native of China. The Japanese angelica tree *(A. elata)*, of Japan and Korea, is similar to the Chinese kind but has narrower leaflets and its flower clusters are shorter and have spreading branches. The Japanese angelica tree is also taller; it reaches a maximum height of 50 feet.

Kalopanax

One eastern Asiatic species is the sole representative of this genus. *Kalopanax pictus* is a tree up to 80 feet tall with lobed, hand-shaped, toothed leaves up to 1 foot across. Its tiny whitish flowers are in small ball-shaped groups, several of which form an umbel 6 to 8 inches in diameter. The fruits, small and black, occur in globular clusters. A handsome deciduous ornamental, this species is native to Japan, China and Korea.

Pseudopanax

Six natives of New Zealand and temperate South America belong here. The lancewood *(P. crassifolium)* of New Zealand is sometimes 60 feet in height with a trunk up to 20 inches through. It is remarkable for the great variance in the size and shape of its leaves at different stages of its growth. After passing though four distinct variations as a quite young plant it develops rigid, sharp-tipped, sharp-toothed, drooping leaves that depend from the upper parts of the stem like the ribs of a half-open umbrella; these leaves, dark green with yellowish midribs, are a half-inch wide and up to 3½ feet long. The tree continues to develop leaves of this type for fifteen or twenty years and then begins producing broader leaves that have three to five long-stalked leaflets. Finally, it has comparatively broad, undivided leaves with few or no teeth. The flowers of the lancewood are in terminal branched umbels.

Kalopanax pictus (Gerd Daümel)

Schefflera

Including species that some authorities segregate in the genus *Brassaia*, *Schefflera* has two hundred tropical and subtropical evergreens, many of which are epiphytic shrubs and climbers; comparatively few are terrestrial or become trees. All have large leaves consisting of several leaflets palmately arranged. Their fragrant flowers are succeeded by red, yellow or purple-black berries. *Schefflera volkensii* of East Africa is an evergreen tree 80 feet in height that often begins life as an epiphyte. Its leaves consist of five to seven untoothed leaflets up to 6 inches in length. Its small yellow flowers form clusters 10 inches long. Probably the best known is the Queensland umbrella tree *(S. actinophylla)*, a sparsely branched native of Australia, New Guinea and Java that attains a height of 100 feet or even more. Its glossy leaves, each with up to sixteen stalked, toothed leaflets arising from a common point at the end of the main leaf stalk, arch downward like the ribs of an umbrella; the leaflets are up to 1 foot long. The leaves are

279

Flowering dogwood. Cornus florida (Andreas Feininger)

clustered toward the branch ends. The small purplish red flowers occur in several terminal radiating branches from 3 to 4 feet long. The berries are purplish black. In recent years this species has become very popular for cultivating in pots and tubs.

CORNACEAE—DOGWOOD FAMILY

About a dozen genera and a hundred species are in the dogwood family. They are widely distributed, particularly in temperate regions. Almost all are woody plants; they include trees, shrubs, and a few lianas. The flowers have four or five sepals and petals and the fruits are berry-like.

Cornus—Dogwood

Most dogwoods are shrubs, but a few are trees. Although all bear flowers, the term flowering dogwood is usually restricted to those which have their clusters of tiny flowers surrounded by large, showy, petal-like bracts. Here belong *C. florida, C. nuttallii, C. capitata* and *C. kousa.*

Other dogwoods, such as *C. mas* and *C. officinalis,* have bracts surrounding their flower clusters but they are small, leafy and do not add conspicuously to the attractiveness of the inflorescences. Some species are without floral bracts. With one exception, dogwoods are natives of the Northern Hemisphere; *C. peruviana* is at home in Peru. The group is circumboreal. Nearly all dogwoods are deciduous; most have opposite leaves. Helpful in identifying them is the fact that the veins of the leaves all curve inward toward the leaf tips. The flowers, with their petals and other parts in fours, are small and always in clusters. The fruits, which vary considerably in appearance according to kind, are often decorative. Some say the name derives from the use made of an infusion of its bark, which was employed to wash mangy dogs, but a more likely explanation is that it is a corruption of dag wood or dagger wood, a name that was first applied to *Euonymus* because of its use for skewering meat and was later transferred to *Cornus.* The eastern American flowering dogwood (*C. florida*) is one of the most beautiful of all flowering trees. In spring its branches are laden, before its leaves unfold, with four-bracted inflorescences each 3 to 4 inches in diameter. Typically, the bracts are white but trees with pink bracts occur and are propagated and planted by gardeners. Even in winter this tree is beautiful because of its sturdy, pyramidal habit and its habit of developing tiers of horizontal branches which, like its trunk, are clothed with rugged bark. The flowers are succeeded by clusters of attractive bright red berry-like fruits. This dogwood, a native from Maine to Florida and Texas, grows to a height of 40 feet, usually in the light shade of taller trees. The wood is especially valued for making shuttles and tool handles. The bark contains a bitter principle which has been used as a substitute for quinine; the bark of the roots yields a scarlet dye.

The western American flowering dogwood (*C. nuttallii*) differs from its eastern relative in that its flower buds in winter are only partially enclosed by the bracts; those of *C. florida* are completely covered. Also, the bracts of *C. nuttallii* often exceed four, which is the normal number in *C. florida.* The western American flowering dogwood is one of the most splendid trees of its region. It sometimes attains a height of 100 feet with a trunk up to 2 feet in diameter. Its crown is pyramidal or rounded. This species usually grows in the shade of coniferous forest from British Columbia to southern California. Its lumber is used for cabinetwork and for tool handles. Another arborescent North American species is the pagoda dogwood, *C. alternifolia.* Flat-topped and growing up to 30 feet high, this has long, slender horizontal branches with many short, erect branchlets. Its leaves are usually alternate but occasionally are in pairs. The tiny cream-colored flowers form flat clusters, without involucral bracts, so that it is not a "flowering dogwood." The flowers are succeeded by red-stemmed, blue-black, berry-like fruits. The pagoda dogwood, native from Nova Scotia to Georgia and Missouri, grows up to a height of 30 feet and has a trunk that may measure 8 inches through.

Two flowering dogwoods of Asia merit attention, the kousa tree *(C. kousa)* of Japan and China and *C. capitata* of western China and the Himalayas. Like American flowering dogwoods, they produce clusters of tiny flowers surrounded by showy, petal-like bracts, four white ones to each flower cluster in the kousa tree, four to six pale yellow bracts in *C. capitata.* The fruits of these Asiatic flowering dogwoods are very different from those of American species; they are raspberry- or strawberry-like in appearance and each contains several seeds embedded in soft pulp. *Cornus capitata,* which attains a height of 40 feet, is evergreen or semi-evergreen and flowers in summer. The kousa tree, also a summer bloomer, rarely exceeds 20 feet in height and is deciduous. Its foliage becomes bright red before it drops in fall.

Unlike all dogwoods except the American *C. alternifolia,* the Asiatic *C. contraversa* has alternate leaves. Growing up to 50 feet in height it develops tiers of horizontal branches and clusters of small white flowers, without involucral bracts, which are followed by blue-black, berry-like fruits. This species occurs in Japan and China and is distinguished from *C. alternifolia* by the fact that the hairs on the undersides of the leaves are not parallel but spread in all directions. The bases of the leaves of the Asiatic kind are also usually rounded rather than wedge-shaped. In its natural range, which includes the Himalayas, China and Japan, *C. macrophylla* grows to a height of 50 feet and in summer bears bractless clusters of creamy white flowers 4 to 6 inches in diameter. The handsome foliage provides the chief attraction of this tree as a landscape subject; its floral display is also attractive. The berry-like fruits are blue-black.

The cornelian-cherry, *C. mas,* is a tree of central and southern Europe and western Asia that has been cultivated since ancient times for its flowers and for its acid, ellipsoid, red fruits that resemble small plums and may be eaten fresh or preserved. Because of the availability of other fruits these are less appreciated now than formerly. The yellow flowers of the cornelian-cherry, which are borne on leafless branches in winter or earliest spring, make a very attractive display. They are in small clusters, each surrounded by an involucre of inconspicuous bracts. Very similar to the cornelian-cherry, and not always easy to distinguish from it, is *C. officinalis,* a native of Japan and Korea. Both species grow to heights of 25 to 30 feet. The leaves of the cornelian-cherry lack the conspicuous tufts of brown hairs which grow in the axils of the veins on the undersides of the leaves of *C. officinalis.*

Griselinia—Broadleaf

This genus, native to New Zealand and South America, consists of six species of trees and shrubs including some epiphytes and some climbers. The broadleaf *(G. littoralis),* one of the commonest New Zealand trees, is esteemed for its very durable lumber. The tree is sometimes 60 feet in height and often has a crooked trunk and branches. It has thick, glossy leaves, 1 to 3 inches long, and small panicles of five-petaled, yellow, silky flowers, the males and females on separate trees.

CHAPTER 29

The Ericales

Most plants in the order Ericales can live only in symbiotic relationship with mycorrhizal fungi associated with their roots. Their pollen grains usually cohere in groups of four.

ERICACEAE—HEATH FAMILY

The heath family, consisting chiefly of shrubs, includes a few vines and trees. Its members have bisexual flowers, usually with twice as many stamens as petals or corolla lobes, and they characteristically flourish in acid soils in temperate regions, although representatives occur in the tropics. It contains about fifty genera and 1350 species.

Arbutus

A few of the twenty species of this Northern Hemisphere genus of evergreens are trees. The most notable are the madrona (*A. menziesii*) of western North America, the strawberry tree (*A. unedo*) of Ireland and southern Europe and *A. andrachne* of the Mediterranean region. They have flaking red bark and terminal panicles of small urn-shaped flowers. The madrona reaches a maximum height of 125 feet with a trunk up to 5 feet through, and has thin bark that peels in long strands. Its shining, oval leaves are about 4 inches long; its white or pinkish flowers are one-fourth of an inch long. The berry-like, orange-red, globular fruits of the madrona, about half an inch in diameter, form loose clusters and are favorites of birds. This is the tallest species of the heath family. The strawberry tree is rarely as tall as 40 feet. It has hairy young shoots, narrowly obovate, toothed leaves up to 4 inches long, and white flowers one-fourth of an inch long. Its orange-red spherical fruits look something like strawberries; they ripen about a year after the flowers fall, so that the tree is in bloom and in fruit at the same time. *Arbutus andrachne*, a native of southeastern Europe, reaches a maximum height of 40 feet. It has oval leaves up to 4 inches long, broader than those of the strawberry tree, and orange-red fruits. It differs from the strawberry tree, too, in having hairless young shoots.

Erica—Tree Heath; Bruyere

The tree heath or bruyere of the Mediterranean region sometimes attains a height of 65 feet. It belongs in a genus of five hundred evergreen species, mostly shrubs, that has a wide natural distribution; characteristically its species grow on acid, peaty soils. The young stems of the tree heath are very hairy; its leaves, one-fourth of an inch long or less, are densely crowded in groups of three. The small flowers are white and have an odor of honey. Briar tobacco pipes are made from the roots of *Erica arborea*; their name is a corruption of the French word *bruyere*.

Oxydendrum—Sorrell Tree; Sourwood

One species native to the eastern United States is the only representative of this genus. A deciduous tree up to 60 feet in height, with a trunk diameter of up to 20 inches, it has oblong lanceolate leaves that are sometimes 8 inches long and that turn brilliant crimson before they are shed in the fall. Its small white flowers are borne in drooping panicles in summer. Its fruits are small grayish capsules. *Oxydendrum arboreum* is an attractive ornamental.

Rhododendron

Among this group of five to six hundred species, mostly shrubs and nearly all of the North Temperate Zone, are a few small trees. *Rhododendron arboreum* of the Himalayas is such a one. It attains a maximum height of 50 feet and has evergreen leaves up to 8 inches long that are green above and silvery beneath. Its red, pink or white bell-shaped flowers, often spotted with brown, are about 1½ inches across and form dense spherical heads. Another Himalayan, *R. barbatum*, is reported to grow up to height of 60 feet; its flowers are dark red.

CHAPTER 30

The Ebenales

The distinctive order of woody plants called Ebenales probably has an ancestry linked to that of the order Theales. Its petals are always joined to form a more or less tubular corolla and the stamens, usually in two to three whorls, are joined to it.

SAPOTACEAE—SAPOTE FAMILY

The members of the sapote family have milky sap, undivided, usually alternate leaves and bisexual flowers, solitary or in clusters. Most are tropical trees of the Old or New Worlds. The family has eight hundred species.

Achras—Sapodilla

This genus of four evergreen species inhabits tropical America and the West Indies. Its most important representative is the sapodilla (*A. zapota*). A native of tropical America, it occasionally attains a height of 100 feet, has glossy elliptic leaves up to 16 inches long, white or pale green, cup-shaped flowers one-half inch in diameter and egg-shaped, russet-brown fruits that are up to 6 inches in diameter and have reddish, edible flesh and from one to several shining brown seeds. The condensed latex from this tree is the most important commercial source of chicle and for a long time was the chief basis of chewing gum. The wood of *Achras* is exceptionally strong and durable; it was employed by the early Mayas for heavy construction and it is still used locally for that purpose and for flooring, railroad crossties and tool handles.

Chrysophyllum—Star-apple

Chiefly natives of the New World, this genus of evergreen trees consists of 150 species. The star-apple *(C. cainito)* is cultivated for its succulent edible fruits and as a shade tree. A native of the West Indies and tropical America, it rarely reaches a height of 100 feet. Its oval leaves, bright blue-green above and coppery and silky on their undersides, are up to 6 inches long. Small five-lobed purplish flowers in clusters are succeeded by globular fruits about 4 inches in diameter that contain, embedded in white, translucent pulp, several brown seeds arranged in a starlike pattern. The satin-leaf *(C. oliviforme)* is a handsome ornamental that occurs in southern Florida and the West Indies. Up to 30 feet in height, it differs from the star-apple in having purple fruits not more than 1¹/₄ inches through and usually containing only one seed; its young twigs, leaf stalks and flower stalks are covered with fine, reddish brown hair. The tiny whitish green flowers form small clusters. Its fruits are made into jelly. Another species of interest is the lechecillo *(C. argenteum)*, a native of the West Indies that sometimes is 25 feet in height. It has clusters of small, greenish yellow flowers that have a peculiar odor. These are followed by edible, dark blue fruits up to three-quarters of an inch long, each with a single seed. The leaves are green above and silvery beneath.

Among African species is another called star-apple *(C. africanum)*, which is cultivated for its edible, pleasantly acid fruits, 2 to 2¹/₂ inches through and reddish or orange in color. The tree attains a height of 70 feet and has more or less elliptic leaves that are up to 12 inches long by one-third as broad and are reddish yellow on their under surfaces; their margins are rolled under. The small-creamy white flowers form crowded clusters. Another African, the white star-apple *(C. albidum)* reaches 140 feet in height, has roughly elliptic leaves up to 1 foot long by one-quarter to one-third as wide and small yellow flowers. The edible, globular, orange fruits, 3 to 4 inches through, contain five seeds. Several other species are natives of tropical Africa.

Mimusops

Here belong more than 120 species of white-flowered, milky-juiced evergreen tropical trees with alternate, undivided, thick leaves. Some botanists segregate certain kinds in a separate genus, *Manilkara.* Notable as the most important source of balata rubber, *M. bidentata,* of tropical America and the West Indies, is a tree up to 100 feet in height with a trunk diameter of 4 feet, and more or less elliptic leaves up to 10 inches long by 4¹/₂ inches wide. It branches horizontally, has a dense crown and small, fragrant, bell-shaped flowers in clusters of three to ten, each with six, eight or more corolla lobes. Its edible fruits, globular or ovoid, are up to 1¹/₄ inches long. The coagulated latex of this tree, called balata rubber, is similar to gutta-percha; it is used for shoe soles, machine belts and as a substitute for chicle. The lumber of *M. balata* is of high quality and is used for heavy construction, railroad crossties, flooring, furniture, cabinetwork, violin bows and a wide variety of other purposes; at one time it was the most important timber tree of Puerto Rico. *Mimusops elengii* of Malaya, India and Ceylon is an 80-foot tree with a straight trunk, branched for most of its length, and forms a dense, rounded crown. Its oval, short-pointed, wavy-edged leaves are up to 6 inches long. In groups of two to six, the star-like flowers, one-half inch wide, spring from the leaf axils; each has eight deeply notched corolla lobes. The ovoid, green to orange, astringent fruits are 1 inch long. The wood of this species is used for boatbuilding, construction, cabinetwork and canes; its bitter bark is used in the distillation of arrack and many parts of the tree are employed medicinally. The red milkwood of South Africa *(M. obovata)* grows up to 50 feet in height with a trunk up to 2 feet in diameter. Its leaves are up to 3 inches long by half as wide. It has beaked, ovoid, orange-red fruits that have a pleasant, persimmon-like flavor. Another South African is the coastal red milkwood, which, as its name implies, is a native of areas near the sea. This kind is usually smaller than the red milkwood and has smaller leaves. Its red fruits, three-quarters of an inch long, are egg-shaped and have sharp-pointed tips. The wood is hard, heavy and strong. The Transvaal red milkwood (*M. zeyheri*) attains a height of about 50 feet; it has elliptic leaves 3 inches long and ovate, blunt-ended, yellow fruits, up to 1 inch long, that have the flavor of persimmons and are tipped with a short bristle.

Palaquium—Gutta Percha Tree

In this genus belong over a hundred species of southeastern Asia, Indo-Malaysia, Taiwan and the Solomon Islands. By far the most important is the gutta percha tree (*P. gutta*) of Malaya, Sumatra and Borneo. An evergreen reaching 100 feet in height, it usually develops a rather flat-topped crown. Its more or less obovate leaves are up to 9 inches long by about one-third as broad and are green above and covered with coppery, silky hairs beneath. The six-petaled, pale green flowers are in clusters and have a sickly, heavy odor of burnt sugar. The pointed, broad-oblong fruits are up to 1¼ inches long. Gutta-percha, an inelastic rubber, is used for insulating marine cables, soles for shoes, machine belts, and other purposes.

Sideroxylon

This is a genus containing a hundred tropical and subtropical species. Good lumber for construction, boatbuilding, furniture and fence posts is produced by the jocuma or false mastic (*S. foetidissimum*), which grows up to a height of about 80 feet and may have a trunk 3 feet in diameter. Its leaf blades are elliptic and up to 4½ inches long by 2½ inches wide. The small yellow flowers, each with five or six petals, are borne singly or in small clusters; they have a peculiar, strong, cheeselike odor. The olive-shaped yellow fruits, which have a sour, unpleasant taste, are eaten by animals; they are ¾ to 1 inch long. This species is a native of Florida, the West Indies, Mexico and Central America. The Queensland hardwood or scrub-crab-apple (*S. australe*) attains a height of 100 feet and a trunk diameter of 3 feet; it produces some of the finest lumber of Australia; the wood is used for turnery, cabinetwork, machine bearings, building, carving and other purposes. This tree has obovate, glossy leaves up to 4 inches long, grayish white flowers in groups of two to six and dark purple, insipid-tasting, ovate fruits up to 2 inches long. It is a native of eastern Australia.

The yellow-box or jungle-plum (*S. pohlmanianum*) of Queensland and New South Wales is sometimes 70 feet in height. It has obovate leaves up to 5 inches long and globular fruits about 1 inch in diameter. Its wood is esteemed for engraving and cabinetwork.

EBENACEAE—EBONY FAMILY

Five hundred species of mostly tropical trees and shrubs comprise the three genera of this family, which is related to the Annonaceae. They have watery sap and usually unisexual flowers, with the females usually solitary and the males clustered. The fruits are technically berries.

Diospyros—Ebony; Persimmon; Guayabota

Ebony wood comes from several of the five hundred species of *Diosypros*, a genus of trees and shrubs that is widely distributed, especially in the tropics and subtropics, and is particularly abundant in Asia. The group has alternate, undivided leaves and usually unisexual flowers. Their fruits have an enlarged, persistent calyx.

The primary source of ebony, the heartwood of the tree, is *D. ebenum* of India and Ceylon. This dense-crowned species attains a height of 60 feet and a trunk diameter of 6 feet. It has lustrous, elliptic leaves up to 3 inches long. The fragrant white flowers open at dusk and fall the next morning. Each of the three-quarter-inch fruits has three to eight seeds. The jet-black heartwood is used for furniture, handles of cutlery, piano keys, chessmen, carving, inlays and opium pipes. Of the numerous New World species of *Diospyros* the only one of commercial significance is the persimmon (*D. virginiana*), a deciduous native of the southeastern United States. It is sometimes 125 feet tall with a trunk diameter of 2½ feet; its lumber is used for shuttles and golf clubs. The persimmon forms a rounded crown, often with drooping branches, and has green twigs. Its pointed ovate, lustrous leaves, up to 6 inches long, turn yellow before they drop in fall. Each tree has flowers of one sex only; the females after pollination produce plumlike, edible yellow or orange fruits about 1½ inches long; until fully ripe these are highly astringent. The black sapote (*D. ebenaster*) is a native of the West Indies and Mexico. Up to 50 feet in height, it has blunt oval leaves up to 8 inches long, small white flowers and edible, olive green fruits that are about the size of oranges and have chocolate brown flesh; in Mexico these are known as guayabota and zapote negro.

The deciduous date-plum (D. lotus), a native from western Asia to Japan, attains a height of 45 feet; it has yellow-brown twigs and ovate, pubescent leaves up to 5 inches long, small reddish or greenish flowers and edible, globular fruits that are about the size of cherries and change from yellow to blue-black as they ripen. Quite distinct is the Japanese date-plum or kaki (D. kaki), a native of China and Japan that is about 40 feet tall and round-headed, and has ovate or oblong leaves up to 5 inches long that are pubescent beneath. It has yellowish white flowers and tomato-like, orange or reddish fruits that have orange flesh and are about 3 inches in diameter. This kind is much cultivated in the Orient and in warm regions elsewhere for its edible fruits. A fine African member of the genus is the jakkalsbessie, West African ebony or Transvaal ebony (D. mespiliformis), which becomes 70 feet tall with a trunk diameter of 3 feet. Graceful, with pendulous branches, this almost evergreen species has lance-shaped leaves up to 6 inches long and 2½ inches broad. Its whitish male and female flowers grow on separate trees. About the size of olives, the fruits are eaten by the natives. The wood is used for furniture, cudgels, tool handles and other purposes. Diospyros mespiliformis occurs over a wide range in Africa. Varying according to the local climate from a low shrub to a tree 25 feet tall, the bloubos or monkey-plum (D. lycioides) commonly has leaves 1 to 1½ inches long and ¼ to ½ inch wide. Its small fragrant, yellow flowers are succeeded by edible yellow, succulent, ovoid fruits about one-half inch long. Under most circumstances this tree is evergreen; it is an important source of fodder. It is a native of the drier parts of South Africa.

STYRACEAE—STORAX FAMILY

The twelve genera and 180 species of the storax family are natives of eastern Asia, Malaysia, North America, tropical America and the Mediterranean region. All are small trees or shrubs with alternate, undivided leaves, bisexual flowers in clusters, petals joined toward their bases, with as many or twice as many stamens as corolla lobes, and single styles. They commonly have stellate hairs.

Halesia—Silverbell; Snowdrop Tree

Six deciduous species of eastern Asia and the southeastern United States constitute Halesia.

They are shrubs or small trees with pendulous, four-lobed, bell-shaped white or, rarely, delicate pink flowers. The light brown fruits are dry and winged. The mountain silverbell (H. monticola) is a tree 90 feet tall, pyramidal when young, round-topped at maturity, and with a trunk sometimes 3 feet in diameter. Its pointed leaves are elliptic to slightly obovate; they turn yellow in fall. Its flowers, 1 inch long, are succeeded by fruits that are usually four-winged. One of the most ornamental of flowering trees, this silverbell is native from Tennessee and North Carolina to Georgia. Rarely exceeding 35 feet in height and often shrubby, the Carolina silverbell (H. caroliniana) has flowers one-half inch long and usually four-winged fruits that are smaller than those of the mountain silverbell which it otherwise resembles. It is native from West Virginia to Florida and Texas. Halesia diptera resembles the Carolina silverbell but its fruits ordinarily are larger and have only two wings and its corolla is more deeply lobed. It blooms less freely than the other kinds.

Pterostyrax—Epaulette Tree

The epaulette tree (P. hispida) is the best-known member of a group of seven deciduous species of trees and shrubs indigenous from Burma to Japan. They have alternate, toothed leaves, panicles of white flowers and ribbed or winged dry fruits. From the nearly related Halesia they differ in having five- to seven-lobed flowers with the divisions of the corolla extending almost to the base. The epaulette tree grows up to 50 feet in height and forms an open head of slender branches. Its oblong leaves are up to 7 inches long. Attractive, five-petaled, creamy-white, fragrant flowers are borne in pendulous panicles up to 10 inches long. The densely bristled fruits are ten-ribbed.

Styrax—Storax

One hundred and thirty deciduous and evergreen shrubs and a few trees, mostly of the warmer parts of Eurasia, Malaysia and America, belong in this genus. Characteristically, their foliage has stellate hairs. The flowers of most kinds have five petals that are joined only at their bases and ten stamens joined to the bottoms of the petals. From the nearly related Halesia and Pterostyrax the genus differs in the relative positions of calyx and fruit; in Styrax the calyx is behind the fruit. Styrax obassia, native to Japan, is a graceful tree that is sometimes 30 feet tall. It has orbicular or broad ovate leaves that are up to 10 inches long. The drooping white flowers, about three-fourths of an inch long, occur in large groups in racemes up to 8 inches long; they have pubescent flower stalks one-half-inch long or less. *Styrax japonica*, also of Japan, is a rather narrow tree that differs from *S. obassia* in having oval to obovate leaves 1 to 3½ inches long and about half as wide as they are long and hairless flower stalks ¾ to 1½ inches long.

CHAPTER 31

The Contortae

Members of the order Contortae usually have opposite leaves, undivided or pinnate, flowers with the petals joined to form a tubular or cup-shaped central portion and stamens joined to the base of the corolla.

OLEACEAE—OLIVE FAMILY

The oleaceae or olive family is a cosmopolitan group represented by twenty-nine genera and six hundred species of trees, shrubs and a few vines. Its members have undivided or pinnate leaves and clusters of flowers that are bisexual or, rarely, unisexual and have two stamens. Familiar genera additional to those discussed below and including species that occasionally are small trees are privet *(Ligustrum)* and lilac *(Syringa)*.

Chionanthus—Fringe Tree
This genus is represented by one species in eastern North America, *C. virginiana*, and one, *C. retusa*, in China. They are small deciduous trees with undivided leaves and white flowers that are truly unisexual or only functionally so, with the sexes usually on separate trees. The blooms form large, feathery panicles. Each flower has four narrowly strap-shaped petals. The fruits are dark blue and grapelike. The American fringe tree differs from the Asiatic kind in having mostly oblong leaves up to 8 inches long and male flowers that have sterile pistils. The male flowers of *Chionanthus retusa* lack pistils and the elliptic or ovate leaves are only about 4 inches long. The American fringe tree attains a height of about 30 feet; the Asiatic species is about 20 feet tall. Both are highly decorative.

Fraxinus—Ash
Among trees of the North Temperate zone ashes are unusual in having opposite and usually compound (that is, each consisting of several leaflets) leaves; in rare instances the leaves have only one leaflet. The flowers appear in dense clusters either before or with the leaves or—in summer when the trees are foliaged—in one group; they may be unisexual or bisexual, as individual trees may also be. The ashes number about seventy species, all deciduous, about half American; a few are shrubs. About three species range into the tropics. The chief uses of ash lumber are for tool handles, agricultural implements, oars, baseball bats, kitchen furniture and interior trim. Characteristically the wood is strong, elastic and shock-resistant.

Commercially the most important American species are the white ash *(F. americana)*, the black ash *(F. nigra)*, and the green ash *(F. pennsylvanica lanceolata)*. These account for 98 percent of ash lumber cut in the United States. The white ash ranges from Nova Scotia to Florida and Texas and grows to 120 feet tall with a trunk 6 feet in diameter. Its branches, stout, erect or spreading, form a round-topped or pyramidal head. Each leaf consists of five to nine, but usually seven, stalked, glabrous leaflets. The black ash, which sometimes attains a height of 90 feet and a trunk diameter of 20 inches, has a narrow head and upright branches. Its leaves, of seven to eleven stalkless leaflets, are covered at first with reddish hairs and at maturity have some tufts of hairs on their midribs below. The green ash is a variety of the red ash *(F. pennsylvanica)* and differs from the latter in its narrower leaves, hairless leaf stalks and other minor botanical details. Both kinds grow to about 60 feet tall with trunks about 2 feet in diameter and leaves of seven to nine leaflets. The green ash is round-topped and has slender, spreading branches. The red ash forms an irregular head with stout, erect branches and has densely pubescent branchlets and leaf stalks. The green ash is a native from Maine to Saskatchewan, Florida and Texas, the red ash from Nova Scotia to Manitoba, Georgia and

Olive. Olea europaea (D. A. Harissiadis)

Mississippi. Closely resembling the white ash, except that it has densely pubescent branchlets and leaf stalks, is *F. biltmoreana,* a tree that rarely exceeds 50 feet in height or a trunk diameter of 1½ feet and is native from New Jersey to Missouri, Georgia and Alabama. Of about the same size is the water ash *(F. caroliniana),* a native of swamps from Virginia to Florida and Texas. It has leaves of five to seven stalked leaflets. The name pumpkin ash *(F. tomentosa)* refers to the soft wood of this species, which attains a height of 120 feet and a trunk diameter of 30 feet. It is native fom New York to Illinois, Florida and Louisiana. A handsome, large-leaved tree, its trunk is usually conspicuously buttressed at its base and its top is narrow and open. Other American ashes worthy of note include the Oregon ash *(F. oregana),* most important of Western species, which grows to a height of 80 feet and may have a trunk 4 feet in diameter. Its shape varies from broad-rounded to narrow-upright. A native of

the Pacific Northwest, its stalked or stalkless leaflets number five to nine to each leaf. The Oregon ash is closely related to a 50-foot native of the southwestern States and adjacent Mexico, *F. velutina,* a species recommended as a street tree for warm, dry climates. This ash has a slender head and a trunk up to 1½ feet in diameter. Each leaf has three to five leaflets.

The blue ash *(F. quadrangulata)* sometimes attains 120 feet in height and, as its botanical name suggests, has four-angled branchlets. Its leaflets number seven to eleven and its trunk may attain 3 feet in diameter. It forms a slender head of spreading branches. The blue ash takes its name from the fact that blue dye can be obtained from the inner bark by crushing it in water. Another American species of which mention must be made is the single-leaf ash *(F. anomola),* a native from Colorado to California. Not more than 20 feet tall, this kind is remarkable because its leaves mostly consist of only a single leaflet, a circumstance which results in an effect most unlike an ash; sometimes it produces leaves with two or three leaflets.

The European ash (*F. excelsior*) is one of the largest deciduous trees of Europe; it attains a maximum height of 140 feet and is native from Great Britain to the Caucasus. It forms a rounded or oval head and usually has nine to eleven leaflets to each leaf. Unlike the American white ash, its foliage does not color attractively in fall. Its large winter buds are pitch black and, among other characteristics, distinguish it from the narrow-leaved ash (*F. angustifolia*), which has brown winter buds and narrower leaves and is a native of the western Mediterranean region. Both species are substantial sources of high-quality lumber and both are attractive ornamentals. The other European of importance is the manna ash (*F. ornus*) which is common in southern Europe and Asia Minor. It is typical of a small group of "flowering ashes" that have showy flowers and bloom in summer when in full leaf. The flowers are showy because they have conspicuous white petals; most other ashes are without petals. The manna ash is so called because a sugary substance called manna is obtained from the trunks by cutting the bark in summer and collecting the exudate, which is used medicinally. This ash grows to a height of about 60 feet and forms a handsome, rounded head. Its stalked leaflets, usually seven, have rust-colored hairs on their undersides. Other "flowering ashes" are natives of Asia but these are less well known. They include *F. longicuspis* of Japan and Korea, which becomes 45 feet tall and has reddish pubescent winter buds and slightly quadrangular branchlets. It is a graceful tree with white flowers, and with leaves of five or, rarely, seven leaflets that turn purple in fall. Also handsome in flower is *F. paxiana*, a large-leaved native of China and the Himalayas, which also has rusty hairy winter buds and squarish twigs, but leaves of seven to nine leaflets. It grows to a height of 60 feet. The Manchurian ash (*F. mandschurica*), native to Japan, Korea and other parts of northeast Asia, is closely related to the American black ash but has leaflets that taper at their bases and are distinctly stalked. It grows 100 feet high and is valued for its lumber.

Olea—Olive

This Old World genus of twenty evergreen species is widely distributed. Its best-known member is the common olive (*O. europaea*), a native of the Mediterranean that is now cultivated in many warm countries. The common olive attains a height of 30 feet, lives to a great age, certainly a thousand years or more, and has ovate or lance-shaped leathery leaves up to 3 inches long that are dark gray-green with silvery undersides. Its small fragrant flowers are greenish. Its fruits are the familiar olives that when ripe are a shining bluish black. They take about twelve months to ripen. Old olive trees frequently have gnarled, twisted, irregularly shaped trunks that are often hollow. The common olive has been cultivated since prehistoric times; frequent reference is made to it by ancient Greek and Roman authors and in the Bible. Olive fruits are eaten raw or pickled, and are the source of one of the most important edible oils. The hard, heavy wood of the common olive is used for canes and turnery.

The wild olive tree (*O. africana*) of South Africa differs from the common olive chiefly in its smaller flowers and fruits. The latter, about a quarter of an inch long, are edible. This shapely, round-crowned tree flourishes in semidesert conditions; in exposed locations it is characteristically stunted and distorted. Its wood is extremely hard and durable. Another South African species is the black ironwood (*O. laurifolia*). Sometimes 80 feet tall with a trunk diameter of $4\frac{1}{2}$ feet, it has a rather small crown of lustrous foliage. Its leaves, up to 4 inches long by $1\frac{1}{2}$ inches wide, have slightly undulating edges. The fragrant, creamy white flowers in terminal clusters, are succeeded by dark purple, succulent fruits $\frac{1}{2}$ to 1 inch long that are eaten by people and by many kinds of birds and animals; even dogs relish them. The hard brown wood is used for piles, railroad ties, tent pegs and other purposes. The maire (*O. cunninghamii*) and the white maire (*O. lanceolata*) of New Zealand produce lumber used for cabinetwork, turnery, construction and railroad cars. The maire, about 70 feet in height, has whitish branches and leathery, linear to lanceolate leaves up to 10 inches long. Its greenish white flowers occur in clusters of ten to fifteen. The white maire, rarely more than 50 feet tall, has white bark, linear to lanceolate leaves up to 6 inches long and unisexual flowers in clusters of six to ten. Its half-inch-long fruits are red or orange.

The ironwood or marblewood (*O. paniculata*) of Australia produces tough, durable lumber that when freshly cut has a fragrance of roses; it is used for staves and turnery. The tree is occasionally 100 feet tall and has lustrous, long-petioled, ovate leaves up to 3 inches long and loose clusters of small, white flowers succeeded by half-inch-long, blue-black fruits. It is a native of eastern Australia, New Caledonia and Lord Howe Island.

Osmanthus

Native of North America, eastern Asia and Polynesia, this genus of opposite-leaved evergreen trees and shrubs consists of about fifteen species. Its small, four-petaled flowers have two stamens. The devilwood (*O. americanus*), native from North Carolina to Florida and Mississippi, is generally less than 70 feet tall and may have a trunk 1 foot in diameter. It has lustrous, elliptic to lanceolate leaves up to 7 inches long and greenish, fragrant flowers that are followed by dark blue fruits one-half inch long. Its lumber is hard, strong and durable. *Osmanthus fragrans*, which rarely exceeds 30 feet in height, has narrow, leathery leaves, 6 inches or less in length and, in the leaf axils, clusters of small, exceedingly fragrant, yellowish white, unisexual flowers, with the males and females on separate trees. The Chinese use the dried flowers of this tree, which is native of Japan, China and the Himalayas, to perfume tea. Rarely more than 25 feet in height and with a trunk up to 1 foot in diameter, the Japanese *O. illicifolius* has leaves coarsely toothed like those of American and English hollies. From hollies *Osmanthus* is easily distinguished by its leaves, which occur in pairs. The leaves of *O. illicifolius* are elliptic, up to 2½ inches long and usually have two to four spiny teeth on each side; they sometimes lack teeth. The flowers are small, white and fragrant, the fruits bluish and up to three-quarters of an inch long. In Japan the wood is used to make small articles of furniture as well as toys and combs. The olapua (*O. sandwicensis*), native to Hawaii, reaches a maximum height of about 60 feet. Its lumber was fashioned by the islanders into digging sticks, spears and other articles. This species has pointed elliptic leaves up to 6 inches long and clusters of bisexual, light yellow flowers in the leaf axils. The fruits, ovoid and about a half-inch long, are dark blue.

LOGANIACEAE—LOGANIA FAMILY

This tropical and subtropical family consists of more than thirty genera and about eight hundred species of trees, shrubs, climbers and herbaceous

Strychnine fruits and flowers. Strychnos nux-vomica (M. Krishnan)

plants. With very few exceptions, they have opposite undivided leaves and clustered bisexual flowers that most commonly have as many stamens as corolla lobes; the stamens are joined to the corolla.

Strychnos—Strychnine Tree

Two hundred species of tropical trees, shrubs and climbers constitute *Strychnos*. Several are esteemed as sources of lumber, tanning materials, edible fruits and arrow poisons; some are used medicinally. Among those employed as arrow poisons, one of the most virulent is the curare poison nut (*S. toxifera*) of Central and South America; this is a vine. Strychnine, one of the deadliest of poisons, is obtained from *S. nux-vomica*, a 50-foot evergreen tree, native to India and other parts of tropical Asia. This species has opposite, ovate, lustrous leaves that grow up to 6 inches long and one-half-inch stalks. Its fragrant, clustered flowers, a half-inch long, are greenish white. The fruits resemble small oranges in size and color; they have hard rind

Devil tree. Alstonia scholaris (M. Krishnan)

and contain soft, white pulp surrounding several disc-shaped seeds. These are the source of strychnine and nux vomica, which are used as poisons and medicinally. From the seeds a yellow-brown dye used for coloring cotton is also obtained. The pulp, which contains traces of the poison, is eaten by flying squirrels and birds. The termite-proof wood of the strychnine tree is used for furniture and agricultural implements. Another native of India and Ceylon, the clearing nut (*S. potatorium*), is about 40 feet in height. It differs from the strychnine tree in having leaves without stalks. Its durable lumber is used for building and agricultural implements. Of the African and Madagascan species, the Natal-orange (*S. spinosa*) is notable because the yellow-brown pulp of its fruits is edible; in Madagascar, an alcoholic beverage is made from it. Some difference of opinion exists as to whether the seeds are poisonous. The Natal-orange does not normally exceed 30 feet in height and is often shorter. It has rigid, horizontal branches and pale-colored recurved spines with black tips. Its broad ovate, smooth leaves are up to 3 inches

long. The greenish white flowers, in terminal clusters, are sweetly fragrant. The globular, hard-shelled fruits are orange-yellow, 4 to 5 inches in diameter, and contain several large disc-shaped seeds. Another species, the fruits of which are used as food, is the African monkey-orange or Kafir-orange (*S. innocua dysophylla*). A small, deciduous tree with ovate, hairy leaves up to 2 inches long, it has yellow flowers succeeded by globular, brown fruits that contain several flat seeds and agreeably flavored pulp that is dried and eaten with honey. The names Kafir-orange and monkey-orange are also applied to other species in South Africa. The hard-pear (*S. henningsii*) of South Africa becomes 60 feet tall and has a compact head. It has short-stalked, pointed, ovate leaves, each with three prominent veins, and axillary clusters of small white flowers. The ovate, orange-red fruits, about a half-inch long, have a solitary seed that contains a poison similar to strychnine.

APOCYNACEAE—DOGBANE FAMILY

Most of this chiefly tropical family of 180 genera and 1500 species are vines; a few small trees, shrubs and herbaceous plants are included. They have undivided leaves and clusters of bisexual flowers with deeply lobed corollas, five stamens and pollen grains that cohere in groups of four.

Alstonia

This Polynesian and Indo-Malaysian genus consists of fifty species with slender leaves that are usually whorled, milky latex, and cylindrical seed pods that hang in pairs and split to release flat, narrowly oblong seeds with tufts of hair at each end. They have straight trunks and tiers of horizontal branches. The most notable species is the devil tree, pali-mara, or milkwood, a native from India and Malaysia to Australia. The species name *scholaris* refers to an old use of the white wood for writing tablets or slates. The devil tree attains a maximum height of about 100 feet and has evergreen elliptic leaves up to 9 inches long and about one-third as broad in whorls of tree to eight; the lower surfaces of the leaves are paler than their top sides. The little greenish white flowers, forming small terminal clusters, are delightfully fragrant, especially at night, and are succeeded by pods 1 to 2 feet long. The lumber of the devil tree is used for shingles, palings, boxes, furniture and coffins. In Malaya the various species of *Alstonia* are called pulai. The commonest, *A. an-*

290

gustiloba, is much like *A. scholaris* but its leaves do not normally exceed 5½ inches in length and its flowers are glabrous, whereas the outsides of the blooms of *A. scholaris* are covered with fine hairs. *Alstonia angustiloba* is sometimes 120 feet tall. The bark of the slender, glabrous Australian quinine tree or bitter bark *(A. constricta)* is used for flavoring beer. It has long-stalked, opposite leaves, yellow flowers and pods up to 8 inches long that contain hairy seeds.

Plumeria—Frangipani

Among the most widely cultivated of tropical flowering trees are two of the seven species of the New World genus *Plumeria;* they are evergreen or deciduous, depending upon local climate. The red plumeria, frangipani or temple flower *(P. rubra)*, like other species of its kind, has copious, caustic, milky sap. It attains a height of 25 feet and has a few stiff, spreading, fleshy branches with foliage crowded toward their tips. The alternate, elliptic leaves are up to 15 inches long and 5 inches broad. They have conspicuous marginal veins and are lustrous green above; their lower surfaces are often hairy. The flowers are red, pink, purplish or, more rarely, white or white with a yellow eye. They form flattish-topped clusters. Each waxy bloom has five overlapping petals and is 2 to 3 inches in diameter. The seed pods, which contain numerous winged seeds, are in twos, the members of each pair widely divergent. *Plumeria rubra* is a native of Mexico and Central America. Its flowers are used for garlands and decorations and, in Hawaii, for leis. The name frangipani is believed to be a corruption of the French *frangipanier,* meaning coagulated milk, and to refer to the thick, white sap. *Plumeria alba,* a native of the West Indies, is called frangipani and also milk tree. It is sometimes 35 feet in height and has lance-shaped, alternate leaves up to 15 inches long and 3 inches wide, shiny green above and densely covered with minute hairs beneath. They are without conspicuous marginal veins but their edges are rolled under. The very fragrant, showy flowers, 1½ to 2 inches in diameter, have five overlapping waxy white petals and a yellow eye; they are in compact flattened clusters. The widely spreading seed pods occur in pairs and contain winged seeds.

Thevetia—Yellow-Oleander

Of the nine tropical American and West Indian species that comprise *Thevetia,* one, the yellow-oleander or be-still tree *(T. peruviana)*, is commonly planted in the tropics as an ornamental; it occasionally attains a height of 30 feet although more often it is shrubby. It has many alternate, nearly stalkless, lustrous, leathery, linear or narrowly lanceolate leaves up to 6 inches long and slightly fragrant, funnel-shaped, yellow (rarely white or pinkish) flowers, 1½ to 3 inches long, in terminal clusters. The slightly triangular fruits, blackish when ripe and 1 to 1½ inches through, contain two to four seeds surrounded by a thin layer of pulp. In the West Indies, the seeds, called lucky seeds or lucky nuts are carried as talismans. They contain an oil that burns well without excessive smoke. All parts of *Thevetia* are poisonous, particularly the milky juice and the seeds.

CHAPTER 32

The Tubiflorae

The very large order of Tubiflorae consists chiefly of herbaceous plants. Its flowers have their petals joined to form a tubular, trumpet-shaped or cup-shaped corolla with the stamens joined to its base. Such familiar plants as morning glory, phlox, tomato, African violet and mint belong here.

BORAGINACEAE—BORAGE FAMILY

The borage family includes one hundred genera with two thousand species of mostly herbaceous perennials. They generally have cylindrical stems, alternate, roughly hairy leaves and bisexual flowers that are usually in coiled sprays but straighten out as the flowers open.

Cordia

Tropical and subtropical trees and shrubs numbering 250 species comprise *Cordia.* They have undivided, alternate leaves and, usually, four-petaled, tubular or bell-shaped bisexual or unisexual flowers in coiled or forked clusters. In the Americas the genus ranges from the southern United States to the Argentine. The geiger tree *C. sebestena)* found in Florida, the West Indies,

Empress tree. Paulownia tomentosa (T. H. Everett)

Mexico, and Central and South America has decorative orange or scarlet blooms in large terminal clusters; it is often planted for ornament. An evergreen, it attains a maximum height of about 35 feet and has ovate leaves up to 8 inches long. Its wood is used for turnery and small articles. Other New World species include the canalete (*C. gerascanthus*) of Central and South America. Larger than the geiger tree, this species is the source of lumber much used locally.

A tree which is native to Central America and Mexico, the 100-foot *C. dodecandria* produces high-grade lumber well adapted for furniture and turnery. This species, the acid fruits of which are edible, is distinguished by its large, rough leaves. *Cordia alliodora* of Mexico, the West Indies and Central America is interesting because of the swellings that commonly develop at the forks of the young twigs; these are inhabited by vicious ants. The specific designation *alliodora* means onion-scented and refers to the garlic-like odor given off by the crushed leaves. The flowers of this kind, which in Central America is called laurel, are white or yellowish

and occur in large clusters. Indians in Mexico use the fruit as food. A very closely allied species is the peterebi or Loro amarillo (*C. trichtoma*), of Argentina. This kind does not have the conspicuous ant-inhabited swellings of *C. alliodora* and its leaves are more hairy, its blooms bigger. It attains a height of 125 feet and a trunk diameter of 4 feet. In Brazil the native species of *Cordia* are called louro. One of the best-known kinds is the freijo or jenny wood (*C. goeldiana*) which is very similar to *C. alliodora*; its wood is popular for general carpentry and shipbuilding; for the latter purpose it substitutes for teak. It is also used for interior trim and furniture. The sebesten (*C. dichotoma*), a native from southeast Asia to Taiwan, the Philippines and northern Australia, attains a height of 60 feet. At first cylindrical in outline, it eventually develops a rounded crown with branches drooping at their extremities. Its leaves are deciduous, ranging from elliptic to almost heart-shaped, and up to 6 inches long by slightly more than half as wide. The flowers, about a third of an inch wide, are white and in lateral clusters. The edible, pulpy, ellipsoid fruits, three-quarters of an inch long, are clear pink and contain a slimy juice.

A native of sandy shores of the Indian and the western Pacific oceans, the kou or sea trumpet (*C. subcordata*) is an evergreen tree that grows up to 50 feet in height and has a dense, spreading crown. Its ovate leaves are 7 inches or less in length by two thirds as broad. The trumpet-shaped flowers, 1½ to 2 inches wide, are orange or pinkish orange; they have six or seven recurved lobes. The almost globular fruits, about 1 to 1¼ inches long and yellow when ripe, are produced in bunches. The wood was used by natives for dishes, cups and other purposes. This is a good shade tree for seashore locations. Indigenous from India to Australia, *Cordia myxa* grows up to 40 feet in height, has elliptic ovate leaves up to 5 inches long and lax clusters of small cream-colored flowers. The flowers and young fruits are used as vegetables; the mucilaginous pulp and the seeds are eaten and the fruit pulp is used as birdlime to trap birds. The wood is one of the best for making

Right: Japanese date-plum. Diospyros kaka (SEF) Overleaf left above: Roble blanco. Tabebuia pentaphylla (Harriet Burkhart) Left below: Frangipani. Plumeria (T. H. Everett) Right: Tabebuia chrysantha (Walter Dawn)

fire by friction. The fiber of the bark is used for caulking and cordage.

VERBENACEAE—VERBENA FAMILY

Herbaceous plants, trees, shrubs and lianas of seventy-five genera and three thousand species are included in the verbena family. The flowers are usually bisexual and clustered; they generally have unequal-sized corolla lobes. Their stems and twigs are often four-angled and the leaves are most often opposite or in whorls of three. This family is predominantly tropical and subtropical. Familiar plants included are verbena, lantana and clerodendron.

Tectona—Teak

Three Indo-Malaysian species constitute this genus. By far the most important is the teak (*T. grandis*). A deciduous tree up to 100 feet in height, this tree is indigenous to India, Java, Sumatra and parts of the Indian Archipelago; extensive forests of it occur in Burma and Thailand. Teak, which is much planted for forestry purposes, has branches in whorls; four-angled, pubescent twigs; and large, opposite or whorled, broad ovate leaves that are often 2 to 3 feet long. The minute white flowers in large panicles are succeeded by small fruits surrounded by papery inflated calyxes. Teakwood is one of the most important of tropical lumbers. Extremely durable and hard, it resists decay even when unprotected by paint or other preservative. It is used for shipbuilding, flooring, greenhouse construction, railroad cars, furniture and piles.

SCROPHULARIACEAE—FIGWORT FAMILY

Most of this cosmopolitan family of 220 genera and three thousand species are herbaceous plants or undershrubs; some are parasites or semiparasites. They have bisexual, usually asymmetrical flowers.

Paulownia—Empress Tree

Seventeen species of deciduous trees of eastern Asia belong here. They have large, opposite leaves resembling those of *Catalpa*, and showy panicles of tubular flowers with five spreading lobes. The fruits are big capsules containing

Jacaranda acutifolia (J. Allan Cash)

winged seeds. The most familiar species is the Empress tree (*P. tomentosa*), a native of China. It is fast-growing, round-headed, about 50 feet tall, and has broad ovate leaves, up to 1 foot long, that are softly hairy on their undersides. The fragrant, foxglove-like flowers are pale violet marked with darker spots in their throats; they are 1¹⁄₂ to 2 inches long. The conspicuous hairy flower buds develop in fall and open in late May. In Japan the wood of the empress tree is used for sandals, boxes and furniture. *Paulownia fargesii* of western China attains a height of 60 feet, has leaves that are hairy on both surfaces and has pale lavender or whitish unspotted flowers about 2¹⁄₂ inches long. With flowers 3 inches long or more and unspotted white or pale lavender, *P. duclouxii* is 60 feet tall; it is a native of central and southwestern China.

BIGNONIACEAE—BIGNONIA FAMILY

This family, which consists chiefly of vines, includes also trees, shrubs and a few herbaceous plants. Composed of 120 genera and 650 species, mostly of the tropics and subtropics, it is widely distributed in both hemispheres and especially abundant in northern South America. Only two genera, however, *Catalpa* and *Campsis*, are common both to the Old and the New World. From nearly related families the Bignoniaceae is distingushed technically by the absence of endosperm in its seeds. Its leaves are usually opposite and the flowers are asymmetrically bell-shaped, cup-shaped or funnel-shaped, showy and bisexual. The seeds may be conspicuously winged.

Catalpa—Indian-bean

One of the handsomest groups of flowering trees, the catalpas are indigenous in North America, the West Indies and eastern Asia. All except the West Indian species are deciduous. Catalpas have large, long-stalked, heart-shaped or coarsely lobed leaves in pairs or in threes and in summer they have showy clusters of asymmetrical bell-shaped flowers at the ends of their branchlets. The flowers are followed by long, slender, cylindrical pods containing many oblong seeds that have a tuft of white hairs at each end. Giant of the Americans is the Western catalpa (*C. speciosa*), a native of the Mississippi Valley that exceeds 100 feet in height and develops a straight trunk sometimes 4 feet in diameter. Its blooms, which occur in clusters of

a few flowers, are about 2½ inches across and are white spotted with brown. Its leaves taper to long points and when bruised have a not unpleasant scent; in these respects it differs from the Indian-bean (*C. bignonioides*), whose leaves are abruptly pointed and, when bruised, are decidedly malodorous. The Indian-bean has many more flowers in each cluster than the Western catalpa but each measures only 1½ inches or slightly more in width. In outline the Western catalpa is pyramidal, whereas the Indian-bean has wide-spreading branches and a roundish top. The wood of the Western catalpa is durable, is easily worked, and is excellent for fence posts; that of the Indian-bean is of no commercial importance. The most important of the West Indian species, the yokewood (*C. longissima*), is most abundant in Haiti where its strong, hard wood is prized for interior trim, flooring and furniture; in Jamaica it is used for boatbuilding. The yokewood is evergreen, grows up to 50 feet high and has narrowly oblong, slender-stemmed leaves and pink-tinted, white flowers. In Cuba and the Bahamas the very fragrant, yellow-flowered, evergreen *C. punctata* is native in swampy lowlands. Attaining a maximum height of about 35 feet, its wood is used to some extent for construction.

Chilopsis—Desert-willow
Flowering-willow

The desert-willow or flowering-willow (*C. linearis*) of dry regions in the southwestern United States and Mexico is the only species in this genus. A deciduous shrub or tree that grows up to 30 feet tall, it has slender leaves that are opposite or alternate and a foot long or less and beautiful, sweet-scented blooms in terminal racemes. The flowers are 1 to 2 inches long and have five-lobed, crimped corollas that are lavender with two stripes of yellow in their throats. The slender seed pods, 6 to 12 inches long, contain numerous seeds furnished with long hairs. The slender, pliable stems are used locally for baskets; the wood serves for fuel and for posts.

Crescentia—Calabash Tree

Five species of tropical American evergreen trees form this genus. The calabash tree (*C. cujete*) is

Above: Calabash tree. Crescentia cujete (J. Allan Cash) Left: Sausage tree fruit. Kigelia Pinnata (Andreas Feininger)

Sausage tree. Kigelia pinnata (Gösta Glasse: Full Hand)

the most important. It reaches a maximum height of about 40 feet and has a few large, horizontal or drooping branches and oblanceolate leaves up to 6 inches long. Its malodorous, bell-shaped yellowish purple blooms open at night. They appear singly or in small clusters on the trunk and on larger branches and are 2 to 3 inches long. The hard-shelled, more or less spherical fruits, 5 to 12 inches in diameter, are technically berries; they are filled with pulp and numerous seeds. The shells of the fruits are used by the natives for making bowls, cups and ornamental articles, often embellished by carving; with the seeds inside them and a handle attached they are converted into the maracas of Latin-American musicians and the hula rattles of Hawaii. The wood is used for boatbuilding and fuel and, in Mexico, the pulp, which is poisonous, is employed medicinally. The Mexican *C. alata* differs in having trifoliate leaves with winged stalks and fruits that rarely exceed 4 inches in diameter.

Cybistax—Prima Vera

The prima vera or gold tree (*C. donnell-smithii*) grows up to 75 feet in height and has a trunk up to 4 feet in diameter. Its deciduous leaves consist of five to seven long-stalked leaflets up to 10 inches long. The yellow blooms, in pyramidal clusters up to 8 inches long, adorn the branch ends. The flowers are more or less bell-shaped, of crepe texture and up to 2 inches long. The wood of this beautiful native of Mexico and Central America is used for cabinetwork and veneer. *Cybistax sprucei* of the Peruvian Andes is cultivated for the blue dye that is obtained from its leaves. The genus *Cybistax* is by some botanists included in *Tabebuia,* a genus which *Cybistax* closely resembles.

1. *Parmentiera edulis*   2. *Jacaranda acutifolia*   3. *Spathodea campanulata*

Dolichandrone

Nine species of Madagascar, East Africa, tropical Asia and Australia belong here. The mangrove trumpet tree (*D. spathacea*) is a narrow-crowned evergreen up to 60 feet in height that inhabits swampy lowlands from India and Malaysia to New Caledonia. It has a massive trunk, which is in old specimens fluted at the base. The leaves are pinnate and have three to nine leaflets; they are 6 to 14 inches long. Opening at dusk, the white trumpet-shaped flowers, 5 to 7 inches long and 3 to 4 inches across the mouth, point obliquely upward; they close at or before sunrise. The 1-inch-wide pods are about 18 inches long; after the seeds have scattered the twisted empty pods remain for a long time on the branches. The corky seeds float readily and are distributed by water. The wood is used for floats for fishnets and other minor purposes.

Jacaranda

Fifty species of trees and shrubs belonging to this genus are natives of Central and South America and the West Indies; most are Brazilian. They have opposite, usually bipinnate, feathery leaves of numerous leaflets and large clusters of blue or violet flowers. The best-known kind, now planted for ornament in most warm countries, is *J. acutifolia*. This Brazilian tree attains a height of about 50 feet; it has finely divided, deciduous foliage and great branched clusters of five-lobed, narrowly bell-shaped, light violet-blue flowers about 2 inches long. The seed pods are flat, wavy-edged discs about 2 inches in diameter that contain many two-winged, thin brown seeds. *Jacaranda copaia*, which has the widest distribution as a native of any species, ranges from British Honduras to Brazil. It sometimes exceeds 80 feet in height and may have a trunk diameter of up to 30 inches. Its huge leaves are composed of numerous small leaflets. Its flowers are bluish or purplish. The light wood of this species is used for interior trim, boxes, coffins and matchsticks.

Kigelia — Sausage Tree

There is only one species of this distinctive genus, a native of tropical Africa. The sausage tree (*K. pinnata*) is a handsome, broad-topped evergreen up to 50 feet tall, with coarse, glossy green, pinnate leaves up to 2 feet long, each consisting of seven to eleven leaflets. Its deep claret-colored, unpleasantly scented flowers open at night. The blooms, irregularly bell-shaped, are strung along pendulous stems, 3 to 6 feet long, and are succeeded by curious sausage-like, hard-shelled fruits up to 20 inches long by 3 or 4 inches in diameter. The fruits, which do not open, contain many seeds embedded in pulp; they are not edible but in Africa are used in native medicine; they can yield a black dye.

Millingtonia—Indian Cork Tree

Southeast Asia is the home of the only species of this genus, the Indian cork tree (*M. hortensis*). Its common name refers to the use of its bark as an inferior kind of cork. This species is an evergreen that grows up to 60 feet in height with

1. *Chilopsis linearis* 2. *Crescentia cujete* 3. *Catalpa bignoniodes (Charles Fracé)*

leaves that much resemble those of *Melia*; they are twice or thrice pinnate and up to 15 inches long. The delicately scented, tubular, waxy white flowers, borne in terminal panicles, are 3¹/₂ to 4¹/₂ inches long and 1¹/₂ to 2 inches wide; their two upper petals are fused up to their middles, while the other three are spreading. The slender seed pods are up to a foot long.

Parmentiera—Candle Tree; Guajilote

Eight species of shrubs or trees—often spiny—consitute this genus, which ranges from Mexico to Colombia. Characteristically their leaves are trifoliate and their bell-shaped flowers are borne in the trunk and larger branches. The candle tree *(P. cereifera)*, a native of Panama, is of interest because of its pendent, yellowish, candle-like fruits, borne in profusion and having an apple-like odor. The tree, well branched to its base, attains a height of 20 feet. Its whitish flowers, each with five wavy-edged lobes, are solitary or in clusters and are 2¹/₂ inches long and 2 inches wide. The leaves consist of three obovate leaflets, up to 2 inches long and attached to a winged stalk. The smooth fruits, which are relished by cattle, are 1 to 4 feet long and about 1 inch in diameter. The guajilote *(P. edulis)*, native to Mexico and Guatemala, attains a height of about 30 feet and is similar to the candle tree except that it has spines at the bases of its leaves, pale green flowers sometimes tinged with purple on their outsides and ridged fruits up to 6 inches long by 1 to 2 inches wide. The fruits are sweet and edible but of inferior quality.

Spathodea—African Tulip Tree; Fountain Tree

Two species, both evergreen, are recognized. The African tulip tree or fountain tree *(S. campanulata)* is a highly decorative native of tropical West Africa that is commonly planted there and in other parts of the tropics as an ornamental. It grows to a height of 70 feet and has a bushy crown. Its opposite, glossy, dark green, pinnate leaves consist of nine to nineteen short-stalked elliptic or oblong leaflets, up to 5¹/₂ inches long by half as wide. Borne in clusters at the extremities of its branchlets, the erect, cup-shaped, orange-scarlet flowers have five lobes narrowly margined with orange-yellow. The blooms are almost 5 inches long by 2 inches wide and have a foxy odor. In the bud stage it secretes so much water that the common name fountain tree is applied to it. It has capsules about 8 inches long by 1¹/₂ inches wide that contain many silvery-winged, 1-inch-wide seeds. The East African *S. nilotica* is a similar but smaller tree. Although its flowers are more brilliant than those of the African tulip tree, it is not as handsome and has foliage that is paler than that of its relative.

Tabebuia

A hundred species are included in *Tabebuia;* they range as natives from Mexico to northern Argentina, and in the West Indies. The limits of the genus are variously defined but most botanists exclude species with pinnate leaves that were once included in *Tabebuia* but that seem to belong more appropriately to *Tecoma. Tabebuia* has undivided or palmately divided leaves. The roble blanco, white-cedar or amapa *(T. penta-phylla)* is a valuable deciduous lumber tree that attains a height of 60 to 90 feet and a trunk diameter of $1\frac{1}{2}$ feet. Its crown is columnar and its leaves are digitate and have up to five slender-stalked leaflets that may be 6 inches long by $2\frac{1}{2}$ wide but are considerably smaller in dry locations; under dry conditions, too, the leaflets may be reduced to one. The tubular flowers, 2 to $3\frac{1}{2}$ inches long, have five spreading lobes and measure $1\frac{3}{4}$ to 3 inches across the face of the bloom; they vary from whitish to purplish but most commonly are deep pink. The flat, narrow fruit capsules may be 5 to almost 12 inches long. The wood of the roble blanco takes a high polish and is used for construction, interior trim, flooring, boatbuilding, furniture, cabinetwork and other purposes. The roble blanco is a native of the West Indies, Mexico, Central America and northern South America. In Brazil the name ipê is applied to many kinds of *Tabebuia*, all of which lose their leaves at blooming time. Among the most highly ornamental kinds is the ipê roxo *(T. heptaphylla)*, which grows up to 60 feet in height and has rose purple blooms. The ipê amarelo *(T. vellosoi)* is a medium-sized tree with brilliant yellow flowers. Attaining a height of 35 to 40 feet, the ipê mandioca *(T. alba)* has paler yellow blooms. Other yellow-flowered kinds for planting in parks and gardens are ipê tabaco *(T. chrysotricha)*, ordinarily not over 45 feet high, and *T. chrysantha* of Venezuela. In Argentina the name lepacho is applied to two or three species, of which the most important, *T. ipe*, attains a height of 125 feet and has a trunk up to 6 feet in diameter. Its rose pink flowers are borne in profusion just before its new leaves appear. The lumber of this tree is used for construction, cabinetwork, and turnery; it also yields a purple dye.

One of the loveliest endemics of Puerto Rico, the roble cimarrón *(T. haemantha)* has evergreen, palmately compound leaves of three to five leathery, broad elliptic, stiff leaflets. Its crimson flowers, slender-tubular with five spreading lobes, are up to 2 inches long and are in erect clusters. This kind has a maximum height of about 20 feet.

Tecoma—Yellow-Elder; Yellow Bells

Sixteen species of trees und shrubs of Florida, the West Indies, Mexico, and Central and South America are assigned to this genus which was formerly named *Stenolobium*. The official flower of the United States Virgin Islands is the yellow-elder or yellow bells *(T. stans)*, a shrub or tree up to 25 feet tall with pinnate leaves up to 8 inches long, of five to thirteen narrow, pointed, toothed leaflets and attractive, yellow, slightly fragrant flowers. This species is native from Florida to Argentina and in the West Indies.

CHAPTER 33

The Rubiales

The *Rubiales* are most abundant in the tropics of the Old World. They usually have opposite leaves.

RUBIACEAE—MADDER FAMILY

The madder family, one of the largest plant families, has five hundred genera and six thousand species; most are tropical. They include trees, shrubs and herbaceous plants that have unlobed leaves and, nearly always, bisexual flowers that are usually pollinated by insects.

Cinchona—Quinine

Forty species of trees and shrubs confined to the Andes, except for one kind that extends also into Central America, constitute *Cinchona*, source of the important drug quinine. The value of cinchona bark as a specific for malaria and other fevers was known to the Indians long before the coming of white man. The earliest recorded use of it by Europeans is in 1630. According to legend, eight years later the wife of the Viceroy of Peru, the Countess of Chinchón, was cured of malaria by the new drug; the generic name of the genus commemorates that lady. Cinchona bark was known as Peruvian bark and, because its virtues were made known so widely by the Jesuits, as Jesuit's bark. The demand for it became so great that under the destructive methods of collecting that were then practiced the forests eventually were threatened with exhaustion. Despite strict laws to prevent seeds or trees leaving the country, in the middle of the nineteenth century both young plants and seeds were

smuggled out of Peru by the British and the Dutch, and trees raised from them and others of later importation formed the basis of cinchona cultivation in India and Java. The species of *Cinchona* are somewhat confused and hybrids between them occur. Those exploited commercially are *C. ledgeriana, C. succirubra, C. officinalis* and *C. calisaya*; the last named was the first to be utilized. Quinine trees are evergreens of medium size with large opposite leaves and yellowish white or pink flowers in clusters.

Coffea—Coffee

Forty species of the Old World tropics constitute the genus *Coffea*, members of which are the source of coffee. Despite the fact that none of the group is a native of the Americas, Brazil, Colombia and other parts of the New World are important centers of coffee cultivation. Three species are of chief significance, Arabian coffee (*C. arabica*), Liberian coffee (*C. liberica*) and Congo coffee (*C. robusta*). By far the most important is the Arabian coffee. This native of Ethiopia is a beautiful evergreen tree up to 30 feet in height, but usually lower, that has horizontal branches and long-pointed, glossy, elliptic leaves 3 to 6 inches long and about one-third as wide as they are long. Pure white, star-like and jasmine-scented, the five-petaled, almost stalkless flowers are about 1¼ inches in diameter; they are borne several together in the leaf axils and are succeeded by fleshy ellipsoid, shining fruits that at first are green but become bright red and finally purple. These berries, about one-half-inch long, usually contain two seeds, each with a flat side; these are de-husked to reveal the kernels or coffee beans that are dried and ground to produce coffee. The stimulating property of the beverage is due to the caffein content of the seeds. The Liberian coffee sometimes is 50 feet in height. A more vigorous tree than the Arabian coffee, it is a native of the west coast of Africa. The sweet-scented flowers of this coffee have six to nine petals and are about 1½ inches long. Its spherical fruits turn from red to nearly black as they ripen; they are 1 inch in diameter. Coffee produced by this species is inferior to Arabian and Congo coffee. Congo coffee (*C. canephora*) resembles Liberian

Above: Arabian coffee berries. Coffea arabica.
Right: Arabian coffee flowers (Both, T. H. Everett)

coffee but is a smaller tree, its flowers are about half as large and its fruits are only one-half-inch in diameter. As its name suggests, Congo coffee is a native of the Congo basin. Several other species of *Coffea* are exploited to a greater or lesser extent as sources of coffee.

Genipa—Genipap; Marmalade-box

On especies, the genipap or marmalade-box (*G. americana*), of this group of six West Indian and tropical American species furnishes edible fruits.

The genipap is a deciduous tree about 60 feet in height that has an erect trunk and opposite, elliptic leaves up to 1 foot long and one-third as broad. Measuring 1 to $1^{1}/_{2}$ inches across, the five-lobed, yellow flowers are in small terminal clusters; they are attractive to bees. The long-stalked, leathery-skinned fruits are brown, lemon-shaped and from $3^{1}/_{2}$ to $4^{1}/_{2}$ inches long. They have sour flesh that is made into a refreshing beverage. Genipap wood is used for furniture, cabinetwork, flooring, boxes and turnery.

Glossary

Anther. The pollen-producing part of a stamen.

Areole. In cactuses a small defined area from which the spines arise.

Axillary cones. Cones that develop from an axil.

Bipinnate. Twice pinnate; with subdivisions diverging from a central axis, and each subdivision divided into leaflets.

Bloom. A waxy coating on various fruits and on some leaves and stems.

Bract. A modified leaf from the axil of which a flower or floral axis arises.

Carpel. A simple pistil or element of a compound pistil; regarded as a modified leaf.

Cauliflory. The production of flowers from the old wood, as in the redbud, chocolate tree and many tropical woods.

Cladode or cladophyll. A branch that has the form and functions of a leaf.

Corolla. The petals of a flower collectively.

Cretaceous. A geological period between the Jurassic and Tertiary.

Cupule. A cup-shaped organ.

Dentate. Having toothlike projections directed outward.

Drupe. A fleshy, one-seeded stone fruit that does not split open, such as a plum.

Epiphytic. An air plant; a plant that grows on another but does not take nourishment from its host.

Gall. A swelling of plant tissues resulting from insect punctures or other irritations.

Glabrous. Smooth, hairless.

Glaucous. Covered with a waxy bloom, e.g. plum, cabbage leaf.

Globose. Nearly spherical.

Inflorescence. A flower cluster.

Involucre. A ring of bracts beneath a flower or flower cluster.

Lanceolate. Narrow and tapering toward the apex.

Medullary. Relating to the pith.

Mucilaginous. Moist, soft and sticky.

Oblanceolate. Tapering toward the base more than toward the apex.

Obovate. Inversely ovate.

Orbicular. Spherical, circular.

Ovary. The part of the pistil that contains the ovules.

Ovate. Egg-shaped with the broad end at the base.

Palmate. Having lobes or divisions radiating from a common point.

Panicle. A flower cluster; a branched raceme.

Papillose. Covered with papillae, soft superficial protuberances.

Pedicel. A slender flower-stalk.

Peduncle. A flower stalk supporting an inflorescence or a solitary flower.

Petiole. A leafstalk.

Phyllode. A petiole taking on the form and function of a leaf.

Pinnate. With leaflets arranged on each side of a common axis.

Pinnatifid. Cleft pinnately, with narrow lobes not extending to the midrib.

Pistillary. Relating to the pistil, the female organ of a flower.

Pistillary cones. Female cones.

Plumose. Having hairs or other parts arranged along an axis like a feather.

Proteaceous. Relating to or resembling the family Proteaceae.

Pubescent. Downy, with short soft hairs.

Raceme. Flower cluster in which single flowers grow individually on small stems at intervals from a longer stem.

Saponaceous. Soaplike.

Sepal. A leaf or division of the calyx.

Serrate. Radiating like the points of a star.

Spathe. A large bract or pair of bracts enclosing a flower cluster.

Stigma. That part of the pistil or style which receives the pollen grains, and on which they germinate.

Stipule. One of a pair of appendages at the base of the leaf in many plants.

Stomate. A breathing pore or aperture in the epidermis.

Style. That part of a pistil or carpel between the ovary and stigma.

Suborbicular. Nearly circular.

Symbiosis. The living together of dissimilar organisms with benefit to one only, or to both, without harm to either.

Tesselated. Checkered in a pattern of small squares.

Topiary. Trees and shrubs sheared into fanciful and ornamental shapes.

Trifoliate. Three-leaved.

Umbel. An inflorescence in which the pedicels appear to spring from one central point.

Vascular. Relating to or furnished with vessels.

Xerophyte. A plant that can subsist on a very small amount of moisture, e.g. a desert plant.

Index